Signs of Power

Signs of Power
The Rise of Cultural Complexity in the Southeast

Edited by
JON L. GIBSON and PHILIP J. CARR

THE UNIVERSITY OF ALABAMA PRESS
Tuscaloosa

Published in part by a grant from Brigham Young University

Cover painting of Caney Mounds by Jon Gibson

Typeface: Goudy and Goudy Sans

∞
The paper on which this book is printed meets the minimum requirements of
American National Standard for Information Science–Permanence of Paper for
Printed Library Materials, ANSI Z39.48–1984.

Library of Congress Cataloging-in-Publication Data

Signs of power : the rise of cultural complexity in the Southeast / edited by Jon L. Gibson
and Philip J. Carr.
    p. cm.
Includes bibliographical references (p.) and index.
  ISBN 0-8173-1391-5 (cloth : alk. paper) — ISBN 0-8173-5085-3 (pbk. : alk. paper)
   1. Mounds—Southern States. 2. Indians of North America—Southern States—
Antiquities. 3. Southern States—Antiquities. I. Gibson, Jon L. II. Carr, Philip J., 1966–
  E78.S65S523 2004
  975'.01—dc22

                                           2003023968

Contents

Figures

Tables

Preface and Acknowledgments

This book was born on a mustard-smeared napkin in a foyer of a New Orleans hotel. It all started innocently enough—Joe Saunders, Bob Connolly, Phil Carr, and Jon Gibson brainstorming about a symposium we wanted to offer to the 1999 Southeastern Archaeological Conference in Pensacola. Well, maybe it was not so innocent: scribbling covered both sides of the napkin. Mainly because Gibson wound up with the napkin and Carr had the pen, they, by default, became the organizers for the symposium that was called "Big Mound Power" but actually turned out to be a rather freewheeling discourse on Archaic hunter-gatherer power and complexity. Thanks to strong performances by the original cast—David Anderson, Sam Brookes, Phil Carr and Lee Stewart, Cheryl Claassen, John Clark, Bob Connolly, Robert Dunnell and Carl Lipo, Jon Gibson, Jose Iriarte, Dick Jefferies, George Milner, Mike Russo, Ken Sassaman, Joe Saunders, Vin Steponaitis, Prentice Thomas and Jan Campbell, Corbett Torrance, Nancy White, and Dolf Widmer—there were few unfilled seats during the session. By sunset, the organizers had been approached about turning the papers into a book, and by nightfall, a poll of the participants found that most were willing to take the next step, and they agreed to a follow-up meeting that would help everybody decide what everybody else was talking about.

That second gathering took place at Poverty Point during the autumnal equinox in 2000. It was a four-day, no-holds-barred, delightful jousting of the minds on major issues of organization and empowerment in simple and intermediate social formations in southern North America. Making the Poverty Point pilgrimage were original participants David Anderson, Sam Brookes, Phil Carr, John Clark, Bob Connolly, Jon Gibson, Mike Russo, Joe Saunders, Lee Stewart, Nancy White, and Dolf Widmer, as well as new invitees George Crothers, Tom Eubanks, and Becky Saunders. What better place to talk about hunter-gatherer complexity than on Poverty Point's ancient grounds? Whether it was carrying on discussions atop the bird mound in the bright sunlight or atop Mound B at night when even the owls fell silent, listening, Poverty Point recharged everyone with enthusiasm for this undertaking.

Now, four years after a scribbled-on napkin started us on our way, the University of Alabama Press has turned our thoughts into a book and a mighty fine-looking one at that. We are much obliged to many fine people who lent a helping hand along the way. John Kelly and Jay Johnson, our reviewers, caught threadbare sections in the manuscript before they reached public eye. Elizabeth Bench-ley, program chair for the fifty-sixth Southeastern Archaeological Conference, made room for the day-long symposium in Pensacola. Commentary by John Clark, George Milner, and Vin Steponaitis, our symposium discussants, helped stew and simmer conference papers into book-worthy servings and earned Meso-americanist Clark an honorary membership in the sodality of Southeastern archaeologists. Dwight Landreneaux, Director of the Louisiana Office of State Parks, gave the okay for the Poverty Point gathering and for videotaping the event. Dennis LaBatt, Manager of the Poverty Point State Historic Site, was our sponsor and host. He provided meeting places, gave us our daily bread and beds, and led the way through the mounds and rings one bright afternoon. His staff shared the giving spirit too. Linda York brought our breakfast fixings every morning; Robert Pickering fried Opelousa catfish caught that very day in the bayou that runs by the rings, proving beyond a shadow of a doubt what really fueled Poverty Point's phenomenal growth. Betty Miller and Gloria Lemon cooked our supper, and David Griffing did the little things that lightened our burden. Joe Saunders and Reca Jones took us to see Lower Jackson and Watson Brake. Michelle Cossey, Louis Courville, Kisha Holmes, and Josetta LeBouef, University of Louisiana, Lafayette, anthropology students past and present, did everything short of reading palms and making short-term loans to keep the meeting running smoothly. Michelle arranged for Geoff Douville to videotape the gathering, and we owe Geoff a shiny doubloon for donating his time, camera, and tapes.

Back at UL Lafayette, archaeology lab assistants Michelle Cossey, Karen Chuter, Melissa Collins, and Kellie Thomassee transcribed audiotapes, compared them with videotapes in order to get speakers properly blamed, and typed the full transcript. Michelle went back through the transcript and replaced preliminary identifications—big cowboy, big fast-talker, blondie, witty guy, pretty dark-haired lady, and good-looking fellow—with given names. Transcribers knew other participants and recognized their voices but sometimes even that did not stop their vivid identifications. The editors had to eliminate some IDs in order to keep our PG-13 rating. At one time, we contemplated including an edited version of the sessions, but after seeing how much work would have been involved, we decided against it.

This book bears scars from rampant worms and viruses, as well as a faulty power source. But all the cyber problems in the world cannot suppress the word, especially when Piper Smith and Lark Goodwin, Gibson's two favorite nieces, recreated lost files from hard copy. Further cleanup of the text and figures for the final draft was aided by Harriet Richardson Seacat and Sarah Mattics, staff members of the University of South Alabama Center for Archaeological Studies.

We editors have been told how self-appreciating it sounds to thank contributors for writing their own book, but neither of us has ever paid much attention to such advice. Our mammas taught us both to say thanks when folks did you a favor. We didn't convert oral presentations into book chapters with wave of wand or cast of spell. Authors did that bit of magic themselves with Logitech keyboard and hard-won data. Salient points ripened under each others' gazes and were served up for a second round of feasting at the Poverty Point miniconference. *Signs of Power* chapters have been tempered with grog from both Pensacola and Poverty Point forerunners. For staying with the effort in the years between Pensacola and Tuscaloosa through conflicting class schedules, contract meetings, fieldwork, grocery shopping, and short periods of sleep, *Signs of Power* authors have the editors' deepest gratitude and hand in friendship. To Dave, Sam, Jan, John, Wildcat George, Gator Mike, Dick, Nittany Lion George, Jim, Bluewater Mike, Ken, Joe, Lee, Prentice, Nancy, and Dolf, Phil and Jon doff their hats and raise their mugs to each of you. Salute, y'all.

Phil thanks Amy and Jon thanks Mary Beth for approving their own sabbaticals from housework, yardwork, and normal life and for sticking by them during their leaves, with love.

Jon L. Gibson
Lake Claiborne, Louisiana

Philip J. Carr
University of South Alabama
Mobile, Alabama

Big Mounds, Big Rings, Big Power

Jon L. Gibson and Philip J. Carr

The ancient monuments . . . consist . . . of elevations and embankments of
earth and stone, erected with great labor and manifest design.
Ephraim Squier and Edwin Davis,
Ancient Monuments of the Mississippi Valley (1848)

Mounds have quickened the pulse of American antiquarians and archaeologists
for generations. They still do. Who among you could stay calm after hacking a
trail through a bottomland-hardwood jungle and suddenly realizing that the in-
cline you're struggling to climb is no natural levee but a lost Indian mound? Or
stand atop a mound on a starlit night with a handful of fellow archaeologists and
keep from getting caught up in what the wind is whispering or help wondering
whether the owl hooting deep in the woods is bird or shilombish?[1] No use pre-
tending, mounds are as magical today as ever. The contributors to this book are
come before you to explain some of that magic.

ANCIENT MOUNDS AND THEIR BUILDERS

Mound builders always have been considered culturally more sophisticated and
evolutionarily more advanced than groups who did not build mounds. But were
they really? What about builders of the very first Archaic mounds? Were they
more socially and politically adept than their hunter-gatherer forefathers and
neighbors or just different? Archaeologists labored long under sway of hunter-
gatherers as short-lived brutes spending every waking moment filling their bellies
(Hobbes 1968 [1651]) or as lay ecologists basking in the leisure afforded by an
almost serendipitous affluence (Sahlins 1968a, 1972). Ethnographically known
hunter-gatherers did not engage in public construction, and only in rare prehistoric instances, such as Poverty Point in the Lower Mississippi Valley and shell
rings on the southern Atlantic coast, were Archaic hunter-gatherers accorded
mound-building motives and skills. Still, such primal cases were considered
atypical, ahistorical—as cases lying outside mainstream cultural developments
and forming exceptions to widely accepted generalizations of Archaic lifeways in
the southeastern United States. Archaeologists were taken with the generalized

foraging model of egalitarian hunter-gatherers going about their business in an efficient, no-nonsense way—so much so, in fact, that they skipped over the fact that the model was based on historically marginalized foragers, not on pristine foragers living in bountiful environments.

The issue of social complexity drives authors' searches here just as it did two centuries ago when antiquarians were trying to explain the enigma of the mounds and their builders. But there is a difference. Our searches are guided by history, not presumptions about complexity as a monolithic sociopolitical condition or cultural developmental stage. To a person, authors herein subscribe to complexity as "that which is composed of many interrelated parts" (Price and Brown 1985:7), as opposed to simplicity, which we construe as sociality having fewer parts. Conceptually, "hunter-gatherer" covers a potentially vast range of variability between traditional views of simple, egalitarian hunter-gatherers and advanced, ranked chiefdoms. Hunter-gatherer complexity has come under fire for making "simple" hunter-gatherers less social, apolitical, and unorganized, perceptions that have dominated traditional views of Archaic foragers. But the discovery of Archaic mounds prompts us to characterize their builders as complex, a wonderfully vague description that highlights that variability while sending us searching for its sources.

Interest in mounds has deepened since it was discovered how old some Louisiana and Florida mounds really are. Today, people do not roll their eyes at claims of 6,000-year-old mounds, but this was not the case a few short years ago. For a half-century, Poverty Point earthworks claimed title as the oldest in the continental United States (Ford and Webb 1956), and they dated to sometime between 1730 and 1350 cal b.c. Claims of even older Archaic mounds were dismissed out of hand for contravening conventional wisdom and, worse, for being seditious. Like the Missouri mule, the archaeological establishment had to be shown the truth and lots of it. Radiocarbon dating and elegance of argument were the capstones, but it was widespread realization that some Archaic fisher-hunter-gatherer groups manifested social formations and practices once accorded only to farming groups that softened skepticism about the early age of mounds. The quiet acceptance of Archaic origin brings us to the point where we can now ask after the sources of power and sociality behind primordial mound building, an impossibility a few years ago. Yet, as is often the case when data run ahead of theorizing, tough questions abound and open new avenues of research regarding relationships and interactions between regions where Archaic mounds were built and those where they were not. But the primary concern is time-honored—just how socially complex Archaic mound builders really were.

While neither complete in coverage nor unified by similar datasets or approaches, the body of research presented in the following pages represents our attempts to get a handle on Southeast Archaic lifeways, some embodying public construction and elaborate stone and bone artifacts and some lacking them (Figure 1.1). We recognize that general characterizations on the scale of regions and periods are as likely to be wrong for specific places and times as they are correct. Syntheses that portray Archaic hunter-gatherers as mobile, egalitarian populations roaming over a sparsely populated land do not always fit the data, as this book bears witness.

ARCHAIC SOCIALITY: TECHNOLOGY AND ARCHITECTURE

The rise of chiefdoms and hereditary social inequality has claimed center stage in contemporary research into Native American cultural complexity. It has not been that long since archaeologists assumed stilled mobility and horticultural economy were essential for chiefdom organization. Mounds and craft specialists were part of the mix as well. We have since learned that structural linkages between these variables are neither simple nor, more important, causal (e.g., Arnold, ed. 1996; Feinman 1995). John Clark and associates have, for example, proposed that some ancient Mesoamerican communities, such as Paso de la Amada, turned to farming sooner than others, because corn was used to make not tortillas but beer for competitive feasting (Clark and Blake 1994). To other researchers, hereditary inequality and foraging were structurally and organizationally incompatible, although the Calusa fisher folk of Florida's Gulf Coast and some salmon-fishing peoples of the northwestern Pacific Coast were long recognized as exceptions. But these were well-documented historic groups. What about Archaic foragers and collectors—the first groups on the North American mainland to deal with matters besides raising a family and finding supper and to leave earth and shell monuments and stone and bone masterpieces to show for it?

Archaic mound and ring building is only the flash point for a broader inquiry on Archaic organization and power. Contributors to this book examine other Archaic technologies and practices regarded as being out of sync with traditional perceptions of hunter-gatherer organization. Their unitary goal is to collect data and infer aspects of hunter-gatherer organization instead of relying on traditional models and perceptions.

Before Poverty Point, some Southeast groups wielded polished-stone and chipped-stone technologies that excelled in craftsmanship and beauty of line and finish. Atlatl weights, particularly bannerstones, were crown jewels of Middle Archaic sites on the Tennessee and Green Rivers during the third and fourth millennia B.C. (Moore 1916). A few unfinished and broken weights came from domestic contexts, but whole objects came from graves or deposits suggesting that their social importance outweighed practical importance in the end (Sassaman 1996). In familiar social groupings, the practical and the social were in-

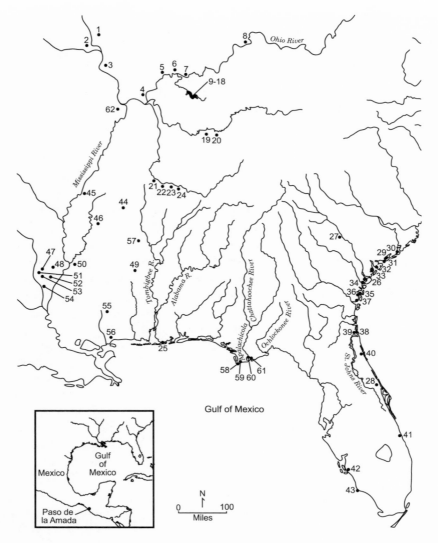

Figure 1.1. Location of key sites discussed in this volume. 1, Koster; 2, Arnold Research Cave; 3, Modoc Rock Shelter; 4, Black Earth; 5, Bluegrass; 6, McCain; 7, Crib Mound; 8, KYANG; 9, Kirkland; 10, Jackson Bluff; 11, Baker; 12, Jimtown Hill; 13, Carlston Annis; 14, Read; 15, Barrett; 16, Butterfield; 17, Ward; 18, Indian Knoll; 19, Anderson; 20, Unnamed; 21, Long Branch; 22, Mulberry Creek; 23, Perry; 24, Little Bear Creek; 25, Van Horn; 26, Bilbo; 27, Stallings Island; 28, Tick Island; 29, Lighthouse Point; 30, Sewee; 31, Fig Island; 32, Coosaw; 33, Sea Pines; 34, Skidaway; 35, Busch Krick; 36, Sapelo; 37, Cannon's Point; 38, Rollins; 39, Oxeye; 40, Guana; 41, Joseph Reed; 42, Bonita Bay; 43, Horr's Island; 44, Humber; 45, Oak; 46, Denton; 47, Frenchman's Bend; 48, Poverty Point; 49, Nanih Waiya; 50, Jaketown; 51, Plum Creek; 52, Insley; 53, Watson Brake; 54, Caney; 55, Keenan Bead Cache; 56, Cedarland/Claiborne; 57, Vaughan; 58, Clark Creek shell midden; 59, Pickalene Midden; 60, Van Horn Creek shell mound; 61, Sam's Cutoff shell mound; 62, Burkett.

separable anyway, and weapons that could send prey and people to the spirit world with a single, swift motion surely carried great power. Robert Hall (1997) proposes symbolic links between ancient atlatls and historic tribal honor badges, courting flutes, and calumets—quite a social registry. But do bannerstones portend transegalitarian social formations? In Chapter 5, George Crothers does not think so.

Beautiful, highly polished, and often engraved bone pins also were fashioned by Middle Archaic peoples from the Tennessee River to Florida's Atlantic coast (Jefferies 1995, 1997), raising the prospect of craft specialization, another traditional indicator of social inequalities. Because pins were numerous and generally discarded with the trash, Richard Jefferies (1997:480) maintains that they were ordinary, everyday items. But, as he maintains in Chapter 4, being commonplace makes them perfect markers for the varied social identities being forged as Middle Archaic collectivities living just south of the Ohio River became less mobile—their movements restricted to ever-smaller territories. In Jefferies's view, reduced residential mobility cut down on access to resources, foods, and spouses and increased security risks and was counterbalanced by formation of intergroup alliances, which birthed movers and shakers and afforded a fertile social milieu for inequalities to take hold. By Jefferies's account, bone pins were not direct measures of social inequality within a collective but of the potential for inequality.

In Chapter 7, Prentice Thomas, Janice Campbell, and James Morehead tackle the twin problems of the age and cultural affiliation of the O'Bryan Ridge phase in Missouri's bootheel—fundamental archaeological homework required before setting out history and sociality. Their excavation at the Burkett site finds that its earliest occupation dated after first mounds in the Lower Mississippi Valley were built and before Poverty Point reached its peak but that its later occupations were logistically well situated to have been involved in the movement of Burlington chert down the Mississippi Valley to Poverty Point. Finding evidence for earthquake activity beneath a multistage mound leads Thomas, Campbell, and Morehead to suggest that Poverty Point–age (and later Woodland) peoples ritualized the spot, which culminated in the mound, perhaps in the manner posited by Crothers in Chapter 5.

Benton Archaic groups living in the hills south of the Tennessee River sometimes cached magnificent oversized bifacial foliates, ornate Turkey Tail bifaces, and atassa (polished-stone effigies) (Johnson and Brookes 1989), which Samuel Brookes in Chapter 6 contends were the work of embedded craft specialists. Brookes also suggests that specialists were responsible for the unusual polished-stone zoomorphs found in a wide band across the Southeast from western Louisiana to central Florida. Shaped in the round, usually from red jasper, these pocketknife-sized beads depict locusts, owls, turtles, frogs, and other four-leggeds (see Brookes, this volume; Connaway et al. 1977), creatures that figure prominently in the lore of historic Southeastern tribes. So far, zoomorphs have not been found in Benton caches or in areas where bone pins are common. With few exceptions, they do not occur in caches, first mounds, or burials. Unlike pins, they are rare and, being representations of those special animals that readily move between the vaults in the native cosmos—land, sky, and water (under-ground)[2]—they are probably amulets or fetishes (Connaway et al. 1977; Webb 1971).

In Chapter 3, Michael Russo argues that some Atlantic and Gulf coastal shell rings were built by transegalitarian peoples, but Nancy White in Chapter 2 finds evidence of only simple shellfish-gathering collectivities along western Florida's Apalachicola River. The many shell heaps, she insists, are not intentionally con-structed mounds but incidentally accumulated refuse left by mobile egalitarian foragers. To White, social inequalities, which disenfranchise individuals or popu-lation segments by restricting access to economic resources, are incompatible with the food bounty of the Apalachicola and the general lack of sedentism. Russo also tackles the public architecture/incidental refuse issue. He proposes that the bigger and more architecturally complex the shell ring, the more so-cially complex its builders. In keeping with social space theory, he argues that closed circles and C-shapes reflect egalitarian formations, while U-shapes and closed circles with dwellings in centrally elevated positions reflect hierarchical social formations.

Philip Carr and Lee Stewart ponder the political-economic implications of the organization of Poverty Point's chipped-stone technology in Chapter 8. They model several different ways that rock might have reached Poverty Point and then search for matches for their expectations among the empirical data. They conclude that indirect acquisition, or exchange, best fits the situations and further propose that independent trade lines run by different lineages produced rock stockpiles that were then corporately shared.

In Chapter 9, Joe Saunders, drawing on his excavations at Louisiana's Watson Brake, Frenchman's Bend Mounds, and Plum Creek Archaic, evaluates evidence for cultivars, sedentism, storage, substantial housing, trade, feasting, burial, and specialized crafts—the usual archaeological correlates of social complexity (e.g., Hayden 1995)—and finds little empirical support for Middle Archaic transegali-tarianism. However, he does find much that recommends Poverty Point trans-egalitarianism, especially in the monumentality of its earthworks. But Kenneth Sassaman and Michael Heckenberger in Chapter 11 contend that Archaic plaza villages evince internalized and institutionalized distinctions between residents of a community and the outside world, the authors' Rubicon for transegalitari-anism. They also suggest that site-to-site consistency in siting and mound posi-tioning indicates that mound building was planned and carried out on a regional scale, not independently by each local collectivity. Why? There is a regular pattern of size downscaling among Middle Archaic mound complexes in northeastern Louisiana, and the hierarchy intimates social and political complexity greater than that encountered in simple egalitarian formations.

Spatial arrangement, proportionality, and numerology of first mounds are also considered in Chapter 10 by John Clark, who finds evidence not only for a standard unit of measurement but also for geometrical layouts and spacing intervals among first-mound complexes from Louisiana to Mexico and Peru, which incorporate multiples of that standard. The numerology, as Clark demonstrates, is familiar: 13s, 20s, 52s, and, yes, the larger numbers too that make up the ritual counts of the Mesoamerican calendar. Finding the same measure and ritual counts across such vast distances may prove to be one of contemporary archaeology's most provocative revelations—it reopens age-old questions about a common "Archaic" cultural base (Spinden 1917) or rather some mighty-old tradition and the history behind it. We think it reasonable to conclude that those who built the works were not simple, ordinary foragers (see Sahlins 1968a).

ARCHAIC SOCIALITY: ORGANIZATION AND POWER

Did it really require transegalitarian societies to mount labor for public construction or industry for special crafts? Could simple egalitarian collectivities have managed? Or, as George Crothers asks in Chapter 5, was corporate society in the traditional sense necessary at all? Underpinning these organizational questions is the issue of power. Power—the capability of getting people to act a certain way or do certain things—permeates sociality in all its guises, but of prime importance for early monument building and fancy artifact crafting is determining how much power resides in varied organizations and can be leveraged by ordinary social means.

In Chapter 12, Randolph Widmer finds that the power behind sociopolitical complexity comes from the appearance of unilineal kin groups with their inherent corporateness and labor potential. For lineages to form, Widmer contends, four children in a group (on average) must survive to be adults in each of four successive generations. He links the required population growth to rises in sea level and shifts in river courses, which, in turn, result in greater food productivity, a boon to wetland fisher-hunter-gatherer baby-makers.

On the other hand, George Crothers in Chapter 5 offers a different perspective on Archaic hunter-gatherer sociality and capacity for action, one that does not depend on degree of group cohesiveness, social complexity, or even concerted effort. From his vantage on Kentucky's Green River, Crothers proposes that dynamic social interactions among individuals or autonomous small groups participating in ritual use of the same spot over and over could account for mounds or produce other extraordinary outcomes—everyone added a little dirt, not to build cohesion but to ritualize participation.

The absence of customary indications of inequality in first mounds leads Jon Gibson (lucky Chapter 13) to recommend that empowerment for mound building comes from a pervasive sense of debt of gratitude, or beneficent obligation, which is not prone to showy exclusionary or self-promoting practices as is competitive obligation. Building on Choctaw tradition about the building of Nanih Waiya, the tribe's sacred mound, he shows that small groups manifesting basically egalitarian relations and corporate makeups could have built Louisiana's Middle Archaic mound complexes. But not so in the case of Poverty Point, which exceeds the labor equivalent of the largest first-mound complexes by a measure of 15 to 20 times.

In Chapter 14, David Anderson sees tribal dynamics in the organization of those Middle Archaic social formations, whose people built big earthworks and shell works and crafted exquisite stone and bone objects. He sees several things being involved—growing populations, increasing sedentism and territorialism, emerging lineages, rising importance of ritual and ceremony, strengthening group-wide ideology, widening intergroup interaction, and stepped-up communal actions. Anderson identifies no prime mover, but neither does he envision the processes having to work collectively to produce tribes. Tribalism results rather from a concatenation of varied combinations of these developments that differ according to time, place, and personality. From the editors' perspective, the right combination seems almost serendipitous. The bottom line—and there is a bottom line, a social threshold—is that social action emphasizes the group and normalizes individual and family matters within the group mentality. Anderson's parting aphorism is worth repeating: "we need to discard outmoded views of hunter-gatherers . . . and begin to explore the richly laden world that really existed."

In Chapter 15, George Milner proposes a solution for why first mounds were built that rings with practicality: "mounds have the virtues of being cheap, permanent, and conspicuous." Milner finds divided opinion on the sociality of first-mound builders—on whether they were organizationally simple or complex—to be a healthy state of affairs, one that will launch new research, new questions, and new answers. He notes that some Archaic groups interacted with each other and others apparently kept to themselves, but he cautions against envisioning interaction exclusively for commercial, ceremonial, or idea-transferal purposes. For innumerable reasons and sometimes for no reason at all, people just do not like each other; interaction among these groups centers on hostility and fighting. But Milner's point is that whether intergroup interaction is friendly or ugly, it brings about practices, institutions, and ethnic awareness, which grow social complexity. People are not what they eat. They are what they do and what they feel they can do.

ASKING IS SIMPLE, PROVIDING ANSWERS IS NOT

Mound building, economic intensification, diminished mobility, intergroup alliance building, exchange, embedded craft specialization, and other processes and practices are consequences of subtle or substantial interactive and organizational changes, which affected not only the number but also the kind and strength of ties within and between Archaic collectivities. Whether Archaic groups who built first mounds and fashioned elaborate artifacts were socially more complex than other hunter-gatherers is interesting only insofar as we can tell how they came to be the way they were and what courses they followed to get that way. George Milner echoes that sentiment: "one should be cautious about basing any argument on the 'original affluent society' notion with its decidedly Rousseauian overtones." The issue of Archaic social complexity is of central concern to the authors of this book, but their contributions are not merely a social registry of simple vs. complex practices or a list of their material archaeological correlates. The authors' interests also embrace the ways and means that some ancient peoples used to embellish their sociality—their power and organization. Asking after Archaic complexity is a simple matter providing answers is not. Seeking those answers, however, gives issue to the chapters in this book.

NOTES

1. In Choctaw tradition, the shilombish is the outside shadow, or the second of the deceased's two souls, which stays near the earthly remains for a time scaring those who venture too close. It takes the form of an owl or fox and can be distinguished from its real counterpart only when its yelps and screeches elicit no response. The cries are dreaded for they portend misfortune and even death to those who hear them or to close relatives or friends. To see a shilombish means certain death.

2. In the traditions of the Cherokee and other Southeastern tribes (Hudson 1984), the cosmos consists of three worlds all encased by a hard, rocklike substance: the upper world represented by the sky, this world represented by the earth, and the underworld lying beneath the earth. Streams and springs are construed as pathways between earth and underworld. The upper world is the world of spirits, and the underworld is backward and chaotic. The earth, or Earth Island, is the familiar world of humans and animals.

2

Late Archaic Fisher-Foragers in the Apalachicola–Lower Chattahoochee Valley, Northwest Florida–South Georgia/Alabama

Nancy Marie White

The archaeological constructs of the Late Archaic and prehistoric cultural complexity are examined here with a discussion of data from the Apalachicola–lower Chattahoochee River valley in northwest Florida, southwest Georgia, and southeast Alabama (Figure 2.1). The Apalachicola is the largest Florida river, originating at the confluence of the Flint and Chattahoochee Rivers, at the Florida-Georgia border, and flowing southward to the Gulf of Mexico. The smaller Flint River begins near Atlanta, and the Chattahoochee comes from the Blue Ridge Mountains of north Georgia. These rivers flow through the karst topography of the Gulf coastal plain to form the largest delta east of Louisiana. The lower Apalachicola Valley is a wilderness of tupelo swamps and estuaries; there are also sheltered bayshores and barrier islands in the Gulf. Late Archaic sites (mostly defined as having produced fiber-tempered pottery) are now known from the islands all the way up the valley. Data from 76 sites (White 2003b) recorded in different environments within the Apalachicola Valley (107 river/navigation miles long) and from more limited riverbank surveys on the lower Chattahoochee (an additional 67 river miles, up to Fort Gaines, Georgia) are summarized here.

WHAT IS THE LATE ARCHAIC?

The traditional view of the Archaic stage in eastern U.S. prehistory was that it paralleled the Old World Mesolithic, a time after the extinction of the Pleistocene megafauna and before the advent of agriculture and pottery, when people were innovating, experimenting with new strategies since their big game–hunting days were over. Ever since Caldwell (1958), typical interpretations have indicated increased efficiency and opportunistic broadening of the range of resources ob-

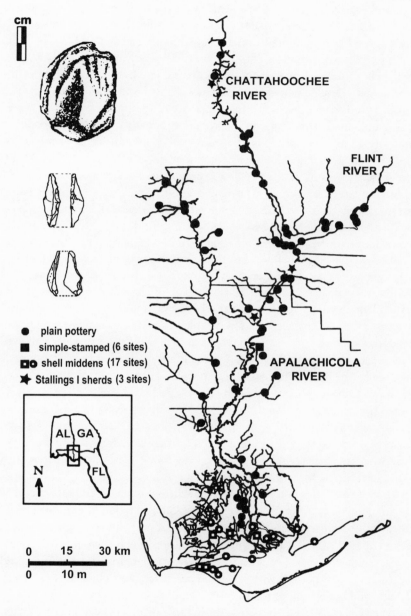

cm

plain pottery
simple-stamped (6 sites)
shell middens (17 sites)
Stallings I sherds (3 sites)

CHATTAHOOCHEE
RIVER

FLINT
RIVER

APALACHICOLA
RIVER

AL GA

N

FL

0   15   30 km

0   10 m

Figure 2.1. Late Archaic sites in the Apalachicola–lower Chattahoochee and lower Flint
River valley region and sample artifacts from coastal shell mounds (clay ball from Clark
Creek shell mound [8Gu60], microtools from Sam's Cutoff shell mound [8Fr754]).

tained, and especially coastal settlement, given the assumed emergence at this time of more useful aquatic environments as a result of rising sea levels, with shellfish and other species now available (e.g., Smith 1986).

Interpretive biases are clear. The stress on efficiency and opportunism produces purely functional models, and the coastal emphasis is a product of increased modern development along coastlines that exposes more sites. Curiously, however, there is also a persistent historical emphasis upon the hunting of terrestrial mammals that prevents our appreciation of early adaptations to aquatic resources (e.g., Walker 2000). Now we know that inland, meals of fish, nuts, and salads were probably quite ancient in the warm, wet, forested New World. For example, Roosevelt and colleagues (1996) have documented Late Pleistocene Amazonian adaptation to aquatic and forest resources, even manipulation of forest species, characterized by stemmed points that are contemporaneous with Clovis elsewhere. At the Monte Verde site in northern Chile, even people who dined on mastodon 13,000 years ago were also munching mushrooms, berries, nuts, potatoes, and shellfish, not to mention various plant leaves (Dillehay 1997). Two other aspects of New World subsistence recently realized are, first, that the earliest domesticated plants were not food crops but utilitarian or "industrial" plants, such as bottle gourd (both in North and South America) and cotton (South America), exploitation of which appeared sometimes long before ceramics or food crop agriculture, and second, that there was knowledge and use of domesticated food crops long before agricultural or even larger-scale horticultural societies emerged. This means that people either did not need to produce food, or did not want to, even though they might have been familiar with gardening. These points are important to keep in mind because we still associate sociocultural complexity with some kind of coordinated, directed group activity. This activity used to be agriculture, or even horticulture, but now we are investigating whether it is mound building or something else and whether it happened as long ago as the Archaic.

Stoltman (1992) has noted our "Archaic schizophrenia" in using the term to mean simultaneously a time period, an ecological adaptation, and a complex of specific artifact forms. In actual practice, "Late Archaic" is now commonly used to mean the hunting-gathering-fishing time during which there is some experimentation with cultivation of already well-known plants in the Midsouth and before which coiled pottery with some temper other than plant fibers is made. The name and dates were formally entrenched by the time archaeologists realized a type of pottery *was* being made during this time. This was fiber-tempered pottery, easily "accepted as an Archaic innovation, presumably because its context seems to be among foragers who had not yet adopted plant cultivation and because its relationship to the subsequent Woodland ceramic tradition is ambiguous" (Stoltman 1992:114). Plus it was easy with old diffusionist models to connect fiber-tempered pottery in the southeastern United States with roughly contemporaneous fiber-tempered ceramics in Colombia, though now we see the oldest New World pottery, in the Brazilian Amazon, is really some 3,000 years earlier and is not fiber-tempered (Roosevelt 1995).

In the northwest Florida region additional, more specific and burdensome terminology has been proposed for the Late Archaic, such as "Norwood phase," "Elliott's Point complex," and "Gulf Formational stage." Each of these has its problems, as each implies that something distinct was going on beyond the generalized adaptation of the Late Archaic. I do not use any of these terms, not only because I am a lumper as far as typologizing is concerned but also because regional variation is poorly understood. In addition, terminology such as "formational" or "formative" is laden with ethnocentric value judgments about what was the "highest-level," most complex, and/or climactic stage in a particular cultural history; as anthropologists we are supposed to get away from this kind of language (as with South American prehistorians' use of neutral "Intermediate" and "Horizon" periods).

TRADITIONAL MODELS: CERAMICS AND OTHER EVIDENCE

The Late Archaic in northwest Florida was thought to be concentrated on the coast and recognized by the presence of fiber-tempered ceramics (Milanich 1994), but there is much confusion of terms and types. The usually plain or simple-stamped, thick, fiber-tempered pottery first called St. Simons Plain or Orange ware (Bullen 1958; Willey 1949) was relabeled Norwood (Phelps 1965), a term that then somehow automatically became a phase name. Norwood is the most poorly defined of several taxa of Southeastern fiber-tempered ceramics, yet the term has been used mostly without question for decades. Shannon (1986, 1987) suggested that Norwood pottery is not distinctive enough to be a separate type. Indeed, he thought *all* the types of fiber-tempered ceramics in the Southeast are products of local typologies instead of resulting from consideration of a whole regional tradition. His attribute analysis of sherds from all the major Southeastern fiber-tempered ceramic series showed they all overlap or are indistinguishable from each other (Shannon 1986; this is, of course, characteristic of many pottery types of all periods!), and his map of distributions of the various types shows more about which archaeologists were working where, and when, than about prehistoric cultural groups (Shannon 1987:9). Sassaman's (1993:17) map of major fiber-tempered pottery traditions has a gap for most of Florida and for the entire Gulf Coast. Many archaeologists still see the earliest ceramics in northwest Florida as "moving in" after having been developed elsewhere. But "major traditions" are just those that were described first and published more. Fiber-tempered wares are just as early in northwest Florida as anywhere else and are very much like all the other early pottery in the Southeast. We should abandon the term *Norwood* and use generic type names.

A study of metric and other attributes of fiber-tempered ceramics from 23 sites investigated by the University of South Florida field program in the Apalachicola Valley (White 2003b) demonstrates this lack of distinctiveness. For example, nearly all of some 200 sherds have some sand in the paste like most fiber-tempered types (Shannon 1986, 1987), which were often originally defined that way (e.g., Wheeler Plain in Alabama; Heimlich 1952:8). A few Apalachicola sherds have grog in the paste as well and most have mica, which is naturally characteristic of clays in this valley. Simple-stamping occurs on sherds mostly from a few coastal/estuarine sites. There are no data indicating that plain-surfaced or less-sandy-paste sherds are stratigraphically earlier, attractive as it may be to see adding sand and simple-stamping as logical transitions to Early Woodland types.

Pots were thick-walled and hand-built, with straight vertical sides and flat bottoms. They were big—a half-vessel recovered from the Sopchoppy Valley to the east of the Apalachicola indicates that a complete pot would have weighed over 10 pounds (Kimbrough 1999). Fiber in the sherds, identified as Spanish moss (*Tillandsia usneoides*), sometimes remains intact; one bit from a sherd from Sam's Cutoff shell mound (8Fr754; see Figure 1.1) in the lower Apalachicola, which also produced chert microtools, was AMS-dated to 3720 ± 60 B.P. or 2290–1930 cal B.C. (2 sigma, Beta-68513; White and Estabrook 1994).

There are just a handful of incised and punctated Stallings Island–type sherds in the middle and upper Apalachicola and on the lower Chattahoochee, well away from the coast. Interior riverine routes appear to be the channels for transport of this pottery; Atlantic coastal types may have actually been brought into the valley from the north, where interaction with the peoples making them would have been easier and closer. The distribution and flow patterns of water across the landscape were probably major structuring principles for Late Archaic life.

So far, there is little else known to be diagnostic of either the ceramic or preceramic Late Archaic, except for chert microtools and clay balls. The few lithic remains other than microtools include stemmed and notched points. Sherds of steatite vessels with notched or ticked lips appear at a few sites from the coast all the way inland. No steatite cooking slabs are known. At least one engraved bone pin has come from a Late Archaic shell midden, from a possibly preceramic level. One jasper bead was recovered at a barrier island site. A clay figurine fragment (or adorno) from possibly the Late Archaic component of Clark Creek shell mound (8Gu60; see Figure 1.1) is reminiscent of Poverty Point figurines. It is a pointed human head with slit eyes (White 1994a).

DISTRIBUTION OF SITES IN TIME AND SPACE

Of the 76 Late Archaic sites in the Apalachicola–lower Chattahoochee Valley, the only ones known to be mounds are also in the coastal/estuarine wetland area, and they are all mounded shell middens on or near streams. Whether coastal or inland, the sites usually have later prehistoric components. Those two or three that do not are perhaps in locations that ceased to be suitable for habitation because of changes in water resources. On the coast, the one shell mound known not to have any later components, Sam's Cutoff, is the only one not today situated in the river swamp. Instead, it is in the middle of the sawgrass marsh, closer to the open water of Apalachicola Bay, and nearly submerged because of rising sea level. Inland Late Archaic components are on either immediate stream banks or old meanders, and they are usually deeply buried by one or two meters of alluvium. Worse, continual fluvial movement has meant constant reworking of riverine lowlands, so that earlier Late Archaic components may often have been redeposited and mixed with later materials. All these factors have made the inland Late Archaic harder to see.

There are only six good dates for Late Archaic sites in this valley. They range from 2900 to 800 cal b.c. (White 1994b, 2003b). This compares well with current dates for fiber-tempered ceramics elsewhere in the Southeast and makes it unnecessary to invoke any immigration of pottery or people from elsewhere.

PEOPLE, SETTLEMENTS, AND SUBSISTENCE

Only three Late Archaic burials are known from the region, all in lower valley shell middens. None has grave goods; two are flexed and the third was too decayed to tell (White 1994a, 1994b, 2003a). One is a young woman, the other two adult men. All were very shallow, perhaps because digging through shell is hard to do. Not only are there no socioeconomic indicators for these burials but also they are located within what is presumably the garbage pile. However, the question remains as to where the rest of the Late Archaic people ended up, not to mention what is different between here and the interior riverine cemeteries of the Midsouth at this time.

Subsistence at lower delta shell middens clearly emphasizes wetland environments. Freshwater fish, shellfish, and turtles predominate in faunal assemblages from tested sites, where bone is well preserved because it is shielded from the acidic soils by the alkaline shell (White 1994a, 1994b, 2003a). Where faunal remains are available for inland sites, though terrestrial species are present, aquatic animals from shellfish to turtles and muskrat are well represented (Bullen 1958). We may be underestimating the importance of the use of aquatic

resources because artifacts such as nets and lines are not preserved. My hypothesis is that Late Archaic adaptations here emphasized wetland resources and that
the dynamism of such environments may have required small, mobile societies
and precluded precocious complexity.

However, there are no data as yet concerning populations, households, or
sedentism. Gross settlement data, of course, provide only static patterns, ignoring
dynamic social relationships within the span of some two millennia. Some
(more simplistic) models assume that periodic aggregations typical of complex
hunter-gatherers must have taken place at larger sites. Flexible social and spatial
boundaries are said to prohibit hoarding of both information and resources,
maintaining egalitarian organization. Only at aggregation sites might there be
such hoarding (Root 1983). But sites distinctively larger than the rest are not
yet identifiable in this valley. Even if they were, they could be produced by repeated use through time by the same small groups.

There are so far no seasonality data either from any sites, but pronounced
seasonal flooding and differential availability of resources characterize all the
valley environments. Furthermore, the size of the useful subsistence landscape
was probably greater than we imagine in this watery wilderness, while the social
landscape may have been smaller. The standard measure of a subsistence catch-
ment area as a 12-km radius or two-hour walk from a site was developed in such
places as the open Kalahari desert (e.g., Lee 1969). Different standards are essential if travel was mostly by water and in forested, more hidden landscapes
where you can go and get things faster but cannot see people coming from miles
away unless you are out on the open bay or on a long, straight stretch of stream
channel.

POVERTY POINT RELATIONS

Lazarus (1958) recorded the extension into northwest Florida of sites producing
Poverty Point–type artifacts and named it the Elliott's Point complex, with jus-
tification for a new name apparently being the modern political boundary of the
Florida state line. Calvin Jones (1993) tabulated some 90 Elliott's Point sites
in the Florida panhandle with a diverse array of fired clay objects. The Apalachicola delta area seems to be the easternmost contiguous extent of the distribution of such materials, though some clay balls have been collected from Atlantic coastal sites and from a site on Tampa Bay (McGee and Wheeler 1994;
Milanich 1994; Small 1966), as well as from the Georgia coast (Webb 1968:
300). However, clay cooking balls may not necessarily indicate Poverty Point
connections in time or space.

All the Apalachicola sites with Poverty Point–type materials are in the coastal/estuarine area, and all are shell mounds/middens. These sites have micro-tools, clay balls, and occasionally other items. A jasper disc bead from Pickalene Midden (8Fr363; see Figure 1.1) on St. Vincent Island in the Gulf is the only fancy lapidary specimen known. At Van Horn Creek shell mound (8Fr744; see Figure 1.1), debitage and cores indicate a microtool manufacturing locus (one of the few suggestions of different site function). Six sites have produced Poverty Point–type clay balls/objects, and many more also have characteristic amorphous clay chunks, in concentrations suggesting they were used for the same type of cooking.

In sum, we now know of one diagnostic Poverty Point item, plus a few dozen clay balls, piles of clay chunks, and hundreds of microtools at lower Apalachicola Valley sites, suggesting more of a subsistence similarity with Poverty Point than economic interaction. The data could easily fit Jackson's (1991) trade-fair model, with selected rarer things (such as the jasper bead) filtering down the rivers and along the coastal area incorporating the Apalachicola delta, along with ideas, which travel more rapidly, flowing over to result in local production of such characteristic items as microtools and clay balls. A map of the continuous distribution of diagnostic Poverty Point artifacts in Late Archaic sites from the Mississippi Valley across the whole northern Gulf Coast would probably show them associated with low wetlands everywhere. Something about wetland adaptation perhaps made it useful to have these artifacts.

The small size of microtools is sometimes thought to have been due to conservation of a scarce resource, but chert, agatized coral, and other lithic raw materials are readily available in the Apalachicola Valley. Another hypothesis has been that microtools are for manufacturing shell artifacts, but shell items from the Apalachicola shell mounds are few (as compared with peninsular Florida). I believe microtools were for woodworking, to make the kinds of artifacts needed to obtain aquatic resources. It might have been not only efficient but also imperative to make as many items as possible out of wood in a forested wetland environment of river swamp, coast, and estuary. Things lost from the boat or the shore would float and could be recovered. (I am struck by the practicality of this hypothesis every field season as crucial equipment is lost over the side of the boat.) Use-wear studies of microtools could confirm such a hypothesis.

The connections with Poverty Point manifested in the northwest Florida region are suggested to be from the use of similar artifacts for similar utilitarian functions in the coastal and estuarine wetlands. Late Archaic populations inland upriver on the Apalachicola, exploiting perhaps more terrestrial environments, do not use some distinctive coastal artifacts such as clay objects and microtools, but they share the same basic plain pottery (though apparently not the simple-stamped version) and probably also some emphasis upon aquatic re-

sources. The inland water sources are different, faster flowing streams. Comparison of specific aquatic species available/utilized from the coast–estuary–river
mouth zone to the interior will be an avenue for further research.

THE MOUND ISSUE

No Late Archaic earthen mounds are known in the Apalachicola–lower Chattahoochee Valley, but most of the Late Archaic sites in the lower valley are shell
mounds, mostly of *Rangia* clams but sometimes of oyster (none are shell rings;
most are curvilinear elevations paralleling stream banks or old channels). Other
sites on the coast, mostly mainland and barrier island bayshore sites, are labeled
shell middens because the shell is not piled high but distributed horizontally.
They may have once been more mounded before erosion or modern development (most shell middens have been mined for road fill).

   We are left with the problem of shell midden/shell mound differentiation and
also the question of whether shell mounds are deliberately built up, using shell
as construction material, or whether they are accumulations of food garbage that
over time make dry, high ground (Claassen 1991a; Waselkov 1987). The standard matrix is usually solid shell with little soil. Even if they were deliberately
constructed out of food garbage, it would be hard to recognize basketloads of
white shells piled on top of other white shells. Most likely they were ever-growing
garbage piles, useful because it is easy to find the high white dry ground in the
river swamp (even today, when the military in Florida uses shell mounds as
bombing practice targets). While it is reasonable to hypothesize stilt houses in
the wetlands such as are known elsewhere, so far there is no real evidence for
even a post mold in the Apalachicola shell mounds. If people were not living
there, some other activity may have been going on. Voorhies and colleagues
(1991) found floors in preceramic shell mounds dating to 3000 B.C. on the
Mexican Pacific coast that indicate not habitation but perhaps shrimp-processing
stations for people with complex settlement-subsistence systems.

   This discussion has assumed that current environments and climate are not
enormously different from those prevailing 4,000 years ago. This may be an un-
founded assumption, but the Apalachicola shell mound faunal assemblages differ
little from Archaic through later levels, suggesting similar environments through
historic times. Through space, there is interesting variability from west to east.
Lower delta shell mounds on the west side show a continuous sequence of freshwater aquatic species, but on the east side Late Archaic deposits are associated
more with oyster and more saltwater fish, while later deposits are *Rangia* clams
and more freshwater species. This is interpreted as a consequence of the fluvial
shifts, as the eastward-migrating river channel brought more fresh water after
the end of the Late Archaic (Donoghue and White 1994; White 2003a).

The reason for building mounds in any Archaic setting in the Southeast could simply be for uplift above the low wet ground. Everywhere we find them, Archaic mounds are in some low alluvial valley or coastal wetland situation where the terrain is not very much above sea level (there is a correlation in the Southeast between the distribution of Archaic mound sites and the elevation zones on the standard Gulf hurricane tracking map). Much of one's established way of life is disturbed by flooding. You can see farther on top of a higher elevation, keep your food and feet from rotting and your fuel dry, and set up a living space that will last longer and be able to be revisited often. The evidence keeps mounting for continual, multiseasonal or year-round occupation of Archaic mounds. It is not necessary to call mound building cultural elaboration, wasteful behavior (Hamilton 1999), or unprecedented group activity, and thus something beyond the realm of utilitarian function, until we can demonstrate that it was not just utilitarian.

POWER, LABOR, AND INEQUALITY

Behavior as complicated as sedentary living and mound building can now be pushed back to the Middle Archaic or earlier (e.g., Russo 1994a, 1994b; Saunders et al. 1997); prehistoric peoples always turn out to have been far more sophisticated and skilled than we moderns think. However, we assume that deliberate construction of mounds requires some centralized direction and thus mounds are evidence of cultural complexity, specifically, of political and social inequalities, if not economic as well. The symposium in which this paper was originally presented was entitled "Big Mound Power" on the basis of assumptions of centralized authority, control, and competition that mounds are supposed to embody.

But in this postprocessual age, we cannot forget about function. If mounds are just ways to get high and stay dry, whether constructed rapidly with piles of earth or shell or slowly by accumulating garbage, this can be done with minimal planning or leadership. If there are burials or cremations or offerings in them, it may be just standard for any large group project as part of the general worldview of ancient America. In visualizing the Late Archaic, I must take a devil's advocate view, not because people were not clever enough to come up with more complex society but because, well, why should they? Why should leveling mechanisms break down and more work be required of most people for less opportunity or lower status?

The problem is with the assumption of hierarchical organization and direction. Yes, there is enormous variability in the complexity and organization of forager societies (e.g., Gregg 1991; Kelly 1995; Price and Brown 1985). The latest way of recognizing this is through various Marxist and other analyses that emphasize labor, the division thereof, and the capture of large amounts. But we cannot assume (e.g., Price and Feinman 1995:4) the automatic presence of inequality in all human societies that then becomes amplified; instead we must assume equality until inequality is demonstrated and look for the different *kinds* of inequality.

The only basic inequality *always* present is the differing ability to make a living based on age, because children cannot do complex, heavy tasks. This is where we should start in looking at division of labor. (Why do we not see this as obvious before we go looking for sex/gender differences, even? We also assume children buried with wealth have ascribed status rather than achieved, though we know little of what they might have accomplished, especially in spiritual realms, at an early age.) But even the very basic subsistence inequalities supposedly always present in forager society that have to do with sharing hard-to-get foods such as meat (Speth 1990) are mitigated in emphasizing aquatic resources that children too can net or pick up. Children's subsistence chores could even include helping parents fashion clay balls for cooking. This might explain the range of cute shapes and small fingerprints on many of the Poverty Point objects and would have given kids a fun, safe job to play at away from sharp knives and fire.

Turning to gender, some models see gender inequality, manifested in the division of labor, as the basis of all inequality in hunter-gatherer societies, but there is little good evidence. It is time to throw out sociobiological models of gender and escape that tyranny of the ethnographic record, which was obtained when intensive agriculture and incredibly early, enormously rapid, postcontact change in the Southeast made unreliable the comparisons with Late Archaic foragers living thousands of years earlier. We must dump the gender stereotypes and continuing Western bias that require rigid divisions of labor cross-culturally (e.g., Bruhns and Stothert 1999; Kent 1998:14). We now have plenty of examples of women hunting and otherwise traveling with heavy loads great distances from base camps, of men gathering plants, and lots of other extremely flexible scenarios from potentially equally appropriate ethnographic data (Brumbach and Jarvenpa 1997; Conkey and Williams 1991; Dahlberg 1981; Estioko-Griffin 1986; Martin and Voorhies 1975; Stange 1998). As Karen Bruhns (1991:427–428) reminds us, the only activities universally restricted to a specific sex are insemination and conception.

Even ethnographic analogy from the contact period, as inappropriate as it may be, does not show the narrow division of labor traditionally hypothesized. Florida Indian women were recorded obtaining both plants and animals, including fish and alligators. And *third*-gender berdaches who were usually wives (Le Moyne's "curly-haired hermaphrodites") did heavy labor, medical, and other unusual jobs (Callender and Kochems 1983; Lorant 1946:69, 81).

Furthermore, a division of labor by gender would not necessarily mean inequality in the sense of a power differential. In the presumably matrilineal Southeast, at least for later periods, there might have been more of a complementarity in the power structure. There is just starting to be some thought about the power of later prehistoric women, whose families centered the household, one of the basic units of archaeological investigation (Bruhns and Stothert 1999; Kent 1999; Trocolli 1999; White 1999). For foragers, women's power could also include spiritual associations with reproduction and menstruation. One study suggests Yurok hunter-gatherers in California scheduled subsistence behavior and mobility in accordance with women's synchronous monthly cycles (Buckley 1988).

Moving on to the next level of understanding inequality, newer models invoke competition vs. alliances and "self-aggrandizers" or "accumulators," opportunistic individuals who scheme, persuade, and otherwise accumulate supporters, wealth, and power (e.g., Clark and Blake 1996; Hayden 1995). These individuals are assumed to exist in any human society (a huge and not well-founded assumption); they are clever enough to devise strategies for achieving prestige and wealth at the expense of everyone else. They have become popular figures in trendy discussions of "agency" in the prehistoric past.

It is nearly impossible to find these self-aggrandizing individuals in the archaeological record and, also, such models may be highly inappropriate for the Archaic Southeast. They are products of the recent Western capitalist milieu in which the theorists are living, with the emphasis upon markets, maximization of capital investment, and world economic issues that are supposed to concern everyone but in reality are far removed from most people (the majority of Americans do not own stocks, for example). They also result from the continuing and perniciously hidden but unchanging sexism and hierarchy in the division of labor in our own society. It is hard to recognize the bias in such models when the situation is assumed to be so natural. Keller (1985) has noted how biologists stubbornly insist on explaining life processes hierarchically: reproduction in slime molds is modeled as a process directed by a few master cells, even though there is no evidence for such cells. Evolution toward greater complexity in human societies may be no more natural or predetermined than evolution toward less complexity.

MODELS OF HIERARCHY VS. EGALITARIAN COMMUNITY

To find opportunistic individuals in prehistory requires unambiguous ways of identifying them, as well as identifying the risk-leveling mechanisms that may prevent them, i.e., group opinion in traditional societies that often serves to sanction individuals who would put themselves first. Ethnographies of hunter-gatherers and even horticulturalists are full of descriptions of such safeguards. Furthermore, big projects can get done in other ways besides under direction of hierarchical leadership. How about the barn-raising or ladies' auxiliary model of production, in which everyone knows what to do and does it, for the good of the group, and so the structure gets erected, decorated, and filled with food for the feast without the need for centralized power? Nuer pastoralists in East Africa, devoid of centralized political leadership (much to the consternation of colonial powers) gathered to build ceremonial mounds of earth and debris, 50–60 feet high, with elephant tusks planted around the base and summit, to which they brought oxen for sacrifice to honor the sky god and his prophet (Evans-Pritchard 1940:186, 222). Mounds are built in many other places in the world by non-sedentary populations (Kurgan burial mounds of prehistoric pastoralists on the west Asiatic steppes come to mind).

What about a model for early mounds that does not require sedentism, hierarchy, or anything other than the process of community gathering, and perhaps trying to rise above the flood level, carried on for a very long time in a stable environment? Every year/month/season each person/family shows up with a covered dish, a basketload of soil, an eye for potential mates, and a prayer to help build the communal earthworks. Because the river channel for some reason does not move for a long while, the buildup gets considerable in a few places such as Poverty Point or Watson Brake (there are doubtless others still unrecognized); perhaps later the work becomes transformed into ritual.

Mounds can be built for utilitarian reasons, which I think we have to assume for the small Late Archaic shell mounds in northwest Florida. There are similar shell mounds along the coastal wetlands westward through Louisiana and Texas, but most of them may be different from the earlier earthen mounds such as Watson Brake. We now know the megalithic monuments of Europe did not originate with eastern Mediterranean civilizations and diffuse westward but instead were built earlier and for many different reasons. Similarly, we should assume until proven otherwise that mounds in the Southeast were independently raised for different reasons in many different places and that all did not necessarily originate with some precocious north Louisiana folks. Russo (1994b:106–107) notes that hierarchy is not necessary to build a mound, nor does there have to be a great labor cost for just dumping garbage every day to build it. We need not postulate a food surplus either for people to be able to construct mounds. If hunter-gatherers only need work a couple days a week to make a living, even in difficult environments such as southern Africa or northern Australia (as in Sahlins's [1972] "original affluent society"), in the bountiful Southeast they should have had plenty of time to build a mound or other construction, for utilitarian, social, and/or ideological reasons, without diminishing their food-getting capacities.

Other requirements for the emergence of hierarchy pushed forward by aggrandizing individuals are, alternately, rich environments with the potential for intensifying labor to obtain more resources or stressed environments in which opportunistic leaders gain power by providing resources. We have moved from simply environmental explanations of stress or demographic pressure (e.g., Price and Brown 1985) to a combination of just the right environments and just the right social roles, or just the social roles evolving in themselves (Arnold, ed. 1996; Hayden 1995), but there is still little clarity about how to see all this in the archaeological record. One possible power differential, that of men over women, as expressed by rape, is correlated with resource stress, as analyzed by Peggy Sanday, while rape-free societies are found more in environments with re-source stability (Benderly 1982; Sanday 1981). But most of the aggrandizer-type models do not spend time demonstrating gender inequality, taking it as a given. A recent work on Midwestern Archaic mortuary sites (Pleger 2000) attempting to find "aggrandizers in transegalitarian societies" concluded there were none, since most of the exotic grave goods were buried with younger adult females, who could never be so powerful!

In looking at early complexity among Southeastern foragers, we must distin-guish social from economic inequality, or ranked from stratified society (Fried 1967). Stratification is based on differential access to economic resources, not just indicators of social prestige (and material culture may be different from what we expect: remember garbology studies showed the poorest people consuming the most bread and liquor [Rathje 1974], and conspicuous consumption may include showering expensive goods on the powerless by the wealthy [Kehoe 1999]). We must look not for the first status differentiation but rather for when and how it became institutionalized, when differences became inherited, thus providing the foundation for not only the emergence of social and political hier-archy (Price and Feinman 1995:4) but also real economic stratification. Social differentiation may mean having special titles, clothing and jewelry, a bigger house, rights to speak first or name children or even decide when to move or to use religious paraphernalia to bring up the spirits. Economic differentiation means some people eat better, have warm blankets, labor little to get a drink of water, live longer, and avoid getting beaten up regularly, while others do not.

Having said all this, I still have no idea how to get testable hypotheses for divisions of labor, let alone economic power differentials. The sex, gender, or age of the maker and user of an artifact is not yet determinable, though with DNA studies some of this may come. Meanwhile, there is lately much more evidence that forager strategies are nothing if they are not both flexible and diverse. If the emphasis upon aquatic resources is real in the Late Archaic, perhaps this may explain the lack of any indication of sedentism, mounds, and unequal power in the archaeological record of the Apalachicola Valley system. The reasons go back to labor and environments. Fish, shellfish, and turtles, the largest component of the shell mound faunal assemblages, and other aquatic resources are not as difficult to obtain as terrestrial mammals and birds. For example, they can be collected by hand, spear, or gig in shallow water, by hook and line, or by net. Turtles can be picked up by hand. Much of the process requires group effort, with netting, propelling the boat, and carrying the containers. We are not talking about harpooning whales here. The near-coastal, bayshore, estuarine, and river swamp aquatic resources can be obtained by people of all sizes, strengths, sexes, and ages. This contrasts with hunting deer, for example, which may require more dangerous weapons, stealth, strength, and stamina.

Besides the richness of the Apalachicola Valley aquatic environments, the dynamism of its landscapes also mitigates against sedentism and possibly therefore rigid social organization. Whether from hurricanes, annual river floods, or other forces, frequently changing habitats may have made settlement for any length of time impossible. The long-term use of shell mounds from Archaic through Mississippian times probably represents old sites being rediscovered by later peoples, not continuous use. Meehan's (1982) amazing ethnography of Australian coastal hunter-gatherers shows that the variables around which everything is geared are the seasons, whether directly, because of wind and water, or indirectly, because of mosquitoes or other conditions. It may be easy to shift habitation sites often if you are extremely mobile because of the comparative swiftness of transport by water. Steatite bowls and 10-pound pots are far less trouble in the canoe than on your back. Perhaps fiber-tempered pottery is flat-bottomed for stability in the boat.

SUMMARY: NO BIG POWER, JUST THE GOOD LIFE

In the Apalachicola/lower Chattahoochee Valley region, work still lags far behind the great progress that has been made in Louisiana and the Poverty Point, Stallings Island, and south Florida areas. Current data suggest that ceramic Late Archaic settlements in all types of environments, from coast to interior, emphasize aquatic resources. The only mounds are of shells, and they are in the coastal/estuarine/lower river swamp areas. These are also the sites that have Poverty Point–related artifacts and simple-stamped fiber-tempered pottery in addition to the plain fiber-tempered ceramics. The dates suggest this adaptation lasts from perhaps 4000 to after 2000 B.C., with little discernible change. Relationships with Poverty Point may be simply from similarity of subsistence practices in low wetlands and the outer edges of exchange networks. Little is known of the preceramic Archaic, with only hints that life was much the same before as after pottery.

There is still little evidence from which to infer anything about social organization beyond basic egalitarian foraging. The suggestion of lithic specialization at Van Horn Creek shell mound might reflect site function, but we are far from demonstrating craft specialization, redistribution of products, relationships with subsistence (let alone subsistence stress), or other social aspects that might indicate any complexity (e.g., Arnold 1987:251–253). As for mounds, there are none until the Middle Woodland (the archaeological construct named Swift Creek–early Weeden Island, after its two ceramic traditions), when burial mounds occur from inland to the coast. Evidence for sedentism is not present until the Mississippian, and even then may not be characteristic of coastal shell middens because of the greater dynamism of the landforms.

Seemingly precocious developments elsewhere in the Southeast, such as large-scale mound building, may be signs of growing Archaic sociopolitical complexity and emergence of differential amounts of power for some people, but they may also be evidence of just general group activities carried out without need of hierarchical direction. While a few material items related to these precocious cultures appear in the lower Apalachicola delta during the Late Archaic, they suggest nothing more (or less) than functional equivalence of subsistence systems and sporadic long-distance social interaction. In the lush watery environments of the Apalachicola–lower Chattahoochee Valley, resource abundance and lack of sedentism as a result of ever-changing surroundings appear to have fostered complex scheduling but reasonably egalitarian society during the Late Archaic. Conservatism, resistance to change, is typical when resources are dependable and group life is successful.

ACKNOWLEDGMENTS

I thank Phil Carr and Jon Gibson for their hospitality in inviting me to participate in the 1999 Southeastern Archaeological Conference symposium and in the wonderful gathering at Poverty Point. Others whom I appreciate are John O'Hear, who reminded me of the example of Nuer mound building that we all read in grad school; Mary Beth Fitts, who drew the clay ball; Laura Weant, who drew the microtools; and Eric Eyles, who helped draw the map.

3

Measuring Shell Rings for Social Inequality

Michael Russo

Two basic interpretations of shell rings vie for archaeological acceptance. One posits that rings are the daily subsistence refuse incidentally tossed behind or underfoot of households (Trinkley 1997; Waring and Larson 1968:273; cf. White, this volume). The other suggests that shell rings are among the earliest examples of large-scale public architecture in North America, intentionally built for ritual and ceremony (Cable 1997; Waring 1968a:243). The incidental refuse theory asserts that the symmetrical, circular shape of the shell rings, as well as their happenstance construction, reflects an egalitarian ethic (Trinkley 1985). Habitation evenly placed around circles symbolizes and supports the idea that each household is socially equal to its neighbor.

Conversely, the public architecture theory states that large-scale construction involves expenditures of energy beyond the access of individuals or families in egalitarian societies. It requires an increased scale of political organization typical of ranked societies. Individuals or groups serve in leadership roles to motivate and manage the large numbers of people needed to build the monuments. The efforts are rewarded in greater social cohesion for the group and a reinforced, higher social status for the leaders (Abrams 1989). The level of organization in societies that build such large-scale public works is widely varied and is certainly not limited to states or chiefdoms (Abrams 1989; Russo 1991).

As earlier, large-scale architecture (mounds, earthworks, shell rings) is discovered (Russo 1994b; Saunders 1994, this volume; Saunders et al. 1994), archaeologists have argued that monumental architecture by itself is not sufficient evidence of social inequality to warrant reclassification of the traditional view of Archaic people as egalitarian (Gibson, this volume; Saunders, this volume). Corroboration of inequality should be sought in other markers of social ranking, such as those that serve as evidence of social complexity in Woodland and Mississippian societies. The lack of horticulture/agriculture, the paucity/absence of exotic or esteemed items, and little or no evidence of storage facilities, structures, craft specialization, feasting, burial goods, and burials in mounds lead to the conclusion early mound/shell ring builders did not participate in hierarchically ranked societies (Russo 1991, 1994b; Saunders, this volume). For shell rings in particular, what appear to be strictly quotidian artifacts (e.g., ceramics, shell tools), living floors (as seen in crushed bands of shells), and large pits filled only with shell refuse (interpreted as shellfish/fish steaming pits and hot fire/meat roasting pits) have all been viewed as evidence that shell rings were places of daily living, not places of ceremony (Russo 1991, 1994b; Trinkley 1980:313, 338–339; cf. White, this volume).

Of course, this hyperskeptical view assumes, a priori, that Archaic builders of large-scale architecture would have to have been socially complex in the same ways evidenced by Woodland and Mississippian builders of large-scale architecture. It further assumes that shell rings could not have been used both as a place of daily living and as a place of ceremony. It is a normative stance (sensu Kuhn 1970) that dismisses the architecture as aberration in order to preserve the operative paradigm of Archaic as egalitarian. In such an approach the presumption is made that if the Archaic builders were indeed socially ranked, then subsequent Southeastern cultural traits that normal archaeologists accept as defining social complexity may be found in some exact or recognizably ancestral form in the Archaic. It does not allow for the waxing/waning of a variety of forms of complex social organization that may have resulted in the discontinuity of at least some organizational and material traits between the Archaic and Woodland/Mississippian cultures.

So little investigation has been undertaken on either shell rings or Archaic mounds that any number of the traditional markers of rank may simply have not yet been found. But sufficient work has been completed to suggest that Archaic monumental architecture does differ from Woodland/Mississippian in the absence/paucity of burials, artifacts, and residences suggestive of differential ranking among the community members. This material depauperation is seen as evidence of an egalitarian ethic, in which status differentiation was kept level, and, as such, archaeologists have been compelled to explain away the ostensibly nonegalitarian, large-scale architecture. Archaic monumental architecture is thus seen as being propelled by periodic, voluntary, corporate behavior (Gibson, this volume), as the result of palimpsests of numerous small-scale daily activities (Trinkley 1980), as facilitated by short-term managers whose power and prestige were tolerated by the egalitarian society only for short times or in critical situations (Russo 1994b), or as, somehow, not outside the organizational abilities of egalitarian hunter-gatherers (Saunders, this volume). I believe these efforts to preserve our long-held view of the Archaic as a time of egalitarian bands, while understandable as a normal process associated with paradigm shifts, serve to thwart investigation of the social complexities inherent in numerous Archaic cultures. For Southeastern archaeology, a tradition steeped in the unilineal, tripartite social organizational classification scheme (bands, tribes, chiefdoms), cultures apparently organized differently have been difficult to envision. Consequently, egalitarian bands seem the best fit for societies constructing large-scale public architecture 4,000 to 7,000 years ago.

In this chapter, I suggest that the artifactual, subsistence, and architectural records of Archaic cultures that built shell rings evidence social inequalities. However, the evidence is not necessarily isomorphic with that typically associated with late Southeastern prehistoric societies. I present theoretical grounding for interpreting the evidence. In lieu of classifying ring builders along a progressive, unilineal evolutionary scale, I suggest that archaeologists may be better served by viewing the cultures as transegalitarian (Clark and Blake 1994; Hayden 1995). Aside from its teleological overtones, the term suffices to describe mound/ring-building Archaic cultures with aspects of both simple and complex modes of social organization. The rise of social complexity from egalitarian roots has been the focus of many papers (e.g., Arnold 1995; Arnold, ed. 1996; Hayden 1995; Kelly 1995; Widmer, this volume). While I briefly touch on and reference this subject, my primary objective is to examine possible ways to recognize incipient aspects of social inequality in archaeological remains from shell ring sites.

FEASTING AND CEREMONY AMONG TRANSEGALITARIANS

To date, archaeologists have discovered that Archaic cultures did not practice agriculture, bury ranked individuals, extensively trade in exotic goods from distant lands, or store prized goods or foods in pits at their shell ring sites. While positive evidence of such activities has been linked to ranked societies, to assume that socially complex societies must necessarily practice any or all of these behaviors is to dismiss the ethnographic archaeological record laden with complex societies that do not. Evidence of daily maintenance activities (e.g., food refuse, cooking pits, hearths, broken pots, clay balls, shell tools), on the other hand, is ubiquitous at shell rings. Such evidence has been used to support the notion of the sites as utilitarian camps or villages, which, in the absence of status goods, were egalitarian. However, this approach implies that socially ranked societies did not engage in cooking, consumption, and garbage disposal on a quotidian level. Of course, members of ranked societies eat, and, if shellfish is a major part of their diet, we should expect to find the remains of such endeavors wherever that food was prepared, eaten, gifted, and/or disposed of. In determining whether shell rings were places of daily meals among equals or places of ceremony

among socially diverse peoples, care must be taken to recognize that a clean dichotomy may not exist. The simple presence of daily maintenance activities at a
site does not equate with a strictly nonceremonial use of a site. In the ethnographic record, many minimally socially complex societies perform ritual and
ceremony at their daily living sites (e.g., Heckenberger et al. 1999; Schiefenhövel
and Bell-Krannhals 1996) and/or practice daily maintenance at certain times at
otherwise unoccupied ceremonial sites (e.g., Dillehay 1990). Both kinds of sites
are ceremonial sites, and if the ceremonies persist for extensive periods at either
site type, we may, under specific circumstances, expect great difficulty in distinguishing among strictly ceremonial sites, strictly village sites, or a combination
thereof in the material record (Hayden 2001).

Regardless of whether shell rings are primarily village sites or solely ceremonial sites, members of ring societies were preparing, consuming, and discarding
shell and other food refuse at the sites often in great quantities suggestive of
large-scale feasting. Feasts occur at every level of socioeconomic complexity, in
egalitarian, transegalitarian, chiefly, and state societies.[1] Feasts represent the
communal consumption of foods and may be differentiated from daily meals by
the quantity and quality of foods eaten, the places where consumption takes
place, and the categories of people involved. In all societies, regardless of their
level of social complexity, people of certain categories or statuses may be excluded from feasts or otherwise feast differently from others. Age and gender
groups may feast in different places and at different times from each other. Certain people may prepare foods while others consume it. Specific instruments
used in preparation, consumption, and presentation of food may serve to differentiate high from low status, male from female, and kinship or ethnic groups
from each other.

The consumption of food is not the only nor necessarily the primary function
of feasting. Feasting is ritual. The greater society is meant to participate in, view,
or be excluded from all feasts for specific social reasons. These reasons may be
subtle or overtly symbolic events in which the distribution of food is intended to
bring prestige and power to the feast's host. In these cases, feasts serve to obtain,
maintain, and transform structures of power (Dietler 2001:70). Other reasons
for feasting may seemingly be more functional. For example, feasts may serve to
distribute or redistribute foodstuffs designed to feed the community. However,
even in these cases, status and prestige may be obtained by those who bring in,
or give away, the most, the biggest, the rarest, or otherwise valued resources.

Like all rituals, feasts are symbolic representations of social relations (Dietler
2001:71). As such, the archaeological remains of feasts can be used to identify
asymmetries in the social order of communities. Differences in the kinds, quantities, and location of material remains associated with differences in social status

may be reflected in the archaeological record. Because of their shapes and constituents (i.e., the refuse of feasts and other meals), shell rings provide ideal laboratories for testing theories of social inequality as reflected in feasting activities.

The ritual aspects attendant with feasts need not be highly elaborate, especially in egalitarian societies where ethics of sharing and equality may prohibit
ostentatious display by productive individuals, such as the best hunter or the
best fisher (Kelly 1995:296–297). In transegalitarian societies, egalitarian ethics
often linger and displays of unequal empowerment among members may be pro-
scribed or tolerated only under specific social circumstances such as at feasts or
in other rituals. Under such conditions, evidence of feasting may be harder to
distinguish from quotidian fare than in more highly ranked societies. This seems
to be the case at shell rings where artifacts recovered are generally utilitarian,
relatively sparse, and seemingly found throughout all areas of shell deposits. In
comparison, the same may be said of the distribution of artifacts in contemporary nonring midden sites. Consequently, seemingly little in the artifactual record serves to identify shell rings as somehow special-purpose, ritual, or ceremonial sites distinguishable from contemporary habitation sites. It is primarily the
shape, size, and distribution of shell that sets ring sites apart from other contemporary shell sites.

SHELL RING SHAPES

For Woodland and Mississippian landscapes, archaeologists have typically used
measurements of mounds as markers of social position. Height and volume mark
rank—the bigger the mound, the more status in the political hierarchy (e.g.,
Cahokia). Shape identifies type (e.g., household, temple, burial). Distribution
indicates hierarchy (e.g., surrounding mounds being subordinate to the largest
central mound). Why these same criteria have not been applied to shell rings
can be linked to at least two factors. One is the theoretical shortsightedness that
has assumed a priori that Archaic folks were not hierarchically organized. Not
only has evidence of status as reflected in material remains gone unrecognized,
but also a clear picture of the political relation of rings to each other and other
site types in regional settlement patterns has rarely been discussed (cf. Sassaman
1993). Despite the fact that rings are often found in groups with other rings,
with other shell middens, and, occasionally, with mounds, analogues to hierarchically infused concepts such as temple mounds, burial mounds, villages, ceremonial centers, and so on are rarely applied to shell rings and their contemporary site types (e.g., Cable 1997; Michie 1976; Sassaman 1993).

The second factor is that shell rings are typically viewed as massive, uniformly
constructed features not possessing separate and distinct components imbued
with social meaning. Whether archaeologists see rings as happenstance con-

structs or as purposefully built ceremonial monuments, the basic two features remain the same—the ring itself and the interior plaza. Archaeologists have generally focused their attentions on the strata and microconstituents—artifacts and fauna—in preference to systematic studies of the structure and geometry of shell rings (cf. Cable 1997; cf. Heide 2002; Hemmings 1970; Marrinan 1975; Russo 1991; cf. Russo 2002; cf. Russo and Heide 2001; Waring and Larson 1968). No uniformly recognized nomenclature exists for the variety of shapes and site features found at ring sites (in this chapter, a problem not completely remedied with concision) aside from descriptive terms such as exterior and interior (cf. Russo 2002; Trinkley 1985).

As their name implies, rings have long been viewed by archaeologists as perfect circles. The idea of rings containing both symmetrical circles of shell and vacant central plazas was forwarded early on (Drayton 1972 [1802]:57; McKinley 1873:423) and continues to hold the public's and archaeologists' imaginations to the present (e.g., Cable 1997; Hemmings 1970; Moore 1897:71–73; Trinkley 1985:102, 117; Waring 1968a:246; Waring and Larson 1968:268, 273). However, even a cursory examination of the prototypical rings of Georgia and South Carolina reveals that none are either perfectly circular or symmetrical. Of the 22 South Carolina and Georgia shell rings mapped or sketched sufficiently, only seven approach anything close to a closed circle; eight are open, or C-shaped; one is a closed oval; two are figure eights; one is U-shaped; and three are "rings" whose shapes defy easy description (Heide 2002; Russo and Heide 2001; see also Figure 3.1 for the footprints of seven of the rings that have been contour mapped).

Preconceptions of shell ring symmetry are so pervasive that where no such symmetry exists, archaeologists tend to apply it (e.g., front covers in Lawrence 1989, 1991). I note, however, that most references to rings as symmetrical circles with vacant centers come from general observations and sketch maps rather than systematic and objective measures of topography or excavations (e.g., Hemmings's front cover drawing in Lawrence 1991; McKinley 1873; Moore 1897). When topographic maps are made of the same sites, asymmetries in construction usually appear. For example, McKinley's (1873:423) observation that Sapelo Ring 1 was a "big circle" and Moore's (1897:71) observation that it was "one of those symmetrical works of the aborigines," plus Hemmings's (Lawrence 1991) and Moore's (1897) idealized sketch maps, contrast with the irregular contours provided by Simpkins's (1975) map (Figure 3.2). While at least part of this asymmetry is likely due to modern disturbance, the Sapelo contour map demonstrates that the ring actually varies widely in shape and height along its circumference in places not attributable to borrowing or erosion. Sapelo's tallest point is 6.25 m (arbitrarily assigned elevations), attained in one position on the southwest portions of the ring, while another point rises to 6 m on the northwest. Elsewhere

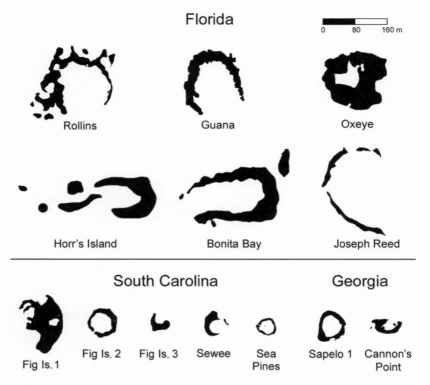

Figure 3.1. Footprints of contour-mapped shell rings.

on top of the ring, the highest elevations are only 4.5 to 5 m (on the south and east sides), or about 15 to 25 percent lower (Figure 3.2). While archaeologists have suggested that southeast portions of the site may have been quarried in modern times (Simpkins 1975; Figure 3.2b), the areas specifically postulated as having been mined do not account for all of the ring's topographical variation.

Similar variation in ring height is found at Cannon's Point, where ring-top elevations reach nearly 50 percent higher on the northwest than on most of the remaining ring (Figure 3.3; DePratter 1976:131, 1979; Marrinan 1975:26, Figure 4). At both the Fig Island 2 and Fig Island 3 rings, the differential is up to 40 percent from the highest elevations on top of the ring to the lowest (Figure 3.4). The Sea Pines ring extends only 60 cm above the land on which it lies, but uppermost sections of the ring are 50 percent higher than the lower sections (Figure 3.5). At Sewee, the differential ranges between 20 and 60 percent, though disturbance may account for the lowest elevations (Figure 3.6).

Postdepositional impacts have undoubtedly affected all extant shell rings to

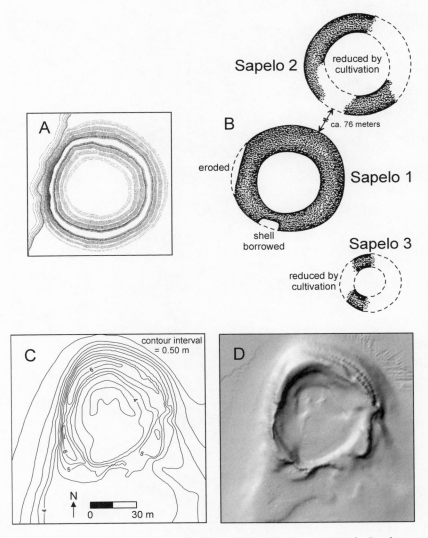

Figure 3.2. Sapelo shell rings. a, Sapelo 1 sketch map, after Moore 1897; b, Sapelo 1, 2, and 3 sketch map, after Hemmings in Lawrence 1991:front cover, p. iv; c, Sapelo 1 surface topography map, after Simpkins 1975; d, Sapelo 1 shaded relief map, derived from contour map in Simpkins 1975.

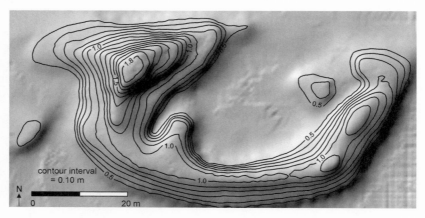

Figure 3.3. Cannon's Point shell ring surface topography and shaded relief map, derived from Marrinan 1975:26.

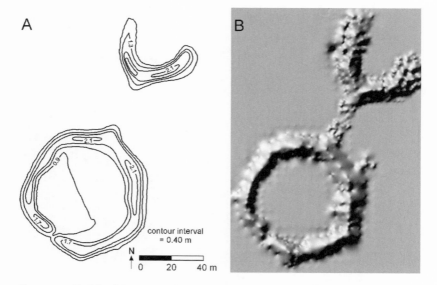

Figure 3.4. Fig Island Rings 2 and 3. a, Surface topography map, after Hemmings 1970; b, shaded relief map based on thickness of shell deposits, after Heide 2002.

varying degrees. At Sewee, a sketch map by Hemmings (front cover in Lawrence 1989) presumed that erosion accounted for the opening in the east side of the ring (Figure 3.6). However, soil cores reveal that the opening is likely not an erosional effect (Cable 1995:112; Gardner 1992:49) but an original design feature. At Sapelo, Simpkins (1975) speculated that the steep sides on the west side

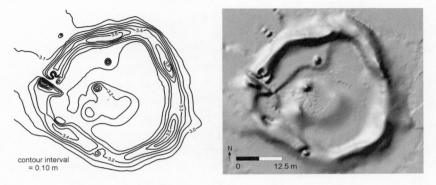

Figure 3.5. Sea Pines shell ring surface topography map and shaded relief map, derived from Trinkley 1980:39.

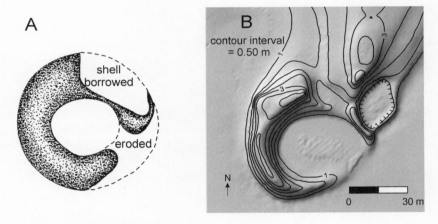

Figure 3.6. Sewee shell ring. a, Sketch map, after Hemmings in Lawrence 1989, 1991:iv; b, surface topography/shaded relief map, after Edwards 1965.

of the mound, sides no other archaeologist had ever posited as disturbed at all, were the result of borrowing for tabby construction (Figure 3.2c). It will be a continuing challenge for archaeologists to distinguish those architectural portions of rings designed by their builders from those wrought by nature, time, and subsequent cultures. Although ad hoc speculations on the causes of ring features abound, few systematic attempts to understand their origins have been undertaken (e.g., Russo and Saunders 1999).

While some shell ring vertical and horizontal asymmetries can be attributed to postdepositional erosion and mining, I posit below that most regularities and irregularities in the geometry of shell rings were conscious decisions that group members made in construction. Even if one assumes that shell was simply deposited underfoot at sites where domiciles were arranged in circles, this decision was made by individuals and the greater group. They decided to deposit the shell in a circle and not at a nearby or distant garbage dump, not in a plaza, and not in a single, conical pile. Being sentient humans, they were well aware that dumping resulted in a raised midden and that the shape of the midden was circular. Efforts were not made to deconstruct or abandon the ring once it was realized what was happening. Shell rings were not accidents. Rings were long-lived well after their geometric character was first observable.

Ring geometry was planned among members of social groups. Where to deposit shell; how much to put in one place and how much in another; how high to pile; where not to deposit—all were individual actions promoted and constrained by social relations among ring builders. The great quantities of shells found at rings were the refuse of myriad feasts, both large and small, feasts that held social importance to their hosts and participants. In the ethnographic record, individuals capable of accumulating more food function as hosts. As hosts they use feasts to distribute wealth, receive gifts, gain power and prestige, repay debt, or obtain the debt of others. Feasts held in public forums such as plazas variably serve to display wealth, symbolize debt relations, or reify social competitions. These asymmetries in social relations—host/guest, giver/recipient, lender/debtor, challenger/challenged—may be directly reflected in the asymmetries of the ring itself. In economies where food is the currency of power, hosts and other high-status members could influence the location and accumulation of shell, the most durable symbol of accumulatory abilities and concomitant social rank. Conversely, those less able, or otherwise unsanctioned by the social group, would not be positioned to gain and distribute shell in the specific social and highly public setting of the shell ring. In the following discussion, theories derived from social psychology and anthropological accounts of feasting are used to support these propositions.

SOCIAL SPACE THEORY

Personal space—the distance from others and the position relative to others that people take—is psychologically and socially defined differently among cultures. However, there appears to be some universality to spacing among people who gather in small public groups. When people gather for the purpose of communicating among themselves, they often form into circles and ovals. In such formations, they typically face the center to visually correspond with one another. Members of groups who perceive themselves and/or are perceived by others as leaders or as otherwise dominant will place themselves relatively more distant from others, for example, in the center of the circle or at ends of oval tables, whereas other group members will seat themselves more equally spaced and across from each other (Sommer 1961). By placing themselves apart, the dominant members enhance their visual and symbolic sway over the others. In small groups placed in U-shaped formations around tables, dominant members tend to sit at the end of the table facing the door (Hare and Bales 1963). When nondominant members are forced to sit in that "head" position, they tend to assume more leadership roles than when placed elsewhere in the group (Howells and Becker 1962). These observations have been made cross-culturally and suggest that physical location is an important criterion in establishing rank in small groups and, in fact, may have universal relevance among all human cultures (Grøn 1991).

In small groups aligned in circular or oval formations, specific placement of members takes on added importance when varied work tasks are assigned. Individuals tend to divide into smaller working cells and place themselves opposite those cells with contrasting ideas or approaches. This serves two ends. One, each member of a working cell can see and directly communicate with each member of the opposing cell (Hare and Bales 1963; Steinzor 1950). The positioning enhances visual communication, and the entire group is privy to the interchange between opposing ideas. And two, when not communicating with opposite work cells, members within working cells gain intimacy with each other (Grøn 1991). That is, distance to each cell member is minimized, voices are lowered, the larger group is excluded from oral communication, and feelings of interpersonal relatedness are enhanced.

Grøn (1991) has suggested that these behaviors in small-group formations are reflected ethnographically and archaeologically within both household and community patterns (sensu Chang 1958:298) among egalitarian and incipiently complex societies. Within small dwellings, and in particular circular dwellings, residents eat, sleep, and work in personal areas, all facing the nonoccupied center of the house. This facilitates visual and oral communication within the household. Higher ranked individuals (usually the alpha male) most often sit directly across from the entranceway, in part to be more distant from the elements (e.g., wind and rain) and house traffic but also to obtain a dominant view of the center communal space and entranceway. Lower ranked individuals (e.g., women, nonconsanguineous relatives) usually occupy places nearer the entranceway. In larger houses, the patterns vary more, but most frequently the more distant relatives are placed farther from those in the more prominent positions nearer the head of the household. Of course, the distances individuals place between themselves varies among cultures, but studies have found that the same relative order exists among circular household cultures, suggesting some universality (Grøn 1991).

Positioning for symbolic and visual communication, rank, and social interaction found among small groups and ethnographically observed households also extends to small circular and arc-shaped settlements (Grøn 1991:105). Archaeological and ethnographic community patterns indicate that the physical distance between and location among households in small circular, oval, and U-shaped communities generally reflects their social relation to one another. Close kin and socially aligned individuals and families tend to place their households adjacent to each other. Such positioning imparts sympathy and interaction among neighbors, while at the same time socially separates subgroups from less related groups within the community. Related household groupings often place themselves opposite less related or rival groupings. Within each grouping a central household is typically flanked by households of decreasing relatedness with increasing distance from the center (e.g., Parkington and Mills 1991).

U-shaped villages follow a similar arrangement. Households of less relatedness or lower social rank are located within and adjacent to similarly ascribed households. These are opposed to other kin/household groupings on the facing arm of the U, which, in hierarchical societies, may hold higher rank. In either arm, however, the more distantly related or socially lower ranked households are found at the open ends of the U, positions physically and symbolically on the periphery of community interaction. Such positions lie outside direct interaction with the social and communications nexuses of their group and most distant from the visually dominant position at the closed end of the U (Grøn 1991).

Grøn's model does not predict that small communities defined as egalitarian, transegalitarian, and simple chiefdoms will always form settlements in circular or semicircular patterns. Rather, it suggests that when they do, positions of rank and intragroup relationships may be associated with specific locations within the circle or arc. Those positions will vary depending on the kind and level of hierarchy in the community. The level of hierarchy may be discerned from the shape of the settlement as well as the distribution and character of households. Dwellings arranged in crescents, circles, or ovals with open central areas are often, although not always, associated with egalitarian groups. Those that are most egalitarian, that is, those that have households of equal size and status, will space dwellings equally distant from each other (Figure 3.7a). In less egalitarian communities with opposing kin alliances, with dual leaders, or with more than one highly ranked household, the ranked domiciles may be situated directly across from each other or in separate positions around the central plaza (Figures 3.7b and 3.7c). Kin and other subgroups that are socially linked with these dominant households vie for position on either side of them (Figures 3.7c and 3.7d).

Single leaders or dominant lineages in more hierarchically organized communities may express their rank in a number of ways. In a circular village, their dwellings may be situated in the center of the circle where they command "pas-

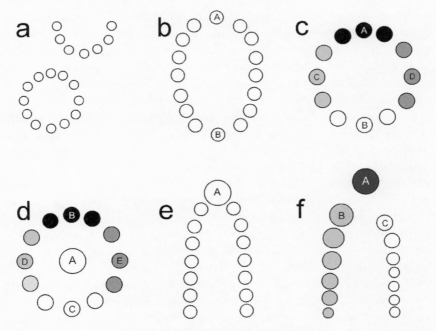

Figure 3.7. Idealized locations of households and status positions (uppercase letters) in arcuate communities (after Grøn 1991). A = primary status positions. Shade intensities denote relatedness among subgroups. Size of circles denotes relative status, with larger circles reflecting the greater status.

sive contact effect" and visual and symbolic dominance over the circled community (Figure 3.7d) (Grøn 1991). In a C- or U-shaped village, the prestige position lies directly opposite the village opening (Figure 3.7e). Psychologically this station imparts dominance over the community, an impression reinforced by allowing no individual or lineage in opposition to it (i.e., only the empty opening opposes it). Persons occupying these positions may place themselves physically higher, more distant, or in larger or more elaborate domiciles to symbolize status distinctions (Figure 3.7f) (Grøn 1991:107, 108). Lying midpoint between arms of the U and possible opposing factions in the community, the position serves as the nexus of visual and oral communication. Control of information equals power. As in other ranked arcuate communities, secondary prestige positions may lie nearest the primary position (Figure 3.7f). Multiple levels of inequalities and subgroup affiliations may be present as reflected in differences in house size and other material symbols within the arms of the U, as well as in proximity to ranked positions (Figure 3.7f).

Grøn (1991; also see Trinkley 1985) has suggested that circular and C-shaped settlements are commonly found among egalitarian societies, while the U shape befits more hierarchical social formations. Exceptions to the rule are apparent, however. The circle with an elevated or centrally positioned dwelling, for example, indicates some form of hierarchical social organization (e.g., Grøn 1991:108; Malinowski 1929). Unfortunately for archaeologists, there is no one-to-one equivalence between a U- or C-shaped settlement plan and a community's organizational complexity, and other archaeological features attributable to social ranking (or its absence) need to be compared with the geometry of circular and semicircular settlement patterns. In terms of households, for example, consideration of the kinds, sizes, locations, and spacing, as well as material content, can provide support in determining social ranking predicted by the model outlined above. The abundant and measurable refuse of feasts found at shell rings provides one such material.

FEASTING THEORY AND SHELL RINGS

Shell rings are typically made up of large piles of conformable shell containing little to moderate amounts of soil. These are placed adjacent to, as well as on top of, one another. Thinner layers of crushed shell with more soil may or may not overlap and underlie the piles. Intermixed among these strata may be lenses of shell, distinguishable from their surrounding contexts in terms of species, sizes of individual shells, soil content, or other traits. Below the shell ring is usually an earth midden with little or no shell. The midden may contain pits as well as other features (e.g., posts, hearths). "Piles," "layers," "lenses," and "pits" are the terms of normative shell ring studies. Few archaeologists have ventured to assign human actions to any of these archaeological terms. Those few have labeled the thin layers as "occupation floors" (Trinkley 1997) or "capping" episodes (Cable 1997). Pits have been interpreted as roasting or steaming pits (Trinkley 1997) and post molds as domicile remains (McMichael 1982; Russo 1991; Trinkley 1997). But large piles and small lenses have generally escaped praxeological interpretation (cf. Russo and Heide 2002; Russo and Saunders 1999). When talking of faunal remains found in rings, archaeologists list the species found in middens (Calmes 1967:27; Marrinan 1975; Trinkley 1985) but may not bother to mention that these species might represent the remains of human food (Calmes 1968:46; Edwards 1965; Hemmings 1970) or may outright deny that they do (Dickel 1992:161). They hint that "features," "lenses," or "deposits" of shell in rings are connected to food gathering, but do not speculate as to what social mechanisms may have been involved between the gathering of shellfish for food and deposition of shell as building material (Michie 1976:5).

I suggest that the shell found in piles, lenses, and other features in shell rings represents the epiphenomena of interactions among people. Small- and large-scale public consumption of food was a medium through which social interaction took place at ring sites. People brought food to the rings, processed it, cooked it, shared it, gifted it, consumed it, and discarded it in front of family, neighbors, and guests. They did not store nor hide food. They did not horde their food and eat in privacy. With its open plaza and raised circular boundary, the ring provided a public forum for all aspects of food preparation, distribution, and disposal. In short, people at shell rings feasted.

Feasts are public rituals. When involving two or more people, food consumption is never solely a biological function but serves myriad social ends. Sharing of food builds trust; giving of food incurs or relieves socioeconomic debt; and wasting of food displays power in the reach for, and maintenance of, social hierarchy. Feasts may be small and mundane or large, overt displays of consumption. By preparing and consuming food in the public forum of the ring, the community affirmed its social relations. By placing the refuse of feasts in large piles at specific locations in the openly public forum of shell rings, the host's actions were memorialized, and feasters received a permanent reminder of the host's prestige and their own indebtedness.

Social aspects of feasts depend both on the kinds of social organization and on the subsistence economies of the participants. Egalitarian, generalized hunter-gatherers typically do not feast on a scope anthropologists recognize as distinct from the totality of individual consumption of daily meals. Because all members are considered potentially equal, egalitarian groups maintain a strong ethic stressing the sharing and distribution of food. Social units are small and consumption is open to public observation, assuring community members that prescribed sharing rules are followed. Because of their inability to consistently predict the amount and kinds of foods they will procure, and because of their limited abilities to store foods, generalized hunter-gatherers probably cannot, on a predictable level, host large-scale feasts in which social units outside their own are invited as guests who are subject to repayment in economic, feast, or other social retribution (Hayden 2001:50). When community-wide feasts are held, they are small because of the nature of the group size and limited resource predictability. Special or ostentatious displays of food that differ from regular meals are not characteristic. The sharing ethic among egalitarian groups suggests that correlates of their consumptive and social behavior should be identifiable in the archaeological record regardless of site type. Although differences in kinds of foods may be found at different site types, the same kinds and distributions of food remains should generally be found at all individual household units.

In contrast, among complex hunter-gatherers and other incipient socially complex groups, feasting behavior is more varied and multipurpose. For example, solidarity feasts serve to strengthen and maintain social bonds and obligations among intragroup and intergroup members. In archaeological contexts, evidence of such solidarity feasts may mimic remains found at egalitarian quotidian sites, with minimal distinctions among participating social units in the forms of food remains and artifacts. We should expect among transegalitarian groups arising out of a hunter-gatherer ancestry, and having not yet obtained any organizational form beyond minimal social ranking, that a strong sharing ethic will persevere. Transegalitarian groups, however, will have developed technologies to produce surplus foods on a predictable basis, establishing the foundation for extracommunity feasting that separates their feasts in scale and kind from smaller egalitarian affairs.

On the basis of ethnographic analogy, Hayden (2001) has identified four general types of feasts in which transegalitarian societies may participate. The "minimally distinctive" feasts include the above-described solidarity feast and other types in which "only the size of the food-preparation and serving materials may differ from [those of] daily meals" (Hayden 2001:54). "Promotional/ alliance" feasts are used to display the host group's success through sharing, giving, and use of ritual paraphernalia, as well as the construction of specialized structures. This serves to incur debt obligations from guests such as marriage and other kin alliances, community alliances, labor, materials, or reciprocal feasts. Promotional feasts are large and differ from a third type, "competitive" feasts, in the artifact realm. Competitive feasts should be evidenced by more costly prestige items and wasted (e.g., intentionally destroyed) materials. Waste of food resources may also be evident since one goal of the competitive feast is to outperform rival hosts. Competitive hosts often construct more substantial structures than promotional hosts. Fourth is the "tribute" feast, usually found only in association with chiefdoms (here included at the upper end of transegalitarian organization) and early state-level societies. These feasts are massive and tend to include all members of society in order to secure obligations on the broadest of scales. The most and rarest of material and food items will be limited to the elite.

How do shell ring builders fit with Hayden's classification of feasters? While shell ring builders undoubtedly hunted a wide range of animals, they depended on shellfish and fish (Russo 1991; Trinkley 1985). In this sense, they were not generalized hunter-gatherers (and presumably egalitarian) living on a marginal economy incapable of producing food surpluses for large-scale feasts (Hayden 2001:43). Rather, they lived in coastal environments that provided nearly ubiquitous faunal resources along every tidal river, creek, and marsh setting. Oysters and other shellfish were bountiful and exploitable year-round in the warm-weather climate of the Southeastern coasts. Although identified as egalitarian (Trinkley 1985), shell ring builders appear to have been complex hunter-gatherers exploiting predictable and intensifiable food resources. They hosted large, small, and numerous feasts, evidence of which is found in their shell rings.

ARCHAEOLOGICAL CORRELATES OF FEASTING AT SHELL RINGS

Understanding the function and structure of shell rings requires understanding the archaeological correlates of feasting vs. daily consumption of food. Correlates of large-scale feasting activity are easily distinguished from those of small-scale domestic meals, particularly those in which the domestic unit is the single nuclear family. On the basis of a wide range of ethnographic examples, Hayden (2001) has suggested that the following food markers of large-scale feasts may be found archaeologically: larger quantities of food items than found in the refuse of quotidian contexts; rare or labor-intensive plant or animal species; and evidence of wasted food items.

Large Quantities

Large quantities of food in the form of shell and other faunal remains of lesser volume typify all shell rings. Massive, undifferentiated shell deposits are found at all extant shell ring sites (Cable 1997; Calmes 1967; Houck 1996; Russo 1991; Russo and Heide 2002; Russo and Saunders 1999; Saunders 2002a; Trinkley 1985:110; Waring and Larson 1968:272). These deposits can be distinguished from the refuse of daily meals found in "occupational floors" in a number of ways. If shell is deposited quickly, as opposed to the gradual accumulation of daily meals discarded underfoot, relatively less evidence should be found of crushing, wind-borne sand, surface fires, artifacts, fauna drawn to exposed shell (e.g., land snails; see Russo 1991), and other subaerial indicators of human or natural activity. That is, the more quickly that shell is piled, the less time these intrusive actions have to occur before the upper portions of the pile seal off the lower. These massive, unconsolidated strata of shell are typically identified as "clean" or "loose," having little to moderate amounts of soil, but always containing mostly shell with oyster usually dominating (i.e., low equitability and diversity) and with little to no evidence of hearths, pits, crushing, or other human activities aside from garbage disposal (e.g., Russo 1991; Saunders 2002a; Waring and Larson 1968). They variably contain charcoal, artifacts, and other faunal remains, but not in the relative abundances of other midden deposits in the ring.

In profile these large, unconsolidated deposits may appear as mounded or level strata. I believe that many of these carry the traits identified above and are the result of feasting, reflecting large-scale and quick deposition. However, determining whether these features are single episodes or otherwise short-term deposits is problematic. I think most of the strata are likely "piles" of shell. The horizontal strata likely represent the tail ends of piles lying adjacent to or overlying other piles. However, because none of these piles have ever been viewed in any aspect but a small shovel test or trench profile, archaeologists may not recognize them as "piles." A complete perimeter of one of these "piles" has yet to be uncovered. The best examples are seen only in two dimensions in the profiles of trenches that crosscut the ring (e.g., Cable 1997; Calmes 1967:fig. 5; McMichael 1982:fig. 6; Russo 1991:fig. 5.3; Russo and Saunders 1999:fig. 4; Saunders 2002a:fig. 22). In these, central piles may stand alone, be overlain by other piles, or have piles and other features such as thin layers of crushed shell/humus/organic soils separating them. Whether these piles are conical in shape, as many of the profiles suggest, or actually other geometric or amorphic shapes extending away from the trench along the perimeter of the ring has never been tested. No large-scale block excavations have ever been undertaken on a ring, except where most of the superior shell in the ring had already been removed (Trinkley 1985).

Regardless of their shape, however, these piles have rarely been described as the material end product of feasts. More culture-free descriptions of actions such as "construction episodes" (Cable 1997), "piling" (Calmes 1967:10), or "heaping" (Dickel 1992:162) typically account for the presence of these shell features. Most often, terms devoid of human intent or action, such as "strata" or "layer," are used, offering the reader little insight as to the origin of the features. Surprisingly, little debate as to the genesis of the piling of shell in rings has arisen. While some think that rings and associated shell mounds were made from quarried shell from other middens (Edwards 1965; McMichael 1982), they offer little convincing evidence in support of the claim (cf. Russo 1991, 2002; cf. Saunders 2002a, 2002b). The most active debate that reflects on the issue involves the argument as to whether shell rings are "intentional" or "incidental" constructions. The incidentalists argue that if the shell was thrown underfoot, more crushing of shell will be evident, along with more midden materials such as ceramic sherds and other artifacts of daily maintenance (Calmes 1967:10; Trinkley 1985). Most archaeologists support this logic (cf. Cable 1997), but it fails to account for the ubiquitous presence of piles of uncrushed shell at all ring sites.

I suggest these piles can be attributable to feasting using the criteria defined above, although other human action might result in similar-looking deposits. Because shellfish was the basic food item in both ceremonial and quotidian contexts of coastal Archaic peoples, piles of discarded shell are found at other site types, including so-called shell-processing sites, habitation sites, and sites with monumental architecture made from quarried shell. In these and all cases of shell piling, context offers the best insight into the characteristics associated with shell deposition and use.

Contexts can be ambiguous, and on a case-by-case basis archaeologists will have to examine shell deposits at ring sites closely to see whether piling of shell was quick and potentially the result of feasting. Unfortunately, we lack precision tools to determine absolutely the length of time in which a pile of shell was deposited. Radiocarbon dating the top and bottom layers of a pile of shell is nearly useless if the goal is to determine the length of time it took to deposit the shell. Few such efforts have been undertaken in shell rings. In one case, the top and bottom of a 1.3-m shell pile were dated to 4470 ± 75 and 4460 ± 105 (uncorrected), respectively (McMichael 1982:105). At other sites, the spans between radiocarbon dates from the top and bottom of rings appear relatively short, particularly if standard deviations are considered (e.g., Russo and Heide 2002; Saunders 2002a). On the surface, these short intervals appear to support the idea of a relatively quick deposit. But given the vagaries of radiocarbon dating and the standard deviations of the dates, it is difficult to interpret from the dates alone whether the pile was built in a week, a year, or hundreds of years. Similar problems arise with other temporal markers such as pottery.

Rare or Labor-Intensive Foods

Hayden (2001:28) defines a feast as any meal between two or more people sharing special foods. "Special foods," of course, are culturally and contextually relative. If, as I suggest, oyster was the mainstay of feasts held at shell rings, at first glance it is hard to see how oyster may have been seen by the feasters as special food. Oyster, after all, is the predominant faunal component of virtually every Late Archaic midden on the Southeast coast, not just shell rings. However, the ritual context of the shell ring itself may have imbued the "specialness" into the otherwise mundane resource. Yams, for example, are a common, everyday food in the Trobriand Islands. When present in a feasting context, however, yams become not only a special food but one inspiring mania for consumption. In the context of ritual, individuals eat yams to the point of vomiting (Malinowski 1929).

But if any food can be considered "special" depending on its context, is Hayden's concept of "special foods" as markers of feasting useful? Perhaps, but it is useful only if the feasting context can be established without reference to the food product. Archaeologists would agree, for example, that food remains found in the ritual contexts of a burial mound were likely special. Similarly, I suggest that shell ring feast remains provide the ritual context for determining piles of oysters to be special-purpose. But oyster piles at shell rings are not the "special" foods Hayden identified as rare or labor-intensive.[2] Perhaps the best candidate for that distinction at shell rings is deer. Compared with other faunal remains, deer are relatively rare in shell rings (always in terms of minimum number of individuals and most often in terms of other measures of abundance). Particularly meaty and rare parts of the deer have been suggested to represent "preferred" items in other Southeastern prehistoric contexts (Hale 1984a; Jackson and Scott 1995; VanDerwarker 1999). The relative rarity of deer in shell rings may, in part, be a reflection of their relative rarity in estuarine environments surrounding shell rings. In this setting deer require more labor to obtain and are certainly a less predictable resource than shellfish and fish. If shell rings are indeed the loci of large-scale feasting of transegalitarian groups, then the model would suggest that deer and favored deer parts, or other rare resources, might be expected to be found in contexts of individuals with the prestige or power to obtain them. Archaeologists need only identify such contexts to test the hypothesis (which I suggest they can do with social space theory).

Unfortunately, complicating the issue of rarity as a marker for feasting is the likelihood that ring sites served multiple purposes. I suggest that some of the confusion as to whether Southeastern shell ring sites are the remains of secular villages or ceremonial centers arises because they likely served both functions (cf. Sassaman 1993). Shell rings exhibit bountiful evidence that they served both as places of domestic activity (Russo 1991; Trinkley 1985) and as ceremonial centers (e.g., Cable 1997; Russo 1991; Russo and Heide 2002; Saunders and Russo 2002). The idea that only two site types, either a village or a ceremonial center, might account for shell rings is somewhat parochial. Transegalitarian societies and incipient chiefdoms commonly mix both functions in circular settlement patterns and other village plans (e.g., Chagnon 1968; Malinowski 1929; Young 1971:235). Full access to plazas may have been limited to specific groups or genders, while the remaining population domiciled in associated habitation areas (e.g., Heckenberger 1996:321). At numerous shell ring sites, contemporary habitation sites, including other shell rings, are commonly found near the rings (e.g., Cable 1997; Russo 1991; Russo et al. 1993; Russo et al. 2002; Saunders and Russo 2002).

Perhaps importantly, at a number of nonring, coastal shell middens, zooarchaeological analysis of fine-screened recovered midden has identified the presumably quotidian meals of Archaic populations as wide ranging in terms of species utilized, but heavily weighted toward estuarine resources (cf. Hale 1984b; Quitmyer and Massaro 1999; Russo and Ste. Claire 1992; Russo et al. 1993). As is the case at shell rings, oysters are a staple at these nonring sites. But contrary to the notion that rare or labor-intensive species were reserved for high-status feasters, the wide range of species in quotidian assemblages, which sometimes includes deer, indicates that these species were also consumed in more mundane contexts. I suggest that daily subsistence remains may, in fact, display greater diversity, including the presence of rare species, than large-scale feasting remains, whether these remains are found at ring or nonring sites. During the annual cycle more time is allotted to daily food procurement than is allotted to feasting procurement and the chances of encountering rare species are increased. Lacking long-term storage capabilities, residents consumed these resources in daily contexts, rather than saving them for more infrequent, large-scale feasting.

Hayden (2001) suggests that restricted consumption of rare foods by the elite at rituals is most often found in tribute feasts, which are typically associated with chiefdoms or more complexly organized societies. With this in mind, the absence of definitive use of rare species in feasting contexts at shell rings might argue for the feasts as solidarity, promotional, or competitive rather than tribute events and, by extension, argue for rings as more structurally egalitarian than chiefly. I am not sure this is the case. Even in the most incipient transegalitarian organization, elite statuses arise, however transitory, and shell ring faunal remains have not been analyzed relative to predicted status locations. Whether rare species are more common at high-status positions has yet to be determined. As Hayden points out, identifying rare feasting foods is difficult in archaeological contexts, and ultimately definitive contextual data, rather than just the infrequent encounter of particular food remains, will be needed to determine the social significance behind rare species. Researchers will be hard put to distinguish whether foods are quotidian or feasting remains, let alone the residue of specific types of feasts. In lieu of detailed studies, today the most definitive indicator of feasting at shell rings is the particular distribution of the remains of the most common food, shellfish, rather than the rarest.

Wasted Food

Hayden (2001:59) suggests that evidence of wasted food and other items of wealth may be present in large-scale feasting sites, particularly at competitive feasts where individuals or groups try to outdo each other in the amount of food they produce, display, give away, and waste. In these settings, wasted food signifies power and elicits prestige. Unfortunately for those studying shell rings, Hayden's ethnographically based examples are largely limited to cultures where domesticated animals and plant foods are produced. Excess plant foods and large animals, such as pigs and cows, are displayed and destroyed or crops are allowed to rot or eaten to excess in order to impress the feasters as to the power the host has over their most valued resource, food.

It might appear that the lack of temporally predictable domesticated resources would preclude shell ring societies from engaging in competitive feasting. Certainly, the largest animals that shell ring builders consistently consumed, such as deer, were not predictable resources that could be summoned for slaughter on command like a family cow. For a feast scheduled for a specific time, the presentation of deer could not be counted on. But shellfish and, to a lesser extent, fish

were found in predictable abundance surrounding every shell ring site. Estuaries
served as storehouses from which feast hosts could draw resources not only to
feed their guests but also to waste excess resources. With the display of great
quantities of shell, feasters would be duly impressed with their host's mastery over
the environment and control over the community's labor force used to exploit it.

This is not to say that oysters or any shellfish were wasted at shell ring sites.
Hayden's model might predict that the display of large numbers of oysters rotting in the sun uneaten, i.e., wasted, would be evidence of competitive feasting.
But to date, no such evidence of massive wasting has been observed in the archaeological record. This suggests at least three possibilities: archaeologists have
missed evidence of competitive feasting, such evidence is obfuscated by its nature
or time, or feasting may not have been competitive in nature or have otherwise
involved the waste of large amounts of food. Of course, oyster (or any animal)
could have been *processed* for its flesh, and that flesh sans shell could have been
publicly displayed to rot. Processing may have taken place off-site, and such acts
of wasting would not have left an archaeological signature at the site of public
display.

FEASTING AND SOCIAL SPACE THEORIES:
EXPECTATIONS AT SHELL RINGS

No shell ring site has been excavated or reported on in sufficient manner to allow full application of either the feasting or social space theory outlined above.
Few rings have been investigated at all, and fewer yet have been reported with
the kinds of structural and zooarchaeological data necessary to identify the distribution of rare food items, wasted food items, or even the relative abundance
of specific food resources across the circumference of a ring. A shovel test here
and there in a ring, a trench across the base of one portion of the ring, or block
excavations of mostly subring deposits typify the range of approaches taken at
ring sites. While these may provide the archaeologist with sufficient data to identify the culture and periods of occupation, such approaches provide insufficient
data to determine whether unequal distribution of food resources occurred at
ring sites. At few ring sites do we know in any detail the internal structure of
one side of a ring compared to the other (Russo 1991; Russo et al. 2002).

The only evidence of feasting correlates that are obtainable from a large number of rings are quantities of shell as manifest in surface topography (e.g., Dickel
1992; Marrinan 1975; Russo 1991; Russo and Saunders 1999; Simpkins 1975)
and shell thickness maps (Heide 2002; Russo et al. 2002). Assuming that rings
are made up mostly of piled-up shell, which I have suggested is an artifact of
feasting, the variability in height on contour maps of shell rings can be used as

a surrogate for confirmed measures of large-scale shell deposits. Combining these maps with Grøn's theory of social spacing of ranked individuals in circular formations, the distribution of shell at ring sites should be found to be more variable in ranked or transegalitarian than in egalitarian social settings. If shell rings were constructed by transegalitarian societies, the form of the ring should also reflect the organization of the society that built it as predicted by Grøn's social space theory. In turn, and as predicted by Hayden's feasting theory, the greatest amount of shell at ring sites should correlate with the location of the individual or group with greatest social ranking as predicted by social space theory. Ultimately, as more investigations are carried out, other standard markers of ranking such as mounds, exotic artifacts, rare foods, and wasted foods may be found to correlate with the prestige positions and the greatest amounts of shell.

Before measuring the shell distribution at rings for evidence of social inequality, however, I suggest that sufficient data have been collected to demonstrate that ring builders were not stereotypical egalitarian, wandering hunters incapable of producing the economic surpluses, leaders, or community efforts necessary for large-scale public architecture. A number of ring sites have been shown to have been occupied throughout the year or over numerous seasons of the year (Russo 1991; Russo and Heide 2002; Russo et al. 1993; Trinkley 1985). In addition, with some rings being associated with ceremonial mounds and others constituting multiple-ring complexes, the size and complexity of certain ring sites is sufficient to argue both for permanent settlement and social hierarchy of at least an incipient level (Dickel 1992; Heide 2003; Hughes 1998; Russo 1991; Russo and Saunders 1999; Russo et al. 2002; Saunders and Russo 2002; Thompson et al. 2002).

These traits alone do not exclude ring builders from consideration as egalitarian in social settings outside rings. Egalitarian societies may exhibit profound inequalities among their members (Kelly 1995; Woodburn 1982) in certain social contexts but not in others. But the architecture of ring complexes does suggest that inequalities at ring sites were of sufficient magnitude that standard egalitarian social leveling mechanisms were not completely effective. Traits not common to egalitarian hunter-gatherers include high population densities, sedentism or restricted mobility, focal exploitation of abundant food resources, and ceremonial feasting complexes (Kelly 1995:302), all of which have been linked to ring sites and associated Late Archaic coastal populations (DePratter and Howard 1980; Miller 1998; Russo 1991, 1992a, 1994b; Russo and Saunders 1999; Trinkley 1980:323–324).

As the name implies, the diachronic trend is for transegalitarian to evolve out of egalitarian societies (Kelly 1995:304). While I believe the totality of evidence leans to this interpretation in the Southeast (i.e., prior to the appearance of ring sites, site settlement seems to have been that of generalized, impermanent hunter-gatherers [e.g., Sassaman 1993]), this does not mean the earliest ring sites are the smallest or least complex. Fig Island, Horr's Island, and Bonita Bay are among the largest and most complex ring sites—but also among the earliest (see Russo and Heide 2002:fig. 10). In order to present some idea of the comparative sizes of groups using the rings, I have calculated population estimates for those ring sites that have maps of surface topography (Table 3.1). For the calculations I have assumed that households 3 to 4 m in diameter, holding three people, were placed on the rings at intervals 2 m apart, based on an artistic interpretation of ring households (Trinkley 1997), the estimate of distribution of households for nonring sites (Sassaman 1997), and evidence of structures from Horr's Island (Russo 1991). These estimates of house size, shape, spacing, and numbers of inhabitants are based on meager data. The estimates assume that the rings were occupied by nuclear families with permanent or semipermanent structures. If this was the case, the figures could underestimate the population at feasts replete with guests. Also, if households held more than three people, the estimates would of course be higher. On the other hand, if the ring normally held gender-specific domiciles (e.g., men's huts), the figures could be overestimates. In any case, the numbers are offered only for heuristic purposes to compare possible population sizes among ring communities in reference to those predicted for transegalitarian and egalitarian groups (Kelly 1995).

Whether rings held permanent or semipermanent households or less intensely occupied structures, their size alone indicates that most shell rings are of scales outside the range of egalitarian societies. The average group size of mobile egalitarian hunter-gatherers is 25 (Kelly 1995:210). Permanently settled populations of greater than 25 individuals are rare among generalized mobile hunter-gatherers. However, populations for settled hunter-gatherers can be quite large—over 1,000 individuals. In the ethnographic record, such societies are, without exception, transegalitarian or more complexly organized. While most of the rings appear to be of sizes capable of holding large populations typical of transegalitarian societies, some estimates reflect size ranges indicative of periodic aggregation communities characteristic of both egalitarian and transegalitarian hunter-gatherers (Kelly 1995). Without supporting evidence of permanent settlement, or definitive evidence of ring use, then, population size alone cannot predict the level of social complexity at ring sites.

At multiple-ring sites, each ring may have served a different function. While daily living may have occurred permanently at rings, it need not have occurred permanently at all rings at a site. Specific kin groups may have occupied rings only at times of ritual, or nearby villages may have been occupied by one portion of the society while other subgroups occupied the rings. This does not mean that the theoretical expectations outlined for social spacing and feasting do not

Table 3.1. Shell ring metrics, ages, and population estimates.

Shell Ring	Plaza[a]		Ring Length			Max	Pop[d]	Av Age	
	Diam	Area (m^2)	Diam[b]	Mid[c]	Peri	Depth		b.p.[e]	
S. Carolina									
Fig Island 1	25	490	100	205	300	5.0	123	3876	(3)
Fig Island 2	55	2,375	90	220	265	1.5	132	4061	(2)
Fig Island 3	30	355	65	95	125	1.2	57	4034	(3)
Sea Pines	40	1,260	55	110	165	0.5	66	3665	(2)
Sewee	40	1,260	65	110	175	1.5	66	3295	(1)
Georgia									
Cannon's Pt.	25x35	875	40x70	235	265	1.7	141	4342	(2)
Sapelo	60	2,375	90	210	285	3.0	126	3860	(2)
Florida									
Oxeye	70	3,850	130	315	520	1.9	189	4517	(3)
Rollins	150	17,665	190	400	550	2.5	240	3527	(6)
Guana	115x140	16,100	150x170	365	420	1.3	219	3730	(2)
Joseph Reed	200	15,700	250	385	440	1.7	231	3272	(6)
Bonita Bay	75x210	15,750	140x230	530	600	1.1	318	4108	(4)
Horr's Island	55x125	6,875	100x160	265	365	4.5	159	4375	(12)

Diam = diameter; Peri = perimeter; Pop = population; Max Depth = maximum shell depth;
Av = average.

a   All linear measures are in meters and based on scaled figures in this chapter. Circular ring measures are given as diameter; more U-shaped rings are given as width/length (w/l) measures. As noted in this chapter, shell rings are not symmetrical. All measures are taken from their greatest variation in the particular aspect.

b   Diameter measures for Oxeye are taken from shell above high tide; perimeter measures are taken from maximum shell below high tide. For rings with attached mounds, rings, and ridges, only the main ring was measured.

c   Mid-ring lengths on U-shaped rings (i.e., circumferences in circular rings) are taken from the tops of rings midway between the plaza edge and the outside perimeter of the shell ring. This is presumably the location of "houses," if they existed. Note that such distribution is hypothetical. No evidence of the sizes or distribution of domestic structures placed on top of shell rings has been identified (cf. Russo 1991; Trinkley 1985).

d   Note population estimates are based on three people per household separated 5 m apart around mid-ring length/circumference on top of shell rings. If greater numbers were applied to households (five is more typical for nuclear families in the ethnographic record [Hayden, personal communication, 2000]), the populations would, of course, increase. If, at larger sites like Fig Island, Horr's Island, and Rollins, all surface areas of attached rings, mounds, and shell ridges, not to mention all or part of the plazas, also contained houses or other people-bearing structures, the potential maximum population estimates would be in the thousands. The figures presented here are estimated minimums, serving to provide evidence for comparison to known population aggregations of hunter-gatherers whose sizes may vary coincident with permanent or impermanent social complexities.

Continued on the next page

Table 3.1 *Continued*

e Radiocarbon dates are based on corrected (conventional) ages found in Russo and Heide
   (2000) for all sites except Guana and Fig Island, the dates for which are based on
   unpublished data. It is unknown whether the date from Sewee is corrected. If
   uncorrected and based on shell, a correction would likely yield an age up to 400 years
   older. Parentheses indicate the number of samples on which the average date was based.

hold if after we gather more data we discover that specific rings were not permanently settled. Social space theory was, after all, built on ethnographic and sociological data of societal subgroups and small groups, not only whole communities. Whether guests and hosts at rings were trading partners, mating groups, kin
groups, lineages, or sodalities, the theoretical assumptions of spacing remain the
same.

However, because Grøn's model of social space is based on small groups,
when communities exceed a certain size, the theoretical premises may not rigor-
ously apply to all rings. Grøn's was a trend study in which some circular and
U-shaped communities did not fit. The possible causes for these misfits were
largely excluded from discussion, but he did postulate that the communities in
his model lay on an isotropic plain. Thus, we may expect that social spacing in
rings may not obtain model predictions if a ring's physical locality encountered
water, severe slope, topographic highs or lows, or other natural or manmade features that interfered with the planned layout. Beyond this environmental cau-
tion, however, I suggest other factors may have interfered with planning. Under
demographic conditions of increasing populations, increases in architectural
complexity may arise and force deviations from planned ring layouts. Under
these conditions, if communities did not split to accommodate their greater
numbers and concomitant social stresses (and this is certainly a possibility), ex-
pansions of rings, or the need to build additional rings or other architecture, may
have emerged. Unplanned population expansion would have been problematic
in closed circles if permanent households occupied the ring. Where did the new
arrivals go? U-shapes, on the other hand, may have been better able to accept
new members because they were open-ended. In either case, as I discuss the various ring sites below, the reader should keep in mind that most of the larger ring
sites are associated with a multiplicity of architectural features such as additional
separate rings, attached rings, concentric rings, linear shell ridges, mounds, sheet
middens, and domicile middens. Not all are shown on the maps I present, but
they can be traced in the cited literature. These indicate, I believe, that ultimately we will need to look at the larger settlements, not just the rings, to understand the functions of the rings. Shell rings reflect the social and power rela-

tions of their communities. As these increased in complexity, so did shell ring sites.

SOUTHEASTERN SHELL RINGS

I suggest, regarding shell rings, that asymmetrical social relations are legitimated in the spatial arrangement of horizontally distributed shell (shape) and vertically distributed shell (height/volume/thickness/depth). To date we have little diachronic control of data obtained from shell rings, and by necessity the model applied to ring sites is synchronic. It assumes that the distribution of shell reflects social relationships that were isometric from initiation to abandonment of the site. In the following, surface topography and shell density maps of shell rings are discussed to determine whether shell is equally distributed, as expected for egalitarian occupations, or whether greater deposits in terms of height or thickness are located in the horizontal settlement plan at positions predicted by social space theory for high-status individuals or groups.

Circular and Semicircular Rings

Shell deposits 90 m or less in diameter and generally circular in shape characterize most rings from Georgia and South Carolina. Together, the two states have more than 50 Archaic shell rings. Unfortunately, few topographic maps exist. In South Carolina, Sea Pines, Stratton Place, Sewee, and Fig Island 1, 2, and 3 have existing contour maps. Of these, the Stratton Place ring was so disturbed at the time it was mapped that analysis of its original shell distribution is precluded (Trinkley 1985). In Georgia, maps of Sapelo 1 and Cannon's Point shell ring indicate some evidence of disturbance. The maps of Skidaway and Busch Krick rings suggest severe disturbance and these sites are not considered here (Crusoe and DePratter 1976:7; Howard and DePratter 1980:251).

Of the mapped, relatively undisturbed rings, four are generally circular, indicating egalitarian organization under model parameters. However, all also evince elevational differences among their shell deposits. At Sapelo 1 and Sewee (Figures 3.2 and 3.6), the highest pilings of shell lie opposite low spots, or openings, as the model predicts for transegalitarian community plans in which prestige positions lie midway between opposing arcs of the ring. Both rings, however, have suffered from quarrying activities during historic times (Cable 1995; Simpkins 1975), perhaps accentuating the differences in shell volume across the rings.

At Sea Pines (Figure 3.5), a similar ring "footprint" exists. However, the opening on the west side of the ring is actually a trench of an archaeological investigation that left behind two spoil piles on either side (Trinkley 1980:38).

Sea Pines is unusual among ring sites in that it contains high spots in its central plaza. If these spots contain in situ shell midden, under the model the elevated and centrally positioned shell would reflect positions of visual dominance and power. However, like the trench opening, the rises may also be associated with spoil from an "old excavation" (Trinkley 1980:39). Alternatively, a recent site visit suggests the high spots are associated with trees in an otherwise largely deforested, well-maintained plaza, offering yet another possibility—height is due, in part, to biological massing associated with tree roots. Until these spots are investigated, the asymmetries in shell distribution that exist at the site are most clearly found on the ring itself. The highest shell (3.65 m) is located in the northwest portion of the ring nearly opposite a lower part of the ring (3.0 m) due south. Under model predictions this suggests a single position of greater status than that opposing it. However, adjacent to the low point in the ring is a relatively higher point directly opposite the highest northwest shell deposit. This southeast point is nearly as tall, suggesting more equal distribution of shell, a possibility reinforced by another high deposit of shell between these poles on the northeast portion of the ring. Only the southwest portion of the site evinces lower-lying deposits of shell overall.

At the generally circular Fig Island 2 ring (Figure 3.4), a similar situation obtains with high shell deposits on the northern and eastern portions of the ring lying opposed to an opening on the southwest side of the ring. However, Hemmings (1970) suggests the opening is an abandoned archaeological trench. Recent testing at the site cannot confirm this (Russo 2002:89; cf. Leigh 2002: 192). No spoil piles of trenching are evident. In either case, asymmetries in shell distribution do exist with the northern and eastern portions of the ring containing greater amounts of shell in terms of height and base width (read volume) than are found on the south and west sides of the ring. At both Sea Pines and Fig Island 2, the "circular" rings are actually more pentagonal or hexagonal in shape with different heights/volumes of shell associated with each side of the polygon (Russo 2002:88).

The two rings that are less circular and more arc-shaped, Fig Island 3 (Figure 3.4) and Cannon's Point (Figure 3.3), exhibit great asymmetries in shell volume across the lengths of their arcs, but the asymmetrical distributions do not match model predictions for status positions. The points of greatest volumes of shell at both rings are not situated centrally, but near the open ends of the arcs, locations at which the model would predict low status. While this distribution of shell is not predicted for position holders who obtain their status solely from within the community, it is predicted for those who obtain status from outside the ring (Grøn 1991:110). That is, the ends of an open C are the first positions outside traders/guests perceive and in this respect are positions ring builders would seek to hold should they seek visual dominance over people outside the community. Alternatively, the model predicts that in circular and arc communities where heightened status among two leaders/groups is found, these groups position themselves across from each other in order not to be placed outside a position of visual/symbolic dominance. Both the Cannon's Point shell ring and Fig Island 3 have their greatest volumes of shell lying in opposition on the east and west ends of the arcs (Figures 3.3 and 3.4).[3]

Large U-Shaped Rings and Ring Complexes

While individual shell rings in Georgia and South Carolina are usually circular or semicircular and under 90 m in diameter, those in Florida are usually U- or C-shaped and exceed 130 m in length. They may also be architecturally complex, having mounds or other rings attached and other shell deposits associated with them. If, however, we consider rings in Georgia and South Carolina as parts of ring complexes and not simply single rings, similar degrees of architectural complexity become apparent. Three sites, Sapelo, Fig Island, and Coosaw, consist of three or more rings and other architectural features, which, taken together, exceed 200 m in length (Heide 2002, 2003; Russo 2002; Thompson et al. 2002). Six Archaic ring sites (three of preceramic and three of ceramic periods) have been identified in Florida (Oxeye, Guana, Rollins, Joseph Reed, Horr's Island, Bonita Bay; Figure 1.1) and are discussed below, from northern rings to southern ones, relative to model evidence of social organization.

Oxeye

The Oxeye site is the oldest (Table 3.1) and smallest of the Florida rings, measuring 160 m in maximum diameter (Figure 3.8). It is also the most circular of the Florida rings, although its original shape has been severely altered by erosion. In fact, most of the ring is buried beneath 1 to 3 m of marsh with only the western portions of the ring lying above the tide line. Tidal erosion has spread the shell eastward making it areally larger today than it likely was when originally constructed. At the time of construction, the ring was perhaps as small as 130 m in diameter and 500 m in circumference.

Due in large part to erosion and burial, testing the site for model expectations is difficult. Currently the tallest portion of the ring lies opposite an opening, as would be predicted by the model for a hierarchically organized society. Whether that opening was an original part of construction or has been opened through tidal erosion is unclear. Grøn (1991) does suggest, however, that the primary prestige position is usually placed on the highest natural topography on an unlevel landscape. Today the highest shell deposits are situated on the west side of the ring where the highest sand deposits underlying the ring exist.

In terms of the differential distribution of artifacts that might be associated with the differential distribution of shell, large units have been excavated only

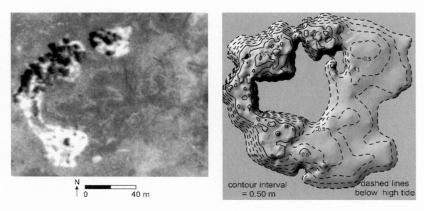

Figure 3.8. Oxeye shell ring. Left, 1943 aerial photograph (white is exposed shell with trees, surrounded by marsh); right, 1998 surface and subsurface shell topography and shaded relief map.

in the western, above-marsh portion of the ring. Consequently comparisons cannot be made with other portions of the ring. However, the excavations have revealed the site to predate the use of pottery in the region, and other artifacts (e.g., shell tools, clay balls) are few.

Guana

Both a surface topography map (Figure 3.9a) and a shell thickness map (Figure 3.9b) have been completed for the Guana shell ring. The former indicates a general U-shaped, albeit somewhat indistinct, ring. The latter measured the actual vertical depths of the shell deposits that make up the ring (determined by extensive probing across the site; Russo et al. 2002). This approach more clearly delimits the shell ring by excluding natural topographic highs and lows that obscure the view of the distribution of shell. The highest portions of the ring exist at the closed end opposite the opening, as the model would predict for a community with social distinctions reflected in the material record. The builders of the western arm were more successful in accumulating shell than those who deposited shell along the eastern arm.

Guana is the only ring that has been excavated in a manner designed to test the spatial distribution of shell and other materials. Excavations have revealed that not only is there more shell but also there are more prestigious and greater numbers of artifacts in the closed end and western arm than in the eastern arm. Both the closed end of the ring and the western arm contain greater numbers of decorated pottery vs. plain than are found in the eastern arm (Russo et al. 2002). Other kinds of artifacts are rare, but those recovered (e.g., carved soapstone and polished bone pins/points) are more common in the higher shell

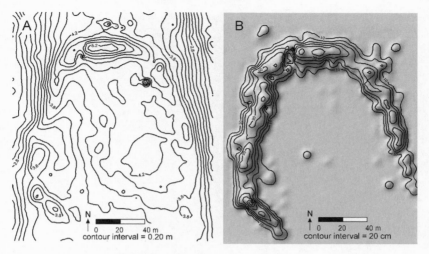

Figure 3.9. Guana shell ring. a, Surface topography map; b, shaded relief/shell thickness map, after Russo et al. 2002.

positions. These data are model predictions for transegalitarian societies. In no position in the ring were differences in artifact distribution, in terms of quality or number, indicative of extreme inequalities in rank among community members as might be typically associated with chiefdoms.

Rollins

The main ring at Rollins is largely circular or C-shaped with a large opening on the southern end (Figure 3.10). The perimeter of the ring, however, is engirdled by smaller, attached rings (Russo and Saunders 1999). The function of these "ringlets" may have been much the same as for the central plaza of the main ring. Largely devoid of shell, both the large and smaller plazas seem to have been used for public ceremony requiring clean, level floors. However, the ringlets contain more pottery than the large central ring, and Ring I yielded abundant shell, vertebrate fauna, evidence of hearths/charcoal, and ceramics from the "plaza." In contrast to the other attached ringlet plazas, this "plaza" seems to have been used as an activity space with dense amounts of refuse deposited underfoot or in pits.

In testing the model, shell deposits are far more extensive on the western side of the ring compared to the eastern side, suggesting social nonuniformity in the accumulation of shell. The numerous attached rings (some as large as individual rings in South Carolina and Georgia) on the western and northern portions of the site indicate that people who built them engaged in social activities requiring exclusion of some portion of the larger community. The naturally high topogra-

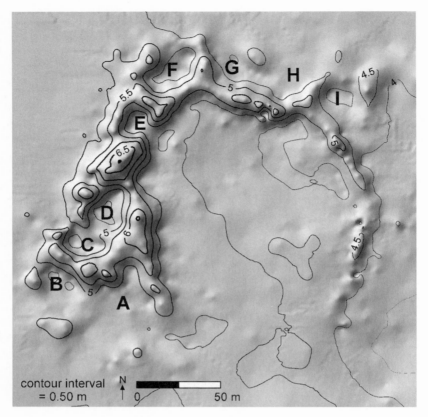

Figure 3.10. Rollins shell ring surface topography and shaded relief map. Attached rings/plazas labeled A–I.

phy lies on the west and north sides of the ring, positions where the highest shell deposits also occur. This indicates that from the initial deposits of shell, groups on the north and west sides held visual and symbolic dominance over the larger community.

The location in the main ring with the single greatest volume and elevation of shell lies between the D and E ringlets (Figure 3.10) on the western arm of the circle. This position is less directly opposite the opening than the more northern portion of the circle where the model would predict the greatest volume of shell to lie. That this position is fairly close to the ideal closed position (somewhere between the G and F ringlets) for visual, communicative, and symbolic dominance perhaps mitigates the misfit somewhat. However, the vast complexity caused by the attachment of the smaller rings to the larger ring brings into question whether social factors other than visual dominance within the main ring affected the decisions for accumulating shell. Whatever functions went on in ringlets D and E, they may have compelled the massive mounding of shell to a greater degree than social factors predicted by the model for simpler, circular community formations.

Like a number of the other rings, Rollins exhibits wide variations in the amounts of shell on one side of the ring vs. another. This suggests social polarities existed in the community that made the ring. These polarities could reflect successful accumulator vs. underachiever, feast host vs. guest, consumer vs. trader, lender vs. debtor, permanent vs. temporary resident, kin group vs. kin group, or any combination of the above. In any of these cases, the ability to accumulate surplus foodstuffs is often shadowed by the ability to transform that accumulation to debt that may, in part, be paid back through material items. On this point, more diverse foods (crab and fish) plus more diverse and greater numbers of artifacts (mainly utilitarian ceramics and bone pins) and oyster have been recovered per unit from the western arm than from the eastern arm (Russo and Saunders 1999; Saunders 1999, 2003).[4]

Joseph Reed

According to local informants, the Joseph Reed shell ring was once a complete circle. Situated on the Atlantic beach, it has suffered from hurricanes, ocean transgression, and daily tides, and only half a circle remains (Figure 3.11; Fryman et al. 1980). While it has extreme variations in shell thickness and height across its remaining arc, the ring has not been investigated sufficiently to determine to what degree these variations are attributable to nature and to what extent they are attributable to its original builders. Dredging from the Intracoastal Waterway has apparently deposited large amounts of shell on its western flank, and at least two modern drainage canals have been cut through its north and western sides. On the south side, Russo and Heide (2002) placed two 1-X-1-m units on the tallest portions of the remaining ring (averaging 1.6 m in shell depth) and one unit on a lower portion (0.9 m deep) on the opposite north side. The higher shell ring areas averaged 11 ceramics per cubic meter, while the less elevated northern unit yielded two ceramics per cubic meter. The higher deposits of Unit 2 also contained the only nonceramic artifacts, two bone pins and one large chert flake from a source at least 200 miles away (Iceland 2000). These limited data hint that greater access to both prestige and utilitarian goods went hand in hand with a greater ability to accumulate food in the form of shellfish.

Horr's Island

Arguably the most complex ring site is found at Horr's Island on Florida's southwest Gulf coast. The main ring/plaza is larger than any single ring in South Carolina or Georgia but not as large as most rings in Florida. Taking into ac-

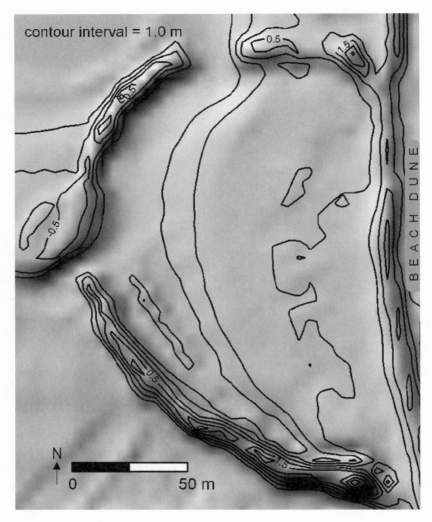

Figure 3.11. Joseph Reed shell ring surface topography and shaded relief map, after Fryman et al. 1980.

count associated mounds (constructed mostly out of shell) and additional shell ridges, however, the site is the largest of Florida's ring sites (Figure 3.12). Because of the unusual topography (the mound/ring complex is situated on top of a very narrow east-west trending parabolic sand dune that slopes from north to south), much of the shell placed on top of the perimeter of the ring has fallen down the sides of the dune. Consequently, the *apparent* volume as seen in ring surface topography (Figure 3.12, top) is greater than the actual deposits of shell (Figure 3.12, bottom). Extensive testing across the site indicates that some of the

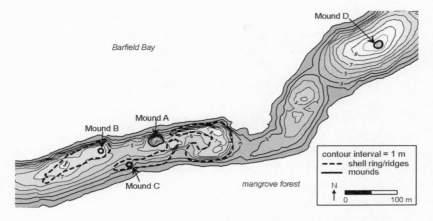

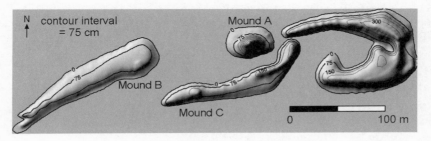

Figure 3.12. Horr's Island shell ring, ridges, and mounds surface topography map (top) and contour and shaded relief/shell thickness map (bottom).

ring deposits extend nearly 4 m deep. As such, they are thicker than most ring deposits in Florida. The deepest deposits are found along the closed end of the ring as the model would predict for a society with differential distributions of wealth and power. Shallower deposits are found on the western end of the northern arm near Mound A.

The complexity of the architectural plan alone suggests a degree of social organization beyond egalitarian. The presence of ceremonial mounds of substantial size indicates at least transegalitarian levels of organization with individuals present in the community capable of compelling others to work for them or the greater public good. Because of the complexity of the plan, most of the site, however, is largely noncircular, precluding the application of the circular-village-plan model to the greater site. Considering the ring as only one of three larger shell deposits at the site, the layout may more fruitfully be approached as a linear or amalgamated village (Grøn 1991), wherein the centralmost position is symbolically and communicatively the most important. In this case, the three mounds (A, B, C) seem to represent the center of the overall site plan.

At the site, each of three mounds (A, B, C) is associated with distinct shell ridge/ring deposits. Mound A may have been associated directly with the shell ring by a relatively thin deposit of shell on the ring's north arm, or it may have been physically linked to a linear ridge of shell to its south. Unfortunately, modern disturbance (a road) interferes with definitive determinations of the original architectural layout. However, the exaggerated piling of shell in the construction of Mound A on or near the end of one of the arms of an open ring reflects similar locations of exaggerated mounding at other rings (e.g., Cannon's Point, Guana, Fig Island 3). The reason for such mounding may likewise be similar to that hypothesized for the other rings, namely, the shifting of social concerns outside the ring (i.e., mounding may have functioned as a symbol of territory or power aimed at rivals, social partners, or trade partners). I have previously suggested that the shell deposits associated with Mounds B and C may have been where guests or groups of lower social rank lived/feasted during times of ceremony. That is, the areas may have served as guest areas or as overflow areas for peoples that the ring site itself could not accommodate (Russo 1991). While this idea is largely speculative, it does fit known parameters for intervillage and intravillage competitive feasting; namely, that lower rank guests or community members display less, even though they may receive substantial food (e.g., Malinowski 1929; Young 1971). If the primary goal of piling shell was to achieve height for display, it may be significant that Mound B and Mound C shell ridges are generally thinner than those found in the shell ring associated with Mound A, suggesting less intense or frequent display.

In terms of artifacts, the Horr's Island site is preceramic, having been occupied centuries before the local adoption of pottery. Also, it is distant from any regional sources of lithics useful in chipped-stone technologies and even more distant from trade routes of the greater Southeast. For these and other reasons, the artifactual residue of the site is restricted, consisting mostly of utilitarian shell tools. Thus few artifacts and fewer obvious prestige artifacts are present to determine whether differential access to wealth is apparent or can be linked to differential positions or varying amounts of shell within the site. To complicate the application of the social space/feasting model to the site, the manners in which the site have been excavated and reported prevent clear understanding of the artifact and overall shell distributions across the site (McMichael 1982; Russo 1991). Ultimately, it is the size of the site, the presence of large ceremonial mounds, and the differential distribution of shellfish remains that are the most definitive indicators of social complexity. Excluding for the moment the problematic Mound A and applying the model to the ring alone, the greatest amount of shell is located at the closed end of the ring—and the ring is U-shaped. Both reflect model predictions for transegalitarian organization. The ring shape and shell distribution thus reflect a social complexity that is found in the greater community itself.

Bonita Bay Shell Works

A few hundred years after Horr's Island was abandoned, another group built a similar west-facing ring 25 miles north. At 240 m in length, it is one of the larger rings but contains fairly thin deposits of shell that are a little over a meter at their thickest (Dickel 1992). As at Horr's Island, the artifact assemblages are characterized by simple, utilitarian shell tools with few exotic or obvious prestige goods (Houck 1996:24). Both sites were placed on sloping, relict sand dunes on whose greatest elevations were deposited the greatest amounts of shell (Houck 1996:30), and both rings are associated with large conical sand/shell mounds (although the cultural association of the Bonita Bay mound to the ring is still in question [Dickel 1992]).

The limited work at Bonita Bay has sought to understand the horizontal and vertical variations in shell seen across the site (Dickel 1992:155–158; Houck 1996:30). Excavations in the closed end of the ring have not been undertaken, but the section of the north arm of the ring nearest to it is situated on a natural topographic high that may extend beneath the closed end. Yet, the closed end, or uppermost status position of a U-shaped ring, is not topographically the highest point in the ring, as the model would predict (Figure 3.13). It is 20 to 40 cm shorter than peak contours at two other locations along the arms. However, this is largely a result of disturbance and postdepositional activity. Portions of the south arm have been buried under 25 cm of sand in historic times (Houck 1996:30), while the closed end appears to have been leveled. Great amounts of crushed shell extend both on the interior and exterior of the ring (Dickel 1992:158). Even though the height of the shell is somewhat reduced, the actual volume (base width times height) of shell seems greatest at the closed end (Figure 3.13).

Comparing ring arms, both shell and artifacts were abundant in the northern arm closest to the modeled high-status, closed end compared with the southern arm, which had horizontally thinner and vertically limited deposits at a point more distant from the closed end of the ring (Houck 1996:7, 15–20, 24, 28, 29). Unfortunately, the methodology used in the recovery, as well as the reporting of artifact and shell distribution, does not allow determination of artifact density per shell volume. However, as predicted by the model, the U-shape and greater volume of shell at the closed end and portions of the northern arm reflect a social organization resulting in unequal accumulation and display of wealth as reflected in food remains.

Fig Island

The structural elaboration and size of shell ring sites in Florida would seem to suggest that the societies that built them were more socially complex than those

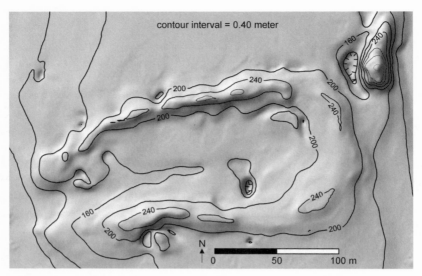

Figure 3.13. Bonita Bay shell ring and mound surface topography and shaded relief map, after Beriault as redrawn by Ferrer in Dickel 1992:143.

that built the smaller, more circular, and structurally simpler rings in South Carolina and Georgia. However, the archaeology of most ring sites in all three states is disappointingly limited, consisting, for the most part, of the recovery of a few artifacts, some sketch maps, and a few shovel tests or excavation units. Even the more intensively investigated sites have had only minor excavations. As archaeologists discover more and more that ring sites do not lie in isolation, clearer understanding can be gained of their organizational complexity as reflected in community layout.

Fig Island Rings 2 and 3 have been known about for decades. Fig Island 2, in particular, was known for its symmetry and simple structure (Hemmings 1970). But recent mapping of shell deposits above and below marsh level has revealed that the ring is actually part of a much larger site with a shell causeway (now buried below the marsh) connecting Fig Island Rings 2 and 3 (cf. Figure 3.4a and 3.4b and Figure 3.14). The angle of the causeway aligns with a narrow opening in the southwest portion of Fig Island 2 and the causeway is centrally located on Fig Island 3. This suggests that architectural intent beyond symbolic and visual dominance (e.g., cosmology, utilitarian function) may have influenced the final shape and orientation of the two rings (cf. Russo 2002).

Even more unexpected is the identification of a massive shell ring east of Fig Island 2 and 3 (Figure 3.14). Fig Island 1 is strikingly similar to Rollins in having a series of rings and shell works attached to a main ring. In another way, it

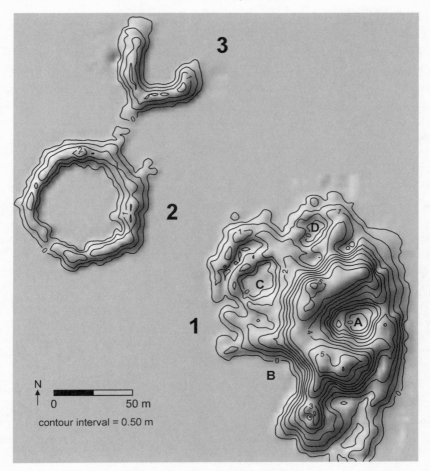

Figure 3.14. Fig Island rings 1, 2, and 3 shell thickness topography and shaded relief map. Letters A–D designate rings/plazas at Fig Island 1.

is similar to Horr's Island with a large shell mound adjoining it on its south side. At over 5 m in height, it is by far the tallest known ring and certainly in volume the largest outside of Florida. The height of the main ring at Fig Island 1 elevated the position holders above occupants at all other rings surrounding it, as well as above any activities that occurred in the ring. More than at any other ring site, visual and symbolic dominance at this ring reached extreme levels. Height was far more important to the builders than providing an arena for the greatest number of spectators. The size of the central plaza is the smallest of all mapped rings, a mere 25 m across. While the ring surrounding it is about the size of Fig Island 2 in *outside* diameter, only people situated on top of the inside of the ring could view the goings-on in the plaza. Beyond this edge, the plaza simply cannot be seen from the top of the ring. In terms of the inside diameter, the top of the ring is about 10 m less than that at Fig Island 2. With the limited surface area on top for viewing, the number of people who could have viewed any activities in the plaza from the top of the ring was smaller than the number who could be accommodated on the potential viewing area found on top of Fig Island 2.

While today the main ring of Fig Island 1 appears almost C-shaped, originally the ring may have been more circular. Tidal erosion may have undercut its eastern side, resulting in a lower shell height and thinner eastern ring wall, but it is still a closed circle of shell (cf. Hemmings 1970:10, who posits historic quarrying for the ring's shape). In the social space model, the most prestigious position in a closed circular formation is its highest point. Two equally high points existed on top of the ring, with the largest elevated area occurring on the south side. This position lies adjacent to a causeway that leads directly to a large shell mound. That mound is not centrally located in the site. It lies distant from all other shell works and rings at the site. It is in the horizontal and vertical distribution of these ring and mound features that, perhaps more than any other ring site, Fig Island is reminiscent of Woodland/Mississippian ceremonial mound complexes where social hierarchy is reflected in the height and separateness of mounded structures.

Like most ceramic-bearing shell rings, decorated and plain pottery, shell tools, and bone pins represent the majority of artifacts recovered from the Fig Island rings (Saunders 2002a). Significantly, while pottery is fairly common in the smaller shell rings, a single 2-×-2-m unit placed in the upper meter of the Fig Island 1 ring recovered very little, contrary to model expectations of a high-status accumulator. Unlike the smaller rings at Fig Island that appear to have resulted from palimpsests of individual episodes of feasting, the shell deposits in the larger ring are devoid of discernible feasting episodes. This suggests a different method of deposition, at least at the lone unit that has been excavated (Saunders 2002a, 2002b). Combined with the paucity of artifacts, the featureless deposition of shells suggests rapid collection of shell and placement within the ring without activities or a time interval between deposits sufficient to allow the accidental deposition of artifacts to occur. In other words, the upper levels of the large ring seem to have predominantly been a construction project designed to achieve height rapidly, rather than a construction project resulting solely from the refuse of periodic, in situ feasting activities (Russo 2002; Saunders 2002a). The idea of living/feasting in the plaza and throwing one's garbage behind domiciles to build the ring is highly unlikely given the steep sloped interior of the ring walls—it is a long way to throw. But even to carry the shell from the plaza up the steep slopes of the interior of the ring would have been difficult. More likely, as the ring rose in height, shell was brought in from the outside and taken to the top of the ring for deposition via egresses provided by less steep shell ramps on the western and northern sides of the ring. Alternatively, it might have been brought by canoe and taken up less severe slopes on the east side if, as discussed, they existed in the past. The nature of shell deposition—massive amounts in short periods of time—is reminiscent of the kinds of deposition found in capping episodes of Mound A at Horr's Island. There, I have suggested that the mound was a community project requiring at least temporary leadership of a status sufficient to compel massive labor contributions from the populace (Russo 1991). Here, the magnitude of the construction project is significantly larger.

THE MODEL OF SOCIAL SPACE AND FEASTING AT SHELL RINGS

The model presented here cannot, of course, anticipate all construction decisions that occurred at the numerous and widely varied ring sites. Rather, it is intended to provide a method for gaining insight into the variability exhibited in the shapes, volumes, and elevations of shell rings by applying universal patterns of spacing observed in the behaviors of small groups and feasting and other social interaction within circular communities. As such, the larger the group, i.e., the larger the ring, the less cleanly characteristics obtained from small group behaviors may be applied. As groups gain in size they, perforce, gain in the numbers and kinds of social mechanisms and roles individuals and groups adopt to maintain societal coherence. At some point in the evolution of communities at large ring sites like Fig Island and Horr's Island, public works projects went beyond those that were directly guided by passive communication or position-dominance needs, and new and different social needs were added to the mix that governed architectural decisions.

The model is most productive in providing corroboration of social complexity in cultural contexts where traditional markers of complexity are ambiguous or lacking. In large ring sites, of course, traditional markers in the form of large public works including ceremonial mounds may be present and sufficient to demonstrate a level of social organization beyond egalitarianism. However, as I have cited, not all archaeologists view large-scale public works as being beyond the scope of simply organized hunter-gatherers. In these cases, and even in the simplest of shell ring formations, social space theory provides apperception for archaeologists in search of signs of inequality, while feasting theory provides the kinds of evidence archaeologists should look at—differences in kinds, qualities, and distributions of food remains and associated paraphernalia. When expected characteristics of food remains (more, bigger, special, rare) match expected positions of relative rank within a shell ring, then confirmation of model predictions is attained. When they do not, alternative hypotheses need to be explored.

For the most part, all shell rings described above have revealed positive correlations between modeled hierarchical ring positions and volume of food remains (i.e., shell). A few have provided additional support for social inequalities in the form of artifact kinds, densities, and distributions, to indicate that transegalitarian rather than egalitarian groups constructed, occupied, and feasted at those rings at which other evidence of ranking may or may not be present. Southeastern archaeologists accustomed to classifying cultural groups as chiefly, tribal, big men, or band level societies may be unenthusiastic about using the term *transegalitarian* to describe ranked societies, since the other and like terms may be subsumed under it. But the use of the term does not preclude other taxonomies. Rather, it serves to distinguish ring builders from strictly egalitarian societies until finer distinctions can be determined as more data are obtained.

At Horr's Island, it is tempting to posit that separate lineage segments resided at the ring, at ridge B, and at ridge C and that the mounds associated with them served as segmentary markers. At Fig Island, it is tempting to view the mound attached to Fig Island 1 as a chiefly residence and the extraordinarily tall and steep-sided ring as a monument to his/her power. At Rollins, the attached rings may have held audiences for sodality rituals whose total members were too few or too exclusive for a more general audience serviced by the main plaza. The variety of shell ring shapes and sizes suggests that no one interpretation of their use or of the social organizations that guided their construction will likely fit them all. It also suggests that we have a long way to go if we are to understand the processes behind the appearance, development, and disappearance of ringbuilding societies.

I suggest that archaeologists seeking correlates of hierarchical social organization in the Archaic need to look beyond markers traditionally linked to Woodland big men and Mississippian chiefdoms (e.g., exotic trade items, prestige burial goods, tributary architecture). It is not that such items have not been or may not be found at shell rings (some already have), but clearly this view of what constitutes evidence of social hierarchy in the Southeastern archaeological record prevents us from finding incipient ranking in any cultures other than those of latter prehistory. It affords us little opportunity to explore the varied social record of transegalitarianism that characterizes much of Southeastern prehistory (Anderson 2002, this volume).

In all societies, individuals and groups seek the material and social privileges that come with status. Those that successfully gain status may ultimately gain great power and begin a process of cultural change that ends in permanent social ranking. But this end result is certainly not guaranteed. For every individual seeking selective advantage, the greater community will act to prevent that individual from gaining it if it is not in their own best self-interest. This is particularly true in egalitarian societies where equality is the dominant organizing principle. Egalitarian societies invent and impose social mechanisms to prevent any disadvantages that status procurement by others may impose on the remaining members of the community. Despite the long-held notion that evidence of social distinctions is lacking in the Archaic record, the archaeologist need only look to the refuse left behind by the battles between these aggrandizers and social levelers for evidence of such distinctions. The gain and maintenance of coveted positions in a public forum; the ability to accumulate large quantities of food for the greater community and personal advantage; and the acquiescence of communities, otherwise insistent on humility and sharing, to the ostentatious display of individual accumulatory prowess—these are all markers that reflect the dynamic social relations among Archaic builders of shell rings. It is likely that these markers are to be found in other archaeological contexts of the period if only we look for them.

NOTES

1. Hayden (2001:43) distinguishes between complex hunter-gatherers who are capable of obtaining surpluses and accumulating wealth through distribution in large-scale feasts and most generalized hunter-gatherers who cannot normally obtain and store surplus foods for feasts. Consequently, planning in advance for large feasts is not possible among most generalized hunter-gatherers. In addition, the concept of "giving" or "hosting" a feast is antithetical to egalitarian sharing ethics.

2. The reader should be aware that labor intensity for the collection of animals has never been satisfactorily determined for prehistoric Late Archaic coastal populations. I am not sure it could be. Typically, as here, a logical argument is offered in place of actual measures of effort; cf. Sassaman (1993:216), who sees shellfish collecting for these populations as "time-consuming, if not labor-intensive."

3. At Fig Island 3, as a result of extreme erosion, the western arm of the crescent has been reduced elevationally and its shell distributed downstream (north) of its original position. Either interpretation of the social significance of shell at these rings must be weighed against the obvious erosional disturbance at the sites. Also, the topographically high western and eastern deposits at Cannon's Point shell ring may be later deposits over a smaller ring buried beneath the marsh (Marrinan 1975).

4. Faunal analysis has yet to be completed from the 1998 Russo and Saunders ex-

cavations on the eastern arm of the ring, i.e., the 1-x-1-m unit 3197 and its associated 50-x-50-cm column sample. However, I observed very little vertebrate fauna and mostly oyster in the unit and column sample. Saunders (2003) reports that the eastern arm averaged 147 sherds (including small sherds less than one-half inch in size), weighing 303 g, while the western arm yielded an average of 2,949 sherds weighing 8,700 g per cubic meter.

4
Regional-Scale Interaction Networks and the Emergence of Cultural Complexity along the Northern Margins of the Southeast

Richard W. Jefferies

The emergence of culturally complex hunter-gatherer societies has been a topic of great anthropological interest for at least the past 15 years (Arnold, ed. 1996; Johnson and Earle 1987; Price and Brown 1985). In 1985, James Brown published a seminal article on the emergence of cultural complexity in the prehistoric American Midwest. He suggested several indicators of emerging hunter-gatherer complexity including the appearance of permanent habitations, food storage facilities, plant domestication, cemeteries, and interregional exchange. Although the conditions, causes, and consequences of increased hunter-gatherer complexity have been topics of considerable debate, Brown (1985:201–202) proposed that it usually occurred where a sedentary way of life was practiced for at least part of the year. A major prerequisite for sedentism appears to be the ability to successfully exploit nearby, year-round food resources having the potential to produce a surplus (Hayden 1996:52). Agriculture, once considered the primary factor in the emergence of complexity, is now seen as an indirect consequence of a more sedentary lifestyle.

The combined effects of increased sedentism and smaller group territories created many new social and environmental challenges for these increasingly complex hunter-gatherers. Perhaps foremost among them was the maintenance of intergroup social connections in the face of declining mobility and the potential for increased exclusivity of territorial use. Also, resource fluctuation had to be managed in new ways, and relations with other regional hunter-gatherers had to be regulated (Renouf 1991:100).

The loss of risk-reducing and security measures practiced by more mobile hunter-gatherers may have been mitigated by changes in the nature of intergroup social interaction. Robert Kelly (1991:143) suggests that in regions where resource fluctuations are spatially heterogeneous, social relationships often serve as useful risk-reducing strategies. One possible response to decreased mobility may have been the establishment of more formal social ties with other local groups, perhaps through a network of trading partners living in nearby as well as distant settlements (Brose 1979; Brown 1985; Jefferies 1997; Marquardt 1985).

Kelly suggests that in highly mobile groups, individuals maintained their own relationships with other groups through individual exchange and acts of sharing. In contrast, in more sedentary groups, one or two people established and maintained social ties with another group, perhaps through marriage, and everyone else maintained their relationship with that group through these individuals (Kelly 1991:143–144). It is conceivable that within any one group, certain members would maintain social ties with partners living in a number of nearby and distant groups (Wiessner 1982a), creating a web of social relations across the landscape. The resulting regional social interaction networks could have served as the conduits through which critical information, materials, and mates moved from one local group to another.

Individuals who gained access to other local groups served as the funnel through which the members of one group had access to the resources of another. Once in this position, a group intermediary had to maintain a delicate balance between the needs and resources of his or her group and those of the other group(s). In the process, these "middle persons" may have gained prestige or power within their local group, thereby elevating their social standing and establishing a certain degree of social inequality (Kelly 1991:144–145).

As Kelly (1991:145) points out, one implication of this model is that non-egalitarian societies developed in clusters, not in isolation, since there had to be equivalent social positions in other local groups that participated in these networks. This trend is reflected in the archaeological record of the North American midcontinent. In this area, the first evidence for the emergence of cultural complexity, as defined by Brown (1985), is not uniformly distributed across the landscape. Instead, these traits first appear at Middle to Late Holocene sites in certain parts of the region, but not in others (Jefferies 1996; Sassaman 1995). The reasons behind this spatial variability are still unclear but appear to be partially related to the heterogeneous distribution of regional subsistence resources (Brown and Vierra 1983:169–170).

Once a social network was operational, it would be to the benefit of all participants for group interaction and exchange to take place on a regular basis, thereby ensuring a steady flow of information and resources. In turn, this would reinforce the elevated social position of the intermediaries. One consequence of increased interaction among these scattered local groups would be decreased social distance among some of their members. More intensive social interaction and integration should be expressed by a greater sharing of ideas, including how to manufacture and decorate certain items in their material culture inventory (Braun and Plog 1982:510). The adoption of common technologies and styles may also reflect attempts of local groups to express their affiliation with other network participants (Wobst 1977:323). Wobst (1977) suggests that attributes expressing such social information would usually appear on items that are publicly displayed.

THE EMERGENCE OF SOCIAL NETWORKS

Using Brown's (1985) criteria for the emergence of cultural complexity, it appears that by approximately 6000 B.P., or shortly thereafter, relatively complex hunter-gatherer societies were developing in several parts of the greater Southeast and southern Midwest including the central Tennessee–upper Tombigbee River valleys (Bense 1987; Johnson and Brookes 1989), the St. Johns River valley (Milanich 1994; Piatek 1994), the Savannah River valley (Sassaman 1994; Sassaman et al. 1988), and the central Mississippi–lower Ohio River valleys (Jefferies 1996, 1997). By this time, some groups that inhabited these areas were gradually abandoning the residential-mobility strategy used during the previous millennia and replacing it with a logistically organized one often associated with a collector subsistence strategy (Binford 1980). This transition appears to have brought about substantial changes in the distribution and movement of people over the Mid-Holocene landscape, including smaller home ranges and multiseasonal occupation base camps.

Prior to ca. 6000 B.P., archaeologically visible indicators of intergroup exchange and interaction are limited to a few examples of exotic materials found at widely scattered sites (Ahler 1991:6). These rare occurrences probably reflect the periodic encounters of isolated, highly mobile hunter-gatherer groups (Anderson 1990:181).

It is not until the appearance of other signs of sedentism and cultural complexity that we see indications for the formation of larger regional-scale social networks. Evidence of this transition in the upper Southeast and southern Midwest is marked by the appearance of region-wide bone and flaked-stone artifact styles and technologies, usually at what have been interpreted as multiseasonal base camps (Cook 1976; Jefferies 1995, 1996). Analyses of the spatial distribution of these artifacts and their attributes provide a means for investigating the scale, intensity, and duration of Middle to Late Holocene hunter-gatherer regional networks (Jefferies 1997; Johnson and Brookes 1989; Sassaman et al. 1988).

BONE PINS IN THE SOUTHERN MIDWEST

As discussed elsewhere (Jefferies 1995, 1996, 1997), analyses of carved and engraved bone pins from a number of late Middle Archaic sites have been used to

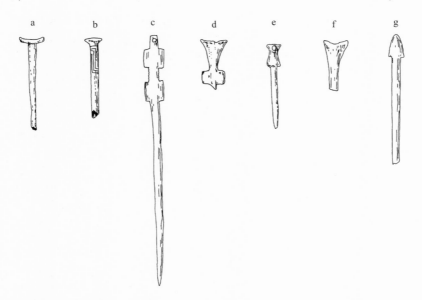

Figure 4.1. Southern Midwest region pin head types.

explore the nature of Mid-Holocene social interaction and integration in the southern Midwest (Figure 1.1). Limited technological data suggest that many of the pins were manufactured from the long bones of the white-tailed deer (Breitburg 1982:923–924). Cook's (1976) analysis of the manufacturing trajectory of late Middle Archaic bone pins from the Koster site in west-central Illinois demonstrated that deer metapodials were incised and split to remove long sections of the bone. The removed pieces were then ground flat, incised along the long axis, split into smaller pieces, and finally ground and polished to form the pin (Cook 1976:38). Bader's (1992) study of similar pins from the Kentucky Air National Guard site (KYANG), located at the Falls of the Ohio River in Kentucky, supports Cook's assessment.

Bader's (1992:280) functional analysis of the KYANG site pins reveals no use-related striae of any kind, suggesting that they were not employed for any heavy-duty tasks. Pins like these are sometimes found in the head area of burials, suggesting that they were used to hold hair arrangements in place (Webb 1974:167, 170, 172, 222). Others appear to have been used to fasten clothing or burial wraps.

Examination of more than 140 bone pins from the eight sites located in the southern Midwest region (Koster, Arnold Research Cave, Modoc Rock Shelter, Black Earth, Bluegrass, McCain, Crib Mound, KYANG; Figure 1.1) revealed that most could be assigned to one of seven types (Figure 4.1) on the basis of differences in pin head shape (Jefferies 1997). Each head type occurred at a minimum of three sites. The crutch-top head style (Figure 4.1a) is the most widely distributed of the seven types, occurring at six sites ranging from west-central Illinois to the Falls of the Ohio in north-central Kentucky. Engraving was rarely observed on this pin type.

T-top pins (Figure 4.1b), characterized by an expanded head shaped by grinding, were also widely distributed across the region, occurring at five of the seven sites. The shafts of more than 80 percent of the t-top pins were engraved with one of several complex designs. Other pin types, such as cruciform (Figure 4.1c), fishtailed-cruciform (Figure 4.1d), and double-expanded (Figure 4.1e), while not as common, were found at sites throughout the southern Midwest region (Jefferies 1997).

Additional information on regional interaction and exchange came from the engraved designs found on the head and shaft portions of some pins (Jefferies 1997). The designs, represented on approximately 43 percent of the specimens and associated with six of the seven head types, are formed by various combinations of single and multiple rectilinear lines and dots. Some of the designs are very simple, consisting of only a few lines; others are much more complex (Jefferies 1997:fig. 7).

Examination of the spatial distribution of different types of engraved designs revealed some regional preferences, but as with the head types, most were found throughout the project area (Jefferies 1997). Even very complex, infrequently occurring examples exhibited a high degree of similarity.

In summary, many of the head types and engraving styles discussed above occur at roughly contemporaneous sites (ca. 6000–5000 B.P.) distributed over a broad region that minimally extended 500 km along the northern margins of the Southeast.

The appearance of localized and distinct artifact styles, like the bone pins discussed here, indicates relatively intensive social interaction among Middle and Late Holocene groups that inhabited the southern Midwest region. The spatial distribution of pins having these technological and stylistic attributes suggests that the efforts of increasingly sedentary local hunter-gatherer groups to maintain or intensify their social ties with other groups in the region were successful and that the network that helped promote this social integration covered an extensive area (Jefferies 1997:477).

Although the distribution of different bone pin styles within the southern Midwest region suggests a high level of intraregional interaction, the specific form (or forms) of this interaction is difficult to identify. One possibility is that each local group that lived in the region manufactured one style of pin. The presence of multiple pin styles at a site would indicate the exchange of pins between members of different local groups, the movement of marriage partners who wore the pins from one group to another, or other activities involving the actual movement of pins from where they were made to where they were ultimately discarded. Another scenario is that each local group manufactured a variety of pin styles, reflecting the sharing of ideas with other local groups concerning how pins should be made, as well as many other cultural attributes that distinguished them from members of other, more distant regional groups (Jefferies 1997). Recent seriation of head types and engraved designs by White (1999) suggests that variation in pin style may be partially attributable to temporal factors (i.e., different styles made at different times).

Whatever the reason, repeated interaction among neighboring local groups eventually resulted in the broadening of cultural identity and the formation of a larger, more complex regional group. Radiocarbon dates indicate interaction among network groups continued for nearly 1,000 years. Similar developments have been documented by Johnson and Brookes (1989), Sassaman et al. (1988), and others for contemporary groups that lived farther to the Southeast.

The similarity of bone pins found throughout the southern Midwest raises many interesting questions concerning the extent of this hypothetical regional network and the boundaries of the broader regional group it helped define. Was it an open network with no clearly defined boundaries? Did groups participating in the network interact with all the other groups or just their nearest neighbors?

INTERREGIONAL PERSPECTIVES

As a means of further evaluating the size and organization of Middle to Late Holocene social networks in the midcontinent, as well as the usefulness of using bone pin technological and stylistic attributes to investigate them, pins from an additional 20 contemporary sites located outside the southern Midwest region were examined. Pins from 10 sites located immediately south of the Ohio River along Kentucky's Green River make up part of this sample, while the remaining specimens come from sites located farther to the south in Tennessee, Georgia, Alabama, and Florida (Figure 1.1).

Green River Region

The Green River region of Kentucky, located ca. 200 km south of the southern Midwest region, is well known for the numerous Archaic sites located along its banks (Moore 1916; Webb 1950a, 1950b, 1974; Webb and Haag 1940). Many Green River sites are large shell middens containing abundant bone artifacts, including numerous examples of bone pins (Webb 1950a:381–382, 1950b:324–335, 1974:282–307; Webb and Haag 1939:20–24).

Green River sites included in this stage of analysis consist of those having late Middle Archaic radiocarbon dates (between 6000 and 5000 B.P.) or relatively high percentages (26–91 percent) and/or large quantities (24–317) of diagnostic late Middle Archaic hafted bifaces (Matanzas, Godar, Big Sandy II). The presence of late Middle Archaic bifaces was based on analyses done by Hensley (1994) as part of her chronological assessment of Green River Archaic sites. Comparison of Hensley's classification of late Middle Archaic hafted bifaces and the approach used in this study indicated that the results were generally comparable (Milner and Jefferies 1998:125).

Using these criteria, bone pins from 10 sites scattered along a 75-km section of the Green River were selected for analysis. All sites were excavated as part of Depression-era archaeological projects; the bone artifacts from these sites are curated at the University of Kentucky's William S. Webb Museum of Anthropology. The 10 sites yielded an average of more than 2,000 bone artifacts, ranging from 23 to more than 11,000 items per site. Considering the numerous bone implements found, if pins were used and discarded at these sites, they should be represented in the museum's collections. The search for bone pins consisted of (1) examining the museum's collections of bone artifacts from the 10 sites, (2) checking photographs of bone artifacts from each site, and (3) consulting museum catalog cards.

The first collections analyzed came from four sites (Kirkland [15McL12], Jackson Bluff [15Oh12], Baker [15Mu12], and Jimtown Hill [15Oh19]; Figure 1.1) having primarily late Middle Archaic components. The percentage of late Middle Archaic hafted bifaces from these sites ranged from 75 to 91 percent of all temporally diagnostic bifaces. Examination of the collections revealed that while probable bone pins were present, the shapes of most specimens retained the original contours of the bones from which they were manufactured. Pins were simply sharpened on one end, with little effort made to shape or decorate the head or shaft portions. Pin heads, when present, usually were the unmodified or slightly modified proximal ends of the bone. Pin shafts showed considerable polish, probably caused by wear, but little engraving was noted. Implements resembling these relatively simple bone tools were also common at sites in the southern Midwest region (Breitburg 1982; Cook 1976). No pins resembling the highly decorated types found at sites in the southern Midwest region were identified.

The second group of Green River pins to be analyzed came from six sites (Carlston Annis [15Bt5], Read [15Bt10], Barrett [15McL4], Butterfield [15McL7], Ward [15McL11], and Indian Knoll [15Oh2]; Figure 1.1) known primarily for their Late Archaic occupations but also containing numerous late Middle Archaic hafted bifaces (50–317). Depression-era archaeologists classified many of the bone artifacts from these sites as pins (Webb 1950b:301, 1974:238–239; Webb and Haag 1940:96); however, most were represented by minimally modified fragmentary or complete mammal or bird bones.

In contrast, the head portions of a few pins from Ward (15McL11), Indian Knoll (15Oh2), and Carlston Annis (15Bt5) match types found north of the Ohio River in the southern Midwest region. Most of these specimens fall into the crutch-top head type (Figure 4.1a), the least technologically complex and most widely distributed of the seven types defined for the southern Midwest region (Jefferies 1997:table 2). At least five crutch-top pins were documented at Indian Knoll (Figure 4.2a–c), all appearing to have come from general midden contexts (Moore 1916:fig. 8).

One example of a double-expanded head type (Figure 4.2d) was also found at Indian Knoll (Moore 1916:fig. 8). Double-expanded pins occurred at five of the seven sites in the southern Midwest region (Jefferies 1997:table 2). A single example of a fishtailed-cruciform pin (Figure 4.2e) was found at the Ward site (15McL11) in McLean County (Webb and Haag 1940:fig. 24). Fishtailed-cruciform pins were identified at five of the seven sites in the southern Midwest region (Jefferies 1997:table 2).

While the Green River sites yielded some bone pins with heads resembling those types found in the southern Midwest region, they were rare. Hundreds of pins were examined, and carved heads like those from the southern Midwest region were identified on fewer than 10 specimens. Most of these came from either the Indian Knoll or Ward site.

Likewise, examination of pin shafts and heads revealed very little engraving. In fact, Webb (1974:292) notes that engraved hair pins were rare at Indian Knoll, stating that "[s]ince hair pins were presumptively ornamental as well as useful, one would expect to find bone carving on hair pins if the art was known" (Webb 1974:292). One notable exception is an Indian Knoll pin with an engraved spiral design that encircles the shaft three times (Webb 1974:292). The pin head has a cylindrical shell bead attached, and the bone shaft has been drilled transversely. This pin style has not been documented in the southern Midwest region.

Despite the rarity of engraved pins, other bone artifacts from Indian Knoll and other Green River Archaic sites were engraved (Webb 1974:fig. 51). The engraved designs found on these objects, however, differ from those on most bone pins from the southern Midwest region (Moore 1916:fig. 6). The shafts of several Green River pins were decorated by painting instead of engraving (Webb 1974:292–294, fig. 48c).

Analysis of the Green River pins indicates that while a few were carved and engraved like those from the southern Midwest region, most were not. In fact, highly stylized bone pins of any type were rare. Most items that could have functioned as pins were minimally modified and exhibited many of the morphological characteristics of the bones from which they were manufactured.

The few elaborate Green River Archaic pins substantially differ from those

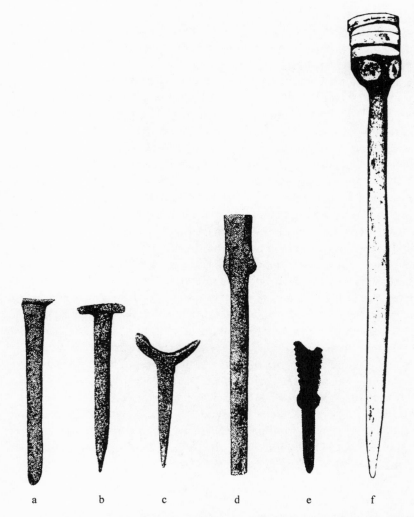

a b c d e f

Figure 4.2. Bone pins from Green River, Kentucky, Archaic sites (images used by permission of the University of Alabama Press [a–d] and William S. Webb Museum of Anthropology, University of Kentucky [e–f]).

found in the southern Midwest region. For example, some have expanded, flat heads that have been shaped by grinding and polishing (Webb 1974:291). Webb (1974:238) reports 62 examples of this pin type from Indian Knoll. While the technology employed to make these pins appears to resemble that used in the southern Midwest region, the end product is considerably different.

Other Indian Knoll pins represent clearly distinctive technologies from those documented in the southern Midwest region. Moore (1916:fig. 8) and Webb (1974:292) report at least seven pins with heads formed by attaching various sizes of shell beads to the top of the pin shaft with asphaltum (Figure 4.2f). In some cases, several shell beads were stacked on top of the bone shaft and held in place by the asphaltum. For other pins, the pin shaft was inserted in a ball of asphaltum and shell beads were placed on the top and/or sides of the asphaltum (Moore 1916). To date, no pins made using this technology are known for the southern Midwest region. Unfortunately, because of the difficulty of dating specific artifacts at these stratigraphically complex, multicomponent sites, it is unclear whether the presence of these distinctive pin-manufacturing technologies in the Green River region is attributable to cultural or temporal factors.

Differences in bone pin style and technology documented in the southern Midwest and Green River regions suggest that distinct social networks existed in these two parts of the midcontinent from ca. 6000 to 4500 B.P. The apparently low level of interaction between hunter-gatherer groups inhabiting these two regions suggests that a social boundary of some type existed near the Ohio River. The occurrence of virtually identical engraved bone pins at late Middle Archaic sites in southern Illinois and eastern Missouri indicates that the Mississippi River did not stop the flow of information and materials (Cook 1976:fig. 23), so the apparent lack of interaction between the southern Midwest and the Green River regions is probably not solely due to the physical presence of the Ohio River.

Regional cultural distinctions suggested by differences in bone pin technology and style are supported by other research, particularly that of Nance (1988: 147), who has proposed that by the Late Archaic, the Green River region was emerging as a "regional sphere of influence." On the basis of artifact type and style similarities, he suggests that Archaic cultural manifestations in western Kentucky were more closely affiliated with groups to the south, not to the north across the Ohio River (Nance 1988:147).

Southeastern Sites

To further evaluate the appropriateness of using bone pins to define the size, organization, and boundaries of Archaic period social networks, published illustrations of bone pins from an additional 10 sites located to the south and east of the southern Midwest and Green River regions were examined. Sites included in this part of the study are located along the middle Tennessee River (Perry, Long Branch, Mulberry Creek [Webb and DeJarnette 1942], Little Bear Creek [Jolly 1969]); the middle Cumberland River (Anderson [Dowd 1989], an unnamed site [Dowd 1970]); the Savannah River (Stallings Island [Claflin 1931], Bilbo [Waring 1968b]); the St. Johns River (Tick Island [Jahn and Bullen 1978]); and the Florida Gulf coast (Van Horn Creek [White 1992]) (Figure 1.1), and they contain cultural deposits that are roughly contemporary with those at the southern Midwest and Green River sites. Although the bone pins shown in these reports do not represent all of the specimens from these sites, elaborately carved and/or decorated pins are commonly illustrated. As with the southern Midwest and Green River pins, most of the Southeastern pins came from sites exhibiting evidence for decreased group mobility and multiseasonal occupations.

Examination of the Southeastern pins revealed, not surprisingly, a tremendous amount of technological and stylistic variability. Burned pin fragments from the Middle Archaic Anderson site in central Tennessee were decorated using various combinations of engraving, painting, and perforating (Dowd 1989: 139). The Anderson pins were associated with two cremations that also contained a variety of exotic items including conch shell cups and marine shell and cannel coal beads (Dowd 1989:93, 102). These artifacts indicate that Anderson site inhabitants were interacting with neighboring and/or distant Middle Archaic groups by ca. 6500 B.P.

Farther east, Depression-era excavations at several Savannah River Archaic sites yielded numerous decorated bone pins. Waring (1968b) assigned 85 bone pins from the Late Archaic Bilbo site near Savannah to four pin types. Although lacking the distinctive head shapes found at many southern Midwest and some Green River sites, the shafts of the Bilbo pins were decorated with both simple and complex engraved designs including horizontal and diagonal banding, cross-hatching, chevrons, zig-zags, and curvilinear designs (Figure 4.3a–f). Waring (1968b:169) states that some specimens resemble those from Stallings Island, located 250 km up the Savannah River, as well as pins from Archaic shell middens along the Georgia and South Carolina coasts. Waring (1968b: 169) compares two of the pins to similar specimens found in the Green River region (Ward site). Archaic shell middens along the nearby Ogeechee River have also yielded similar pins (Roshto 1985).

Claflin's (1931) investigations at the Stallings Island site produced several specimens that he described as having "decidedly nail-like heads" that resemble what are now called crutch-top pins (Figure 4.3g–h). Several of the Stallings pins exhibit finely engraved designs, while the shafts of other specimens are decorated with painted designs (Claflin 1931:24, plates 37 and 38).

The excavation of Middle and Late Archaic shell middens along the St. Johns River in northeast Florida yielded thousands of bone pins (Jahn and Bullen 1978; Purdy 1996). Although many of these sites were "excavated" prior to the adoption of scientific techniques (Moore 1892, 1893, cited in Bullen 1961), most of the pins appear to be associated with the late Middle Archaic Mount Taylor and the Late Archaic Orange components (Milanich and Fairbanks 1980:151, 155). Jahn and Bullen (1978:17) note the similarity of engraved designs on bone pins and fiber-tempered Orange Incised pottery.

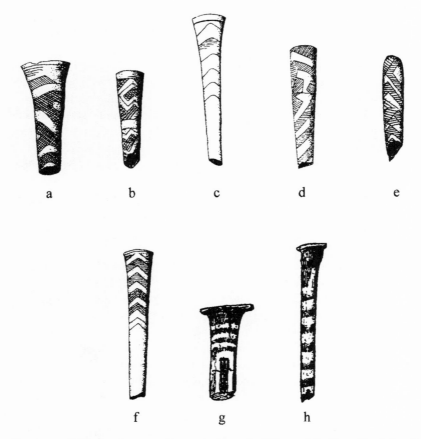

a   b   c   d   e

f   g   h

Figure 4.3. Carved and engraved bone pins from the Bilbo and Stallings Island sites (images used by permission of the Peabody Museum, Harvard University).

Investigations at one of the St. Johns River sites, Tick Island, yielded examples of the crutch-top and expanded-head pin types first defined in the southern Midwest region. Other pins have very distinctive heads and decoration, sharply distinguishing them from pins found in the midcontinent. The shafts and heads of some Tick Island pins were decorated with simple or complex rectilinear or curvilinear incised lines (Purdy 1996:plate 10).

DISCUSSION

Analysis of pins from the 20 Green River and Southeastern sites revealed important new data on the distribution of pin manufacturing technologies and styles, as well as the relationships between pin distributions and the size, boundaries, and organization of Middle to Late Holocene social networks. First, the crutch-top pin type, initially defined for the southern Midwest region, is much more widely distributed than first thought (Koster, Black Earth, Bluegrass, McCain, Crib Mound, KYANG, Indian Knoll, Long Branch, Perry, Stallings Island, and Tick Island; Figure 1.1). Examples of crutch-top pins were documented in a variety of Middle and Late Archaic contexts in the Green River region, the middle Tennessee River valley, the middle Savannah River valley, and the St. Johns River valley, indicating that this pin type was manufactured throughout much of the Midwest and Southeast. Also, several pins from the Tick Island site in Florida resemble the southern Midwest expanded-head type, even down to the designs engraved on the pin shafts. The broad geographic distribution of these pin types, particularly the crutch-top, reduces their utility for defining regionally distinct social networks. On the other hand, their distribution may reflect broader patterns of *inter*regional interaction. In contrast, other pin types defined for the southern Midwest region, such as the t-top, cruciform, fishtailed-cruciform, and double-expanded types, appear to be geographically restricted, making them distinctive markers of the southern Midwest regional network.

Pins exhibiting painted shaft designs like the specimen from the Green River region also occur in the middle Cumberland valley (Anderson) (Dowd 1989: plate 30), the middle Tennessee valley (Little Bear Creek) (Jolly 1969:fig. 2), and the middle Savannah River valley (Stallings Island) (Claflin 1931:plate 38). Painted designs usually consist of horizontal or diagonal banding or a combination of banding and curvilinear designs such as spirals or concentric circles (Claflin 1931:38; Dowd 1989; Jolly 1969). The distribution of painted pins (Indian Knoll, Anderson, Little Bear Creek, and Stallings Island; Figure 1.1), although based on a small sample, suggests that this decorative technique was more commonly used by groups that lived south of the Ohio River. No examples are known for the southern Midwest region. Ritchie (1932:plates VIII, XI) reports several painted bone and antler artifacts from the Lamoka Lake site in New York, but this decorative technique does not appear to have been used on bone pins at that site.

SUMMARY AND CONCLUSIONS

Bone pin technological and stylistic attributes have been used to investigate the emergence of organizationally complex Middle to Late Holocene hunter-gatherer societies that once inhabited areas along the northern margins of the Southeast. As a means of examining the scale and intensity of interaction within and between regional groups, the attributes of pins found at sites in the southern Midwest region were compared with those from sites in Kentucky's Green River region, as well as more distant Southeastern sites. Results of this research suggest

the following: (1) the widespread distribution of certain pin types sharing similar technological and stylistic attributes in the southern Midwest region indicates that Middle to Late Holocene groups living in that area participated in
a regional-scale network that promoted social interaction and integration; (2)
radiocarbon dates associated with these pins indicate that these groups maintained some level of social interaction for at least 1,000 years; (3) while bone
pins were commonly used by contemporary Green River Archaic groups living
south of the Ohio River, most were not elaborately carved and/or engraved, suggesting that bone pins were not a popular medium for expressing social information; (4) the more elaborate pins that were manufactured in the Green River
region do not conform to types identified in the southern Midwest region; and
(5) in most cases, Green River pins that do match pins from the southern Midwest region were crutch-top pins, the most common and widely distributed type
used in this study.

It is much more difficult to identify the kind(s) and intensity of interaction that took place within and between these regional groups. Nevertheless,
differences in bone pin technology and style suggest that regionally distinct social networks existed in the southern Midwest and Green River regions during
the Middle to Late Holocene. The apparently low level of interaction between
groups inhabiting these two regions suggests that some type of social boundary
existed in the vicinity of the Ohio River and that groups living to the south
maintained stronger affiliations with other southern groups. The occurrence of
virtually identical bone pins at late Middle Archaic sites in Illinois and Missouri
indicates that the Mississippi River did not stop interaction (Cook 1976:fig. 23),
so the apparent lack of interaction between the southern Midwest and Green
River regions is probably not solely attributable to the physical presence of the
Ohio River.

Examination of hundreds of pins from other Southeastern sites revealed a
wide range of technological and stylistic diversity. Some types whose occurrence
was once thought to be limited to the southern Midwest region, particularly the
crutch-top type, have a much wider geographic distribution. The broad spatial
distribution of these pin types reduces their utility for discerning patterns of regional interaction. In contrast, most of the pin types defined for the southern
Midwest region do not occur outside that region, suggesting that their distributions may be indicative of regional patterns of social interaction and integration.

In addition, analysis of the Southeastern pins revealed some styles and technologies that are currently unknown in the southern Midwest region. The distribution of these attributes may be useful for studying the emergence of regional-
scale social networks in the interior and coastal Southeast.

The results of this study suggest that the development of more complex
hunter-gatherer societies in the southern Midwest brought with it a restructuring

of intergroup relations and a more broadly defined cultural identity. Decreased group mobility and smaller territories meant that new ways had to be put into place to ensure that needed materials and information continued to be available. The appearance of similar kinds of bone pins throughout the southern Midwest region indicates that exchange and interaction among local groups intensified during the Middle to Late Holocene. Repeated interaction with neighboring groups eventually resulted in the broadening of cultural identity and the formation of a larger, more complex social group. If access to the resources of other groups was restricted to certain individuals, then these intermediaries were privy to information and resources not available to others. This privilege may have contributed toward the increased status and prestige of those people, ultimately creating a mechanism for the development of greater social inequality among group members.

Studies by Johnson and Brookes (1989), Sassaman et al. (1988), and others suggest that social changes discussed in this chapter occurred elsewhere in the Southeast during the Middle to Late Holocene. Although evidence of these changes is not always reflected by the groups' bone tool technology, the similarity of other artifact types (flaked stone, ground stone, shell, and so on) suggests that similar processes were under way. In contrast, evidence for these changes does not exist in many parts of the study area, suggesting that the organizational complexity of the Middle to Late Holocene social landscape was quite variable.

Despite these potential problems, limiting factors, and restrictions, if done carefully, analyses of bone pin stylistic and morphological attributes have the potential to provide new insights into the emergence of regional-scale hunter-gatherer social networks throughout much of middle and southeastern North America. We have only started to scratch the surface with these interesting artifacts.

ACKNOWLEDGMENTS

I would like to thank the William S. Webb Museum of Anthropology, University of Kentucky; the Peabody Museum, Harvard University; and the University of Alabama Press for giving me permission to use the images in Figures 4.2 and 4.3. Victor D. Thompson, Department of Anthropology, University of Kentucky, performed the necessary computer manipulations to produce the figures. I also would like to acknowledge the assistance of the many researchers who have provided me with bone pin data over the past 10 years, particularly my colleagues at the Center for Archaeological Investigations at Southern Illinois University–Carbondale, the Illinois State Museum, Indiana State University, Indiana University, and the University of Louisville. Without their assistance, none of this work would have been possible.

5

The Green River in Comparison to the Lower Mississippi Valley during the Archaic

To Build Mounds or Not to Build Mounds?

George M. Crothers

In the mid-latitude regions of North America along the Illinois, Ohio, and Tennessee river systems, Archaic period hunters and gatherers created extensive, deeply stratified middens exemplified by sites such as Koster and Black Earth in Illinois, Indian Knoll in Kentucky, and Eva in Tennessee. Many archaeologists interpret these sites as evidence of increased sedentary behavior and complex social interaction à la Price and Brown (1985). Why did this collective behavior not result in mound construction in the mid-latitude regions of North America, as it did at Watson Brake and other early mound sites in the lower Mississippi River valley and in Florida? How do we explain the differences? Here, I reflect on the archaeological variability and possible organizational differences between the lower Mississippi River valley and the middle Green River valley of west-central Kentucky during the Archaic.

The Green River, a tributary of the Ohio River, is well known for its large number of Archaic shell midden sites, including Indian Knoll (Webb 1946), Carlston Annis (Marquardt and Watson 1983; Webb 1950b), and a number of other large sites (Figure 1.1; see Crothers 1999 for a summary). For a period lasting possibly 2,000 years (ca. 5000–3000 radiocarbon years or 6500–4500 calibrated years before present), hunters and gatherers repeatedly occupied a number of sites on the Green River and engaged in large-scale production and consumption of food items. The food most conspicuously consumed was fresh-water shellfish, but a host of other food resources commonly found in the Eastern Woodlands were utilized as well: deer, squirrel, rabbit, turkey, fish, turtle, hickory nut, other small mammals, and wild plants. The large midden deposits that resulted are prominent on the landscape even today, and in current archaeological parlance are often referred to as shell mounds. This is an unfortunate use of the term *mound*. Although some of the middens do create artificial mounds on the landscape, more than 50 years of investigations have failed to demonstrate that these "mounds" are purposeful monuments in the sense the term *mound* normally connotes in archaeology. William Webb and the WPA-era archaeologists who excavated the largest number of these sites generally referred to them (more accurately but perhaps less scientifically sounding) as "shell heaps," specifically to distinguish them from burial and geometric mounds known for Adena and later prehistoric periods in Kentucky. (See also Russo's [1994b:94] distinction between shell mounds and intentionally constructed ritual mounds.)

Claassen (e.g., 1991a, 1992) interprets the Green River middens as purposeful burial mound construction. Although I believe Claassen's hypothesis fails to account for the full range of archaeological material associated with these sites (see Morey and Crothers 1998), she does point out that many archaeologists have not taken into account the large number of burials interred in these midden sites. For example, over 1,100 burials were removed from the Indian Knoll site alone. It is clear that these sites are about more than just food production. In the ecological approach taken by many processual archaeologists, however, emphasis has been on subsistence and paleoenvironmental data. I have argued that large midden sites were as much a part of a cultural landscape as they were part of a natural landscape (Crothers 1999). Although river shoals initially may have been favored because of their rich riverine resources, over time midden locations became venerated, independent of their natural capital. In a similar vein, Gibson (2000:183) argues in the case of Poverty Point that ceremony and ritual were inseparable parts of everyday native life. Whether one wants to describe particular activities at any given site as sacred or secular, Gibson suggests sites such as Poverty Point and Watson Brake—and, I would add, the deep shell middens of the Green River—were spiritual places to their original inhabitants.

What then should we make of the difference between earthen or ritual Archaic mound construction in the southeastern United States and large Archaic midden formation in the mid-latitude regions of the United States? Both appear to be the result of large social formations, construed as more complex and reflecting greater sedentary behavior than typically associated with hunter-gatherer societies. Russo (1994b) has argued, rightly I believe, that progressive evolutionary models have hindered our explanation of large social endeavors during the Archaic. I also follow Russo in believing that large earthen construction works

did not necessarily require a level of social organization beyond egalitarian sequential hierarchies or temporary heterarchical relations (Crumley 1987; Johnson 1982). That is, group actions necessary to complete any large-scale mound construction project need not be linked to minority rule by permanently ranked office holders as is often assumed for southeastern mound builders. Large-scale *public works* can be built under the direction of ad hoc groups or through group agreements that are initiated at basal social units (e.g., nuclear families) and sequentially extended to the sum of those units [Russo 1994b:106, emphasis added].

Russo (1991), for example, suggests that mound construction at Horr's Island, Florida, was a public work for integrating society. While a permanently ranked leader was not necessary for ritual mound construction, public works of this magnitude functioned in Archaic societies, as they do in state societies, to counter internal stress and provide a purpose for societal cohesion.

The key term is *public works*. How do we define an Archaic public? Is public a concept compatible with Archaic hunters and gatherers? What is the nature of the social group in the Archaic period? In the same vein that progressive evolutionary models of interpretation hinder explanation of Archaic mound construction, I would argue that the modern concept of society hinders explanation of hunter-gatherer interaction in the Archaic. Implicit in the discussion of lower Mississippi River valley mound construction and mid-continental midden formation are two assumptions: that Archaic period hunters and gatherers realized distinct societies and that sedentary behavior is a necessary condition of large social formations.

Ingold (1996, 1999) questions whether hunters and gatherers live in societies at all. Whereas hunters and gatherers exhibit a distinctive form of sociality based on common features of immediacy, sharing, and autonomy, this is incompatible with the modern concept of society conceived as a distinct community with interlocking interests defined by the institutional structures of a state. In other words, hunter-gatherers exist in "societies" for those seeking to exert control over them, but not for the hunter-gatherers themselves (Ingold 1999:408).

AN ARCHAIC PERIOD FORAGING MODE OF PRODUCTION

Elsewhere, Bernbeck and I (Crothers and Bernbeck 2003) critique the concept of complexity as a social or economic variable that has little value and propose an immediate-return forager system to explain Green River Archaic hunter-gatherer behavior without recourse to progressive evolutionary arguments. We term this model a "foraging mode of production" (sensu Leacock and Lee 1982; see also Bernbeck 1991) and propose it as a theoretical model that predicts certain types of behavior, institutionalized forms of interaction, and a social organization distinct from sedentary, corporate social formations. These ideas, of course, are not original with us (see Crothers and Bernbeck 2003 for the theoretical background), but our purpose is to propose an alternative model that we believe, at least in the case of the Green River Archaic, more fully accounts for our present understanding of the archaeological record.

In brief, a foraging mode of production is based on dynamic and complex social interaction among relatively autonomous foragers; economic production is based on immediate consumption (this is Woodburn's [1980] concept of an immediate-return economic system); rights to property and resources are open (ownership in the Western sense extends only to present use); and mobility is the primary means of responding to a variable environment. We use the term *environment* as an all-inclusive concept; that is, individuals base their decision making not only on productivity of the natural environment but also on the actions of other humans in that environment.

A successful foraging mode of production depends upon open property rights and mobility. To give up mobility is to begin constructing exclusive property rights. The institutional structure of foragers enables mobility and constrains the development of exclusive property rights. While this property-less forager world and "cavalier" attitude to material possessions is anathema to corporate, sedentary societies, it is the source of autonomous individual action among foragers. Sahlins (1998) termed hunters and gatherers the "original affluent society" to make the point that hunters and gatherers have a different worldview—one governed by limited wants in an environment that provides unlimited means—in contrast to a Western notion of "affluent society," in which consumers weigh unlimited wants against limited means.

Bird-David (1990, 1998) uses metaphorical models termed the "cosmic economy of sharing" and "nature is a bank" as a way of understanding hunter-gatherer economic behavior and captures the essential features of a foraging mode of production. Property has no meaning beyond its immediate use, and foragers bank future production in their knowledge of the environment to provide resources. All of this is to say that hunters and gatherers (modern or premodern) are neither isolated from nor incognizant of the larger world around them (sensu Wilmsen 1989). It does imply, however, that hunters and gatherers hold a common institutional structure that enables a foraging mode of production. Some of these institutions may be as old as anatomically modern *Homo sapiens,* even if remaining hunters and gatherers today are encapsulated and marginalized by modern states; their institutional structure is coherent and fully functional, and prehistorically it was extremely successful.

Hunter-gatherer mobility takes two forms: locational mobility and group flux (Crothers and Bernbeck 2003). Locational mobility is simply the recurring and largely regular, often seasonal, relocation by whole groups. Driven primarily by ecological considerations, patterns of locational mobility are largely derived from environmental patterns. Over time, these patterns may reflect broad environmental changes. In contrast, group flux is characterized by frequent and largely unpredictable change in composition of inhabitants at any one camp or location. Driven primarily by sociological considerations, individual movements may appear chaotic or unpatterned. Archaeologically, we cannot address this form of mobility at the individual level. For the hunter-gatherer, however, it is an important aspect of autonomy that institutionally is reinforced by open property rights and likewise provides incentives not to invest labor in complex technology or material accumulation (North 1990). What results is a very dynamic system of interaction. Hunter-gatherer institutional structure enables fluid group composition, flexible social relations, detailed regional knowledge of the environment, and autonomous individual action.

PREHISTORIC HUNTERS AND GATHERERS
IN THE GREEN RIVER VALLEY

Why do I believe that forager interaction, rather than the beginnings of sedentary behavior and the different form of institutional structure that it entails, characterizes the Green River Archaic? Most important is the archaeology of shell midden sites. These sites are composed of massive amounts of shell, sandstone, and organically enriched sediment deposited over relatively short intervals. Postdepositional trampling and mixing of the deposits do not appear to be significant. Burial placement is random, often overlapping or intersecting earlier burials. All sites lack evidence of permanent or semipermanent structures or facilities. The two most common features are large, burned clay hearths and clusters of sandstone (fire-cracked) rock, presumably the result of mass processing of resources. One is left with an impression of multiple, large-scale events, intensive collection of resources, and production and consumption of large amounts of food, but occupation that is of relatively short duration.

It may be that these sites were more or less permanently occupied or at least seasonally occupied (i.e., locational mobility; e.g., when harvesting shellfish and fishing are most productive or when the nut mast ripens), but by different combinations of people (i.e., group flux). A foraging mode of production posits that autonomous hunters and gatherers were free to come and go, calculating where resources were most productive, and to determine with whom they wanted to associate. No one owned the "shell midden" or, more properly, the river shoal that was the source of rich resources, and anyone was free to take unused resources. Likewise, no one would deny access to unused resources, as long as the intervening party followed conventional etiquette in asking.

Presumably, these site locations attracted large gatherings because of their concentrated resources, especially at seasonally predictable times when pooled labor provided an economy of scale in processing. However, other events also likely determined use of these sites, such as the death of an individual that may have required a feast as part of burial ritual. The random nature of events occasioned by social gatherings (birth, puberty, marriage, death, etc.) adds an unpredictable element to any underlying patterns of site use and occupation. It may be that resources at these sites were drawn upon throughout the year without any fixed group continuously occupying a site.

A similar argument can be made about the general egalitarian behavior represented by the distribution of grave goods. Among human burials, potential status items such as atlatls and bannerstones are just as likely to have been placed with children or women as with men (however, see Rothschild 1979; Winters 1968 for attempts to discern patterns). There was also the peculiar behavior (by Western standards) of burying people within their refuse. I interpret this as further evidence that individuals did not inhabit the shell middens for extended lengths of time. With sedentary behavior comes structure and order to living arrangements. Refuse is separated from living areas, burial grounds are separated from both, and bodies are interred in order.

Shell midden sites reflect a celebration of the productivity of the river and its shoals, a resource that provided in life and perhaps in death. Ingold (1996, 2000) writes cogently about the hunter-gatherer perception of the environment that is foreign to the Western scientific dichotomy of society and nature. In Western perception, human beings exist in two planes: society composed of other persons and nature composed of nonhuman animals, plants, and inanimate objects. The Western mind is detached from nature and literally must construct a mental representation of it prior to engagement. In hunter-gatherer perception, human beings exist as a part of the environment (in a single plane) along with other people, nonhuman animals, plants, and inanimate objects. Apprehension of nature is not a matter of construction but of engagement (Ingold 1996:121). In a metaphorical sense, the structure of shell midden sites reflects the engagement of individuals in the environment, not apart from or superior to the environment.

In the history of Archaic period research, shell midden sites have always been enigmatic. First, we struggled to comprehend the incredibly dense deposits of shell and midden in the Green River sites—accumulations that seemed inconceivable if they were the products of small hunter-gatherer groups. Later, we were perplexed that sedentary groups would live on refuse heaps, interring their dead within the very refuse deposits they dwelled upon, suggesting instead that middens really had nothing to do with subsistence and everything to do with burial mound construction. Archaeological interpretation suffered, first, from the progressive evolutionary paradigm in which densely deposited midden must be the result of permanent habitation and, second, from the notion of society as a given condition of human sociality rather than an artificial and relatively recent institutional construct. In the former paradigm, sedentary behavior was thought to be a preferred condition of human society. In the latter, we assumed that humans have always lived in well-defined societies. Rather than trying to explain why hunters and gatherers lack the institutional structure of organized pluralities, we should be trying to explain why humans live in societies at all.

ARCHAEOLOGY OF THE GREEN RIVER VALLEY IN COMPARISON TO THE LOWER MISSISSIPPI RIVER VALLEY

This brings us back to my original question: Does the intentional construction of mounds at Watson Brake and other early mound sites in Louisiana and the Gulf coastal area during the Archaic, which culminates with Poverty Point, represent a different organizational form of human sociality than a foraging mode of production? The easy way out of this question is to claim that we do not yet know enough to answer it. It has only been in the past decade that even the occurrence of Archaic mound construction has been widely accepted (Russo 1994b). We have learned a great deal about Poverty Point layout and construction, artifact types, and relationship to other sites (Gibson 2000) and are now beginning to learn more about Watson Brake and the earliest mound sites (Saunders et al. 1997). On the basis of what we do know at this stage, there are some interesting comparisons between the lower Mississippi River sites and the Green River sites to begin answering the question in more detail.

First, sites in both areas contain deep middens resulting from exploitation of riverine resources. In the case of the Green River, this includes shellfish and fish, although the exact contribution of each is difficult to quantify. In the lower Mississippi River valley, fish was the dominant subsistence item with shellfish contributing only a minor amount. In both cases, other terrestrial vertebrates also contributed significantly to the diet (deer being the most important). Nuts (hickory/pecan, walnut, and acorn) likewise contributed an important but difficult to quantify component of the overall subsistence in both areas. However, in both cases, site location is determined by proximity to riverine resources. In the Green River, it was shoals for collecting shellfish and in the lower Mississippi River oxbows with large fish stocks. Also, in both cases, there appears to have been a seasonal element to site use: warm-water shellfish collecting in the Green and periodic flooding that replenished fish in oxbows and ponds in the lower Mississippi. Presumably both areas also had a second seasonal element: fall ripening of the nut mast.

After subsistence remains, the second-largest contributions to the midden are sandstone (or fire-cracked rock) in the Green River sites and Poverty Point objects (or baked loess cooking balls) in the lower Mississippi River sites. Both technologies would have been relatively labor intensive but subject to an economy of scale with mass production, at least in the processing of nuts.

Artifact manufacture was an important endeavor in both areas. In the Green River sites, production of shell and bone beads and other more utilitarian bone tools (fishhooks, pins, awls, and so on) is common. Flintknapping appears to have been geared toward late-stage biface manufacturing and maintenance. An array of projectile points, knives, drills, and scrapers is common, but the amount of debitage is less than expected for the number of finished tools. Similarly, ground-stone tool production does not appear to have been significant, but finished ground-stone artifacts are common, especially grinding and pounding implements. Bannerstones are predominantly found in burial contexts. Exotic materials (copper, marine shell, and nonlocal chert), while consistently present in sites, are rare and most commonly found in burial contexts as well.

Poverty Point appears to have a much wider range of artifact types and material manufacturing debris. Pottery, absent at the Green River sites except as later intrusive material, appears to have been made at Poverty Point, but it is rare. Stone vessels are much more common at Poverty Point than pottery, but these too are absent from the Green River. Likewise, plummets are common at Poverty Point but are absent in the Green River. There is a similar range of cutting, grinding, and pounding implements at Poverty Point sites and Green River sites, but presently it is difficult to compare ratios of finished tools to production debris between regions. Perhaps the only stone artifact type more prevalent in the Green River region than in the lower Mississippi Valley is bannerstones.

We lack good comparable data, but my feeling is that bone tools and manufacturing debris may be more prevalent in the Green River. Shell bead manufacture dominates at the Green River sites, whereas stone beads appear to be dominant at the lower Mississippi River sites. Decorated bone pins are another artifact type of significant manufacture in the Green River region that is absent or insignificant in the lower Mississippi River valley (see Jefferies, this volume).

In sum, the Green River region and the lower Mississippi River region appear to have distinct stylistic and technological trajectories or, in other words, one does not appear to be derived from the other in any short-term historical sense. However, this still leaves the original question: Does the Poverty Point phenomenon represent a different form of social organization, i.e., something other than a foraging mode of production such as Bernbeck and I have hypothesized for the Green River?

Both regions lack consistent evidence of permanent structures or long-term facilities. This is most perplexing at Poverty Point sites because the construction of large earthworks would seem to go along with permanent residence. The Green River sites contain large numbers of burials, whereas the Poverty Point sites lack any. Perhaps this has to do with the large-scale WPA-era excavations at the Green River sites vs. the more limited excavations at Poverty Point and other early mound sites, but the lack of burials from the lower Mississippi River sites is still a major quandary.

It is not inconceivable to me that extensive midden could accumulate at sites like Watson Brake, and even Poverty Point, without permanent residence by the same group. In other words, midden is a product of a forager mode of production that experienced considerable group flux. While this could explain the large accumulation of everyday living debris without investment in long-term structures and features (as in the case of the Green River), it does not seem compatible with mound construction. As Russo (1994b) suggests, large-scale mound construction could be done under the direction of ad hoc groups or through group agreements that are initiated at basal social units without direction from a controlling authority. If the purpose of mound construction was indeed for integrating society (i.e., as a public work), as Russo also suggests, then early mound construction does represent a new form of social organization by hunters and gatherers.

Why was it necessary to integrate society at these early mound sites? Was it to counter outside threats? Was it to ritualize the act of ownership in land or resources? Did it signify belonging to an exclusive society? Perhaps we have in the lower Mississippi River valley the first attempts at large-scale societal integration, and perhaps Gibson (1974) was not very far off the mark when he called Poverty Point North America's first chiefdom. This cooperative endeavor may not have required permanently ranked office holders, but it suggests that someone or some leadership body provided direction and originated mound construction even if ad hoc and for temporary purposes. Whatever form this process took, it required an element of control over the means of production. In the lower Mississippi River valley, control would have been over access to particularly good fishing locations in the bayous. The extension of property rights to future yields of a resource requires new forms of institutional organization, very different from what is hypothesized as a foraging mode of production. For example, see Wolf's (1982) discussion of the kin-ordered mode of production vis-à-vis the tributary mode of production. Exclusive (communal) property-rights institutions entail new organizations for negotiating, monitoring, and enforcing rights of access.

Let me now propose, in rough outline, another possibility for explaining early mound construction in the lower Mississippi River valley that does not rely upon corporate, social formation. The layout of each mound site did have significance; there was a design to each construction. Each design, however, rather than originating with one or a few individuals who directed its implementation, was a shared pattern of activity that ritualized a specific use of space. An individual or a small group visiting a particular site took part in that activity, which included procurement and consumption of resources along with a host of other reasons for social interaction but which also included symbolic acts of moving sediment to specific areas. Each person followed a tradition in which they added sediment to a location according to those who came before them, and this in turn led the next person to follow suit. No one designed the layout of mounds, but everyone contributed to the final design. The design had an important meaning, not as a monument but rather as an act of participation. It was clearly a social phenomenon in which many individuals took part, not to build social cohesion but rather to ritualize participation. Participation was not predetermined by membership in society but by individual decision to participate. In this manner, hunters and gatherers participated in a form of self-organization.

It is not a coincidence that the earliest mound construction—the largest example of hunter-gatherer organization—to occur in North America took place in the lower Mississippi River valley. It is today one of the most productive agricultural areas on the continent and was in the past one of the richest natural environments. The Green River valley, while a very productive environment, could not sustain a harvest of natural resources on the scale of a Poverty Point without damage to its ecology. There is tantalizing evidence, although not sufficiently quantified yet, that local shellfish populations represented in the midden deposits experienced something approaching ecological collapse as a result of high rates of harvest during the Archaic. Periodic flooding of the lower Mississippi River valley provided a nearly inexhaustible supply of fish in the backwaters and bayous. This feature of the environment likely drew unprecedented numbers of hunters and gatherers to the otherwise stone-deficient environment. The early mound sites of the lower Mississippi River valley were symbolic of the natural abundance of the region that supported a foraging mode of production and the unprecedented scale of social interaction that hunters and gatherers were able to obtain.

I am not claiming that early mound construction in North America is best explained as forager interaction, only that we should consider it as an alternative. The proof will lie in our ability to interpret differing evidence of institutional forms of social structure in the archaeological record. From my view, Archaic sites in the lower Mississippi River valley share similar characteristics with those of the Green River—extensive midden deposition and a lack of permanent structures and facilities. On the basis of burial data, the Green River populations appear to have an egalitarian social structure. This information is lacking from the lower Mississippi River region. There was a vigorous trade in stone resources and other exotic artifacts at Poverty Point, many of them decorative as well as utilitarian. This widespread movement of material may be more representative of the locational mobility of Archaic hunters and gatherers in the lower Mississippi River valley than of a formal economic trade in scarce resources. Jackson (1991) describes Poverty Point as a trade fair. I am reluctant to ascribe that level of organized economic activity in a forager mode of production, but there would have been an important element of information exchange among highly mobile hunters and gatherers anywhere they came together in large pluralities.

The question for the future comes back to an age-old question of anthropology: What is the nature of the social group among Archaic hunters and gatherers? I have argued that we cannot assume that society as we define it in sedentary, agricultural, and state-level organizations is also a feature of hunters and gatherers. Certainly, hunters and gatherers participated in large social formations; the question is to what degree social relationships were binding and institutionalized. The concept of a forager mode of production assumes that corporate, institutionalized social relationships are not a natural condition of human sociality but must be constructed and artificially maintained.

The more immediate problem is to ascertain whether ritual mound construction in the lower Mississippi River valley was a difference in the scale of forager interaction or a difference of kind in social organization. Ultimately, I believe this will come down to our ability to identify differing forms of property relations among Archaic period groups. Differing forms of institutional property rights should be manifest in varying degrees of technological investment, allocation of labor to delayed-return production, and the creation of a tributary class. It is interesting to note that ultimately whatever form of organization was responsible for the construction of early mound sites that culminated with Poverty Point, it was nearly 2,500 years before that feat was achieved again in North America (north of the Rio Grande). Few would argue that the later prehistoric societies that constructed large platform and temple mounds contained chiefly classes. If Poverty Point was simply a step in the gradual development of hierarchical organization, then it behooves us to explain what happened in that 2,500-year gap.

6

Cultural Complexity in the Middle Archaic of Mississippi

Samuel O. Brookes

Mississippi is often thought of as a poor state. From an economic standpoint, this is true. However, if one were to argue from a cultural perspective, Mississippi would have to be thought of as a very wealthy state. The musical heritage of this relatively small state is second to none. Mississippi is the birthplace of country music, blues, and rock and roll. The literary heritage is also without peer. Writers William Faulkner, Eudora Welty, Richard Wright, Shelby Foote, and Tennessee Williams have called Mississippi home. The state is also known for its athletes, its food, its politicians, and its beautiful women. Considering this richness of culture in modern times, it should come as no surprise that the state is just as rich in archaeological resources. Mississippi's first citizens and their works were every bit as outstanding as its current ones, from the Middle Archaic accretional middens along the Tombigbee River, to the giant Emerald Mound at the end of the Natchez Trace, to the Grand Village of the Natchez Indians. With such a diversity of riches, one could hardly expect the state to have a monotonous landscape. Mississippi is again blessed with a richness of landforms, and here we might quote William Faulkner's (1954:34) wonderful description of the state:

> In the beginning it was virgin—to the west, along the Big River, the alluvial swamps threaded by black almost motionless bayous and impenetrable with cane and buckvine and cypress and ash and oak and gum; to the east, the hardwood ridges and prairies where the Appalachian mountains died and buffalo grazed; to the south, the pine barrens and the moss-hung liveoaks and the greater swamps less of earth than water and lurking with alligators and water moccasins, where Louisiana in its time would begin.
>
> And where in the beginning the predecessors crept with their simple artifacts, and built the mounds and vanished, bequeathing only the mounds

in which the succeeding recordable Algonquian stock would leave the skulls of their warriors and chiefs and babies and slain bears, and the shards of pots, and hammer- and arrow-heads and now and then a heavy silver Spanish spur.

Of course Faulkner took some liberties with the archaeology, especially the Spanish silver spur; such artifacts, while having been sought by many, have never been found. Also, his term "simple artifacts" is misleading. As it will be shown in this chapter, some of these artifacts are incredibly complex, if not in form then in meaning. Yet, his association of mounds with some of the earlier native people has turned out to be remarkably prescient. His division of the state into three primary areas, while probably not acceptable to a geomorphologist, is adequate for our purpose. Mississippi can thus be divided into three main physiographic regions. To the east are the uplands or hills. This area includes the black prairie and holds together well as an archaeological unit. To the west is what Faulkner called the "big woods." The Yazoo Basin, known to Mississippians as the Delta, is today nearly devoid of trees, having been cleared for agriculture in the twentieth century. Delta National Forest is the only bottomland hardwood forest in the National Forest system and provides one a glimpse of what the area probably looked like in prehistoric times. The piney woods of south Mississippi are the third part of the triumvirate. These areas stretch from south-central Mississippi to the Gulf Coast. In addition to the landforms one must consider the waterways. The Mississippi River should be thought of as an interstate highway. Many of the streams from the uplands flow west across the Yazoo Basin and into the Mississippi River. Further, many of the streams of Arkansas flow east out of the mountains, with their lodes of rock, into the Mississippi River. The significance of this lies in the fact that the streams connect broad expanses of terrain to the "Big River." In the uplands, east of the Pontotoc Ridge, some streams flow east into the Tombigbee and thence south to the Gulf of Mexico. The Pearl River of central Mississippi flows south to the Gulf, so the people in the interior of the state are often only a ridge or two away from a swift route to another part of the state or region. They then have access to either the Mississippi River or the Gulf of Mexico. Thus, the region itself gave rise to many of the exchange routes that were later used by prehistoric peoples. Finally, we must also consider that the flora and fauna of the regions, as well as the raw materials contained therein, differed widely, prompting the native populace to engage in exchange.

MIDDLE ARCHAIC PREDECESSORS

To discuss the Middle Archaic, I must begin with a brief discussion of some aspects of earlier cultures. The Middle Archaic inhabitants of Mississippi were the biological and cultural descendants of people who had lived in the region for thousands of years. While the culture of the Middle Archaic people is causing a mild revolution in archaeological thought because of its complexity, it did not arise in a vacuum. This culture was handed down for thousands of years, and while many of the elements are new items added by the Middle Archaic people, some elements go far back in time to the Paleoindians.

Mississippi at the end of the Ice Age must have been a wondrous place that would appear totally unfamiliar to anyone alive today. The Pleistocene mega-fauna were present, albeit in ever-decreasing numbers. To the north, the melting of the ice, the concomitant rise in sea level, the fields of stagnant ice, and the occasional jokulhlaup (a catastrophic flood caused when an ice dam gives way, releasing the waters of a glacial lake) must have made the early people very cautious, not only of large, dangerous animals but of their surroundings as well. These Paleoindians were the first people to enter into the Southeast and thence into Mississippi. We know from projectile-point raw material types and distribution that this initial penetration was from the north. Groups came south from the Tennessee River area and south down the Mississippi River, then eastward up the tributary streams (McGahey 1987). Evidence suggests that Paleoindians settled over most of Mississippi, and the various Archaic peoples are their lineal descendants. The Paleoindians thus represent the only mass migration of people into the area, save for one minor episode during the latter part of the Early Archaic period. When we talk of the cultural complexity of the Middle Archaic folks of the Mid-Holocene period, we are speaking of cultural traditions that have been in place for roughly 8,000 years. It is important to note that the Paleoindians, as Shott (1990:10) states, "faced not only a daunting range of rapid and problematic environmental change, but did so lacking the structural support(s)—decades if not generations of accumulated material knowledge and lore, and preexisting land-use patterns—that are taken for granted by modern foragers and which can spell the difference between survival and doom in unforgiving habitats." People learned to adapt to this new environment, and by the end of the Paleoindian period the region had changed greatly, the ice had disappeared, and the flora and fauna were of the modern variety.

We can look to the Paleoindians of the region for cultural complexity. Dan Morse (1997) has demonstrated this in Arkansas with his excavations at the Sloan site. I do not feel the discovery of a Late Paleoindian cemetery is that unusual per se, rather it is most likely part of a much older cultural tradition. What is complex at Sloan, in my opinion, is an artifact type: the Sloan point. Sloan points are oversize bifaces that show no signs of use wear. They are made of Burlington chert from the Crescent quarries in Missouri. Sloan points are known from Missouri, Illinois, and Arkansas, some being found up to 400 km from the source of the material. They occur as single finds, in caches, and, as at

Sloan, in graves. Walthall and Koldehoff (1998:266) state that Sloan points exhibit "particularly fine workmanship, requiring considerable labor and skill for their production." They stop short of suggesting that specialists made these artifacts. Sloan points are distinguished by their large size, excellent workmanship, thinness, and deposition in special contexts such as burials and caches. Sloan points are special artifacts that appear out of place in the toolkit of late Paleo-indians, much as the swords of the Knights of Columbus appear as anachronisms to us today. "Cults of the Long Blade"—what do they mean?

It must be noted that the Sloan points are a type of oversize Dalton biface. Work by Morse (1973) and Goodyear (1974) has demonstrated the Dalton point is in reality a projectile-point/knife. The patterned resharpening is mostly a result of the knife function of the implement. To date, no evidence of warfare has ever been suggested for this time period. The Dalton point therefore functioned as a hunting weapon, rather than as a weapon of war. Thus the oversize Sloan point was created with a ritual hunting conception. It was not used for hunting per se, but rather for a ritual aspect of the hunt. I would suggest these artifacts are "atassa," ritual dance knives. Atassa, as they are called by the Creek Indians (Howard 1968:76), comprise a variety of artifact forms. In this chapter I will discuss two varieties. Oversize chipped bifaces with no signs of use or resharpening and effigy bifaces of ground and polished stone are considered atassa, or ritual dance knives. I make the distinction between the chipped specimens and the ground and polished examples because all of the latter are ritually killed. In the Mississippian era, war clubs are also considered atassa, though none of these forms are known from the Middle Archaic. I have made this argument for the oversize bifaces of the Middle Archaic (Brookes 1997) and here suggest the Sloan points are the earliest of this type of ideotechnic artifact. It would be useful to expand on the work done by Walthall and Koldehoff to keep plotting the distribution and, where possible, the context of this artifact type. It is of interest to note that the Sloan point has never been found in Mississippi. Is this because we are located too far south of the source material and therefore outside the exchange network that distributed the points, or is there some other factor at play here? It appears to me that Sloan points could easily be made of Fort Payne chert or other raw material that is of large size and available within the region, yet such is not the case. Is it possible that a Sloan point is special because specialists in Illinois made it from Burlington chert? We could begin to ask such questions as, how many people in a group owned Sloan points? Were they in fact a status symbol for an individual or was their importance related to their usage in ritual behavior that benefited the entire group or a portion of the group such as hunters? What was the manner of their ultimate disposal?

Yerkes and Gaertner (1997:71) have suggested that oversize Dalton points at Sloan were specifically manufactured as burial offerings. Morse (1997:90) excavated one Sloan point in association with several other Dalton artifacts. He interpreted this artifact cluster as representing two possible grave lots at the Sloan site, which he argues convincingly is a Dalton cemetery. The oversize Dalton points at the Sloan site also appear to be ideotechnic artifacts (Yerkes and Gaertner 1997:71). Thus we have two different types of ideotechnic artifacts in the late Pleistocene, both of which are representative of hunting artifacts. It is of interest that four of the oversize Dalton points at Sloan were in association with the single Sloan point recovered there. This would suggest a similar function and possibly that the artifacts were part of a set.

THE MIDDLE ARCHAIC OF MISSISSIPPI

I hope that I have demonstrated that ideotechnic artifacts did not suddenly appear with the Middle Archaic. Oversize ritual knives, representing hunting activities, are present in Paleoindian times. Having titled this chapter "Cultural Complexity in the Middle Archaic of Mississippi" it is only fitting that I should eventually broach that topic. Of all the culture periods in Mississippi, the Middle Archaic is one of the best dated and most studied, ranking right up there with the Mississippian and Historic periods. This is due largely to the Tennessee-Tombigbee waterway project of the late 1970s and early 1980s. One of the major accomplishments of that study was the Midden Mound project, a multimillion-dollar study of Middle Archaic period accretional middens along the Tombigbee River. Excavations were conducted at 11 sites, with the majority (nine) being located northeast of Tupelo, Mississippi. Most of the sites excavated contained Benton culture artifacts. Meeks (1999) employed over 30 radiocarbon assays to suggest a date of 4000–3000 B.C. for the Benton culture. Earlier dates appear to be associated with White Springs/Sykes points, which are ancestral to, and partially coeval with, Benton.

The Benton culture then falls squarely into the Hypsithermal, a period when the climate was much warmer and drier than today (Pielou 1991:269). The Midden Mound study suggested one of the effects of the Hypsithermal was reduced discharge in rivers and streams, eolian erosion in the uplands, and the covering of the gravel bars by silt (Bense 1987:397). Bense did state that gravel was available in the adjacent tributary stream valleys, but the percentage of Fort Payne chert use goes from 5 percent of pre-Benton bifaces to greater than 75 percent of Benton bifaces, suggesting that local raw material depletion was the prime factor in the shift. I had originally thought that high-quality Fort Payne chert was desired for Benton bifaces because it could produce larger points. Such is not the case, for in the southern reaches of Mississippi, large bifaces were produced at this time using generally inferior quartzites, silicified sandstone, and limonites. While the ability to produce large bifaces is an impor-

tant consideration in the use of these materials, the deciding factor appears to
have been that the local gravel sources were covered with silt from eolian erosion. The good-quality chert in the north is located in the uplands, as is the
poor-quality material in the south; hence both were available when the preferred
material, local gravel in streambeds, was unavailable. After 3000 B.C. the climate
shifted to an essentially modern regime and the gravel bars were once again
available to flintknappers. Consequently, after Benton the percentage of Fort
Payne chert use goes back to 6 percent (Sparks 1987:13–28). This is striking,
as Fort Payne chert is far superior to local gravel, yet after the Middle Archaic it
is rarely if ever used. A similar situation has been observed in south Mississippi,
where the sandstones, quartzites, and limonites drop out and are replaced by
local gravel after 3000 B.C. Size does appear to be a factor in biface manufacture
during this time. However, it is just as likely that large bifaces were produced
because, not only did people have the means to produce them, but also, having
to journey to upland quarries or exchange material to acquire bifaces, it would
behoove them to curate the artifact as long as possible. Larger bifaces would ensure a longer life for the tool as the user could resharpen it more times than a
shorter biface.

OVERSIZE BIFACES

Jay Johnson and I discussed Benton bifaces and some unusual artifacts from the
Middle Archaic from northeast Mississippi (Johnson and Brookes 1989). Oversize Bentons, oversize Cache blades, and Turkey Tails have some similarities to
Sloan points. These blades are all made from a single type of chert—this time
it is Fort Payne—and are quite well made. While larger than most examples of
the type, the oversize bifaces are also thinner. Width, thinness, and length are
not the only factors that make these bifaces stand out. The workmanship and
technological skill exhibited on oversize bifaces is unmatched by any chipped-
stone artifacts in the state. Johnson and I suspect specialists were doing the
knapping, as the size, thinness, and flaking patterns are unequaled elsewhere in
the state on any time level. In one instance, a large thin biface was made from
a preform that had a hole the size of a quarter in the center of the rock. This
piece of material would have been rejected out of hand by most knappers, but it
appears in this instance the hole was desired as it showcased the skill of the
knapper. Further, the hole is also a sure sign that the blade in question would
suffer no use as a knife or spear, as it would so weaken the blade as to render it
useless for heavy cutting or piercing. Let me add, these special bifaces show no
signs of use wear/resharpening or breakage and are usually found in caches.

　　We suspect some oversize bifaces may have been placed with burials, though
this has not been demonstrated in Mississippi. In Tennessee, at Eva (Lewis and

Lewis 1961:140), two oversize Benton bifaces were found with female burials. Both these points, called "daggers" by Lewis and Lewis, were placed at the waist. Also in Tennessee, a cache of five Benton bifaces, a Turkey Tail preform, and a bone bead was found at the shoulder of a male burial (Dowd 1989:99). Dowd remarks that the blades were "neatly stacked." In Alabama, a cache of five Turkey Tails was found with the burial of a dwarf (Craig 1958). These objects were alongside the pelvis and had been carefully stacked according to length with the longest placed on the bottom. These artifacts are special pieces and were given special treatment. I bring all this up again to point out that oversize bifaces of nonutilitarian purpose are present in Late Paleoindian and Middle Archaic times. Also, there is some evidence to indicate that sets of knives rather than individual examples were often placed in caches and/or burials. Finally, it must be pointed out here that of the caches we discussed (Johnson and Brookes 1989), a professional archaeologist excavated only one, the Beech site cache. That cache is unusual in that all 11 bifaces were ceremonially broken. Nancy White (personal communication, 2000), who excavated the cache, suggested that the cache had been placed in a bag or container of some sort. This is interesting because it suggests that this cache contained unhafted bifaces. At any rate, it remains as the only cache of such bifaces found in the Midden Mound project. The remaining caches were plowed up in fields or dug up by relic hunters at smaller sites on tributary streams away from the Tombigbee River. The implications are that the Midden Mound project missed the ceremonial aspect of Benton culture because of sampling error. It appears that such ceremonial activity took place away from the large base camps along the Tombigbee River. Howard (1968) notes a similar situation for the Creek dance grounds, which are located away from villages and are only occupied for ritual dance purposes. This situation is similar to what is often referred to as a "vacant ceremonial center" by researchers in the eastern United States.

The Benton caches also yielded evidence of another class of artifact that, while rare, has a long history in the Southeast. Ground and polished effigies of oversize bifaces are known from the Middle Archaic and the Mississippian, a span of over 5,000 years. It should be noted here that the oversize chipped-stone bifaces of the Paleoindian and Middle Archaic are also present in the Mississippian. It could be that these occurrences, separated in time and space as they are, represent independent invention.

However, what purpose could such artifacts serve? As has been tediously pointed out, these are all nonutilitarian artifacts. Adding a new wrinkle, however, is that the ground and polished effigies (hereinafter referred to as atassa) are always ceremonially broken, or killed. This is significant as the ground and polished objects are sturdier than the oversize flaked-stone points in caches. The chipped-stone points are almost always unbroken. It often took quite a bit of effort to kill the atassa, indicating that this was an important action that needed to be carried out. Brown (1996:469–488) describes ground and polished effigy bifaces from Spiro of which all examples were ceremonially killed. It is generally believed that special artifacts are killed to release spirits contained in the artifact.

The material of the atassa in north Mississippi is a coarse claystone or siltstone from an unknown source. Some examples are more than 60 cm in length. Cache blades, stemmed points, notched points, and Turkey Tail–effigy atassa are known. Not only are the ground-stone atassa found in both Middle Archaic and Mississippian contexts, but also all known examples have been ritually killed. The implication here is that this is probably not a case of independent invention but rather a cultural tradition that was passed down for centuries.

I (Brookes 1997) have argued that the atassa are ritual knives used in dance ceremonies. Such artifacts are illustrated and described by Howard (1968) and are used by modern Creek Indians today. The dances are an important part of the culture of many Southeastern tribes. In earlier times, the Choctaw only danced at night, and whites were not allowed to view these dances (Swanton 1931:223). Further, Bushnell (1909:20) reports that the Choctaw of Bayou Lacomb, Louisiana, would perform a series of dances in a certain order. The Choctaw villages always had an open place or square, similar to Creek village layouts, where dances and other ceremonies were held (Swanton 1931:221). Choctaw dances were said to be very similar to dances of the Chickasaw and Creek (Swanton 1931:223). One of these dances that was present in both Creek and Choctaw dance repertoires is the *Iskitini hila,* or horned owl dance (Swanton 1931:223). Thallis Lewis (personal communication, 1996), a full-blooded Choctaw, informs me that the Choctaw today have a repertoire of over 30 dances, but many more have been forgotten. The presence of atassa in the Mississippian is a part of what we call the Southeastern Ceremonial Complex or Southern Cult. The presence of atassa in the Middle Archaic suggests to me a portion of that corpus of religious symbolism and belief goes far back in time.

BANNERSTONES

A recent article by Sassaman (1996) concerning Mid-Holocene bannerstones is full of data related to cultural complexity in the Middle Archaic. Bannerstones have long been a subject of discussion among Eastern archaeologists, though in recent years far too many people, both archaeologists and amateurs alike, are apt to simply classify them as atlatl weights and move on. Were they atlatl weights? I think not, for several reasons. As Sassaman (1996:63) has pointed out, bannerstones are not evenly distributed across the Carolinas. It would appear that if bannerstones were an important part of an atlatl, then bannerstones would be found where atlatls are used. Such is not the case: bannerstones do not occur in Australia, Asia, Africa, Europe, South America, western and central Canada, or western North America. They are only found in eastern North America. Also, no atlatls have ever been found with bannerstones attached. This idea sprang from the Green River Archaic sites where bannerstones were found in alignment with antler hooks. These hooks were thought to represent part of a composite atlatl. When complete atlatls have been found, they have tended to be one-piece, not composite, tools. At the Green River sites, it was noted that bannerstones and hooks were often associated with females and infants. Several theories have been put forth to explain this pattern. Another important aspect of their distribution is that seldom are these so-called atlatls associated with pro-jectile points. That they occur in burials cannot be argued. Douglass (1882) found them in caches in Florida mounds, and C. B. Moore (1894) also found them in Florida mounds, where they appear to be an ornament associated with burials.

The authoritative work on the subject of bannerstones is by Byron Knoblock (1939). Knoblock placed bannerstones into types and then used a set of three classes of each type to further divide them. Class C was considered by Knoblock to be the ultimate or final form. Class C specimens are always manufactured from a specific type of stone. Thus Mississippi Valley Butterfly bannerstones are always made of quartz, while Double Notch Butterfly bannerstones are always made from banded slate. Knoblock illustrates a knobbed lunate bannerstone, one of a group of 12 excavated from a mound in Illinois, that was ceremonially killed. All 12 (class C specimens made from banded slate) were broken into four to eight pieces, all pieces were present, and the bannerstones were accompanied by eight copper axes, along with the skeletal remains (Knoblock 1939:34). The fact that specific types of bannerstones were manufactured from a specific type of raw material strongly suggests a special class of artifact. Ceremonial breakage, mound burial, burial with humans, and caching further lend support to the idea that these may not be functional tools. Ceremonial breakage is known from Mis-sissippi as well with siltstone bannerstones being broken and deposited at the Oak site in Itawamba County (White et al. 1983:88), immediately adjacent to the site that produced a cache containing ceremonially killed oversize Bentons, a double-notch Benton, and a Turkey Tail. Bannerstones were also traded over great distances, so they, too, are a part of the Middle Archaic exchange network. Finally, let me add that bannerstones occur in northeast Mississippi with Benton artifacts. Bannerstones are rare in the Yazoo Basin with the Denton culture sites. They are even rarer in the Natchez Bluffs, south Mississippi, and the Gulf Coast area of Mississippi during the Middle Archaic, with only four examples recorded, including a "frog" effigy bannerstone from Jefferson County, Missis-sippi (Brown 1992:201). Bannerstones make an appearance on the Gulf Coast in the Late Archaic period, but they only occur at the Claiborne site—strange for such an important tool as an atlatl weight.

BEADS

One of the questions frequently asked about this time period is, were there specialists? The answer is yes. John Connaway's (1981) article on the Keenan bead cache is one of the most important, and most overlooked, lithic studies in Southeastern archaeology. The Keenan cache consists of 449 unfinished stone beads in every stage of manufacture from unmodified raw material to completely carved and polished with drilling started. Also included in the cache are several classic Middle Archaic effigy beads. Connaway's article is important for five reasons. First, the bead preforms comprise a new artifact type. For studies of site function, it is important to distinguish between bead blanks and drills, which is how bead blanks have been classified in the past. Some of the bead blanks are bifaces, some are trifaces, and some are quatrefaces. These latter two forms should be easy to recognize and should alert researchers that they are dealing with bead manufacturing.

Second, the cache demonstrates aspects of Middle Archaic technology never before demonstrated. The bead blanks, after being flaked to desired shape, were hafted and turned on a lathe. It is probable that this was a simple lathe, but the technology was there. Also the beads were drilled, often from one end, with a small chert bit from a microblade. Some beads are in excess of 9 cm in length. This suggests that drilling was not done by twirling a bit that was loosely held in the hand. A drill press of sorts, well braced and solid, would be needed for such an operation. It is possible that the bow was used in this process, though it could be that a pump drill, perhaps used with a spindle whorl, was employed in the manufacturing process. At any rate, the manufacture of stone beads in the Middle Archaic was far more complex than previously suspected.

Third, the fact that 449 beads were found in the cache suggests a specialist was involved in the manufacture of the beads. Such is also suggested by work at the Denton site (Connaway et al. 1977) (Figure 1.1). The zoomorphic specimens from Denton are well made from hard, carefully selected stone. The preforms at the site are usually of coarse stone that is poorly worked, more often into rough oval pendants rather than beads. The technology of the zoomorphic beads is quite different from that of most of the lapidary specimens from Denton. This, coupled with the fact that a lathe and sophisticated drilling apparatus were involved, would suggest a specialist. The time to manufacture and maintain the sophisticated drilling apparatus used on zoomorphic and some other beads would likely require a specialist. Further, the sheer number of beads in the Keenan cache suggests bead working was a near full-time endeavor for some people.

Finally, a comparison of the Denton lapidary industry with the zoomorphic beads at the site is striking. Zoomorphic beads are usually made of imported stone. They are finely carved and highly polished. The majority of beads and pendants at Denton are of poor-quality local stone, crudely shaped and polished, and rarely carved. The 80-odd zoomorphic beads now known are so strikingly similar that probably no more than a very few people were involved in the manufacture of the beads.

Fourth, the fact that the distinctive zoomorphic beads are found in five states, Louisiana, Arkansas, Tennessee, Alabama, and Mississippi, with the latter yielding the majority (nearly 50) of the known examples, indicates that the beads were being made and put into the Middle Archaic exchange network. Since so many of the beads have been found in Mississippi, and the remainder are all from adjacent states, it is suggested that zoomorphic beads were made in Mississippi.

And fifth, the placement of the beads in the pit at Keenan suggests a ritual scene. To quote Charles Rau, who in 1878 described the cache in his article "The Stock-in-Trade of an Aboriginal Lapidary," the large effigy piece "lay flat on the bottom of the hole, the long and cylindrical beads were placed on end, on and around it, as closely as possible and the smaller objects were spread over them in a rather promiscuous way" (Rau 1878:297–298). The careful placement of the beads is reminiscent of the careful placement of artifacts with burials. Rau's title for his article suggests that, 121 years ago, he thought a specialist was at work. I had originally thought that the cache indicated that finished artifacts, not raw materials, were moving in the exchange network. Such is not exactly the case, for Rolingson and Howard (1997) have shown that several beads and pendants from Mississippi (usually effigies) are made from imported stone, generally from the eastern Ouachita Mountains, though one specimen is from the Appalachians. The exchange networks were complex in the Middle Archaic (Gibson 1994a; Jefferies 1996; Johnson 1994). Evidence for specialists using lathes has also turned up at a site recently located in Warren County, Mississippi. This again is in the southwestern quarter of the state, where bead specialists seem to have been present. In addition to the Keenan cache bead specialists, there were specialists involved in the manufacture of the oversize bifaces of the Benton caches.

CRAFT SPECIALISTS

At this point, I must address craft specialization. I have argued earlier in this chapter that, as evidenced by their superior workmanship, specialists produced the oversize bifaces of the Middle Archaic. It is also my opinion that this is the case with the Sloan points of the Paleoindian period and the swords and other eccentric flints of the Mississippian period. I feel this is the case not only because of the workmanship but also because of the raw materials involved. Certain raw materials were used for certain types of bifaces. This fact indicates that bifaces were not being produced over a wide area by talented artisans but were being made in a few areas by craft specialists. To be sure, these were not full-time specialists, but when certain artifacts were required, it was this group of people, and no one else, who manufactured the items. Likewise the makers of zoomorphic beads were craft specialists. Analysis of the Keenan bead cache, discussed above, demonstrates that specialists were involved in making some, though not all, categories of beads. The Denton site provides an excellent demonstration of this fact. To date, 24 zoomorphic beads have been found there (John Connaway, personal communication, 2001). Most are of imported rock and all exhibit superior design, carving, engraving, and polishing. The zoomorphic beads are all finished. Many of the other specimens of the Denton lapidary are unfinished. The great majority of the Denton lapidary consists of poor-quality beads and pendants of coarse stone that have been rudely shaped (if at all) and then drilled with a large chipped-stone drill. In contrast, the zoomorphic beads are carefully drilled with microdrills. The implication is that the zoomorphic beads at Denton are all imports, made by specialists and transported to Denton as a part of the Middle Archaic exchange network. It appears then, that specialists were involved in producing some types of both stone beads and bifaces. Both classes of artifacts produced by specialists are ideotechnic artifacts. Specialists are necessary not only for their skill in flaking or carving but also for their power or magic, which becomes a part of the artifact.

Zoomorphic beads are a unique trait of the Middle Archaic in Mississippi. Specimens are known from the surrounding states, but I have argued the evidence suggests a few specialists in southwest Mississippi were making and exchanging the beads. In earlier papers, I have described several classes of these beads, but here I would like to focus on one class of bead, the owl bead. Several owl beads are known; the image portrayed is an eared owl sitting on a stump. One example from Hinds County, Mississippi, has feathers and claws engraved on it. There are four varieties of eared owl: the great horned owl, the long-eared owl, the short-eared owl, and the screech owl. All of the eared owls are found in Mississippi and Louisiana, though the long-eared owl and short-eared owl only winter here. The owl symbolism, noted first in the Middle Archaic with owl effigy beads, continues into the Late Archaic with the famous Poverty Point period fat owl pendants. Owl symbolism continues in the Mississippian period with effigies of eared owls on bowl rims, this form being most common at the Humber site in Coahoma County, Mississippi (Figure 1.1). At this point, we should remember the horned owl dance of both the Creeks and the Choctaw. Hudson describes the long-eared owl as commonly being thought of as a witch.

It is of interest to note that the Mississippi Choctaw today do not like to discuss owls. When they hear an owl, they often call a shaman to determine whether this is in fact an owl or a witch (Ken Carleton, personal communication, 1999). The screech owl, an eared owl, is the most common type encountered by the Choctaw today. The modern Choctaw word for witch is the old word for "war prophets" (Ken Carleton, personal communication, 1999). War prophets were respected and powerful people; they also carried stuffed owls with them. Owl symbolism goes back at least as far as the Middle Archaic. The modern Choctaw and many other Southeastern groups believe in "Little People." Little People sometimes kidnap children, who later return to the group as shamans. When speaking of Little People, we should remember the Middle Archaic dwarf from Alabama with his cache of big Turkey Tail blades. Modern Native American beliefs seem to go far back in time. I would argue continuity back to the Middle Archaic at the very least.

Connaway's work at the Denton site is ongoing. To date, 24 zoomorphic beads have been recovered from this site. In addition to the Denton-style point cluster, several Benton points, two Elk River points, and an Aberdeen-style triple-grooved axe have been recovered, indicating exchange with Benton groups in northeast Mississippi. As previously stated, it appears the zoomorphic beads were all imports to the site from the south. Denton seems to have been what Ian Brown (1999:134) refers to as a node of interaction. Denton is in a good location near where the Tallahatchie and Yokona Rivers combine. The geomorphology of Denton indicates it was occupied while it was on an active course of the old Ohio-Mississippi River meander. There is some question as to whether the site originally had mounds. Denton site B, referred to by Connaway et al. (1977) as a small mound, is immediately east of the site. This small area has yielded several unusual artifacts. A large chipped blade that could fall into the atassa category and fragments of two others, all from imported stone, have been recovered from this area (Connaway et al. 1977:37). An unusual bannerstone was recovered from the area, as well as a finely wrought tubular stone bead (Connaway et al. 1977:81). Lithic debris, which literally covers the main portion of the Denton site, is lacking on Denton site B. It is possible that Denton site B does represent a mound, but further testing will be required to substantiate this.

DISTRIBUTIONAL DATA

Mississippi, like Gaul, can be divided into three parts during the Middle Archaic period. The northeast section has Benton points of blue-gray Fort Payne chert. Shuttle-type bannerstones are present, and zoomorphic beads occur. Large chipped and ground and polished atassa are present. At this time we know of only one instance of mound building, though large accretional midden mounds are common in floodplains. Interestingly, caches of atassa do not usually occur on these large middens along the major streams, but rather on smaller sites farther up tributary streams. Grooved axes are present. Evidence suggests the triple-grooved Aberdeen style is slightly later than the full-grooved style. Chipped-stone adzes are common. There is abundant evidence for participation in the exchange networks, with Benton points and Fort Payne chert bifaces being found over a wide area. In addition, zoomorphic beads and Tallahatta quartzite points were being brought into northeast Mississippi from the southwest and southeast, respectively. The Vaughan mound in Lowndes County, Mississippi, is a Middle Archaic burial mound (Atkinson 1974).

The Natchez Bluffs and Yazoo Basin contain examples of the Denton point type. The majority of these points are made of yellow-tan chert of the Citronelle formation. Mississippi Valley Crescent and Southern Humped bannerstones are present though rare, with several examples decorated by engraving or carving. Chipped-stone and ground-stone atassa are present but are also rare. Zoomorphic beads occur but are clustered at the Denton site. Data suggest the zoomorphic forms are imported from the south, while local lapidary efforts pale in comparison to those of the southern specialists. Ground and polished celts made from quartzite and rhyolite are present. Chipped-stone adzes are present. Evidence for interaction includes Fort Payne Benton and Elk River points, the atassa points of imported cherts and slate, polished celts of quartzite and rhyolite, and an Aberdeen-style grooved axe of sandstone. The zoomorphic beads are also considered to be imports. Mound building is possible at Denton site B.

The Gulf Coast and southwest Mississippi area is characterized by what we call Crain points; Gagliano (1963:113) called them broad spade-shaped points. They occur along with the St. Tammany and St. Helena tool types. The Pickwick/Ledbetter cluster of bifaces occurs over the entire state and appears to represent a specialized knife form. In fact, similar stemmed blades are found all the way up the east coast to Massachusetts. Ground and polished celts are present. Chipped-stone adzes are common, with some showing some grinding and polishing. Bead making appears to be an important activity with specialists at a few sites making large numbers of stone beads. Bannerstones are rare in the Middle Archaic period on the Gulf Coast and in south Mississippi. Participation in the exchange network is demonstrated by the presence of zoomorphic beads. Several of these beads have been reported from the Gulf Coast area, but what are very rare in this region are the oversize bifaces. This is strange because large flakable stone is one of the major resources the area lacks. Why the coast folks were not getting good imported chert is a real mystery, especially when one considers the large amount of stone being transported in the exchange networks.

Four probable Middle Archaic mounds are known from this part of Mississippi. A group of three mounds was present on the Gulf Coast in what is today a residential neighborhood in Pascagoula. When two of these mounds were leveled, a group of 14 stone beads was found. One of these is a classic Middle Archaic effigy bead. Another mound has recently been located in Lincoln County, Mississippi, with several carbon 14 dates in the vicinity of 3000 B.C. (Kevin Bruce, personal communication, 2001). Further, the Monte Sano mound is located not far to the south of the Lincoln County mound.

The three regions of Mississippi have different artifact complexes and use different types of raw material for their manufacture. They all participate in the Middle Archaic exchange network but to differing degrees. The exchange network appears disjointed and uneven. Further, both sacred and secular objects are moving within the exchange system. The atassa of northeast Mississippi suggest elaborate dance rituals that we have little evidence for elsewhere.

I would suggest that there is a musical tradition among the Middle Archaic folks that we are missing altogether. I know that as I leave the urban areas of Mississippi in my truck on various jaunts, I encounter areas where country music is the only sort played. I do not doubt something of this order prevailed in early times, though to archaeologists today these boundaries are marked by projectile point styles. I wonder, too, if there were not linguistic boundaries. The distribution of Evans projectile points serves as an excellent example of prehistoric boundaries. Evans points are a diagnostic for Middle Archaic sites in Louisiana and Arkansas. To date we have documented three Evans points from Mississippi. The specimens from Mississippi are from along the Mississippi River: two from Natchez and one from Vicksburg. This suggests to me the river was a boundary, not a barrier. Today when you cross it, you can immediately buy liquor in grocery stores and find liquor and beer that is unavailable on the east bank. It serves as a boundary, not a barrier. There is also a difference in the language and music of the two banks, though the food is similar. I would bet this was the case in the Middle Archaic. I just wish I could prove it.

CONCLUSION

Cultural complexity in the Middle Archaic now seems almost a given. In a prophetic statement Jay Johnson (1987:204) equated blade cores, long-distance trade networks, and mound building with complex societies. At the time he pointed out that this was confined to two periods in the Yazoo Basin, Late Archaic Poverty Point and Early Mississippian. While this chapter has ventured outside the Yazoo Basin, it can now be stated that there are four periods with such complexity. Middle Archaic and Middle Woodland can now be added to Poverty Point and Mississippian.

In a presented paper, Gibson and Carr (1999) put forth four preconditions for mound building by hunter-gatherers. The first of these is an intensifiable food source. While there is no doubt that the hunting of deer and other mammals was important, the fish and shellfish resources of the region should not be overlooked. The trapping of smaller game and the exploitation of a variety of plant foods, coupled with the hunting of large game and shellfish procurement, provide one the food source requirement. Also it may be noted that most sites in the Middle Archaic period are closer to water sources than earlier and later sites, and it becomes apparent that the intensification of the food source was not fortuitous.

The second precondition was a missing resource. Here, we have an interesting dichotomy. As has been pointed out in this chapter, exchange networks existed over a large part of the state and region. Cherts and other flakable stone were certainly being exchanged but so were some other special items. Bannerstones, beads, effigy pendants, and effigy beads were being exchanged over large areas. These items are not necessities but rather are ideotechnic artifacts, and there is evidence that these items were made by specialists. Thus the exchange networks seem to have originated not to move rock into rock-poor areas, but to move sacred artifacts with power into areas away from the point of origin of these items. To be sure, there were people in most groups who could have made these items, but these items are desired because the makers are special; that is, the makers have a special power and that power passes into the artifact itself. Perhaps the most interesting aspect of all this is that the Gulf Coast, a rock-poor area if there ever was one, does not get good imported rock in the Middle Archaic, yet it gets effigy beads. What is coming to the Gulf Coast is not a necessity but power in the form of ideotechnic artifacts. Also of note is that oversize knives, commonly associated with hunting/butchering, are in fact ideotechnic artifacts. These ideotechnic artifacts also appear to be associated with ritual dance and death. In the later periods, the ideotechnic clubs associated with warfare join the ideotechnic knives. We have little evidence for warfare in the Middle Archaic, hence the atassa of this earlier period represent hunting knives rather than the swords and war clubs of the later Mississippian period.

The third precondition is the networking that concentrates power in the hands of a few. Again the ritual nature of the artifacts is important here with their power and tie-in to dance ritual and perhaps burial ritual. Dance ritual demands space, and the mounds and plazas provide defined ritual space for the proper use of the artifacts. The mounds can also serve as special places for the powerful (people and artifacts) to come together with the not so powerful for the transference, or sharing, of power. Let us not forget that with the ritual objects we are not just dealing with "big men" but also with other people who at least some of the time have status and, arguably, power. This group most certainly includes some dwarves and females as evidenced by burial accompaniments. These latter two groups are not often thought of in terms of power among hunter-gatherers, but the evidence suggests otherwise. Then there are the shamans, the ultimate brokers of power. The shamans are both desired and feared. Their power is great and the ritual ceremonialism of the Middle Archaic with the mounds and the ideotechnic accouterments suggests that at this point in time they were powerful indeed.

The fourth precondition is balanced reciprocity. Here I would refer to Howard's (1968) wonderful description of the dance ritual of the Creeks in the 1960s. Howard (1968:passim) describes the shaman removing from beneath the chief's bench the boxes containing the atassa (ritual dance knives), shell rattles, and other ceremonial equipment. The atassa were then given to the two senior matrons, who were not allowed to put them down until the dance was finished. When the dance was completed, the atassa were handed back to the shaman and placed in the box and delivered back beneath the chief's bench. The square ground where the dances occurred had a mound and was a gathering place for groups from several villages. This ritual was recorded in 1965 and presumably is occurring to this day. There is power: the chief, the shaman, and the matrons are all special people, at least on this occasion. They all participate in a ritual that involves a sharing of power. The sharing continues with the sharing of food and, at times, ritual feasting. The coming together of groups of people also serves to create alliances and the possibility for trading partners. While there are social aspects to these activities, the ideotechnic artifacts represent power and remind all of the solemnity of the occasion.

I hope this chapter has demonstrated that the trappings (artifacts) of power are prevalent in the Middle Archaic and have their origin even further back in the Paleoindian period. Some of these same special types of artifacts are found in the Mississippian cultures of the thirteenth through sixteenth centuries and occur up to present times. What we are witnessing with the mounds and special artifacts of the Middle Archaic is a part of a rich cultural tradition dealing with the supernatural that goes far back in time and is still with us today, albeit in modified form.

7

The Burkett Site (23MI20)

Implications for Cultural Complexity and Origins

Prentice M. Thomas, Jr., L. Janice Campbell, and James R. Morehead

The nature and complexity of Late Archaic O'Bryan Ridge manifestations and their relationship to Poverty Point culture in the Lower Mississippi Valley have been controversial topics for more than half a century. When baked clay objects and other trappings of material culture similar to those in Poverty Point assemblages were first identified at sites in the Cairo Lowlands of southeastern Missouri, Stephen Williams characterized them as a regional variant of Poverty Point (S. Williams 1954). Questions over the strength of the relationship led Phillips (1970) to finesse the issue by referring to O'Bryan Ridge as a phase of the Poverty Point period. In his seminal work on Poverty Point, Webb (1977) viewed O'Bryan Ridge as having some contact or relationship with Poverty Point, but he did not regard it as an integral part of the culture—a position reversed in the second edition of the same study (Webb 1982). At a Poverty Point conference in the mid-1980s, Williams reflected again on the O'Bryan Ridge phase, commenting that it was probably earlier than Poverty Point (S. Williams 1991).

The relationship of O'Bryan Ridge to Poverty Point is a crucial concern addressed here. On the one hand, complexity is enhanced for the former if it is an integral element of Poverty Point. On the other hand, if O'Bryan Ridge is only a peripheral trading partner, or indirectly and weakly related to the southern complex, this would affect a consideration of the complexity of the southeastern Missouri components and the scope of Poverty Point influence would warrant reexamination.

THE BURKETT SITE AND THE O'BRYAN RIDGE PHASE

Burkett (23MI20) is the type site for the O'Bryan Ridge phase, which was formulated in the mid-1950s when that site and a nearby neighbor, Weems

(23MI25), yielded a suite of artifacts that mirrored some of the assemblage traits of the Poverty Point site (S. Williams 1954). Burkett was investigated between 1964 and 1966 by Hopgood, whose effort recovered baked clay ball fragments and chipped-stone artifacts, seemingly more evidence linking the site with Poverty Point (Hopgood 1967). Similar items were found at Weems by J. R. Williams (1967), who was also the first researcher to broach the subject of mounds, confirming a conical one was present at Weems and hinting of one at Burkett. However, neither Hopgood nor J. R. Williams elaborated upon the O'Bryan Ridge phase data; the focus of both researchers was on the later Woodland component. The issue of mound building was also left largely unaddressed.

Over two decades would pass before Burkett was examined again, this time by Mid-Continental Research Associates (MCRA), who conducted geomorphological and cultural resources investigations of the New Madrid Floodway for the Memphis District Corps of Engineers (Lafferty and Hess 1996). As part of the work, MCRA investigated both the Burkett and Weems sites and substantiated not only the presence of the O'Bryan Ridge phase components but also the significance of both properties.

This evaluation led to the first large-scale opportunity to explore the archaeological manifestation of the O'Bryan Ridge phase in 1999 when Prentice Thomas and Associates, Inc. (PTA) was tasked by the Memphis District to conduct data recovery at the Burkett site. The primary objective was to confirm the stratigraphic separation of O'Bryan Ridge phase materials below ceramic deposits across the site. With this confirmed, three specific issues guided research related to the O'Bryan Ridge phase deposits: (1) to define assemblage traits, (2) to establish the chronology of the O'Bryan Ridge phase, and (3) to ascertain the cultural affinity of the mound. The work also provided the long-awaited chance to explore the cultural complexity of O'Bryan Ridge and its external ties to Poverty Point culture.

SETTING

O'Bryan Ridge rises sharply above the Mississippi River floodplain in the vicinity of Burkett, with an absolute elevation of 315 feet above mean sea level (amsl) at the highest point on the site to 300 feet amsl in the nearby floodplain. The Mississippi River has occupied the same meander belt between Thebes Gap and a point 35 miles north of Memphis since about 10,000 B.P. (Saucier 1994:253). O'Bryan Ridge, the setting for both the Burkett site and its contemporaneous neighbor, Weems, is believed to have been formed by proximal overbank deposits from Fisk Meander Channel (FMC) I shortly after the formation of the Charleston Fan (Lafferty 1998; Porter and Guccione 1996). Citing the recovery of an Early Archaic point on O'Bryan Ridge, Lafferty (1998) suggests that the

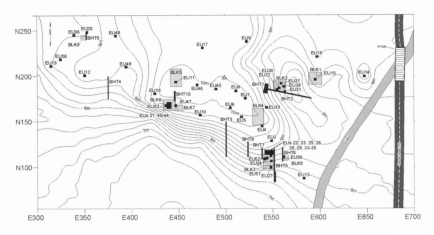

Figure 7.1. Contour map of the Burkett site showing PTA's investigations.

landform dates to at least 7000 to 5000 B.C. Radiocarbon dates on cores submitted by MCRA have established that FMC J, which scallops O'Bryan Ridge from
the south, formed by 5000 B.P. (Lafferty and Hess 1996).

DATA RECOVERY AT THE BURKETT SITE

PTA's initial field procedures included excavation of backhoe trenches and 2-by-
2-m units to examine site stratigraphy, internal variation, and artifact content,
followed by mechanical stripping of large blocks to expose sub–plow zone features (Figure 7.1).

It quickly became clear that Burkett would live up to its reputation as a significant site. Excellent evidence for the relative stratigraphic position of O'Bryan
Ridge phase materials underlying ceramic-bearing Woodland levels was derived
from Block 3, which was placed adjacent to a backhoe cut that had exposed a
rich intact midden. The richest deposits associated with the O'Bryan Ridge
phase occupation were found in the midden at depths below 50 to 60 cm. The
block excavations also revealed evidence of a graben, which is a down-thrown
fault block from earthquake activity. On the basis of a paleoseismology study
conducted by Tuttle (2002) on this graben and other seismic evidence at the
site, earthquakes were determined to have taken place at Burkett during the Late
Archaic and later occupations. The ongoing occupation in light of such catastrophic events begged for greater consideration in assessing the cultural complexity of the O'Bryan Ridge phase.

The issue of mound building also spoke to the concern of complexity, and
confirmation of whether a mound had been present at Burkett was a driving

force in the site's investigation. Besides J. R. Williams's reference to a mound, a local informant told MCRA that the mound at Burkett had been leveled by an overzealous farm manager (Lafferty and Hess 1996). Credible evidence of the presence of a mound was also found on a 1931 floodway map on which a 4- or 5-foot-high, roughly circular mound was clearly depicted. No surficial trace of the mound was present in 1999 when PTA began its work. However, by taking distance and angle readings from known points, the location of the mound was identified by PTA and overlaid by Blocks 6 and 7 (see Figure 7.1). Excavations in these blocks revealed remnants of the mound in stratigraphic profile and, as will be discussed, additional evidence of earthquake activity (see Mound Chronology section, below).

THE O'BRYAN RIDGE INVENTORY AT BURKETT

The O'Bryan Ridge component at Burkett yielded 309 chipped-stone tools, 4,247 pieces of debitage, 14 ground, pecked, or polished items, and 340 baked clay objects. The Burkett point type accounts for two-thirds of the 30 identifiable points recovered (Figure 7.2), and another 23 percent are very similar types like Gary. Virtually all of the other bifaces are unidentifiable fragments (66 of 76). The single most common formal uniface class is piercer, though none of the examples could be characterized as Jaketown perforators.

Detailed analyses of the O'Bryan Ridge chipped-stone industry have indicated complex structuring in the chipped-stone facies, which is particularly true of the most common raw material categories and certain major tool categories. For example, there are statistically significant associations between Cobden chert and points and Mill Creek chert and nonpoint bifaces, as well as a definite tendency for formal unifaces to be made from Mounds gravel, a plentiful local resource. Core reduction strategies revealed a wide repertoire, including bifacial, blade, opposed platform, discoidal, and blocky/amorphous[1] approaches. However, when initial, exhausted, and unsortable core fragments are discounted, the blocky/amorphous approach is the most prominent, followed distantly by single platform cores (another simple, possibly related approach); minimal evidence was found of other, more controlled reduction types, blade cores included. Researchers have observed a strong, positive relationship between blocky/amorphous cores and sedentism, the association being fairly well documented in Mississippian age societies (e.g., Johnson 1987; Koldehoff 1987; Parry and Kelly 1987). Does this mean that the O'Bryan Ridge phase occupants were sedentary? Not necessarily, since such cores are also strongly associated with easy access to large quantities of raw material (Custer 1987; Johnson 1987).[2] Of the 18 blocky/amorphous cores identified in O'Bryan Ridge phase contexts, 15 are of the very local and accessible Mounds gravel.

Figure 7.2. Examples of Burkett points.

Lapidary items are represented by only one jasper bead, but a variety of fine ground-stone remains have been reported by local collectors (Webb 1982; S. Williams 1991). The lack of context data for these items leaves their association with the O'Bryan Ridge component indeterminate, though probable.

Most of the 340 baked clay objects (Figure 7.3) are amorphous, biconical,

0   5
                                 cm

Figure 7.3. Examples of baked clay objects.

and spheroid, the shapes reported as most common by previous workers at Burkett and Weems alike. The variety of shapes is, however, limited in comparison
with the variety found at classic Poverty Point sites (cf. Webb 1982).

Notable in the floral collection is the dominance of mast crops, particularly
hickory and walnut, while acorns are very rare and pecans were not observed at
all. Cultigens were not recovered. The faunal remains are—to the extent that
they may be identified at all—dominated by large mammal bone, specifically
white-tailed deer. Turtle is next most common, and after that identifiable remains are almost nil. The impression is one of seasonal occupation.

The distribution of various artifact classes displays interesting patterns. The
greatest concentration of O'Bryan Ridge phase materials, seen across widely disparate artifact classes, was in Block 3. A secondary concentration of chipped-
stone tools and debitage was identified in the far northwestern part of the site
near Block 9. Except for a few baked clay objects found just above a hearth in
Block 6, there are virtually no O'Bryan Ridge artifacts of note where the mound
formerly stood.

It is tempting to aggregate all these considerations and conclude that the
O'Bryan Ridge phase was indeed a complex society. However, as is the case for
blocky/amorphous cores and sedentism, there are other explanations that cannot be excluded in the assessment of O'Bryan Ridge society. The consistent
structuring of major tool and raw material categories does not necessarily translate into evidence of general social complexity or strong, long-distance relation-

ships; as a case in point, Paleoindian chipped-stone assemblages typically exhibit highly structured lithic technologies and exotic raw materials, but neither of these characteristics is considered evidence of social complexity or trade.

CHRONOLOGY AND THE O'BRYAN RIDGE PHASE

In the complete absence of dates, S. Williams (1991) offered his "best guess" that the O'Bryan Ridge phase began close to 2000 B.C. and may have ended at or before classic Poverty Point, around 1000 B.C. Since he made that prophetic statement, 13 dates have been obtained from contexts relevant to the study of O'Bryan Ridge phase components. Three of these were obtained by PTA from the Burkett site (reported as standard radiocarbon ages). Beta-140461, on carbonized nutshell, yielded a date of 4260 ± 70 B.P. or 2310 B.C. A small hearth in Block 3 produced carbonized nutshell (Beta-140463) that yielded an age of 3960 ± 80 B.P. (2010 B.C.). Beta-135123, on charcoal from a clay-lined hearth near the mound, yielded a date of 4000 ± 50 B.P. (2050 B.C.). These dates are numbingly close to the predictions of Williams and well in agreement with a date of 3920 ± 100 B.P. (1970 B.C.) reported by Lafferty and Hess (1996) from the Late Archaic Renaud site (23MI621). Four comparable radiocarbon dates are available on O'Bryan Ridge phase deposits from Burkett's close neighbor, the Weems site—4710 ± 90 B.P. (2200 B.C.), 4330 ± 70 B.P. (2380 B.C.), 4290 ± 130 B.P. (2340 B.C.), and 4210 ± 70 B.P. (2260 B.C.).

The remaining five dates were provided by Panamerican Consultants, Inc. (PCI) from 23MI605, with point estimates as old as 3420 ± 50 B.P. (1470 B.C.) to as recent as 3120 ± 60 B.P. (1170 B.C.). PCI's dates are consistently later than those from Burkett, Renaud, and Weems, falling within the range of early Poverty Point sites like Teoc Creek (22CR504) in the Upper Yazoo Basin of Mississippi (cf. Webb 1982), as well as the Mule Road and Labras Lake phases in the American Bottom (Chapman et al. 1999). Site 23MI605 was referred to by PCI as Late Archaic, without specific reference to the O'Bryan Ridge phase or Poverty Point culture.

MOUND CHRONOLOGY

None of the deposits in the mound were suitable for radiocarbon dating, so a series of Oxidized Carbon Ratio (OCR) samples was taken from excavation levels above, within, and at the base of the mound remnant in excavation unit 47 and submitted to Archaeology Consulting Team, Inc., for processing (ACT samples 4203 through 4207). The OCR procedure rests on determining the degree of biochemical degradation of organic carbon and charcoal incorporated into sediments, a process assumed to be linear through time (Frink 1995). OCR has been cross-checked against associated diagnostics and radiocarbon assays, which have yielded comparable dates, though it is subject to various constraints (e.g., sediments in caves, rockshelters, and reducing environments generally yield uninterpretable results). The OCR method has been employed in conjunction with radiocarbon to date the important deposits at Watson Brake (16OU175) (Saunders et al. 1997) and the Poverty Point type site (16WC5) (Gibson 1997), but it has its critics (cf. Killick et al. 1999; also the response by Frink 1999).

The OCR results from excavation unit 47 were perplexing, particularly in view of the carbon 14 date from Feature 145. The order of ACT-4204 through ACT-4206 is consistent with loading from a single borrow pit yielding an inverted time series—oldest on top, youngest on the bottom (Table 7.1). The position of the baked clay objects and sherds, plus the age of some of the fills, suggests this part of the mound was not Archaic. In particular, ACT-4204 was from a level dominated by baked clay objects and without sherds; the OCR point estimate of 1280 b.c. is not conflicting. The date for the layer below could be Late Archaic or Early Woodland, depending on which end of the range one finds most plausible—the presence of sherds argues for the latter. The coup de grâce comes from two Baytown sherds in the 60 to 65 cm level, a submound context.

In an attempt to shed more light on the mound construction, a second series of OCR dates was executed on sediments from excavation unit 57, excavated solely to gather additional OCR samples. Rather than clarifying the picture as hoped, the results were again perplexing, best appreciated by a comparison of the dates themselves (Table 7.2) with the profile of excavation unit 57 (Figure 7.4).

This is a curious sequence of dates for a loaded profile as there are no temporal inversions in the fill. The color-texture sequence is unlike that of any soil described in the county soil manual. Neither is it credible as the product of pedogenesis in a natural deposit, nor does it resemble the effects of pedogenesis in mound fill that has resulted in normal horizon sequences in mounds of Archaic age (cf. Saunders et al. 1994). The thinness of the layers, particularly the clay-textured layers, suggests that these strata are at the edge of the mound and may reflect disturbance and slopewash. The sequence of dates could be consistent with fairly steady accretion between 1810 and 350 b.c. It would also be extraordinarily slow for construction—there are only 26 cm of sediment between the top of the upper date of 350 b.c. at 19 to 20 cm and the bottom of the earliest date, 1810 b.c., at 44 to 45 cm. As dissimilar as the color-texture sequence is to pedogenesis, the date sequence is still more difficult to reconcile with mound construction practice. Taken at face value, ACT-4771, ACT-4772, and ACT-4773 would imply three accretion episodes over a period of 480 years, which added a grand total of about 6 cm to the height of the mound! The most plausible interpretation of this sequence is that ACT-4775 reflects

Table 7.1. OCR dates for sediments from excavation unit 47, 23MI20

Sample Depth	ACT #	Artifact Depth	BCOs*	Sherds	OCR Date	Calendric Date and Range†
19-20 cm	4203	15-20 cm	0	0	2403±72 B.P.	450 B.C.; 590-310 B.C.
29-30 cm	4204	20-30 cm	12	0	3228±96 B.P.	1280 B.C.; 1480-1080 B.C.
39-40 cm	4205	30-40 cm	3	2	2687±80 B.P.	750 B.C.; 910-590 B.C.
44-45 cm	4206	40-50 cm	7	0	2620±78 B.P.	670 B.C.; 830-510 B.C.
54-55 cm	4207	50-60 cm	0	0	3481±104 B.P.	1530 B.C.; 1730-1330 B.C.
n/a	n/a	60+ cm	1	3	n/a	n/a

BCOs = Baked clay objects.

*Chipped stone is disregarded due to lack of diagnostics.

†Both the calendric date and the range are rounded off to the nearest decade; the range is approximately 2 sigma.

Table 7.2. OCR dates for sediments from excavation unit 57, 23MI20

Sample Depth	ACT #	Soil Texture	Color	OCR Date	Calendric Date and Range†
9-10 cm	4767	Sand	10YR 4/4	480±14 B.P.	A.D. 1470; A.D. 1440-1500
14-15 cm	4768	Sand*	10YR 5/6	1772±53 B.P.	A.D. 180; A.D. 80-180
19-20 cm	4769	Clay loam‡	10YR 4/3	2304±69 B.P.	350 B.C.; 490-210 B.C.
24-25 cm	4770	Sand‡	10YR 3/6	2510±75 B.P.	560 B.C.; 720-400 B.C.
29-30 cm	4771	Silty clay‡	2.5Y 7/2	2817±84 B.P.	870 B.C.; 1030-710 B.C.
31-32 cm	4772	Clay‡	10YR 3/2	3012±90 B.P.	1060 B.C.; 1240-880 B.C.
34-35 cm	4773	Sand*	10YR 5/4	3304±99 B.P.	1350 B.C.; 1550-1150 B.C.
39-40 cm	4774	Sand*	10YR 5/4	3450+103 B.P.	1500 B.C.; 1700-1300 B.C.
44-45 cm	4775	Clay loam	10YR 3/2	3755±112 B.P.	1810 B.C.; 2030-1590 B.C.

*Possible sand blows

‡Fills?

†Dates rounded to nearest decade.

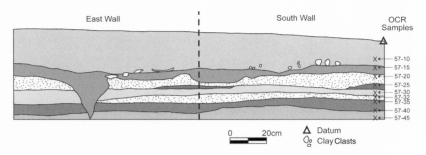

Figure 7.4. East and south profiles of excavation unit 57 showing plow zone and mound and submound deposits, along with sand blows from earthquake activity.

the age of the upper part of the terrace Bt and that ACT-4773 and ACT-4774, which overlap at 1 sigma, represent a single liquefaction event ca. 1425 B.C. The thin clayey layers above it may reflect one or more construction episodes; they overlap considerably and average about 965 B.C. Above that are sands that probably reflect a liquefaction event about 560 B.C., an Early Woodland time frame. Another clay loam cap dated to 350 B.C. is surmounted by additional sand suspected to be due to yet another liquefaction event at about A.D. 180.

An explanation that incorporates both series of dates would be that the mound was initiated in the Late Archaic and was positioned above sand from a liquefaction event. The loaded sediments were periodically disturbed, washed down the apron, and subjected to some pedogenesis, but not enough to result in the development of diagnostic soil horizons. Later liquefaction events occurred in Early and Middle Woodland time frames, and the earlier of these may have impacted the mound and provoked additional clay loading as evidenced by ACT-4769. At this time, the mound was extended to the vicinity of excavation unit 47, accounting for the radically different series of dates from that area.

The above reconstruction contains a number of "if . . . then" propositions in the chain of events. It is conceivable that if any link fails, the entire reconstruction might disintegrate. The explanation proffered is speculative but logical, consistent with the data, and the most plausible, given the assumption the dates are substantially correct.

This interpretation implies long-term treatment of the site and mound area as a special precinct. Is this credible? Why not? Investigations at Poverty Point itself have determined that mound building spanned a long period of time, of which the Poverty Point period was but the latter half. Therefore, a few hundred years of post–O'Bryan Ridge phase use, maintenance, and additional construction by Woodland peoples seems comparatively minor.

WHY BUILD A MOUND ON AN EARTHQUAKE FISSURE?

It is realistic to assume that earthquake activity, which was widespread over the New Madrid region during prehistoric and historic times, had cultural signifi-cance that related to religious beliefs, as well as political and social interaction between populations. Swanton (1931:35–37, 100) discusses origin myths in which Native American ancestors emerged from a hole or cave in the earth (e.g., Nanih Waiya). Such beliefs may have counterparts, if not roots, well into prehistory when natural events such as earthquakes demanded explanation.

It is probable that populations also gathered ritually to cover the openings created by earthquake events. The occurrence of mound construction over earthquake activity has been documented elsewhere in the Cairo Lowlands at Towosahgy (23MI2), where Mound A was placed over a seismic event dated to A.D. 400 (Saucier 1990).

The dates on the sand blows in excavation unit 57 and the initial layers of mound construction can be used to foster an argument, hypothetical though it may be, that Late Archaic groups remaining in the area but no longer living at the Burkett site were responsible for the initial stages of mound construction at the Burkett site after a seismic episode. Moreover, some settings that experi-enced the effects of earthquakes, such as the Burkett site, may have been aban-doned as habitation centers but continued to be part of the settlement sphere, perhaps with ritual or ceremonial connections. Additionally, the mound vicinity as a sacred precinct would explain the scarcity of artifacts there. The accumula-tion of more dates from contemporaneous sites will be useful in revisiting the issue of mound construction and natural phenomena among the Late Archaic populations of southeastern Missouri.

THE O'BRYAN RIDGE PHASE AND POVERTY POINT CULTURE

The findings from the Burkett site argue against a close relationship between O'Bryan Ridge phase populations and Poverty Point culture. The radiocarbon dates from the Burkett site, as well as from Weems, and MCRA's dates from Renaud (Lafferty and Hess 1996) predate those from the Poverty Point site by a considerable margin. This temporal range supports S. Williams's (1991) belief that O'Bryan Ridge was earlier than Poverty Point.

This interpretation is backed up by the suite of artifacts. The large, stemmed dart points, predominantly of the Burkett type, are reminiscent of Hale points, which have been reported from the Poverty Point site, as well as Late Archaic contexts along the Gulf Coast, in the Yazoo Basin, and in the Lauderdale focus of the Tennessee River shell middens (Webb 1982:49). At the type site in Louisiana, distribution studies suggest that Hale points are associated with a restricted pre–Poverty Point occupation (Webb 1982:66). For the most part the hallmark projectile points of Poverty Point, such as Motley, Pontchartrain, and Delhi, are uncommon or lacking in O'Bryan Ridge components. Steatite and the lamellar microlith and lapidary industries, other trademark elements of the Poverty Point culture, are infrequent at best. The lithic differences are profound in themselves and the comparisons summarized in Table 7.3.

Other aspects of the assemblage underscore more difference than similarity as well. The baked clay objects in O'Bryan Ridge phase components are mostly amorphous, spheroid, or biconical. Webb (1982) suggested the possibility that large biconicals and spheroids may represent early forms of Poverty Point objects, an observation that might be useful in correlating the early radiocarbon dates from some O'Bryan Ridge phase sites with developing patterns and traits at Poverty Point.

Involvement in trade is evident in the presence of a few items, but the O'Bryan Ridge phase assemblages do not bear the "showcase" of exotic goods that established Poverty Point culture as one intensively involved in the long-distance exchange and redistribution of material goods.

CONCLUSIONS

The O'Bryan Ridge phase of the Cairo Lowlands does not seem to be related directly to classic Poverty Point culture. The evidence collected to date overwhelmingly supports its being antecedent to Poverty Point. This finding alone means that a reconsideration of the phase is mandated, and many characterizations formulated on the premise that it was part of the Poverty Point sphere of influence have to be rethought. When the direct tie with Poverty Point is removed, one factor we believed would contribute to societal complexity is removed. There are, however, other factors.

Development of exchange systems is also regarded as a feature of complex societies. Although limited in comparison with later Poverty Point trade networks, the presence of exotic items at the Burkett site indicates involvement in long-distance exchange. Situated by FMC J, the topographic feature O'Bryan Ridge would have been in a strategic location for riverine and overland travel. Any sites on that ridge would have been in the tight spot of the hourglass for movement up the Mississippi River to the St. Louis area and southern Illinois, as well as for movement up the Ohio River. If local O'Bryan Ridge phase entrepreneurs could control the transportation routes, they may have been in a position to control access to critical goods, among them Burlington or Crescent Hills cherts around St. Louis. Though exotics like Burlington were not dominant in the Burkett collection, this does not rule out the site occupants' having

Table 7.3. Lithic industries at Poverty Point (16WC5) and Burkett (23MI20)

Characteristic	Poverty Point	Burkett	Comment(s)
Dominant points	Gary (25%)	Burkett (>60%)	Burkett is like Hale, which was a mere 2% at 16WC5; Gary is 6.7% of the identifiable O'Bryan Ridge phase points at Burkett
Other points	Pontchartrain (12.4%)	No equivalent	Narrow Burkett points are similar but lack the elongated lamellar retouch that is definitive for Pontchartrain
	Motley (12%)	No equivalent	
Controlled reduction	Bladelet cores	Bifacial cores	Bifaces appear to have done double duty at Burkett, acting both as tools and as cores
Formal unifaces	Jaketown perforators made on bladelets are the most common form	Perforators are most common, but not Jaketown style	Perforators at Burkett are very dissimilar to those of the Poverty Point culture — serrated and denticulated pieces (often made on biface trimming flakes) are the next most common unifacial tool at Burkett but are very rare at Poverty Point
Ground stone	Steatite vessels, celts, lapidary industry	Abraders, pitted stones, and fragments	No steatite vessels, sparse lapidary items at Burkett
Raw materials	Arkansas novaculite, "northern gray flint," and local [Citronelle] gravel	Burlington exotic; Cobden and Mill Creek chert are nearly local; Mounds gravel is local	No large-scale import of exotic stone at Burkett — at Burkett, the utilization of exotic Burlington chert and local Mounds gravel are different — Gibson (1997) noted no difference in the usage of local and exotic stone at Poverty Point

been instrumental in the movement of such goods between geographically disparate populations.

Mound construction is traditionally viewed as another feature of complex societies, a supposed sign of the growth of religious centers and creation of public works. A mound was inarguably present at Burkett, and there is circumstantial evidence that at least a portion of it was constructed by O'Bryan Ridge phase groups. Clearly, the erection of a mound implies societal ability to organize labor for its construction, either voluntarily or not. If the work force for mound construction was conscripted, a logical conjecture is that the society was nonegalitarian. In other words, an individual or individuals had the power to mobilize the labor, reflecting social stratification, which is yet another feature of complex societies. Moreover, the mound location atop an earthquake feature has been interpreted as deliberate and thus suggests elements of ceremonialism in the O'Bryan Ridge phase culture.

Taken as a whole, the characteristics of the Burkett site include various features of complex societies. O'Bryan Ridge phase culture appears to qualify as a complex society, although the features are limited and perhaps even indicative of emergent or initial development.

At this point, the issue of the relationship of the O'Bryan Ridge phase to Poverty Point has been resolved—it was not directly related to the florescent era of the latter. The issue of the nature of complexity in O'Bryan Ridge phase culture has been addressed but not resolved. This question requires more intensive investigation of O'Bryan Ridge phase sites. The current results represent, however, a good foundation on which to build interpretations of societal complexity and begin to rethink the cultural relations of the O'Bryan Ridge phase.

ACKNOWLEDGMENTS

We thank Matt Paré and Gray Rackley for the graphic illustrations and Erica Meyer for her editorial review prior to submission to the University of Alabama Press. We also appreciate peer review comments, verbal input from Stephen Williams and James Hopgood, and the efforts of everyone who contributed to the investigation at Burkett in the field and laboratory.

NOTES

1. Also referred to as expedient core technology.

2. Blocky/amorphous cores have been identified in Paleoindian through protohistoric components in the gravel-rich deposits of west-central Louisiana (Morehead et al. 1999).

8

Poverty Point Chipped-Stone Tool Raw Materials

Inferring Social and Economic Strategies

Philip J. Carr and Lee H. Stewart

It is easy to become awed by the Poverty Point site located in northeast Louisiana (Figure 1.1). Poverty Point was occupied by hunter-gatherers but included a built landscape with a geometric layout suggestive of master planning (Clark, this volume; Gibson 1973:69, 1987:19–22). Additionally, an interesting array of material culture indicative of intense and wide-scale trade and significant production activities was present. These aspects are what have made the Poverty Point site one of the mysteries of archaeology and have ensured its inclusion in all overviews of Southeastern prehistory. Many of the basic questions concerning the nature of the site occupation are still debated, as are other aspects of the inhabitants' lifeways.

The built landscape of Poverty Point includes six concentric earth embankments and Mound A (Gibson 1974, 1994b). These embankments are impressive in scale and are 1.2 km apart at the ends. Not particularly tall today (1–2 m), these embankments have been variously impacted since their construction. The embankments are divided by five crosscutting corridors into six sectors with Mound A at one end of the central corridor. Mound A is suggested to represent a flying bird and measures approximately 21 m high and 216 m from head to tail. Additional mounds, the "causeway" embankment, and other artificial features compose the Poverty Point site and further demonstrate the impressiveness of the built landscape. The Poverty Point site was arguably planned and required the organization of a significant amount of labor to build (Clark, this volume; Gibson 2000).

The material culture recovered from the Poverty Point site is remarkable in diversity and quantity (Gibson 1974; Webb 1968). The assemblage includes a wide variety of personal items such as cylindrical, tubular, and disc-shaped beads, ground-stone pendants in geometric and zoomorphic shapes, and perforated human and animal teeth. The number of utilitarian items such as projectile points, atlatl weights, plummets, and clay balls is impressive, but the amount of chipped-stone tool debris is staggering. Gibson (1998a) estimates that there are 70 metric tons of exotic chipped-stone artifacts at Poverty Point. In addition to nonlocal chert and other raw materials for chipped-stone tool manufacture, trade materials include copper, galena, hematite, magnetite, and a remarkable amount of soapstone. Attempting to grasp the magnitude and diversity of Poverty Point material culture is not an easy task, and we must admit to being somewhat awed by the variety of raw materials evident in even a single 10-cm level of a 1-×-1-m unit.

The pendulum can swing from incredulity to a more sober perspective on the Poverty Point landscape and assemblage. While impressive now, it must be kept in mind that the earthworks and artifacts represent a lengthy occupation. The exact span is debated, but Gibson (1998a:319) suggests the major occupation was between 1730 and 1350 cal B.C. That is, if the Poverty Point site was occupied for X years and by Y number of people, then the amount of labor per week each individual would need to devote to landscape modifications or procuring raw materials may appear much more reasonable. For example, Gibson (1987:16–19) calculates that 100 laborers working daily could have built the Poverty Point earthworks in 23.5 years, but these figures are proposed as labor equivalents and not a reflection of the actual time span for mound construction.

Such an exercise can help put things in perspective, which is certainly needed for interpreting a site such as Poverty Point. However, if taken too literally, it can remove human action. Can we truly imagine people carrying X basketloads of dirt per day for almost 24 years? In terms of the amount of artifacts, can trade trips be made in a day or can such trips be ensured to take place on any regular schedule? Gibson (1987) rightly presents his labor equivalent as a heuristic and not as reflecting human action. In order to answer questions about how the occupants of Poverty Point might go about modifying their landscape or procuring raw materials, more context from a variety of data classes is needed.

Focusing on the uniqueness and enormity leads to seeing the people of Poverty Point as somehow outside the rest of prehistory and not being expected to fit our explanations. On the other hand, making the people of Poverty Point mindless automatons can be equally stultifying to understanding how they lived. We suggest that in order to understand the Poverty Point site and its people, a research strategy is needed that involves detailed analyses of individual classes of data and then assembling diverse lines of evidence to address a specific question. If each line of evidence supports a certain interpretation, then it can be accepted. If not, further investigation is necessary to resolve the ambiguity. Once a certain interpretation of a specific aspect of the Poverty Point lifeway is accepted, it provides the context for addressing new questions. After several such investigations are conducted, a general picture of life emerges. Forming this general picture will not end the cycle as each new investigation provides insight and cause for reconsidering previous interpretations. This strategy essentially models the efforts of Jon Gibson over the past 30 years and stands in contrast to more abstract discussions of the Poverty Point site and its people.

Here, we will provide a brief example of the first aspect of this approach and demonstrate its utility. While we have confidence in the research strategy for providing an understanding of Poverty Point and its people, the more extensive analyses we suggest will take significant amounts of time. This is particularly true given the size of the Poverty Point site and assemblage. One of us (LHS) is continuing this research as part of a Master's thesis. Despite the size of this task, we see this as the only means of deriving accurate answers for the questions we pose. Otherwise, equifinality will prove impossible to overcome.

When one considers how the lifeways of Archaic hunter-gatherers are generally described, it is easy to see why Poverty Point has caused such discussion. It is not uncommon to read that Archaic hunter-gatherers lived in small campsites, moved on a seasonal basis, and had an egalitarian social system. The "tyranny of the ethnographic record" (Wobst 1978) and the "San-itization" of the archaeological record (Isaac 1990) are readily apparent. The recent realization that the generalized foraging model based on ethnographic work with the !Kung San Bushmen has had a disproportionate effect on interpretations of the archaeological record has freed archaeologists to think in new ways (Kelly 1995). While the value of the ethnographic record cannot be denied for demonstrating how various cultural aspects are integrated and providing examples of cultural practices, it is increasingly recognized that archaeologists must consider the possibility that the behavior of prehistoric hunter-gatherers has no recorded ethnographic analog. The Poverty Point site and the culture that produced it might be one such example.

Gibson (1974) set the course for Poverty Point research when he made the case that it represented the first North American chiefdom. Additionally, he argued against the interpretation of significant Mesoamerican influence as previously postulated by Webb (1968) and Ford (1969). Gibson (1974:99) estimated between 4,000 and 5,000 people lived at Poverty Point with small villages (35–60 people) in the surrounding area. His evidence for redistribution and a chiefly lineage included exotic raw materials, production of ornaments, and distribution of these items (Gibson 1974:100–104). These issues of demography/nature of occupation, settlement pattern, political organization, and trade are the foci of subsequent Poverty Point research. It is noted that Gibson (1987, 1998, 2000, this volume) has collected new data and revised his thinking of these issues. The demography/nature of occupation of Poverty Point was characterized by Gibson

(1987) as the "great town" vs. "vacant ceremonial center" debate and involves the aforementioned issues as well, especially political organization. The great town argument is for a significant, year-round occupation of Poverty Point by thousands of people living in a socially differentiated society. For example, Williams and Brain (1983:399) apparently view Poverty Point as occupied by a substantial population and see "control of the society by an elite." Likewise, Kidder (1991:48) suggests a stratified and "presumably chiefdom level of political organization" through an examination of site types and reconstructed settlement hierarchy. On the other side, the vacant ceremonial center argument holds that Poverty Point was not occupied year round but rather visited periodically, and social relations were of a basic egalitarian nature with no chiefly elite. Jackson (1991) has provided an argument for a specific type of this case, which he refers to as an "Intersocietal Trade Fair." He views Poverty Point as a periodic, large, and spatially and temporally predictable gathering of unrelated hunter-gatherers (Jackson 1991:266). In addition to noting the wide variety of exotic materials at Poverty Point as evidence to support the trade fair model, Jackson suggests that the environment could not have supported the large population postulated in the great town model. Gibson (1987) used the Poverty Point earthworks as evidence to investigate this argument, but failed to resolve it with the data at hand and concluded more excavations at Poverty Point are needed. He argues, however, that the large population of the great town model could have been supported by the availability of fish (Gibson 1987:24).

In a recent publication, Gibson (1998a) examines several core components within 3.5 km of the rings and periphery components up to 40 km from the site to provide an alternative interpretation to the chiefly elite as part of the great town model. Gibson (1998a:328) argues that the Poverty Point earthworks and exotic trade materials indicate a corporate political strategy. In such a corporate strategy, "power is shared across different groups and sectors of society" (Blanton et al. 1996:2). This is not equivalent to egalitarian relations, because power sharing can be uneven or differ in the contexts in which it is exercised, but rather it is where one individual or subgroup does not have monopoly control over sources of power. Gibson (1998a:329) suggests that the Poverty Point earthworks and local distribution of exotic raw materials indicate a "group first, or team, mentality" that exemplifies corporate behavior.

This discussion demonstrates the diversity of interpretations of how the inhabitants of Poverty Point were organized and who, if anyone, exercised power. This goes beyond a general lack of agreement, as some interpretations are polar opposites. New data are needed to resolve these debates and should be derived from a variety of artifact classes. We will turn to the related issue of trade and later present data from our analysis of a small sample of the chipped-stone tool assemblage.

Trade, as a major focus of Poverty Point investigations, is obviously interrelated with the great town vs. vacant ceremonial center debate. However, researchers on the same side of this debate differ in their specific interpretations of the role of exotic materials and how trade was carried out. It is generally assumed that most exotic materials such as copper, galena, hematite, and magnetite were brought by "trade or travel in dugouts or rafts down the three great rivers: the Mississippi, the Ohio, and the Arkansas" (Walthall et al. 1982). Lafferty (1994:181) suggests that characteristics of the Mississippi River and its tributaries are "highly relevant to the structure and nature of trade and the growth of prehistoric centers." In particular, he suggests that the low gradient of the Mississippi River allowed for a lower cost in moving trade items up the river than that for other drainages. Gibson (1974, 1994b) maintains that the Poverty Point site was strategically located below the confluence of six major rivers, which are presumed to have served as trade routes.

Addressing Poverty Point exchange, Gibson (1994b:148–150) categorizes materials as local (within 100 km: Citronelle gravels, Catahoula sandstone, and quartzite), distant (100–300 km: novaculite, quartz crystals, magnetite/hematite, and possibly greenstone), and long distant (over 300 km: copper, galena, steatite, Dover/Fort Payne flint, Gray Northern Flint, and exotic white chert). While it is recognized that chert distributions are more extensive than shown, Figure 8.1 (after Gibson 1994b:fig. 1) shows the general location of the geologic sources for lithic materials identified in the Poverty Point assemblage. Trade managers are envisioned as operating within "intraregional and interregional ceremonial and perhaps diplomatic contexts, both internal and foreign affairs wrapped up in formalized shared or copied ritual experience" (Gibson 1994b:161). This view is elaborated in subsequent works (Gibson 1996a, 1999).

Gibson (1998a:332–334) sees exchange of exotics as a basic part of the political economy and through time entrepreneurial traders using rock giveaways to exaggerate social inequalities. At one time, Gibson (1974) argued for redistribution of such items as plummets and atlatl weights, but later he suggested that exotic chipped-stone tools were distributed locally in a much more utilitarian manner without control by elites (Gibson 1998a). In a differing view, Williams and Brain (1983:399) suggest that at Poverty Point a "professional group of prehistoric 'voyageurs' may have been employed full-time to gather and transport materials from their sources . . . the Poverty Point agents must have been extractors, not traders." In contrast, Bruseth (1991:22–23) characterizes Poverty Point as one of several "gateway communities" that controlled trade in an area. On the basis of a study of galena from Poverty Point and related sites, it was suggested that Poverty Point represents a "large regional exchange center" that "would have received disproportionate quantities of exotic commodities through a directional exchange medium" (Walthall et al. 1982:142). In con-

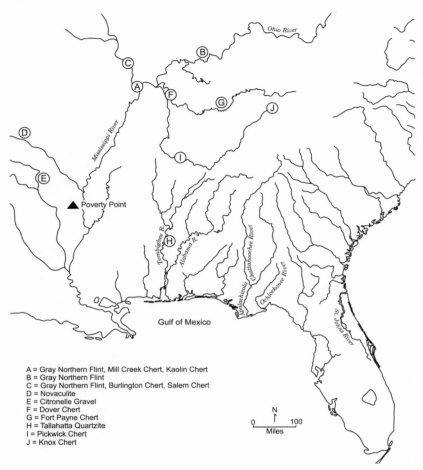

Figure 8.1. General source locations for lithic materials identified in the Poverty Point assemblage (after Gibson 1994b:fig. 1).

trast, the Intersocietal Trade Fair as postulated by Jackson (1991) has Poverty Point not as a gateway or regional exchange center but as a known aggregation site where hunter-gatherers from various groups engaged in exchange. Interestingly, Webb (1991:3) sees a probable role for direct trade, trade through intermediaries, and centrally controlled trade in the evidence from Poverty Point.

It is clear that the manner one views the demography/nature of occupation of Poverty Point provides something of a foundation for how the social-political organization is interpreted and vice versa. The manner that trade is conceptualized by different researchers is generally derived from this foundation and reflects the diversity of ideas concerning organization and power at Poverty Point. On the other hand, an understanding of trade can provide the context for more accurately characterizing the manner that power was distributed and labor organized.

We see utility in the research by Gibson (1987) wherein one line of data, the earthworks, is used to consider the question of great town vs. vacant ceremonial center. Although he failed to resolve the debate at that time, such detailed analyses are needed if we are ever to move beyond presenting alternative scenarios based as much on preconceived notions as on data. We attempt to emulate that research through an examination of the chipped-stone tool assemblage and consideration of trade. Further, we see great utility in Gibson's (1998a) discussion of temporal change at Poverty Point, but this is beyond the scope of this chapter.

RESEARCH APPROACH

The approach that we suggest here is nothing new but simply represents a commitment to a series of steps to ensure an accurate understanding of prehistoric behavior. We are essentially advocating a falsificationist strategy that involves bringing multiple lines of evidence to bear on the same research question. This ambitious research approach will not be accomplished in a single study but is a long-term strategy for better understanding the archaeological record of Poverty Point and any other site.

The Poverty Point site obviously offers a wide variety of data and artifact classes for use in a multiple lines of evidence approach. Here, we will only explore one such line of evidence: chipped-stone tool raw materials. The questions we consider are the manner raw materials were acquired by inhabitants of the Poverty Point site and how this reflects the social-political organization. Additional lines of evidence explored in the future could be based on other artifact classes such as cooking balls, soapstone, earthworks, or artifact styles.

The lack of consensus concerning the nature of site occupation, political organization, and trade means that there is not a solid context for situating the current study. A variety of possible scenarios are examined here and evaluated on the basis of preliminary evidence from the chipped-stone tool assemblage. The number of scenarios is not exhaustive as this study represents a first step in a long-term research project and a more detailed analysis of a larger sample may cause reconsideration of how individual scenarios are evaluated.

We adopt an organization of technology approach to the analysis of the chipped-stone tool raw materials (Carr 1994). In brief, this approach suggests that artifact form and distribution are reflective of the technological, social, and economic strategies employed by a group of people given a particular set of environmental conditions, especially raw material availability (Nelson 1991:59).

One assumption of this approach is that when everything else is equal, people will choose to minimize effort and maximize return.

Researchers generally discuss two mechanisms for lithic materials to enter a site: direct and indirect acquisition (Meltzer 1989:12). Direct acquisition involves individuals of a group going to a source area, either a primary or secondary geologic context, to obtain raw materials and then transporting them to a site. Conversely, indirect acquisition is the situation in which stone is acquired by one group from a source and transferred to another group. Indirect acquisition is synonymous with exchange. These mechanisms should not be confused with Binford's (1979) distinction between direct and embedded procurement that involves whether stone procurement was the secondary or primary activity of a particular foray.

It is not a simple task to determine whether materials were acquired directly or indirectly. In an excellent discussion of this issue, Meltzer (1989:30) concludes, "there do not seem to be clear cut rules for sorting direct from indirect acquisition in any deterministic fashion." While lawlike generalizations may not be possible, detailed data combined with knowledge of historical factors and the general economic and social strategies employed by a group can allow one to make a case for either direct or indirect acquisition. Consensus among researchers of the nature of such economic and social strategies is limited for the occupants of Poverty Point, and we have generated only preliminary data for lithic materials. Here, we will outline more specifically some of the ways that stone was acquired and later compare these scenarios with the available data. These scenarios are presented at a relatively general scale and a more nuanced consideration would refine the expectations and results, but our goal at this time is not to come to a conclusion concerning the lifeways of Poverty Point people but to suggest possibilities for further consideration.

Previous researchers have documented that the Poverty Point site is in an area completely devoid of what is traditionally termed local lithic raw materials. The closest source of lithic material for the manufacture of chipped-stone tools is gravel chert located 40 km west of Poverty Point (Gibson 1994b). Consider this choice of site location in comparison to that of Watson Brake (Saunders, this volume), which is situated at a source of local gravel chert (Johnson 2000). While there are alternative materials to stone for the manufacture of tools, such as deer antler for projectile points, stone was an important part of the economy despite not being readily available.

DIRECT ACQUISITION

Direct acquisition is the most straightforward way that stone materials reached an archaeological site. In this case, residents of the Poverty Point site acquired

Table 8.1. Implications for various occupation scenarios for direct acquisition

	Quantity	Quality	Diversity	Form	Local
Foragers	Small	Available	Low	CT	Low
Aggregation	Medium	Medium/High	High	CT	Low
Collectors	Medium	High	Medium	PR	High
Trade fair	Small	Medium/High	High	CT/PR	Low
Voyageurs	Large	High	Medium	CT/PR	High

CT = Curated tools; PR = partially reduced.

materials at a primary outcrop or secondary geologic deposit. This could either be direct procurement, in which individuals went to the geologic source for the explicit purpose of obtaining stone, or embedded procurement, in which stone acquisition was incidental to other activities. Implications for the direct acquisition of stone by Poverty Point inhabitants are shown in Table 8.1.

If Poverty Point was occupied seasonally by a group of foragers (sensu Binford 1980), then we might expect that these individuals procured stone before moving to the Poverty Point site. They would have known they were moving to a site without stone in the immediate area. These individuals would have organized their movements to ensure that adequate stone was brought to the site and would have "geared up" with the best quality materials available by manufacturing curated tools for immediate use. Citronelle gravel sources are effectively beyond what is considered a normal range for foraging so this type of stone would only be at the site as part of gearing-up efforts prior to establishing residence.

If Poverty Point was an aggregation site for multiple bands of foragers, we might expect a greater diversity of stone sources to have been acquired before they moved to Poverty Point. This is because each band would journey from a different section of the home range. In other respects, lithic material usage is expected to be relatively similar to that of a forager residence. The one exception is that foragers at an aggregation site would likely plan on some trading of lithic material. However, trade in bulk of chippable stone is not likely because of the constraints of high residential mobility.

The occupation of Poverty Point by more residentially stable collectors would result in task groups directly procuring stone from geologic sources or in embedded stone procurement during logistical forays. These collectors would also gear up prior to taking residence at Poverty Point, bringing finished tools of nonlocal materials. In overall amount, collectors are expected to make the greatest use of immediate sources and would have engaged in stockpiling of those materials (sensu Parry and Kelly 1987).

The Intersocietal Trade Fair model is expected to show similar patterns to those of an aggregation site, but this model would result in the greatest diversity

Table 8.2. Implications for various occupation scenarios for indirect acquisition

	Quantity	Quality	Diversity	Form	Local
Down-line	Medium	Medium/High	High	CT	High
Trade at source	Large	Medium/High	High	CT/PR	Medium/High
Nonlocal traders	Large	Medium/High	High	CT/PR	High
Elite directed	Medium	High	Medium	CT	Medium/High

CT = Curated tools; PR = partially reduced.

of lithic materials through direct acquisition. That is, individuals are expected to have directly acquired the majority of lithic materials prior to moving to Poverty Point to conduct extensive trading. The lack of long-term use of the site as postulated in the model would mean little to no use of local materials, except in the case of groups in the general area gearing up prior to occupying Poverty Point.

The final example of direct acquisition considered here is the sedentary "voyageurs" model (sensu Williams and Brain 1983) in which a special group of Poverty Point occupants extract materials from distant sources. Presumably, these voyageurs would procure only the highest quality materials and return with finished tools or partially manufactured tools in order to maximize the load for each trip.

INDIRECT ACQUISITION

Indirect acquisition can produce an even wider array of potential scenarios for lithic material acquisition by the occupants of the Poverty Point site, but only a few examples are considered here (Table 8.2). For each of these scenarios, it is assumed that indirect acquisition indicates a residentially sedentary population at Poverty Point.

Classic down-the-line trading would result in a small quantity of extralocal materials because of the distance that they are moved and the potential number of hands through which the items are passed. This would result in a heavy dependence on local gravel sources by the residents of Poverty Point. Extralocal materials should enter the site as finished tools. In this scenario, flake debris density of these extralocal sources would be low and represent predominately the late stages of reduction.

In the case most similar to direct acquisition, occupants of Poverty Point might go to the geologic source but, because they have crossed territorial boundaries, engage in exchange for the materials with people who consider that source within their territory. Nonlocal materials would enter the site as tools or partially reduced in order to ensure the bargain. Site occupants would likely need to supplement the lithic material supply with local gravel sources.

Indirect acquisition might be in the form of individuals from other groups coming to trade directly with Poverty Point occupants. Traders are expected to bring materials of medium to high quality that are partially reduced or fashioned into finished tools in order to demonstrate that quality. Depending on another group to supply stone for tools is potentially unreliable and some use of local sources is expected in order to counter this.

The final form of indirect acquisition considered here is that directed by elites. The trade of materials from one important site or node to another that is directed by elites for their benefit is expected to involve finished tools of the highest quality materials. Use of local materials is expected by individuals who do not benefit from the distribution of these nonlocal materials.

POVERTY POINT CHIPPED-STONE TOOL RAW MATERIALS

In discussing our analysis of the chipped-stone tool assemblage from the Poverty Point site with various archaeologists, we have been surprised at the amount of resistance to the possibility that raw materials originated from sources other than relatively local gravel bars. This is surprising given the general acceptance of the trade of other materials such as galena and soapstone. For example, Bass (1981) argues that gray and white cherts found in the Poverty Point assemblage are available in the local gravels. However, her study was restricted to microliths and she does not confirm the presence of specific chert types, such as Fort Payne, Dover, Burlington, and so on, in the local gravel sources. In another example, Gibson (1994b:132) found that "when occasional chunks or large flakes are found, they inevitably exhibit outcrop or large-nodule characteristics . . . rarely seen in local gravels." We would ask the question, if the materials from Poverty Point that are classified as exotic are readily available in local gravel bars, why are other Archaic hunter-gatherers in the area not making more use of this source? Both in this study and the work by Gibson (1994b), chalky cortex is identified on some pieces, and this cortex is not found on chert from secondary deposits far from the primary geologic source. While more research is needed to understand what lithic materials were available in gravel bars, an a priori conclusion that all or the majority of the chippable stone in the Poverty Point assemblage was acquired from secondary gravel sources is not supported by available data.

LITHIC MATERIAL IDENTIFICATION

James Ford and Clarence Webb (1956) knew that the lithic materials from Poverty Point represented materials outside their expertise to identify, and they sought help from experts in other regions. For example, a gray chert with a waxy, glasslike surface was sent to Raymond Baby (Ohio State Museum), Irving Peith-mann (Southern Illinois University), and Glenn Black (Indiana Historical So-ciety) for identification and two of these researchers expressed confidence that some of the gray stone was Harrison County chert from Indiana. Ford and Webb (1956:125–126) established 12 source areas for Poverty Point exotic materials, of which six were considered as the origin of some of the chipped-stone tool raw materials. Conn (1976) also worked with numerous archaeologists and geolo-gists from eastern North America to identify chert types in the Poverty Point assemblage. He concluded that lithic materials came to the site from five geo-graphic areas: west-central Arkansas, the southern Illinois–eastern Missouri area, the upper Ohio River valley, the Tennessee River valley, and locally. In the surface sample of materials he analyzed, two-thirds were from distant sources. However, the small size of local gravel cherts and the flakes produced from such nodules might preclude their collection from the surface. This makes the high percentage of nonlocal chert somewhat suspect and in need of testing with a screened collection from excavations.

The greatest sustained effort in the identification of lithic materials in the Poverty Point assemblage has been conducted by Gibson (1974, 1994b, 1998a). Recognizing the potential problems with macroscopic identification of lithic ma-terial types and the difficulty in making comparisons between analysts, Gibson (1994b) uses some relatively broad, descriptive categories such as "Gray North-ern Flint" and "exotic white chert." He also has identified specific chert types such as Mill Creek (Illinois), Flint Ridge (Ohio), and Pickwick (Alabama). In his analysis of 3,046 pieces of chipped stone, Gibson (1994b:table 4) reports 47.3 percent local gravel, 0.4 percent orthoquartzite, 3.3 percent novaculite, 26.7 percent Gray Northern Flint, 12.8 percent exotic white chert, and 9.4 per-cent other exotic chert (see Figure 8.1 for general source locations).

ANALYSIS

We began our investigation of the Poverty Point lithic assemblage much as pre-vious researchers have as an attempt to better characterize the specifics of the source areas for the chipped-stone tool lithic materials. Because of the immen-sity of the collection, we employed a macroscopic approach. Also, as with pre-vious researchers, we sought the aid of regional experts in chipped-stone tool raw materials to either confirm our assignment of a specific source or contra-dict it.

After consulting with regional experts and building a comparative collection based on geological materials as well as specimens drawn from the Poverty Point assemblage, each of us worked to identify the raw materials from a unit-level bag. Next, the other person worked through the identified materials and noted any questionable assignments. These were then discussed and a final decision was made. An "Other" category was employed for materials that did not appear similar to any in our comparative collections or for which we could not agree on the assignment. Many of the unidentified artifacts are small pieces of flake debris that lack the diagnostic characteristics needed to make a definite decision.

Here, we report on the analysis of 1,021 pieces of flake debris from Units N5656/E5146 and N5653/E5163. These units were excavated under the supervision of Gibson and were screened through one-quarter-inch mesh. To supplement this sample, we also provide data from the examination of flake debris surface-collected at Poverty Point. The analysis of the surface collection was conducted by only one of us (PJC).

As witness to our cautious approach and the difficulty in identifying small pieces of flake debris, 31.8 percent (n = 325) of the material from the unit excavations is classified as Other. The next highest percentage is for Gray Northern Flint (20.2 percent; n = 206). We initially attempted to divide this category into specific chert types such as Cobden-Dongola, St. Genevieve, and so on, but the task was too difficult. Additionally, some of these cherts have expansive geographic ranges and are referred to differently in various states, which exacerbates the identification problem. We did feel confident in sorting Dover and Fort Payne chert from the Gray Northern Flint category, as did Gibson (1998a), and these materials make up 10.5 percent (n = 107) and 8.0 percent (n = 82) of the assemblage, respectively. Local gravel chert (13.5 percent; n = 138) and Burlington chert (12.5 percent; n = 128) make up a larger percentage of the assemblage than either Fort Payne or Dover. The remaining materials all occur in very small percentages: Mill Creek chert (1.1 percent; n = 11) novaculite (0.9 percent; n = 9), Kaolin chert (0.6 percent; n = 6), Salem chert (0.4 percent; n = 4), Fern Glenn chert (0.2 percent; n = 2), Johns Valley shale (0.1 percent; n = 1), Knox chert (0.1 percent; n = 1), and Tallahatta quartzite (0.1 percent; n = 1). General source areas for these materials are shown in Figure 8.1.

Nearly all of the flakes from the surface-collected sample (n = 1,024) are larger than those from the unit excavations. We do not suggest that the percentages of particular materials are comparable between the two samples or that these are representative of the site. However, the surface-collected assemblage does provide some interesting insights into the question of gravel sources and quality of the materials. Despite the larger size of the majority of these flakes, 27.5 percent (n = 282) are classified as Other. Gray Northern Flint makes up 37.9 percent (n = 389) and, interestingly, 15.7 percent (n = 61) of the Gray Northern Flint exhibits primary cortex. This latter characteristic indicates procurement of this material was from the primary geologic source, not from river gravel bars. Dover (13.4 percent; n = 137), Fort Payne (10.4 percent; n = 107), and Burlington (6.7 percent; n = 68) cherts are the next most abundant in the sample. As was the case with the Gray Northern Flint, some of each also exhibit primary cortex (Dover, 3.6 percent; Fort Payne, 0.9 percent; Burlington, 0.1 percent). The most interesting aspect of the Burlington sample is the high percentage that is low quality (46.4 percent; n = 32). The quality of the Burlington chert was not assessed in the sample from the unit excavations, but one of the regional experts remarked on its less-than-desirable flaking qualities. The remaining lithic materials all occur in low percentages, and these include novaculite (1.7 percent; n = 18), local gravel (1.4 percent, n = 14), Mill Creek chert (0.3 percent; n = 3), Bigby Cannon chert (0.3 percent; n = 3), Kaolin chert (0.2 percent; n = 2), and crystal quartz (0.1 percent; n = 1). While a formal technological analysis was not undertaken, a surprising amount of the flake debris exhibits characteristics indicative of early-stage reduction. Coupled with the large size, this suggests that not all of the lithic material reaching the site was modified before arrival.

Much work remains before specific conclusions can be drawn concerning the use of specific source areas through time (i.e., sorting out the Gray Northern Flint category), the contribution of primary vs. secondary sources, and in what form particular materials entered the site and, then, how these materials were reduced after arrival. Answers to these questions will greatly clarify our understanding of the acquisition of raw materials as well as the economic and social strategies in use. On the basis of our work and that by Gibson, we are comfortable in making four broad statements concerning the chipped-stone tool assemblage from Poverty Point: (1) large quantities of chipped stone entered the Poverty Point site; (2) a great diversity of lithic materials is represented and the materials were derived from a variety of source areas; (3) there is considerable variation in the quality of the chipped-stone tool raw materials; and (4) at least some of the chipped-stone tool raw materials entered the site with little or no modification.

Direct Acquisition

The expectations based on the direct acquisition scenarios do not closely fit the data presented here. The majority involved residentially mobile hunter-gatherers and the quantity of materials was expected to be small or medium. In contrast, the great quantity of chipped stone at Poverty Point fits only the voyageurs model under direct acquisition in which materials would be stockpiled for long-term use. However, none of the scenarios were expected to include low-quality materials, which are present in the assemblage. With regard to the diversity of materials, the data fit best with the high expectations for an aggregation site or the trade fair model. On the other hand, all of these scenarios were expected to involve materials entering the site as tools or minimally as partially reduced, and this does not fit the data. Finally, the use of local gravels does not fit with the trade fair scenario. Overall, the data presented here do not strongly support any of the direct acquisition scenarios.

Indirect Acquisition

The scenarios for indirect acquisition fit more closely with the results of our analysis. This is in large part because all of these assume a sedentary residential population, which would suggest the need for a large quantity of lithic materials. Quality and the form of materials are two aspects that still do not fit any of the scenarios discussed. It is hard to imagine a situation in which low-quality lithic materials are brought long distances and in an unreduced or minimally reduced form. This is particularly true if you are going to engage in trade and want to ensure a return on your efforts. Each of these scenarios, except directed trade by elites, is expected to result in a high diversity of lithic materials, as is evidenced by the data. However, a greater use of local gravels is expected in all of the indirect acquisition scenarios than is supported by the data.

In summary, the quantity of lithic material at Poverty Point suggests a sedentary residential group who engaged in stockpiling raw materials. The quality and form of the material do not fit our expectations for traders interested in optimizing their return. The diversity is suggestive of far-flung trade routes, and the relatively low use of local gravels indicates that having to fall back on this smaller-sized material was not often necessary. Taken together, the data do not match any specific indirect acquisition scenario.

DISCUSSION

The diversity of materials represented in the Poverty Point assemblage could be driven by different lineages living at the site establishing their own trade relations with various groups. Perhaps each lineage attempted to build its own stockpile and quantity was more important than quality. The size of the stockpile could be indicative of status or size of the lineage. If one was attempting to maximize the size of the stockpile as opposed to maximizing return through trading, then unmodified lithic material might be desired. For the purpose of a giveaway, however, it is suggested that low-quality materials and unmodified pieces would be ineffective. Engaging in redistribution through giveaways would fit the distribution of lithic materials in the core and periphery of the Poverty Point site as observed by Gibson (1998a).

The scenario we envision need not only involve lineages and giveaways but could simply represent individuals in a corporate political economy in which generalized reciprocity rules over stone. In such a case, adding quantity to the stockpile may be more important than bringing the highest quality material in a modified form. This scenario could include individuals from far-flung regions coming to Poverty Point—but not for trade. These individuals might make the journey for protection (Gibson 1998a) or for the purpose of some other pilgrimage. As a good guest, one brings a gift of stone.

CONCLUSIONS

We have succeeded in demonstrating the role a single line of evidence, chipped-stone tool raw material, can play in examining the efficacy of different scenarios of Poverty Point social and political economy, as well as suggesting new scenarios for study. The chipped-stone tool assemblage needs additional analysis as the sample sizes discussed here are too small to be representative, but the utility of this artifact class for providing pertinent information is clearly illustrated. In addition to increasing the sample size, a more detailed examination of the chipped-stone tools and flake debris is needed. Such an analysis should focus on technological aspects of the lithic assemblage such as how specific raw materials are brought to the site as finished tools, partially reduced tools, unreduced nodules, cores, and so on and how those materials are treated once at Poverty Point. Recent research into levels of stone tool production (Carr and Bradbury 2001) has great potential for aiding in the interpretation of the assemblage. Once this is accomplished for different areas of the site over time, the specific answers will begin to emerge from the lithic analysis.

Much additional work at Poverty Point and with existing assemblages remains to be accomplished. Other lines of data should be investigated to examine the suggestions concerning the corporate nature of the economy and stockpiling/giveaways by lineages or to determine if some other scenario best fits the data.

ACKNOWLEDGMENTS

All contemporary work at Poverty Point owes a great debt to Jon Gibson, and we in particular share that debt. Jon has continually worked to better our understanding of this awesome site and his efforts have resulted in the availability of finely controlled, excavated collections, data to consider, and hypotheses to ponder. Jon also encouraged our interest in specifically working with the Poverty Point collection and provided access to some of his excavated material for this paper and the forthcoming thesis by one of us (LHS). We deeply value Jon as a scholar, researcher, and friend. PJC acknowledges access to the surface-collected material provided by Poverty Point State Park and this was made possible by Robert Connolly and Dennis LaBatt. We thank John Clark for providing comments on an earlier version of this paper and sending us off in a totally new direction, although not one suggested by him. Many thanks are due to our regional lithic experts, Andrew Bradbury and Brad Koldehoff. Their willingness to ponder and argue the geologic origin of hundreds of flakes made this study possible. Andrew also provided comments on an almost complete manuscript as did Amy Young, and their suggestions helped clarify our discussion. All misidentifications and errors of logic are the responsibility of the authors.

9
Are We Fixing to Make the Same Mistake Again?

Joe Saunders

The identification of mounds dating to ca. 5000–6000 B.P. has required archae-ologists to rethink the process of social evolution. The existence of Archaic mounds provides us with one of those rare research opportunities of a win-win situation. Archaic period mounds are significant if they were constructed by societies with social inequality, and they are equally significant if they were constructed by egalitarian cultures. On the one hand, we extend traditional models (social inequality) back almost two thousand years earlier than previ-ously thought; on the other hand, we break the traditional bond between monu-mental architecture and social inequality, an element often considered necessary for the construction of public architecture.

In many respects, the choice we must entertain is an excellent example of Kuhn's proposed growth of knowledge in a normal science (Kuhn 1962). Stan-dard interpretations or theories (paradigms) accommodate new data that do not fit the established explanation (anomalies). Initially the anomalies are treated as unique, exceptions to the rule, or as outliers to the norm. As anomalies accumu-late, adjustments to the established explanation are made, until the anomalous data reach critical mass, forcing researchers to offer alternative explanations that embrace the old as well as the new observations (Lakatos 1970).

In our particular case, traditional models of social evolution have proposed a number of preconditions or co-occurrences that are associated with societies that construct monumental architecture.[1] Initially, various material and social traits included agriculture, pottery, sedentism, trade, and social inequality (Ford and Willey 1941; Fried 1967; Johnson and Earle 1987; Service 1975; Willey and Phillips 1958:146). With the excavations and dating of Jaketown (Ford et al. 1955; Phillips et al. 1951) and Poverty Point (Ford 1954, 1955a, 1955b; Ford and Webb 1956), the precondition/co-occurrence of pottery was aban-doned. Although there was no evidence for plant domestication at Poverty Point, it was viewed as a necessity for sustaining a large population at the site (Willey and Phillips 1958:156). Gradually, however, agriculture was excluded as a prerequisite from the general model (Johnson and Earle 1987; Price and Brown 1985) and for Poverty Point in particular (Gibson 1973; Webb 1982; Williams and Brain 1983), with perhaps the assumed co-occurrence of plant domestication, mound construction, and social inequality being laid to rest with evidence that domesticated plants were at best supplementary foods for later ceramic cultures (Bender 1985a; Kidder and Fritz 1993). Evidence for sedentism at Poverty Point also was challenged (Jackson 1991; Williams and Brain 1983), leaving trade (Gibson 1994c; Lehmann 1991; Smith 1991) as the sole independent variable suggesting an association between monumental architecture and social inequality. Consequently, Poverty Point was considered to be an aberration (Smith 1986). Although the site's existence refuted many of the preconceived notions about social evolution, because it was an outlier, it did not disprove the general model. Besides that, there was trade.

The identification of multiple Archaic mound sites in the Southeast (Connaway et al. 1977; Gagliano 1967; Manuel 1983; Neuman 1985; Russo 1996a; Russo et al. 1991; Russo and Fogleman 1994; Saunders and Allen 1994; Saunders et al. 1997; Saunders et al. 2000; Saunders et al. 2001) has eliminated the anomalous status of Poverty Point.[2] Many sites with monumental architecture date to ca. 5000 years B.P., approximately 1,500 years before Poverty Point. Site testing indicates that the subsistence base was nonagricultural, and, in fact, most of the sites were only occupied seasonally. Furthermore, at least for the Archaic sites in Louisiana, trade was negligible. Therefore, trade too was not a necessary trait, or substitute precondition, for the emergence of social inequality and monumental architecture. These data show that mound sites were constructed without pottery, plant domestication, sedentism, or trade. The only precondition left is social inequality—and among the original traits, the remaining evidence for unequal status among these early mound builders is the mounds themselves, which is circular reasoning. Social inequality is necessary for mound construction because such undertakings require planning, construction, and provisioning, which in turn require leadership. Therefore where you have mounds, you have social inequality. Essentially, we are left with a choice: either social disparity was necessary for mound construction, or it was not. Unfortunately, too often the choice is determined more by one's theoretical preference than by the evidence for the presence or absence of social inequality in the archaeological record.

The purpose of this chapter is to determine whether there is evidence for social inequality among the builders of Archaic mound sites in northeast Louisiana. The thesis is quite simple: if monumental architecture signifies social inequality (Moore 1996; Wason 1994), evidence independent of mounds themselves should exist in other aspects of the archaeological record. The source, cause, or prime mover of social disparity is not important (population pressure, circumscription, environment, abundance, warfare, or others), only the empirical evidence for its social existence. In this study, all theories concerning the origins/causes/sources of inequality are treated equally. The interest is in how various theories define archaeological evidence in nonegalitarian cultures and whether it exists at Archaic mound sites, not the correctness of a theory.

Two mound groups, Watson Brake[3] (Figure 9.1) and Frenchman's Bend Mounds (Figure 9.2), and one open site with one possible small mound (15 m × 0.3 m), Plum Creek Archaic,[4] will be examined for the bulk of that evidence. All three sites are located along the edge of the Pleistocene terrace. Each site is less than 1 km from the location at that time of the Arkansas River channel (Saucier 1994), adjacent to backswamp areas, and within approximately 35 km of one another (Figure 1.1). Radiocarbon assays from in situ midden deposits indicate that the sites are roughly contemporaneous, dating between ca. 5000 and 5700 B.P. They share the same material culture, including Evans points, fired earthen blocks (Saunders et al. 1998), fire-cracked rock, and lithic blade technology. Each site has midden deposits with excellent faunal preservation, although the faunal sample from Frenchman's Bend Mounds was collected using a quarter-inch-mesh screen, while eighth-inch mesh was used at Watson Brake and Plum Creek Archaic. A total of 17 test units (eight 1.5 × 1 m, nine 1 × 1 m) were excavated at Watson Brake, four units (three 1.5 × 1 m, one .5 × .5 m) at Frenchman's Bend Mounds, and one unit (1.5 × 1 m) at Plum Creek Archaic.

THE DATA

Empirical evidence for social inequality can be divided into two groups: categorical and distributional. Categorical data are measured by their presence/absence on sites; distributional data are measured through comparisons among sites. Examples of each are employed here, but the majority are of the categorical type.

CATEGORICAL DATA

Plant Domestication

Although plant domestication no longer is considered a necessary prerequisite for social inequality (Brown 1985; Johnson and Earle 1987; Price and Brown 1985), Price (1995:130) argues that "the initial indications of status differentiation are associated with the beginnings of farming" and, furthermore, that "there are no known examples among prehistoric hunter-gatherers in which hereditary inequality is unequivocally present."

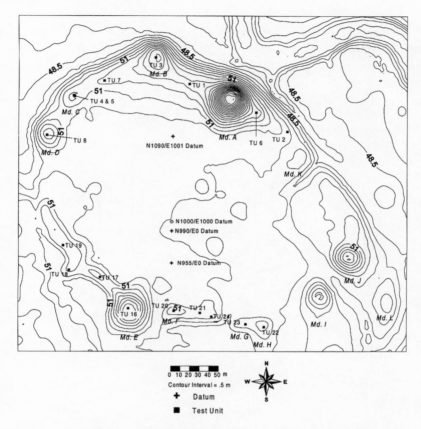

Figure 9.1. Topographic map of Watson Brake. Note possible Mound L southeast of Mound J.

During site occupation of Watson Brake, Frenchman's Bend Mounds, and Plum Creek Archaic, the adjoining floodplains probably contained large tracts of swamps and small streams (Saunders et al. 1994). The ages and locations of the sites match the preadaptive setting for the domestication of goosefoot (*Chenopodium berlandieri*) and marshelder (*Iva annua*) as suggested by Smith (Smith et al. 1992).

Charred seeds from a submound midden and Stage I in Mound B at Watson Brake include goosefoot, possibly marshelder, and knotweed (*Polygonum* spp.). None of the seeds display morphological characteristics suggestive of plant domestication (Saunders et al. 1997). Although these plants may have been "quasi-cultigens" (Smith 1992a), the subsistence economy of Watson Brake (Saunders et al. 1997), Frenchman's Bend Mounds (Russo in Saunders 1993), and Plum Creek Archaic folk was fishing, hunting, and gathering.

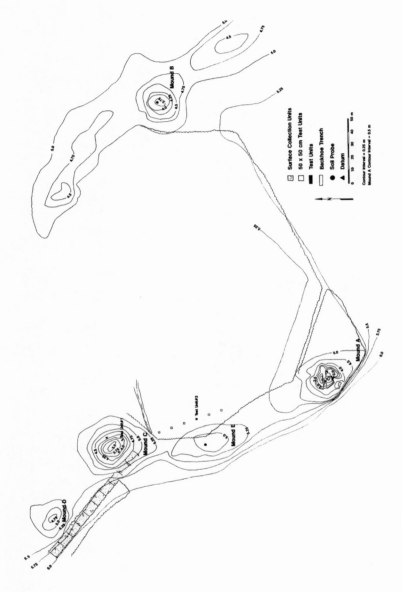

Figure 9.2. Topographic map of Frenchman's Bend Mounds.

Sedentism

Kelly (1995:148) defines sedentism as the condition in which a human group, or at least part of the population, remains at a site year-round. Sedentism is frequently viewed as an indication of social inequality (Brown 1985; Kelly 1992).

The submound midden and Stage I midden from Mound B at Watson Brake contained over 23,000 bone fragments examined by Jackson et al. (2001). Fish remains make up over 50 percent of the assemblage, while upland species (deer, rabbit, squirrel, and turkey) compose about 35 percent of the sample. Freshwater drum is the most abundant species captured. Juvenile drum are common, suggesting fishing occurred during spring spawns. Seasonal analysis of 78 of the 111 fish otoliths from the two middens found that most of the fish were caught in the spring-summer-fall and only 7.6 percent (n = 6) of the seasonally specific specimens were caught in the winter (Stringer 2001). Ageable deer remains suggest fall-winter hunting (Jackson et al. 2001). Floral remains from the submound and Stage I midden in Mound B include species that ripen in spring through fall; among these are goosefoot, marshelder, muscadine, spike rush, and caric sedge.[5] Fall mast crops of hickory and acorn also were recovered (Allen 1996).

The preliminary analysis of over 8,000 bone fragments from Plum Creek Archaic by Sheffield (in Jackson et al. 2001) has identified 80 percent fish and approximately 15 percent mammal remains. As at Watson Brake, drum was the most abundant species captured. The composition of the fauna and preliminary analysis of fish otoliths (Stringer, personnel communication, 2001) suggest a spring-summer-fall occupation at the site.

The size of the faunal assemblage (n = 887) from Frenchman's Bend Mounds is inadequate to assess seasonality. Nevertheless, over 90 percent of the identifiable pieces were of fish. The small sample shows that the economy of the site was based on riverine resources (Russo in Saunders 1993), as at Watson Brake and Plum Creek Archaic.

The data from Watson Brake indicate a predominately spring-summer-fall occupation and less intense site occupation in the winter. Preliminary analysis of the Plum Creek Archaic data also indicates spring-summer-fall site utilization, with no evidence for wintertime occupation.

Storage

Many authors list storage as an important marker for sedentism and social inequality (Arnold 1996a; Brown 1985; Ingold 1983; Johnson and Earle 1987; Keeley 1988; Testart 1982; Woodburn 1982). The most common evidence cited for storage is the presence of pits.

The excavations at Watson Brake revealed one pit in the adjoining platform of Mound A. The pit is in mound fill, between 100 and 130 cm below the surface. It is circular, measuring 30 cm in diameter and approximately 30 cm in depth, with a basin-shaped base. The surface of the feature is not associated with a buried A horizon. However, an Evans point, a bead blank, and a small cluster of fired earthen block fragments occur at approximately the same depth as the top of the pit feature, suggesting an ephemeral occupational surface before mound/platform construction resumed. The contents were organically enriched sediments, very little charcoal, some fire-cracked rock, small pieces of burnt clay, and a possible piece of burnt bone. The ephemeral status of the occupational surface suggests short-term use of the feature, of which storage does not appear to be a logical candidate.

Three irregularly shaped depressions were recorded in the submound/ridge surface at Watson Brake. The depressions extended between 15 and 25 cm into the subsoil of the Prairie terrace. The artifact content of the features was qualitatively similar to the midden matrix. No increase or decrease in the density of fire-cracked rock, charcoal, block fragments, lithics, or bone was detected. The functions of these features are not known, but a natural origin should not be ruled out (e.g., tree fall).

An oval, stepped pit feature was located beneath a shell lens at Plum Creek Archaic. The shell lens was covered by approximately 40–50 cm of midden fill. The top of the pit feature in turn was beneath the shell lens, suggesting a separate depositional event. The pit extended into the Prairie terrace approximately 25 cm. The density of mussel and aquatic snail shell, fire-cracked rock, charcoal, fired earthen block fragments, and lithic debitage was not noticeably greater than artifact recovery from the superimposed shell midden. Its function is unknown. No pit features were observed at Frenchman's Bend Mounds.

Structures

Public architecture is considered one of the most significant attributes of complex social structure (Brown and Price 1985; Feldman 1987; Johnson and Earle 1987; Moore 1996; Price 1995). While no evidence of such was observed at Plum Creek Archaic, provocative data are available from Frenchman's Bend Mounds and there are some equivocal indications at Watson Brake.

Extensive evidence of structures other than earthworks has been recovered at Frenchman's Bend Mounds. A test unit excavation in Mound A exposed a line of three postholes in the submound surface (2Ab horizon). A virtually artifact-free prepared surface of 1–2 cm of silt loam extended at least 2 m (limits of the test units) from one side of the posthole line, suggesting that a floor was associated with the wall of a structure.

A test unit in Mound C defined a sequence of three floors sandwiched between the Pleistocene terrace surface and the base of the mound. The profiles of the three superimposed floors were continuously exposed in the four walls of the 1.5-x-1-m test unit. A cylindrical hearth extended through the three floors into the submound surface, suggesting that the floors were constructed in rapid succession. One small post (ca. 10 cm in diameter) extended through the three floors into the terrace subsoil and two shallow postholes may be associated with the lowermost floor. A soil core from Mound E identified two superimposed floors between the mound base and the Pleistocene surface.

The architectural features at Frenchman's Bend Mounds appear to be non-domestic. Each feature is covered with a mound, suggesting a ceremonial rather than a residential function. The surface of the floor under Mound A was artifact free, while only a few pieces of fire-cracked rock, debitage, cobbles, and bone fragments were found on the three floors beneath Mound C.

At Watson Brake, a mottled surface between the base of Mound B and the submound midden may represent a poorly preserved/constructed floor, but its status is very questionable. One isolated posthole is associated with the feature. Two postholes within 10 cm of one another were located in the subridge surface between Mound A and Mound K. The two postholes extended into the sub-mound surface 20 cm.

Trade

As previously noted, trade has been considered as evidence of social inequality (see Drennan 1996). In contrast to the manifold evidence for trade at Poverty Point (Gibson 1994b, 1994c; Lehmann 1991; Smith 1991; Webb 1982), there are virtually no imported raw materials at Watson Brake (Johnson 2000), no evidence of trade at Frenchman's Bend Mounds, and only one novaculite flake (central Arkansas) at Plum Creek Archaic. Instead of imported material being selected for the production of specific types of artifacts (Gibson 1999, 2000), as seen at Poverty Point, lithic artifacts of all types from the Middle Archaic mound sites were made of local raw material, with an apparent preference for tan chert. Only a few nonlocal artifacts have been recovered from Watson Brake: these include one piece of slate (probable origin is the Ouachita River valley in Arkansas), one novaculite thinning flake, and a hematite plummet of Poverty Point style, which is assumed to be intrusive (ca. 60 cm below the surface in a disturbed area of Mound B, Test Unit 16) and is one of only two genuine Poverty Point artifacts from the site.

Craft Specialization

Microdrills are the most abundant tool at Watson Brake. Johnson (2000) has identified 154 microdrills, 93 microdrill preforms, 70 blades, and 16 blade cores in the Watson Brake lithic assemblage. The chert microdrills were used in stone bead production (Connaway 1981:63; Gibson 1968; Johnson 1993, 1996,

2000). Test Unit 8 excavations into the surface of Stage II, Mound D recovered 73 microdrills (47 percent of this tool type at the site), 51 microdrill preforms (55 percent), six blades (9 percent), and two blade cores (13 percent) (Johnson 2000). The lithic assemblage includes the complete reduction trajectory of micro-drills (see Johnson 1993), suggesting that Mound D was a bead workshop during that phase of mound occupation. However, beads in various stages of manufacture (Connaway 1981) were not recovered from the surface of Stage II, Mound D. In fact, only seven chert beads representing initial, intermediate, and final stages of bead manufacture were found at Watson Brake. It is possible that finished beads were removed from the site or that the microdrills also were used to make beads on perishable material (bone and shell).

Evidence of bead production at Frenchman's Bend Mounds is significantly less. Limited excavations produced one bead fragment, but no microdrills or blade cores. Surface collections include one bead blank, one tubular bead (notched on each end; informant's account), blades, and at least five blade cores.

Direct evidence for bead production at Plum Creek Archaic is absent: no microdrills or beads were recovered. However, 12 blades and five blade cores on local chert were surface-collected, suggesting that microdrill technology was practiced at the site.

Jay Johnson (2000) maintains that the blade/drill technology at Watson Brake did not require a level of specialization; this view is shared by others regarding the manufacture of stone beads (Connaway 1981; Connaway et al. 1977; Williams and Brain 1983). Craft specialization usually indicates economic support for a specialist by his/her society (Brumfiel and Earle 1987; Clark and Parry 1990; Wason 1994). The production of beads at Watson Brake is not of an intensity to suggest that artisans were dependent upon the lapidary industry for economic support. Nearly half of the microdrills were obtained from one provenience at the site and these may represent one episode of drill manufacturing. The remaining microdrills were recovered from a multitude of submound/subridge middens and intermediate stages of ridge and mound construction, suggesting widespread use of microdrills by many people engaged in bead production or that microdrills were used for a variety of purposes.

Feasting

Feasting is viewed as evidence of resource redistribution (Wason 1994) and/or aggrandizement (Clark and Blake 1994; Hayden 1994, 1995) in chiefdoms. The faunal assemblage on the surface of Stage I, Mound B at Watson Brake contained a significantly greater proportion of deer bone by weight and count than occurred in the three preceding levels in the submound midden, leading Jackson (1996) to speculate that the dominance of deer remains indicates feasting refuse. Jackson and Scott (2001:194) suggest that the occurrence of waterfowl at Watson Brake also may reflect ritual feasting. There is no evidence of feasting at Plum Creek Archaic or Frenchman's Bend Mounds (very small faunal assemblage).

Burials/Burial Goods

Burials and associated goods are considered the most reliable means of establishing social inequality among a population (Paynter 1989; Wason 1994). No human burials were uncovered in the earthworks at Watson Brake, Frenchman's Bend Mounds, or Plum Creek Archaic. A few fragments of charred bone were found on the surface of the second floor beneath Mound C at Frenchman's Bend Mounds, but it is not known whether the bone is human (too small for identification). Human remains have been found at Watson Brake. Jackson (1996) identified human bones belonging to at least three individuals: an adult, a child (ca. 3 years), and an infant. None of the remains were articulated, but rather they were incorporated into the submound/mound fill. This pattern may be the result of the unintentional disturbing of burials while collecting midden refuse/fill for mound construction. An alternative explanation may be tied to the social status of the individuals. Ames's (1994) overview of Northwest Coast hunter-gatherers mentions that slaves were rarely buried. This is an intriguing possibility, but it also has a logical extension. If slaves were not afforded burial status, then it may follow that the slave-owners were. Currently, there is no evidence of such burials. No known human remains were found at Plum Creek Archaic.

DISTRIBUTIONAL DATA

Hierarchical Structure—Sequential Social Organization

Johnson (1982) defined two types of hierarchical organization of local communities. Sequential social organization is horizontal, stressing kinship ties and coresident groups. Economic differences between communities are suppressed (see Feinman's [1995] corporate group). Decisions are consensual, and ritual and ceremony play a central role in expressing the solidarity of the community. Consequently, public architecture is used to display space for communal ritual (see Blanton et al. 1996). In contrast, simultaneous social organization is vertical and a small group of individuals exercises integration and control of the community. Economies among communities are more diversified, usually including long-distance trade (see Feinman's [1995] network group). Here, public architecture is focused on individuals. Johnson (1982) speculates that social inequality may be associated with simultaneous hierarchies.

The absence of long-distance trade suggests that the hierarchical structure among Watson Brake (very large mound complex), Frenchman's Bend Mounds

Table 9.1. Food and lithic tools at Watson Brake, Frenchman's Bend Mounds, and Plum Creek Archaic

	Watson Brake	Frenchman's Bend	Plum Creek
Food			
Fish	X	X	X
Mussel	X	X	X
Snail	X	X	X
Deer	X	X	X
Small game	X	X	X
Hickory/pecan	X	X	X
Tools			
Points	X	X	X
Bifaces	X	X	X
Unifaces	X	X	X
Preforms	X	X	X
Ground stone	X	X	X
Flake cores	X	X	X
Blade cores	X	X	X
Blades	X	X	X
Microdrills	X		
Beads	X	X	
Earthen blocks	X	X	X
Elements	16	15	14

(large mound complex), and Plum Creek Archaic (possible small mound site) is sequential. If so, then following Johnson's model there should be little variance in the economic activities among the three sites (suppression of different economic roles in hierarchy). In other words, we should expect a redundancy in artifact assemblages among the sites. Since each site shares a similar ecological setting (same array of foods and lithic raw material) and bears evidence of extended occupation (midden deposits), differences in artifact assemblages are less likely to be attributed to the exploitation of different resources (fish at one site, deer at a second, lithic quarry at a third, and so on) or the range of activities conducted at the site (long-term occupation at one site, ephemeral occupation at a second site, and so on). A comparison of the food and artifacts from the three sites is shown in Table 9.1. The analysis of lithic artifacts from Plum Creek Archaic is not completed and therefore the data are at a "raw" qualitative level.

Granted that the qualitative level of data decreases the probability of variance among the sites, nevertheless a pattern of redundancy is quite evident. The single source of variability among the three sites is the lapidary industry. The variance in artifact recovery methods (quarter-inch screen at Frenchman's Bend Mounds vs. eighth-inch screen for Watson Brake and Plum Creek Archaic) probably explains the lack of microdrills at Frenchman's Bend Mounds. The recovery of one partially drilled jasper bead blank and one broken jasper bead, however, suggests that stone beads were made at the site. Only one 1-×-1.5-m test unit was excavated at Plum Creek Archaic, while seven 1-×-1.5-m test units were excavated at Watson Brake. Therefore the lack of microdrills at Plum Creek Archaic could be a function of sample size. However, microdrills were recovered from each of the 1-×-1.5-m units at Watson Brake, indicating, perhaps, that the lack of microdrills at Plum Creek Archaic is not solely a function of sample size. The lack of stone beads at the site tends to suggest further that bead production did not take place at Plum Creek Archaic. Although limited variability in lithic assemblages does exist among the three sites, overall there appears to be a redundancy of economic activities, suggestive of a sequential hierarchy.

A FINAL CONSIDERATION—POVERTY POINT EARTHWORKS

The absence of plant domestication, sedentism, storage, trade, craft specialization, feasting, and burials and the redundancy of economic activities among three Middle Archaic sites suggest that the early mound builders were egalitarian societies and therefore that the occurrence of monumental architecture alone does not signify social inequality. By the Late Archaic (ca. 4000–2500 B.P.), however, some of the categorical traits absent during the Middle Archaic begin to appear. Does their occurrence signify a shift to a transegalitarian social structure that is expressed in the monumental architecture?

As previously noted, widespread evidence exists for trade at Poverty Point. Other "signatures" of transegalitarian social structure besides trade also have been identified at Poverty Point–age sites. Ford and Webb (1956) recovered human remains associated with Mound B at Poverty Point. Ford et al. (1955) identified a crescent posthole pattern at the Poverty Point–age component at Jaketown in west-central Mississippi (Webb 1982:20). Exnicios and Woodiel (1990) describe a possible posthole pattern (arc) associated with smudge pit features on a Poverty Point ridge. Hillman (1986) identified postholes near the eastern edge of the plaza and Gibson (1989, 1990, 1994d) recorded postholes in his plaza and ridge excavations.

In Webb's (1982) seminal study and definition of the Poverty Point culture, he identifies 11 additional sites in Louisiana that may have Poverty Point–age mounds (Webb 1982:11–12). Among these, three of the sites have one mound (Galloway, Lower Jackson, Motley), two have two mounds (Head, Neimeyer-Dare), one has five mounds (Stelly), and one has six mounds (Caney). Webb also includes four multicomponent mound sites, one with three mounds (Neely), two with five mounds (Insley, Marsden), and one with nine mounds (Mott), that may or may not have mounds that date to Poverty Point times. Research since 1982 (Russo and Fogleman 1994; Saunders et al. 2000; Saunders et al. 2001) shows that three of the sites listed by Webb date to the Middle Archaic: one with a single mound plus a five-mound and a six-mound complex. Excluding also the four multicomponent sites, then Webb's Poverty Point mound sites in Louisiana consist of two single-mound sites,[6] one of which (Motley) many consider to be part of Poverty Point, and two sites with two mounds. Thus, the only site with large-scale monumental earthworks (five mounds and six concentric ridges) is the site of Poverty Point itself. A disproportionate amount of energy was invested in the Poverty Point earthworks, conceivably at the expense of the contemporaneous single- and two-mound sites. This suggests that a hierarchy existed in the Poverty Point society, perhaps with simultaneous vertical social organization as defined by Johnson (1982).

A clear hierarchy does not exist among the Middle Archaic mound sites. Ten mound sites have been radiometrically dated to the Middle Archaic: two of the sites have one mound, four have two mounds, two have five mounds, one has six mounds, and the largest site, Watson Brake, has 11 mounds. By the number of mounds constructed, the sites are more diverse than the Poverty Point sample. Yes, Watson Brake is the largest among the sites, but the amount of energy invested in all of the other nine mound sites exceeds that expended at Watson Brake. For example, a conservative estimate of the volume of dirt used to construct the Watson Brake earthworks is 33,900 m^3 (calculated with the mapping program Surfer 1999). The volume of mound fill at the Middle Archaic single-mound site Lower Jackson[7] (ca. two miles south of Poverty Point) is 8,400 m^3 (Surfer 1999), or approximately 25 percent of the volume of the Watson Brake earthworks. In contrast, Gibson (2000) estimates the volume of the earthworks at Poverty Point to be between 667,000 and 750,000 m^3, a volume that not only dwarfs the other Poverty Point–age mounds but the collective volume of the Middle Archaic mounds as well.

In their study of the sociocultural evolution of Mesoamerica, Blanton et al. (1996) describe an evolutionary trajectory that teetered between two types of power strategies: corporate and exclusionary. The corporate power strategy is shared across groups and sectors of society; the exclusionary power strategy monopolizes sources of power. Blanton et al. (1996:2) suggest that exclusionary strategies may be associated with interactive trade networks among autonomous groups. Through time, a culture may shift from a corporate strategy to an exclusionary strategy and then back to a corporate strategy as the political power/ influence of one group expands through the control of prestige goods. Essentially two factors distinguish the Late Archaic from the Middle Archaic in Louisiana: the emergence of trade of lithics at the beginning of the Late Archaic and the apparent vertical hierarchy between the earthworks at Poverty Point and its con-

Table 9.2. Attributes of social inequality observed at Watson Brake, French-man's Bend, Plum Creek Archaic, and Poverty Point

Attribute	Watson Brake	Frenchman's Bend	Plum Creek	Poverty Point
Plant domestication	--	--	--	--
Sedentism	?	?	?	?
Storage	?	--	?	?
Structures	--	**x**	--	**x**
Trade	--	--	--	**x**
Craft specialization	?	?	?	?
Feasting	?	--	--	?
Burials	--	--	--	**x**
Sequential hierarchy	x	x	x	--
Simultaneous hierarchy	--	--	--	x

Bold = May be significant indication of social inequality.

temporaneous, smaller mound sites. During the Middle Archaic, it appears that mound building was a local expression among self-sufficient groups with the absence of trade and a wide range of variability in the size of earthwork sites. Throughout Louisiana, Middle Archaic people were constructing mounds and sharing stylistic and technological traits in bead and biface production (Johnson 2000). Yet, significant regional variability in other aspects of their material culture coexisted (Saunders and Allen 1998), perhaps suggesting shared regional concepts and local autonomy. Then, after 5000 B.P., mound construction appears to end. Shortly thereafter trade begins, culminating with the emergence of the Poverty Point culture approximately 1,000 years later.

SUMMARY

The intent of this study was to evaluate data from three Middle Archaic sites to see if there is adequate evidence to determine whether social inequality existed among the early mound builders. My concern is that social inequality is being attributed to Middle Archaic cultures solely on the basis of monumental architecture. In the past, archaeology has selected other preconditions for social inequality, only to discover later that the prerequisites were not necessary in many societies—so, are we fixing to make the same mistake again?

My predisposed view was that the data were inadequate to draw such a conclusion. A review of nine commonly accepted indicators for inequality did not conclusively demonstrate that the Watson Brake, Frenchman's Bend Mounds, and Plum Creek Archaic folk were transegalitarian (Table 9.2). Evidence for structures at Frenchman's Bend Mounds is the most significant data to support social inequality, followed by the marginal evidence for a year-round occupation at Watson Brake. Conversely, the lack of long-distance trade and human burials, as well as the apparent sequential social organization, strongly suggests an egalitarian culture of mound builders.

Concerning the evidence of nonresidential structures at Frenchman's Bend Mounds, a study on the occurrence of nondomestic structures among "tribal" societies by Adler and Wilshusen (1990) found that nonresidential facilities existed in 22 of 28 cultures examined. Perhaps the occurrence of the Frenchman's Bend Mounds structures is not as significant as originally suggested. Paul Wason (1994:147) argues that "[t]o claim that a particular structure is solid evidence of inequality means knowing that it could not have been accomplished by an egalitarian society, but just what might an egalitarian society accomplish?"

Poverty Point sites present a different case. Trade, structures, human remains associated with Mound B at Poverty Point, and the disparity in the volume of mound and ridge fill and expended energy at the Poverty Point site vs. other contemporaneous mound sites must be indicative of emerging or established social inequality.

CONCLUSIONS

The collective evidence suggests that the mounds at Watson Brake, Frenchman's Bend Mounds, and Plum Creek Archaic were constructed by seasonal hunter-gatherers of egalitarian status. The richness of the faunal and floral remains, the abundance of locally available raw material, the construction of nonresidential structures, and the production of lapidary items indicate a lifestyle of affluent hunter-gatherers. Middle Archaic mound building appears to be expressed locally by independent corporate groups. In contrast, evidence for social inequality begins to emerge before and during the construction and occupation of Poverty Point. Additional research is necessary to more fully explore these issues. With expanded data a more complete understanding of the social organizations and power base of these Archaic cultures can be achieved.

ACKNOWLEDGMENTS

Funding for the research on Middle Archaic mound sites was provided by the National Geographic Society, the National Park Service, and the Louisiana Division of Archaeology. Thanks to the Gentry family, Bishop Johnston, Plum Creek, Inc., and the Thomas family for allowing research to be conducted on their sites.

NOTES

1. In this chapter, I adopt Trigger's (1990a:119; see Moore 1996:92) definition of monumental architecture as follows: "Its principal defining feature is that its scale and elaboration exceed the requirements of any practical functions that a building [earthen structure] is intended to perform."

2. In the growth of knowledge in normal science, the replacement of an old theory with the new is signaled by inclusion of the new theory in histories or overviews of the field. The "legitimization" of Archaic mounds began with Neuman's (1984:83–84) publication of *An Introduction to Louisiana Archaeology*, in which he addresses Archaic mound sites in Louisiana, and continued later with Jeter and colleagues' overview of archaeology of the Lower Mississippi Valley (Jeter et al. 1989). Interestingly, a paper presentation on Archaic mounds by Gibson and Shenkel (1988) received a hostile reception—resistance remained as late as 1988.

3. At Watson Brake, a probable twelfth mound (L?) is located approximately 40 m to the southeast of the earthen enclosure. If it is a mound, its cultural affiliation currently is unknown.

4. One small, probable mound ca. 40 cm in height and 20 m in diameter is approximately 250 m west of the site. Its cultural affiliation is not established.

5. No remains of winter hackberry (*Vaccinium arboreum*), one of the few winter-specific plants in the area, were recovered. The plant is quite common at Watson Brake.

6. A third Poverty Point–age single-mound site just north of the Arkansas-Louisiana state line has been confirmed by Dr. Marvin Jeter of the Arkansas Archeological Survey (Jackson and Jeter 1994; Jeter, personal communication, 2002).

7. These calculations are of the current condition of the mound. Considerable fill had been removed from the mound summit, so the actual volume of mound fill is underestimated. In contrast, the mounds and ridges at Watson Brake are in pristine condition.

10

Surrounding the Sacred

Geometry and Design of Early Mound Groups as Meaning and Function

John E. Clark

There is one deduction to be drawn from the fact, that the figures entering into these works are of uniform dimensions, which is of considerable importance in its bearing upon the state of knowledge among the people who erected them. It is that *the builders possessed a standard of measurement, and had some means of determining angles.* The most skilful engineer of the day would find it difficult, without the aid of instruments, to lay down an accurate square of the great dimensions of those above represented, measuring as they do more than *four fifths* of a mile in circumference.

E. G. Squier and E. H. Davis,
Ancient Monuments of the Mississippi Valley (1848:61)

Squier and Davis's (1848) fabulous study of early mound groups ranks as the best early archaeological project in the New World; even today, the data presented and preserved are unsurpassed. Yet, a century and a half after the fact, the early promise of their study remains unrealized. In this essay I revisit their inferences that early mound builders had a standard of measurement, geometry, and engineering skills for planning sites. I evaluate these ideas on the earliest mound groups that have just recently come to light and argue that important clues to the meaning of early mounds and their function in societal reproduction and/or evolution are to be found in the technical details of their construction. What kinds of knowledge were required to construct the early mound enclosures? I consider site planning and fundamental principles of geometry as they are reflected in early mound sites in the American Southeast, Mesoamerica, and South America. There are some astounding similarities. The descriptive task undertaken here is sufficiently complex that I refrain from trying to explain what all the noted similarities might mean.

For most of the sites considered, I am an outsider who has merely been playing with maps and looking for patterns and regularities, with only a superficial knowledge of local archaeological problems, field conditions, and issues. Consequently, it is appropriate that I temper my claims to match my ignorance: *the patterns described below are offered as proposals that require further field testing by those more aware of the details of individual cases.* I consider briefly seven sites: Caney Mounds, Watson Brake, and Poverty Point of Louisiana, Claiborne and Cedarland of southern Mississippi, Paso de la Amada of southern Mexico, and Sechín Alto of highland Peru. All these sites are among the earliest mound groups in their regions.

Two assumptions need to be mentioned before I commence the arguments. I start with a presumption of inductive reasoning—that the plan of a planned human work can be inferred after the fact from the finished product itself, all other things being equal. I also assume that the ancients had available, and actually used, simple devices for measuring and establishing mound orientations, sizes, and positions, such as measuring cords, wooden stakes, sight lines, measured paces, plumb-bobs, orientation posts, and so forth. My principal inference in the following work is that the Middle and Late Archaic inhabitants of North and South America shared a common measurement system and logic. The best evidence for this is found in the size and disposition of the mounds themselves.

CANEY MOUNDS, LOUISIANA

All early mound groups from the southeastern United States I consider here share basic features of site layout that are most clearly evident at Caney Mounds. Here I rely on the recent map of this site graciously provided by Joe Saunders; I am also indebted to him for the map of Watson Brake used below, and I rely on his assessments of dating and mound contemporaneity at these sites. They date to about 3400–3000 B.C. (Saunders et al. 1997). In presenting conjectures about these sites, I rely on simple illustrations of geometric features to make my initial points rather than breaking down the geometry into numbers and equations that make the simple rope-and-stick geometry appear more daunting than it really was. Specifically, I will be concerned with circles, squares, rectangles, equilateral triangles, and vesicas—the lanceolate-shaped intersections of identical circles when the center point of each lies on the same line and is intersected by the paired circle, as in a Venn diagram. A vesica of this type inscribes two equilateral triangles placed base to base in a diamond or mirror-image arrangement.

I first saw Saunders's map of the Caney Mounds at the Poverty Point conference in 2000 after having spent a year, off and on, exploring plans from early sites from all over the Americas and after having verified to my own satisfaction the existence of an Archaic period system of measurement. What first caught my eye for the Caney site was the obvious equilateral triangle arrangement of the largest mounds and incorporated natural features, with the apex of this triangle at the center of Mound F and its base defined by the corners of the eastern bluff.

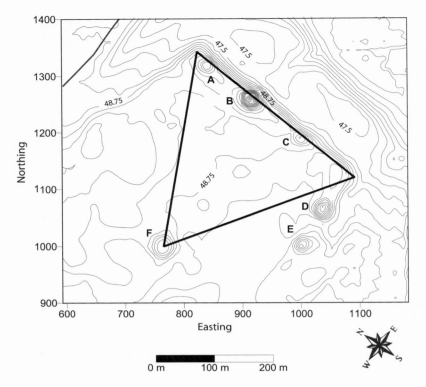

Figure 10.1. Principal triangle at the Caney Mounds complex (map courtesy of Joe Saunders).

Figure 10.1 shows the primary triangle at Caney. The triangle defines the outer edges of the row of mounds and natural rises along the eastern bluff. This equilateral triangle is 346.5 m on a side, or very close to it. This distance represents four units measuring 86.63 m each, an unusual distance that occurs with monotonous regularity at all the sites considered here.

I call the interval of 86.63 m the Archaic *Standard Macro-Unit* (SMU). The primary triangle at Caney is 4 SMU on a side. In turn, each SMU represents 52 *Standard Units* (SU) of 1.666 m. This is not the place to rehearse my full argument for this measure, but I think 1.666 m represents the length of a cord or string held in the outstretched arms, otherwise known as a fathom or wingspan (*braza* in Spanish).[1] This measure also represents the height of the person holding the cord, in this case, the height of a man. The basic standard unit was measured from the male human body and could be divided in half as many times as desired (i.e., 83.3 cm, 41.65 cm, 20.83 cm, and so on) or multiplied endlessly. That the SMU represents 52 (13 × 4) SU is of extreme interest, as I discuss in the concluding section. I discovered this measure based on fine-grained information on posthole patterns and building sizes at Paso de la Amada, Chiapas, Mexico (see below). Subsequent search of the literature revealed that others had previously discovered this precise unit at other American sites (Guillemin-Tarayre 1919a, 1919b; Scholten de D'Éneth 1954, 1956, 1958, 1970, 1977, 1980, 1981, 1985; Smith 1969; Sugiyama 1993). Metrological considerations of eroded earthworks do not inspire confidence in claims for this degree of accuracy, but we can check implications for this level of accuracy over long distances to see whether they hold. This claim is evidenced by the examples and illustrations that follow. I limit my discussion to distances between mounds (either their centers or edges), but the mounds themselves were built according to the same standards—both in vertical and horizontal dimensions (see Smith 1969).

As evident in Figure 10.1, the primary 4-SMU triangle at Caney leaves some mounds unaccounted for. The site appears to be an incomplete oval along the lines of the Watson Brake (see below) and Insley sites (Kidder 1991). Following a suggestion from Ken Sassaman, I considered the alignment of the two largest mounds (B and F) on opposite sides of the plaza. These form the base of a double equilateral triangle inscribed in a vesica with a radius of 3.5 SMU, as shown in Figure 10.2. The base connects the midpoints or summits of these conical mounds. These mirrored equilateral triangles are one-half SMU (43.32 m) shorter than the primary triangle. The curved lines of the vesica delineate the outer edges of the mounds at the southern end of the site, and the sides of the inscribed equilateral triangle pass through the centers of these same mounds. The northern triangle appears unnecessary, but it is implied.

What is quite clear at Caney is that the mounds form an arrangement according to at least two different orientations that converge at the summit of the principal mound on the west edge of the site. In previous efforts to understand early mound groups, I did not consider this possibility; instead, I tried to fit site plans to one major orientation and its minor perpendicular alignment. Aligning the largest mounds at sites such as Caney and Watson Brake did not occur to me in these initial analyses because their shared axes are askew from the overall "oval" geometry of their mound groups. Consideration of the Caney Mounds has prompted me to pay more attention to triangles and triangulation of measuring points.

Figure 10.3a shows the basic pattern of the Caney Mounds; its abstracted template represents a rather complex and apparently arbitrary layout. I have portrayed the issue of orientation too simplistically as dual principal orientations. Figure 10.3b shows eight different orientations; two different systems of triangles, each with four orientations, are involved. These include the three sides of each triangle as well as the lines bisecting their bases. Mirrored vesica triangles merely

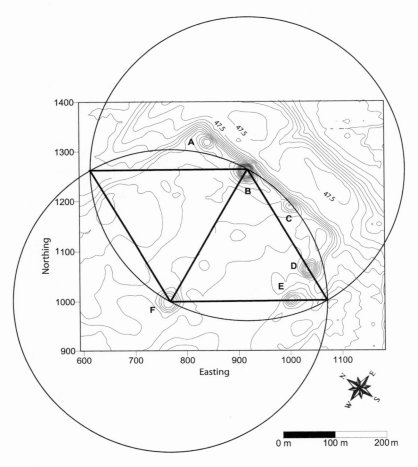

Figure 10.2. Secondary equilateral triangles at Caney Mounds inscribed in a vesica.

repeat the same orientations in both paired members. I consider as the two principal orientations at Caney Mounds those that run through the summit of Mound F, one intersecting the eastern line at its midpoint and the other running through Mound B. The latter becomes the shared baseline of the smaller, double triangles. The mirrored triangles, or vesica pair, share the same orientations but have potentially different, parallel axial lines. Any singular orientation can have many parallel lines. The difference between the two principal orientations at Caney is 10 degrees. For convenience of description, I designate the bisecting line of the primary triangle as the principal orientation and the shorter line connecting the two principal mounds as the secondary orientation. The other feature of the Caney pattern is that the sides of the smaller equilateral triangle define the positions of the other mounds at the southern edge of the site, so mound alignments are found on four of the eight orientation lines.

In terms of site purpose, the arrangement of mounds at Caney according to these orientations suggests that viewing two or more points of the eastern horizon may have been important to the function and meaning of this center. I am unqualified to pursue issues of alignments to visible horizons or to celestial phenomena; I only attempt here to infer major axes of mound arrangements.[2] Arguments for ancient astronomy must await the establishment of the orientations of interest and the lines of sight (see Romain 2000).

WATSON BRAKE, LOUISIANA

In analyzing Watson Brake, I presume that the mounds were contemporaneous, although some were augmented later to increase their heights (Saunders et al. 1997). This site looks like an oval or ellipse at a slightly smaller scale than the Caney Mounds complex. It is important to stress that the mound arrangement fits the vesica form and triangles much better than it does a true ellipse.

If we allow our attention to be drawn to the tallest mounds and the northeastern bluff, we see at Watson Brake a principal triangle such as identified at Caney Mounds (Figure 10.4a). Likewise, we observe the same mirrored equilateral triangles in a vesica arrangement that encompass the northern and southern mounds (Figure 10.4b). The two principal axes are the same and are separated by 10 degrees as at Caney Mounds. The pattern and orientation of the three superimposed equilateral triangles is identical to that at Caney, but at a slightly smaller scale (Figure 10.4c). Whereas at Caney the principal triangle is 4 SMU on a side, that at Watson Brake is 3.5 SMU. Recall that this was the size of the secondary triangles at Caney. The secondary, or smaller, double equilateral triangles at Watson Brake are 3 SMU on a side. In short, we see a decreasing interval of 43.42 m, or half an SMU. On the other hand, if we consider this shorter increment to be the main unit of early sites, then the two triangles at Watson Brake would be better conceptualized as 7 and 6 large units on a side and those at Caney would be 8 and 7 on a side. I explore implications of these numbers in the final section.

The contemporaneous Middle Archaic site of Frenchman's Bend is the same scale as Watson Brake and possibly to the same general plan (see Russo 1996a: 278, fig. 14-9; Sassaman and Heckenberger 2001). At Watson Brake, the southeastern 3-SMU triangle passes through the center points of the paired mounds. The opposite northwestern pair is offset, with Mound C located on the central axis that bisects the mirrored triangles and passes between the two southern mounds. The summits of Mounds A, D, and E form an isosceles triangle, with the equal sides 2.5 SMU in length.

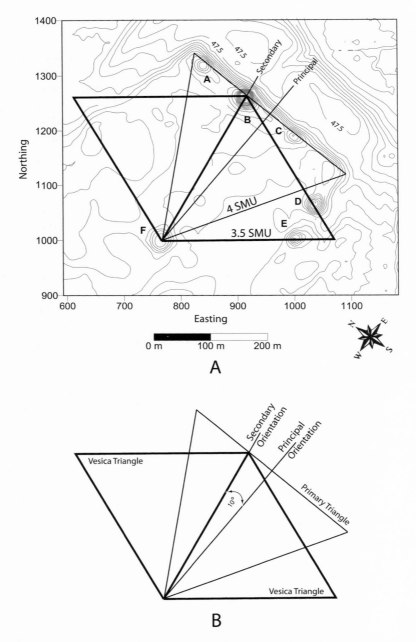

Figure 10.3. Caney Mounds geometry. a, Overlapping triangles and axes of orientation; b, simple template of the overlapping triangles and axes of the Caney Mounds complex.

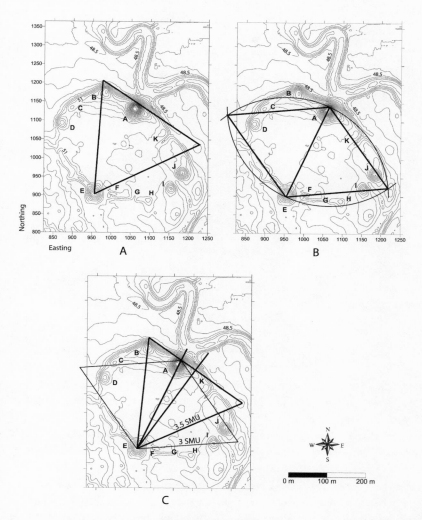

Figure 10.4. Geometry of Watson Brake (map courtesy of Joe Saunders). a, Principal triangle; b, secondary vesica and inscribed equilateral triangles; c, overlapping triangles at Watson Brake showing the Caney pattern.

CEDARLAND AND CLAIBORNE, MISSISSIPPI

I will not dwell long on Cedarland and Claiborne, twin horseshoe-shaped sites
in southern Mississippi (see Bruseth 1991; Webb 1982). They date to the Late
Archaic, about 1400 B.C., and are contemporaneous with Poverty Point. Their
shapes have been somewhat problematic to me in previous attempts to reduce site

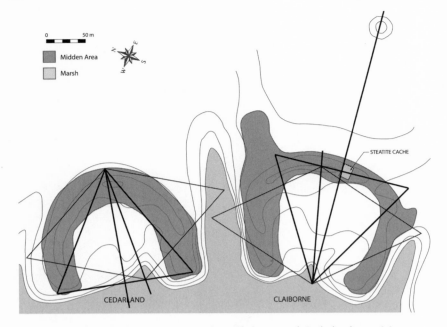

Figure 10.5. Caney templates superimposed on Claiborne and Cedarland sites. Map redrawn from Bruseth (1991:10, fig. 2). The Caney template is shown at one-fourth scale.

plans to simple geometry because the extended arms of the dark midden deposits
at these sites converge or taper rather than open in an arc or remain straight or
U-shaped. Their size is of special interest because they are precisely a fourth the
scale of the Caney Mounds complex. Figure 10.5 shows the template of Caney
triangles, at one-fourth scale, superimposed on the Claiborne and Cedarland
sites. Note that the bisecting line of the principal triangle at Claiborne passes
through the steatite cache and the northern mound. On the basis of current
evidence, there do not appear to be secondary orientations at either Cedarland
or Claiborne that correspond to those of the double triangles at Caney. It is of
interest, however, that the sites form an obvious formal pair and each has a different orientation.

Two things are of particular interest in these examples. First, the basic measurement intervals or increments used in these early sites are consistent for sites
of different scales, places, and possibly functions. This is easily appreciated by
overlaying site maps in a method James Marshall (1995:6) calls "cryptographic
overlay" (see Ford and Webb 1956:18 for an early example of this technique).
Claiborne and Cedarland are a fourth the scale of Caney (see Figure 10.6), and
Caney is at a half scale to Poverty Point (see Figure 10.7). Second, equilateral
triangulation appears to have been the way these sites were laid out. Differences

in scale and possible functions between Caney and Claiborne suggest that small villages were laid out according to the formats of the mound groups, or vice versa. This is an important point of historical significance when considering the creation of the first mound groups and the long lapse between the creation of the earliest ones and the belated building of Poverty Point nearly 2,000 years later. Knowledge of enclosed villages necessarily preceded the construction of Caney Mounds and Watson Brake at 3400 B.C., and it persisted after this period of monumental construction at least until Poverty Point times. This persistence of form and size of mound groups in the absence of a continuous history of building mound enclosures (a gap of more than 1,800 years) suggests that these features were part of everyday village life and architecture and that the mound sites were constructed as special "villages" projected to a cosmic plane in a more permanent form. The model for mound enclosures persisted naturally in pedestrian village construction through many centuries after the initial mound building had ceased.

POVERTY POINT, LOUISIANA

Poverty Point is the site that first captured my interest in Southeast archaeology, for all of the usual reasons and also because it is contemporaneous with Paso de la Amada, a site I am investigating in southern Mexico; both appear to be involved with the same developmental issues of the possible origins of hereditary inequality starting about 1800 B.C. I have whiled away weeks of effort testing possible geometric patterns for Poverty Point from available maps, but none was sufficiently accurate to inspire confidence in any findings until now. Here I rely on Tristram R. Kidder's recent map of Poverty Point and the 1986 "Provisional Edition" of the Pioneer and Epps, Louisiana, 1:24,000 topographic sheets (32091-E4-TF-024, 32091-F-TF-024) for the placement of the Lower Jackson Mound and the Motley Mound vis-à-vis Mounds A and B. My concern has been to get the most accurate data that correctly place the Lower Jackson and Motley Mounds on the same map with the most accurate representation of Poverty Point. I compensated for scale differences and made a composite map from these sources.[3]

I can only begin to explore here the wonderful spatial complexity of Poverty Point and its outliers. Like its Middle Archaic predecessors, Poverty Point was laid out by major axes of orientation, SMUs, and triangulation. In fact, Poverty Point incorporates its Archaic antecedents, Lower Jackson and possibly Mound E (Gibson 1996a:296, 1998a:331, 1998b:19; Saunders et al. 2001), into its overall structure and pattern.[4] Here I first consider the larger plan and then turn to the central core of the site with its concentric arcs.

The oldest axis of Poverty Point, designated here as Principal Orientation 1,

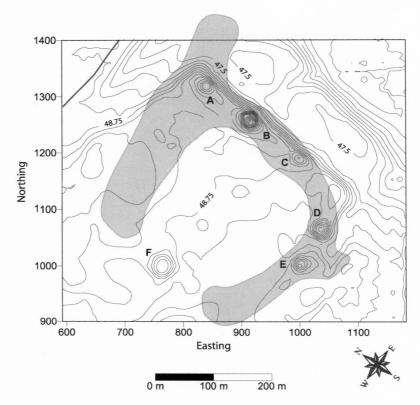

Figure 10.6. Outline of the Claiborne ring superimposed on the Caney Mounds. Claiborne is shown at four times scale.

is defined by a line that passes through Lower Jackson Mound, the Ballcourt Mound (Mound E), Mound A, and Mound B (see Gibson 1987, 1996a:296; Webb 1970). In Figure 10.8 this is shown as a central axis flanked on the east and west by parallel axes spaced at the same distance from the center line. The eastern axis passes through the central plaza of Poverty Point, the southeast avenue, and the northwest corner of Motley Mound. The long axis of the supposed smaller bird effigy at Motley Mound is perpendicular to this axis (Gibson 1998b:25), making the analogous "wing" axes of Mound A and Motley Mound perpendicular to each other (see Ford and Webb 1956:18; Gibson 1987:20). Figure 10.9 shows these same axial lines as defined or laid out by triangulation. The basic equilateral triangles shown are twice the scale of the principal triangle at the Caney Mounds (Figure 10.1), being 693.06 m (8 SMU) on a side. The distance between the parallel axes represents the height of the primary equilat-

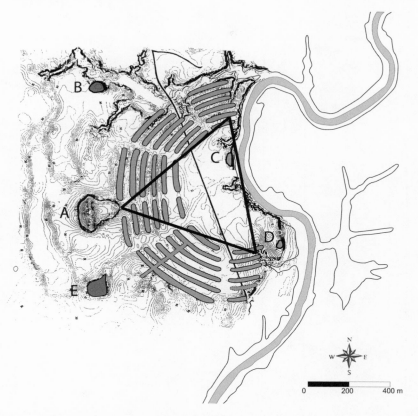

Figure 10.7. Caney Mounds principal triangle at twice scale superimposed on Poverty Point.

eral triangle. The height of an 8-SMU equilateral triangle is 6.9282 SMU, or precisely 360 SU. Thus, the parallel axes are 360 SU apart (600.2 m).

It is striking how neatly these orientations and measurement intervals capture so many essential details of Poverty Point. They account for the locations of Lower Jackson Mound, Mound E (the Ballcourt Mound), Mound A, Mound B, Motley Mound, and the southeast avenue. Figure 10.9 also indicates the number of SMUs. It is 60 SMU from the outside edge of Lower Jackson to the outside corner of Motley Mound, on the eastern parallel axis, and 40 SMU from Lower Jackson to the northern edge of Mound B on the center axis. Distances calculated in large units of 20 appear to have been significant. The main axis also passes through the eastern ramp of Mound A. This point is 32 SMU from Lower Jackson and 28 SMU from Motley Mound. The center point of Mound E is its mirror image, being 28 SMU from Lower Jackson and 32 SMU from Mot-

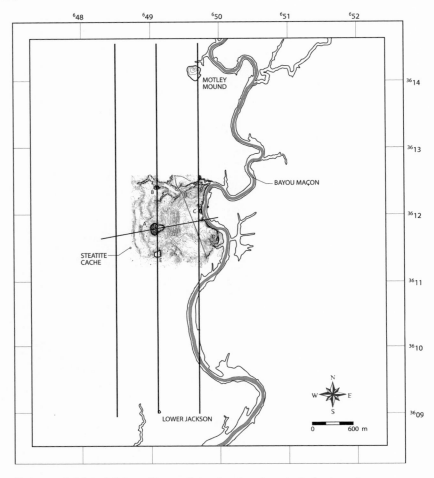

Figure 10.8. Map of Greater Poverty Point showing the principal orientation connecting Lower Jackson Mound and Mounds E, A, and B.

ley Mound. Therefore, the space between Mound E and Mound A represents the central area of Greater Poverty Point. The 60 SMU of total length represent 3,120 SU, or 5.198 km. The stress on marking 28 SMU from both ends of Greater Poverty Point may indicate a concern with lunar counts and phenomena.

A second system of long orientation lines (Principal Orientation 2) also passes through the same measuring point at Lower Jackson Mound and the central point of the plaza (Figure 10.10). The parallel western axis touches the edge of Mound E, passes through the center of the Mound A ramp, and then goes

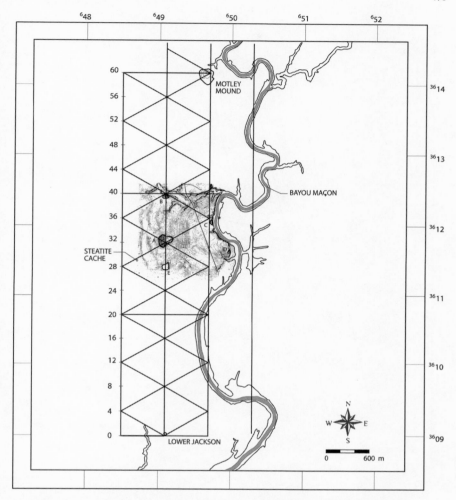

Figure 10.9. Map of Greater Poverty Point showing triangulation along the principal axes shown in Figure 8.

on to the same measuring point already identified in Motley Mound in Figure 10.8. In other words, Motley and Lower Jackson Mounds are in complementary positions at alternate, opposite edges of Greater Poverty Point, and they represent nexus points that are significant for two of the long axial systems and their implied perpendicular alignments.

Figure 10.11 shows the system of orientation at Poverty Point that the concentric arcs are fitted to, designated as Principal Orientation 3. The central axis

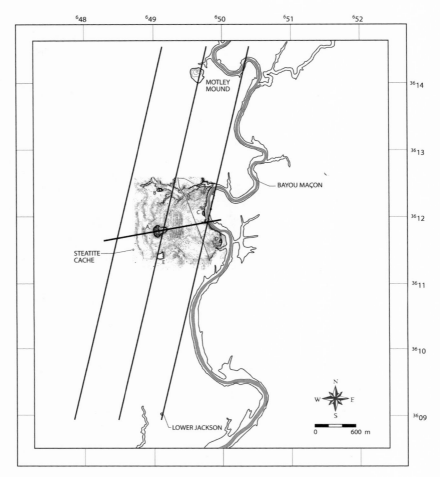

Figure 10.10. Map of Greater Poverty Point showing Principal Orientation 2 and its parallel axial lines.

of this orientation system passes through Mound B, and it is also paralleled by eastern and western axes at the same 600-m interval shown in Figures 10.8 and 10.10. The parallel western axis traverses Lower Jackson (at the same point of the previous axes). As with the other orientations, the spacing between parallel axes is 360 SU. All three systems employ this same spacing, and all initiate at Lower Jackson Mound. I give Lower Jackson pride of place because it is older than the others, dating to the Middle Archaic (Gibson 1996a:296, 1998b:19; Saunders et al. 2001). This distant conjunction of axial lines represents clear evidence that the positions of all the mounds and rings at Poverty Point were

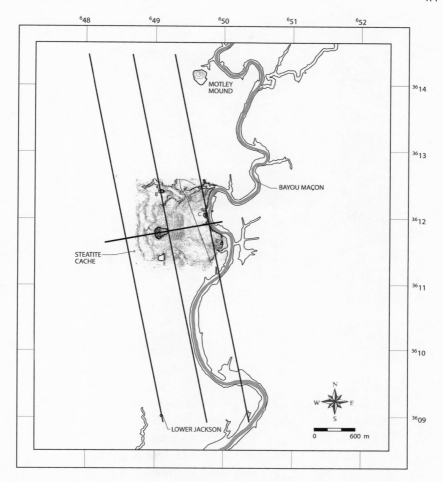

Figure 10.11. Map of Greater Poverty Point showing Principal Orientation 3 and its perpendicular orientation through the central area of the rings.

dependent for their placement on the antecedent position of Lower Jackson Mound. In other words, the position of the earliest mounds, coupled with traditional practices of site layout and measurement, dictated the position, orientations, and arrangements of later mounds. Greater Poverty Point had a significant construction history that is critical to the decipherment of its meaning.

The half rings at Poverty Point and their associated mounds are organized according to ascending, superimposed equilateral triangles (Figure 10.12). As at Caney, these principal triangles open to the east to mounds located along the eastern bluff. Figure 10.13 shows the Caney 4-SMU principal triangle and one

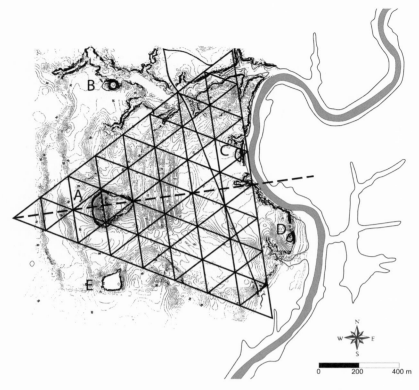

Figure 10.12. Map of Poverty Point (courtesy of T. R. Kidder) showing the system of
nested equilateral triangles. Each small triangle is 2 SMU (173.26 m) on a side.

twice its scale (8 SMU) oriented to the same measuring points and axial alignments. The larger triangle runs from the eastern edge of the Mound A ramp
to both inside corners of the open court. A triangle twice this size includes
Mound A and the outer edges of the rings (Figure 10.12).

These triangles overlap and run in counter directions as well. Each equilateral
triangle contains four others of half size, ad infinitum. Note that the triangles
running from east to west provide clear orientations for defining two avenues
symmetrically flanking the central avenue to Mound A (Figure 10.14), but they,
in fact, did not provide this orientation, as the sides of the equilateral triangle
are too far apart. The flanking avenues are asymmetrically placed. Of the westward triangle, one side goes through the avenue north of Mound A; the southern arm misses the avenue but conforms quite closely with the position of the
raised causeway. The layout of the avenues better conforms to more complex
geometry based on isosceles triangles, as shown in Figure 10.15. My hypothesis
is that the sight line from Lower Jackson Mound, in Principal Orientation 2, to

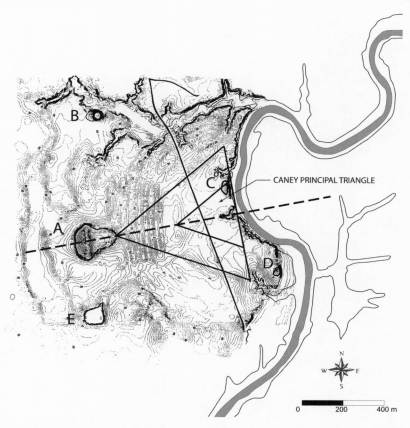

Figure 10.13. Map of Poverty Point showing the Caney principal triangle and one twice its size.

the central measuring point of the Poverty Point plaza is the key for establishing the locations and orientations of all other avenues except the central one connecting Mound A to the center of the plaza. The other three principal avenues are regularly spaced from this first one using two measurements. Figure 10.15 shows a circle of 8 SMU. The isosceles triangles defining the avenues have sides 8 SMU in length (416 SU) and bases just under 7 SMU long (360 SU), the height of the 8-SMU equilateral triangle. The geometry for establishing the avenues is precise and elegant in conception, although it may have been difficult to execute in practice.

   In earlier studies, I tried to fit the Poverty Point rings to circles and arcs. Even with Clarence Webb's (1982:10, fig. 7a) older map, which may have privileged this interpretation more than deserved (see Gibson 1996b:2; Russo 1996a:261), my exploratory exercises were not entirely satisfactory. The court or plaza of Pov-

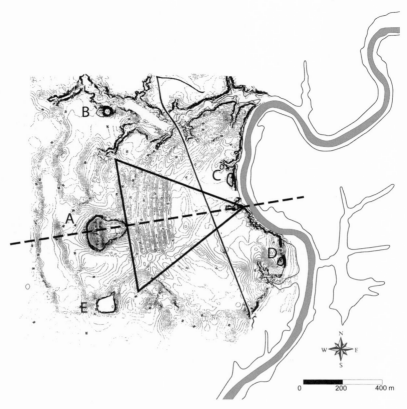

Figure 10.14. Map of Poverty Point showing the correspondence of the equilateral triangle to the location of the avenues.

erty Point's enclosing rings is better defined by a **D**-shape of half hexagons based on the system of nested, equilateral triangles shown in Figure 10.12 or, more specifically, by half hexagons formed by the three contiguous equilateral triangles inscribed in a half circle (Figure 10.16).

I have displayed each alignment at Poverty Point as a separate system (I have not shown them all) to spare the reader the confusion of trying to examine all these lines, their triangulations, and measurements on a single site plan. Singly, each system appears straightforward and simple, and they follow the same spatial logic with different orientations. In combination they implicate a very complex conception of planned space through time and over vast distances (see Figure 10.17). Several measuring points are shared by the three different alignment grids, such as Lower Jackson, Mounds A and B, Motley Mound, and the center of the plaza. The steatite cache is close to some of these orientation lines, so I suspect that a more precise placement on the map could conform to axial

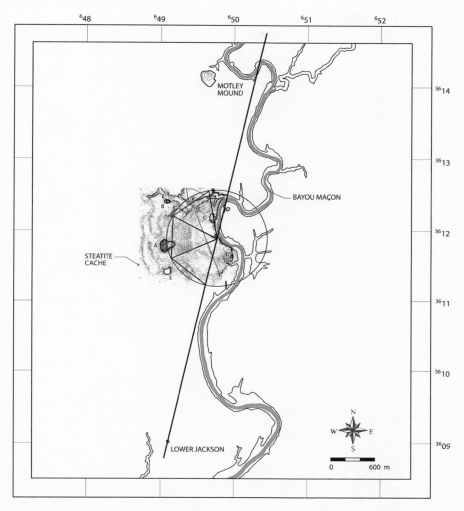

Figure 10.15. Map of Greater Poverty Point showing a hypothesis for the placement of the principal avenues through the rings based on isosceles triangles.

points—perhaps in conjunction with feasting rituals or rituals involved with food preparation and serving.[5] That a similar conjunction point at Claiborne (Figure 10.5) was also marked with a steatite cache (Bruseth 1991:16, fig. 6; see illustration of vessels in Gibson 2000:123, fig. 6.7) is of more than passing interest. Other major orientation or measuring points shown on these Poverty Point maps may be similarly marked with special offerings and should be checked with appropriate methods. The best candidates are those that represent significant and multiple conjunctions, such as Motley Mound, the northern edge

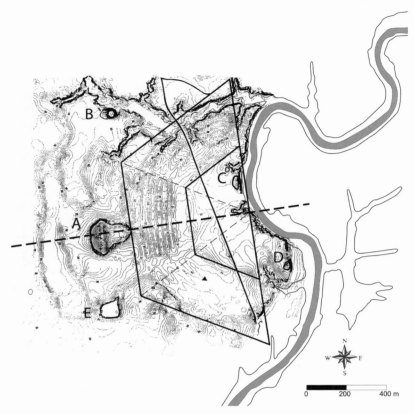

Figure 10.16. Map of Poverty Point showing the correspondence of the central plaza, rings, and edges of the rings to half hexagons defined by 4-SMU and 8-SMU equilateral triangles.

of Mound B, and the central measuring point on the eastern margin of the plaza. How far did the rationalized measures at Poverty Point, its major axes, and measured spaces extend? I have only traced orientations and standard distances between Lower Jackson and Motley Mound, but I would not be surprised to learn that other mounds located north or south were found to conform to the same axial lines and at standard distances in multiples of just over 5 km. Sassaman and Heckenberger (see Chapter 11, this volume) argue persuasively that the Middle Archaic mounds conformed to a regional pattern of site orientation and complementaries.

Figure 10.18 shows the superimposition of the Caney triangles, at twice scale, on Poverty Point. The principal axis passes down the central avenue and through the central measuring point at the eastern edge of the plaza, and the secondary axis forms a tangent to Mound C, the Dunbar Mound. The northern edge of

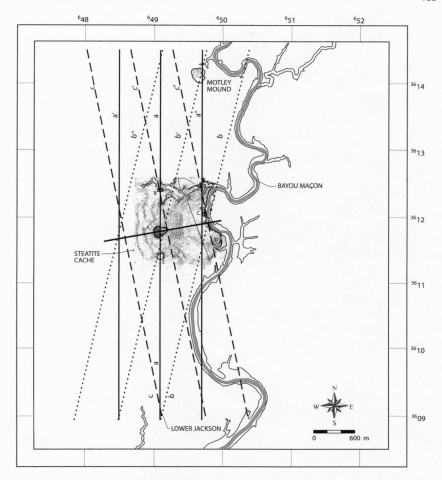

Figure 10.17. Map of Greater Poverty Point showing the three principal orientation systems and the main axial lines.

the vesica triangles parallels the north-central avenue. This is a close fit of the Caney template to Poverty Point, albeit at twice the scale. As discussed below, sites located more distantly in time and space provide even more convincing fits to the Caney triangles.

PASO DE LA AMADA, MEXICO

The Pacific Coast site of Paso de la Amada in southern Mexico is contemporaneous with Poverty Point (ca. 1800–1200 cal B.C.) and at the same spatial scale—but not the same scale of monumentality (Figure 10.19). It is significantly

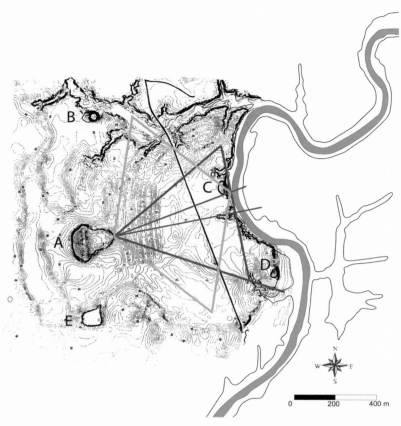

Figure 10.18. Map of Poverty Point showing the superimposition of the Caney Mounds template at double scale.

different in overall conception, sharing more basic features with early sites in South America than with Poverty Point, such as a U-shaped plaza and possible sunken circular courts. Recall that the hypothesis for the Archaic measuring system and increments derives from study of Paso de la Amada, its buildings, and features. In previous work, I thought all the mound placements at Paso de la Amada could be most parsimoniously accounted for by circles and a grid of 86.63-m squares. I returned to the map of this site after looking at Caney and the compelling evidence for the use of large equilateral triangles in the layouts of the Archaic sites in the southeast United States. A principal triangle exactly twice the size of that at Caney defines the southern half of Paso de la Amada, with its apex at the largest, offset mound to the east, Mound 4. Actually, the Paso de la Amada triangle is the same size as that for the Poverty Point rings (Figure 10.13), but oriented from east to west rather than from west to east.

The most investigated mounds at Paso de la Amada are in the southern plaza and consist of Mound 7, a ballcourt 86.63 m long (1 SMU), and a series of superimposed residential platforms at Mound 6 (one-fourth SMU long, or 13 SU) that has been interpreted as a chief's house (Blake 1991). In all my considerations of the Paso de la Amada map and aerial photographs, I could never satisfactorily reconcile the orientation of the residence at Mound 6 to the principal site axis. Reconsidering Paso de la Amada with ideas derived from investigations of sites in the American Southeast, especially of multiple, superimposed orientations, provides a credible explanation. Figure 10.19 shows the Caney triangles, at double scale, on Paso de la Amada. The orientation is reversed, or a mirror image of Caney, but otherwise a remarkable fit for a site so distant in time and space. The two orientations connect all principal mounds at Paso de la Amada (Mounds 1, 3, 4, 6, 7, 20, and 32) and at significant junctions within each mound. The probabilities are astronomical against these correspondences among site layouts being due to accidental convergence.

SECHÍN ALTO, PERU

Even farther afield in the Casma Valley, Peru, the Initial Period (i.e., earliest ceramic period) site of Sechín Alto is of particular interest. Dating to 1800–1200 B.C. (Burger 1992:80; Pozorski and Pozorski 1987:71–75), Sechín Alto is contemporaneous with Poverty Point and Paso de la Amada. Its gigantic stone mounds with prepared facing stones are more massive than those at Poverty Point. Its main mound is the largest construction in the New World on this time horizon, measuring 300 by 250 m at the base and 44 m tall; its early core is constructed of conical adobes with a later facing of granite monoliths and chinking stones (Pozorski and Pozorski 1987:71). Sechín Alto is linear, with a large mound complex in the southernmost sector and a graduated series of contiguous courtyards and sunken circular courts to the north that increase in size from south to north (see Burger 1992:81, fig. 62 for aerial photograph).

There is ample evidence at this site of Archaic SMUs and their subdivisions. In previous attempts to understand this site, I considered circles and squares as the fundamental organizing geometry, for which there is ample evidence. Consideration of the Caney arrangement of overlapping triangles yields more interesting results, however. Figure 10.20 shows the superimposition of Caney triangles on Sechín Alto, as was done for Paso de la Amada and Poverty Point. At double the scale, there are numerous remarkable fits for the Caney triangles—especially as they tangentially delimit the edges of sunken, circular courts. This degree of fit shows that several basic features of measurement are shared with earlier sites in the Southeast but that the site layout follows a different conception of how to put the triangles together.

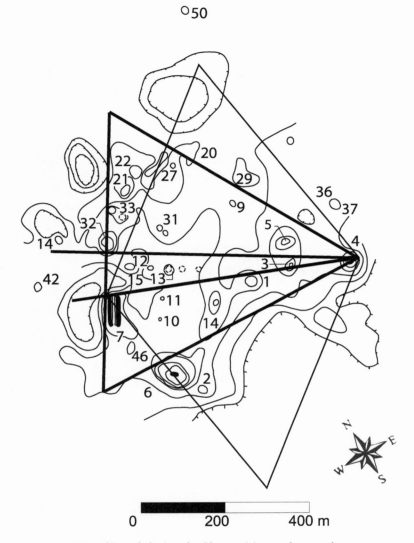

Figure 10.19. Map of Paso de la Amada, Chiapas, Mexico, showing the superimposition of the Caney Mounds template at double scale.

The geometry of Sechín Alto is actually extremely complex. Figure 10.21 shows a different arrangement of the Caney family of triangles fitted to the site plan of Sechín Alto. A series of equilateral triangles, based on incremental increases of 86.63 m, the Standard Macro-Unit, accounts remarkably well for the telescoping or escalating arrangement of plazas and sunken patios. Specific fea-

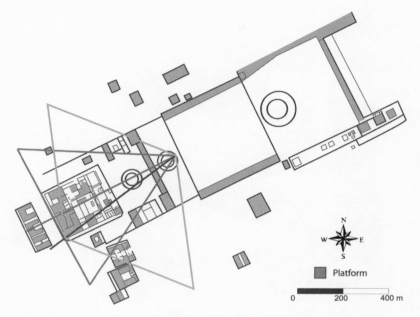

Figure 10.20. Map of Sechín Alto, Peru, showing the superimposition of the Caney
Mounds template at double scale (map redrawn from Burger 1992:80, fig. 61, and Pozorski
and Pozorski 1987:73, fig. 46).

tures of this complexity need not detain us here. For current purposes, it is
sufficient to recognize the use of the same SMU and the same series of equilateral triangles in laying out this sacred South American center. In plan, the
circles and rectangles call themselves to one's attention, but the graduated series
of conjoined rectangular plazas is based on the geometry of equilateral triangles
in regular SMU intervals of 86.63 m and form a progressive series, in SMU
math, of natural numbers (4, 5, 6, and 7). The use of these triangles is too
specific and arbitrary to have been devised by chance in all the places at which
they appear.

SIMILARITIES AND DIFFERENCES

The seven sites showcased here span more than 3,000 years and 3,000 terrestrial
miles. Detailed consideration of the geometric plan of each site could easily fill
a book, so I have had to be selective in what issues to address in making a case
for an extensive Archaic system of site planning and layout. My purpose is to
view the question of early mounds in the American Southeast from a broad perspective. I do not expect every reader to accept all the various proposals, but full

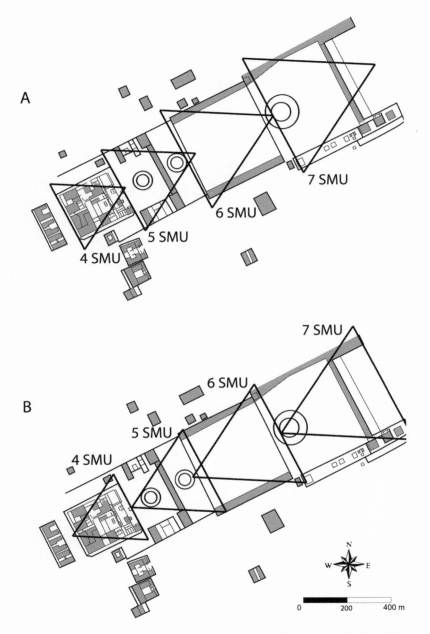

A

7 SMU

6 SMU

5 SMU

4 SMU

B

7 SMU

6 SMU

5 SMU

4 SMU

N
W   E
S

0   200   400 m

Figure 10.21. Maps of Sechín Alto showing the series of equilateral triangles that define its telescoping arrangement of plazas. The 4-SMU triangle is the principal triangle at Caney.

agreement is not necessary for reaching some accord on fundamental issues concerning the construction of early mound groups and their functioning and meaning. I think the evidence is clear that these sites were planned as totalities, at high levels of precision, and constructed over relatively short periods of time. All indicators are that these enclosed spaces served as sacred places. This conjecture is hardly earth-shaking as these sites are presumed to have been special. Consideration of site structure, construction, history, and function and meaning suggests some particular ways in which they may have been special. Because of the nature of archaeological inference, I consider these topics out of their natural order, beginning with issues of construction—the reality of the early mounds and mound groups themselves—and then make a case for patterning and planning from the material evidence. Issues of history are as critical to inferring past use and meaning as are technical requirements, so I deal with issues of history before discussing function and meaning.

Constructing Mound Enclosures

We can achieve needed perspective and requisite humility concerning construction issues of early mound groups by briefly considering how we would build a replica of Poverty Point today—perhaps as a theme park. What work would be needed, in what sequence, and what tools and equipment would we use? Clearly, we would have to start with a detailed blueprint that specified locations of all the mounds, their horizontal extent in any given direction, and their desired heights. If astronomical observations were to be part of this mix, a detailed reconnaissance of the local terrain would have to be undertaken in conjunction with drawing up the plans so that the site as a functional unit would fit local conditions. All of this would require preliminary measurement and calculations at different scales (between the scaled model and the real terrain). Desired alignments and distances between mounds would have to be coordinated to celestial phenomena and visible horizons, while at the same time avoiding swamps and bodies of standing water. Distances and orientations between mounds would have to be calculated. Transferring the blueprint to the ground surface would be our first construction task. Even with modern laser survey technology, this would require some forest clearance, both for clearing lines of sight and, subsequently, for cleaning vegetation away from the areas of designated construction. With older plane table and alidade equipment, initial survey would take months to complete. With primitive instruments it would have taken much longer. It is well to remember that, given its scale, Poverty Point's constructed complexity is only visible from the air rather than from ground level (cf. Gibson 1998b:23). It necessarily follows that it represents a drawing or plan transferred onto the terrestrial plane by basic survey and measuring techniques (cf. Marshall 1987; Morgan 1937).

Equally important would be decisions about where to place borrow pits for mining fill dirt and consolidating clay for building up and surfacing the desired mounds. Even with the modern aids of bulldozers, road graders, and backhoes to replace direct human labor, an earthwork the magnitude of Poverty Point would require months of effort. The initial survey and preliminary clearance of vegetation would also require substantial labor investments. The total project would require close supervision and provisioning—or closer, in case of an accelerated work pace—for sustaining a motivated workforce.

How did the ancients do it? Most assessments of past mound building skip the necessary stages of conceptual work and move directly to issues of moving dirt on the backs of enthusiastic volunteer laborers. This propensity for privileging dirt may be an occupational bias of field archaeologists. We can easily calculate the cubic meters of dirt moved and convert these figures into reasonable estimates of human energy expenditure (see Gibson 1987). Such estimates are critical and useful, but they are only the middle chapter of a much longer and more complicated story. Of equal or greater importance are issues of planning and site survey. I have been concerned in this chapter only with the work of planning as reflected in final products.

As detailed in the following section, the regularities of site configurations considered here provide clear evidence of site planning and precision—in short, of calculation, counting, and mensuration. Necessary prerequisites for these activities are a system for counting and measuring, coupled with knowledge of simple geometry. The intricacies of site configuration and precision, most evident at Poverty Point, show clear evidence for measured intervals and areas and for the use of elemental compass geometry—circles, arcs, vesicas, inscribed equilateral triangles, and rectangles. Plans could have been drawn on a board, or, as James Marshall (1987:40) argues for the later Hopewell, on a "sand table," or with other such simple means such as a model from tied strings, with the use of durable templates (Romain 2000:66–67), or even with sticks as reported for the historic Creek Indians.[6] With some simple code, the plan had to specify distance, direction, interval (proportion), and magnitude of proposed three-dimensional construction at a very small scale (see Romain 2000:66–67), and this plan had to be converted to the desired scale on the ground (by changing the magnitude of base units from the model version to SUs or SMUs). Taller mounds had to be planned for by providing a wider base, and this would have required some understanding of the angle of repose of piled dirt.

I have argued throughout this essay for an anthropocentric measuring system based on the height of a man, or width of his outstretched arms, as measured with strings or cords. String systems are highly flexible, mobile, and incredibly easy to use because lower measurements can be taken by folding the string in

halves or thirds and larger increments are just a matter of nondistracted counting. The actual magnitudes or counted intervals used are another matter entirely
and are independent of the measurement system or its devices for measurement.
Thus, finding the same measured intervals at different sites implicates two quite
different spheres of knowledge. Some basic counts could be recorded on the
string itself by the locations of knots of various sorts. My major claim is for an
Archaic period system of measurement based on an increment of 1.666 m (or
its half or its double) and larger units of 86.63 m (or half or double this). I find
it nothing short of astounding that one can take the long measurement unit of
86.63 m discovered at Paso de la Amada, Mexico, a second millennium B.C. site,
and superimpose this arbitrary length on Middle Archaic sites of the American
Southeast, such as Caney Mounds, and get perfect fits, in whole numbers, of site
parameters and internal structure. It is equally amazing that other investiga-
tors have inductively inferred the two logical permutations of this same basic
measurement system with data from other sites. Scholten de D'Éneth (1954,
1956, 1970, 1977, 1980, 1981, 1985) argues that 3.34 m (1.67 m × 2) was the
"American Unit," with 83.3 cm, the Peruvian *vara* (rod), being a fourth this
measure, and Sugiyama (1993) argues for a unit of about 83 cm (1.66 m/2) for
Teotihuacan, Mexico, virtually the same unit. This is the same system of measurement seen at Caney Mounds, Watson Brake, and Poverty Point. Gibson
(1987:20) makes a clear case for a 43-m unit at Poverty Point; I did not become
aware of this until reaching the same conclusion by a more circuitous logical
route and from different observations.

    In actual practice of marking a site for construction, I think long distances
were measured with long cords of standard length (see Morgan 1937). Critical
points of a proposed site could be easily established by triangulation with two
long cords from points on an already established line, much as archaeologists use
two tape measures to lay out a square excavation unit using Pythagorean geometry. The same spaces could be established with counted paces, but I believe
the degree of precision shown in the measured spaces (see Figures 10.8–10.11,
10.17) over long distances at the largest sites is better explained as having been
accomplished with long cords, use of which is common practice all around
the world, even today (cf. Davis 1983). In actual practice, ancient surveyors/
engineers would have needed a way to get around trees without losing track of
distance and direction, the best way being to burn down the trees or scrub and
to clear the space (Morgan 1937). The Middle and Late Archaic inhabitants of
the American Southeast presumably were adept at making long nets (Gibson
2000:147), so making long measuring cords would certainly have been within
the range of their technological capabilities. Net technology also requires a basic
knowledge of geometry, intervals, linked parallel cords, and counting for making

a mesh of a particular size—the same basic knowledge needed for planning Poverty Point and/or making a simple string model of its principal axes and conjunctions.

The standard unit of measure, whether 83.3 cm, 1.666 m, or 3.333 m, can easily be explained as an independent invention of people of similar stature using the human body to calculate fathoms with the use of strings and simple manipulations of the interval by doubling or halving the string length. This simple hypothesis for Standard Units, however, cannot explain the existence of Standard Macro-Units of 86.63 m (or 43.32 m) that show up at early sites in the southeast United States, Mexico, Peru, and many other places and persisted in some regions up to the Spanish Conquest. The existence of the SMU implies shared concepts of counting and culturally significant numbers, such as 4, 13, 20, and 52. Some of the numbers could be cross-culturally pervasive based on standard features of the human body, such as units of 20. Others, such as 13, are much less obvious and cannot be credibly thought to recur through independent invention. Translating the measured distances at early sites back into their (possible) original native numbers presents some special challenges, but I believe it to be well worth the effort as this information will provide significant insights into aspects of ancient systems of belief (see below).

The actual construction of earthworks required forest clearance, leveling, and then extraction of dirt and clay and their transport by simple means, as described by Gibson (1987, 1996b, 2000:91–94; cf. Morgan 1937). Depending on the work pace and construction interval, this required varying degrees of supervision and/or provisioning of a labor force, social, political, or ritual inducements to labor, job-site responsibilities, leadership, credit for accomplished work, fame, and possibly power. All these issues are of supreme interest and are addressed by other authors in this book. Conjectured solutions to these issues, however, depend on assessments of labor organization, leadership, and site use and function, all of which presuppose knowledge of actual site construction.

Questions of planning and labor time are critical for resolving questions of human energetics because mathematics provides an essentially infinite number of energy solutions to the problem of mound building (see Gibson 1987 for detailed discussion for Poverty Point). For purposes of discussion, suppose that the volume of earth moved to construct a site such as Watson Brake was 100,000 m^3 of fill. If we divide this cumulative sum by conservative estimates for the total length of its occupation and by the number of estimated ambulatory inhabitants, the per capita labor investment per day would be at its hypothetical minimum. If we grant our hypothetical site 200 inhabitants and a 500-year occupation history, each person would have to have moved 1 m^3 of dirt per year, or about 2.8 liters of dirt per day. But this is the mathematics of buying a house on credit with pain levels minimized by reducing payments to the smallest increments and taking an eternity to cover the debt. By such relaxed mathematics we could conclude that the labor requirements were, hypothetically, all other things being equal, not onerous and would not have required any significant supervision as they would barely have exceeded the volume of daily household sweepings. Processual interpretation with such hyperconservative assumptions and calculations would be that there was no real payoff to a person or a community for overseeing the piling up of household sweepings behind one's house until, half a millennium later, a circular earthwork had been created.[7] The math is beyond question, and the assumptions for length of occupation and size of the population can all be reasonable, but nothing else in the equation fits any known reality of human behavior. My point here is that one can make assumptions that preclude a priori any possibility of ever viewing mound construction as socially significant or meaningful, either by grossly overestimating the time taken to do the work or by underestimating the number of tasks involved and/or their difficulty (i.e., thinking that the main task is to heap up dirt).

On the other hand, it is equally easy to err on the side of exuberance. If we calculate that our same earthwork was constructed over a five-year period, it would have required that each inhabitant carry 100 m^3 of mound fill per year and place it in the appropriate spot. This is certainly doable but much more onerous, and it would have required significant adjustments in the work schedules of everyone in the community. Clearly, the possibilities between minimal and maximal estimates should safely bracket the reality we seek, but if we relax these parameters and fail to frame time and labor closely enough, our estimates will serve little useful purpose, even as heuristic exercises. Archaeology can provide details for sorting out energy issues, such as determining the number of construction phases for each mound, their dating, the nature of the imported fill, and the distance it was transported. I believe site structure and other evidence of deliberate planning provide other clues to help us reach better and more realistic approximations of the labor requirements for building mound complexes. Techniques of absolute dating will never be precise enough to narrow the labor window sufficiently to distinguish between 2 and 200 m^3 of labor per person per year. In terms of inferred managerial imperatives, however, there is a world of difference between the two. Low-end estimates generally presume ad hoc construction of mounds, one at a time, with no particular rhyme or reason to the cumulative effect. Evidence discussed here of site structure indicates that models of casual construction, with earthworks being the cumulative coalescence of individual building initiatives, have little merit (cf. Mainfort and Sullivan 1998). Gibson's (1996a:302) comment that "nothing about Poverty Point is ad hoc" clearly applies to its plan and mounds.

Arguments from overall design point to mound groups as preconceived, integrated wholes that were constructed as such. In terms of energy assessments, I believe the evidence of repeated configurations and close attention to measured intervals, orientations, and scales requires that we narrow the labor interval actually taken for site construction, as Gibson (1998a:319) has recently done for Poverty Point. This would, in turn, make their construction a big deal socially. We find their existence today, given the mounds' verified age, of tremendous social and political significance. There is no good reason to believe that the folks who constructed these mounds were any less impressed with their own handiwork than we are. I can well imagine them proudly chanting, as did the Choctaw after erecting a memorial earthen mound at Nanih Waiya to safeguard the bones of their recently deceased ancestors and relatives, "Behold the wonderful work of our hands" (Lincecum 1904:521–522, cited as an appendix in Knight 1989:288–289).

Implied in all this discussion are issues of social organization and the social and psychological prerequisites for motivating a voluntary workforce. As a minimal requirement, workers would have to have been able to see evidence of the magnitude and magnificence of their own work. Projects would have to have been completed sooner rather than later to keep them going, with the evidence of past work being obvious, impressive, and capable of conveying a sense of pride in work accomplished. All these factors are corroded in minimalist math.

Site Planning

As just emphasized, considerations of site planning have significant implications, so it is important to establish a credible case for it. My assertions for planning are based on recognition of repeated patterns within and between sites. One aspect of planning that I have not dealt with here concerns selection of appropriate space. Caney Mounds, Watson Brake, Frenchman's Bend, Insley, Poverty Point, and others appear on bluff locations. Other features of the local landscape were probably also important (see Mainfort and Sullivan 1998; Sassaman and Heckenberger 2001). With reference to basic measurements, bluff sites selected had to be long enough to accommodate the planned mound enclosure. Finding a bluff line that trended north-south may have also been important. These issues of construction-site selection go beyond my immediate purpose here of analyzing mound sites as human artifacts with certain technological, manual, and conceptual requirements.

I started considering issues of site planning five years ago and did my initial work with Paso de la Amada and other Mesoamerican sites (see Clark 2001; Clark and Hansen 2001). On the basis of this work, I claim to have rediscovered several measuring systems and principles of site organization. Here I am concerned with the Archaic system based on SUs of 1.666 m and modular distances of 43.32 m and 86.63 m. As described, these standard increments best explain the sizes and scalar differences characteristic of early Southeast mound groups.

Consideration of Caney Mounds has had a significant impact on my view of geometry, and I have been rethinking my previous work ever since. I have argued for a specific and rather complex arrangement of mounds at Caney and have used this abstracted pattern as a template for evaluating another six sites. Watson Brake is the best fit to the Caney template, and it probably better represents a complete pattern. I never recognized the principal triangle at Watson Brake, however, and I would never have done so because the site is close enough to an oval plan that this impression would have prevailed. As documented in the illustrations, equilateral triangles of various sizes can be fitted nicely to all the sites of the sample. Triangles are actually a simplification of vesica and circle geometry based on standardized radii. Every vesica contains a mirrored pair of equilateral triangles, and every circle contains six. In many cases, the curve or arc of a circle delimits outer edges of mounds whereas the sides of inscribed triangles pass though the mounds' center points (see Figures 10.2 and 10.4).

The other noteworthy characteristic of the Caney Mounds was evidence of dual orientations that converge on the summit point of the western conical mound, with the divergent angle between the two lines being 10 degrees. The longer orientation, the bisecting line of the principal triangle, does not pass over the summit of any mound, so its status as a sight line for celestial observation is dubious. The secondary (i.e., shorter) orientation does connect the two tallest conical mounds, and these are separated by a standard interval. It appears a likely possibility that this is a sight line of celestial significance. Because of the way the site was laid out, however, this sight line between principal mounds is 10 degrees off the main axis. In short, the abstracted Caney template takes account of distance, principal lines of sight, proportions, and conjoined systems of equilateral triangles of different size. It could hardly be more specific and arbitrary. Finding another configuration to match this template, therefore, would not be expected in the hypothetical world of random chance. The remarkable correspondences to the Caney template seen at other sites can only be due to shared experience, whether historical or contemporaneous.

Given their dates and proximity, the correspondences between Caney Mounds and Watson Brake are understandable as a phenomenon of contemporaneous interaction. The same can be claimed for Frenchman's Bend. The noteworthy differences among these sites are scalar and perhaps degree of completeness of mound complexes. The differences in scale between Caney and Watson Brake are not as easily manipulated as those noted among Caney, Claiborne, and Poverty Point, each of these being at a fourth, a half, or twice the scale of the others. In contrast, Watson Brake is 12.5 percent smaller than Caney Mounds, an unusual scalar difference indeed. But this represents a difference of one measurement module of 43.32 m, or one-eighth lineal distance of the principal triangle at Caney. Prior determination of the measurement system and large intervals was critical in determining the shared features of these two sites.

Considerations of Paso de la Amada and Sechín Alto demonstrate the presence of the same measuring system, modular distances, equilateral triangles, triangulation, and principal orientation lines evident at Caney, Watson Brake, and Poverty Point. Minimally, these foreign cases show that many of the organizational principles built into the Southeast sites formed a coherent package of perdurable cultural knowledge and practices that was extensive in time and space. Some historic connections are implicated, but how far back they go remains to be determined.

I have not discussed issues of mound sizes or proportional arrangements of spaces defined by mound configurations. They are equally significant and interesting phenomena, but they presuppose acceptance of the basic principles of layout that I am concerned with in this essay.[8] Proportions are entailed in considerations of standard distances, orientations, and measurement intervals. I forego discussion here of mound architecture, of mound sizes and shapes, and of proportional space to avoid undue extension of my argument. What I have presented should suffice to make a credible case for site planning without attempting to explicate all its complexity. My foil for discussion throughout has been the common notion that mound groups are haphazard arrangements of mounds constructed ad hoc by hunter-fisher-gatherers with too much spare time on their hands. Early mound sites evince significant patterns and repeated structures that could only occur as a result of deliberate planning and careful construction. They had to have been planned from the very beginning according to simple principles of geometry and arithmetic. I refer here largely to internal structure at individual sites. The data from Poverty Point are incontestable proof of significant external planning between and among sites—sites as conceived of as individual entities by archaeologists. Perhaps it would be more appropriate to state that planned, modified, and constructed cultural space included much more than individual mound enclosures. The extent of external planning has yet to be investigated.

I have been arguing for a level of precision for early mound builders that we rarely accord them. As moderns, we have no difficulty in thinking that ancient craftsmanship of small items, such as owl beads or hematite plummets, exhibits mastery of detailed knowledge and skill, but we do not generally accord the largest works of aboriginal hands this kind of presumption of intelligence and design. We should. Aboriginals clearly knew much more, and much earlier, than we give them credit for. This is most clearly evident in the design and construction of their earliest mound enclosures. At Poverty Point I have illustrated major lines of orientation that extended over 5 km (Figures 10.8–10.11). These same axial lines were carefully measured and counted over these same distances. Thus, at Greater Poverty Point, there is evidence of vigesimal arithmetic— counting by 20s. The straight linear distance, along parallel axes, between Lower Jackson Mound and Motley Mound is 60 SMU. It is 40 SMU from Lower Jackson to Mound B (Figure 10.9). The distance between parallel axes, for all three major systems of orientation, is 360 SU. The ability to measure and count was essential, of course, in converting small models or drawings of a site plan into mound constructions on the ground. This is a trite technical imperative of number, distance, and magnitude. Much more was involved.

Measured space is numbered space. Numerical coefficients of distances, a.k.a. numerology, may inform us as to why spaces were constructed as they were and, consequently, what they might mean. In converting modern metrics into Archaic Standard to assess numbers in an aboriginal system, we have to confront the issue of the basic standard unit. As discussed, some sites are scalar versions of others. Was this done by making an appropriate division of the number of units, say from 8 SMU to 4 or 2 SMU? Or was it done by reducing or increasing the length of the standard unit used, say from 83.3 cm to 1.666 m, while keeping counts the same? Any of these standard units would yield the same proportional information to our modern measurements, but not the same numerology. My presumption is that scalar adjustments were effected by manipulating the size of the SU while maintaining the same counts. This hypothesis makes the most sense of scalar differences based on halving or doubling distances.

In the discussion of Caney Mounds, I mentioned that if the SMU were half of what I initially proposed, then all the numbers for the large triangles would be sequential integers: 6, 7, and 8. Later sites were twice this scale. If we suppose that the basic unit of measure during the Middle Archaic was 83.3 cm (a long pace or the length of a string extending from the center of one's chest to the fingers of an outstretched arm) instead of 1.666 m (a fathom or brace), this would allow us to think of these sites as having the same number patterns at different scales. I think this was the case. Messing with inferred numerology, however, is inherently dangerous and self-revelatory, so I will attempt to minimize potential losses by limiting considerations of conjectured native numbers to a few brief examples to show the possibilities of such analyses without exhausting their promise.

The sides of the principal triangle at Caney were described as 4 SMU at the larger SU unit. If the SU was 83.3 cm, then the Caney triangles are 8 and 7 SMU on a side. As previously noted, the height of an 8-SMU equilateral triangle is 6.9282 SMU or 360 SU. At Caney, the principal conical mound along the eastern bluff, Mound B, is offset to the north of the obvious bisection point in such a way that the axis defined by the summits of these mounds measures

7 SMU. Translated into its constitutive units, this is 364 SU. I find this solar year count between the summits of the principal mounds intriguing and do not believe that it is an accidental consequence of my math. Inferences of all the particulars of the Archaic measuring system preceded my encounter with the recent map of the Caney Mounds. My interest in numbered spaces followed my conviction that it is possible to infer native systems of measurement. In no instance have I tried to work backwards from a hypothesis of the possible numerical significance of a distance to an inferred standard unit of measure. I think the builders of the Caney Mounds complex measured an interval away from the intersection of the principal orientation axis with the base of the 8-SMU equilateral triangle to locate the point that corresponded to a 7-SMU diagonal. They could have done this on either side of the axial line of the principal orientation, but they chose to do it on the northern side. Either hypothetical placement would have been fairly easy to calculate with cords. If ancient builders built this solar number into the basic structure of Caney Mounds, this fact would diminish the probability of a possible celestial significance for this orientation and suggest, instead, that the position of Mound B relative to Mound E was dictated by numerological concerns rather than astronomy. Of course, these need not have been mutually exclusive options.

If this number is important for the secondary axis, why the difference at Watson Brake? Recall that this site is one-eighth smaller than Caney Mounds, so the corresponding diagonal between the principal mounds is 6 SMU, or 312 SU, a number that does not appear obviously significant. On the other hand, the principal triangle itself at Watson Brake is 7 SMU on all three sides, the 364 SU count of the solar year.

For Poverty Point I illustrated a series of nested triangles that provides a numerological minefield (Figure 10.12). With a standard unit of 1.666 m, the length of the enclosed plaza is 364 units, and it is twice that to the outside of the rings. This is to say that doubling the size of SU to 3.333 m, the maximum distance between the rings, measured north-south, is 364 SU. All these measures could just as easily be 365, or 370 for that matter, based on the accuracy of the maps I am working with and the archaeology of clay and dirt structures. In making claims for precision I am constrained by the overall evidence of the measurement modules, so I have given them the benefit of the doubt when confronted with a few fuzzy edges of mound sizes due to erosion, vegetation cover, and the like. Consequently, I argue for 364 (7 × 52) rather than the more precise number for the solar year. With a unit of 3.333 m as the SU, the distance between the central measuring point on the eastern edge of the Poverty Point plaza and the western edge of Mound A is just under 5 SMU, or 260 SU. This same number is built into the Caney Mounds and Watson Brake complexes.

At Caney, the perpendicular distance between the secondary axis connecting Mounds B and F and the parallel axial line passing through the summits of Mounds D and E in the southern sector measures 260 SU. Along the eastern bluff, 260 is the distance between the summits of Mounds A and C (Figures 10.1, 10.2). At a fourth this scale, the open area of Cedarland is approximately 260 by 260 SU. At this same scale (83.3 cm for SU), Mound A at Poverty Point is 260 SU in length. This is to say that Mound A is comparable to Claiborne and Cedarland in absolute size.

The variations at Watson Brake are even more interesting, as shown in Figure 10.22. The principal triangle at Watson Brake is 7 SMU (at 83.3 cm for SU) on a side, or 364 SU, and the smaller paired equilateral triangles are 6 SMU on a side, or 312 SU. Bisection of these vesica triangles yields four 3-5-6 right triangles, the height of the bisecting line from the base being 5 SMU, or 260 SU. This same distance was measured along each arm of the southern equilateral triangle to place Mounds I and J. It is 5 SMU (260 SU) from the summit of Mound A to that of Mound J; it is the same distance between the summits of Mounds E and I. As noted previously, the northern pair of mounds, C and D, are not symmetrically placed in accord to the northern triangle of the vesica pair. Rather, Mound D is centrally placed in such a way that the distances from its northern edge to the summits of Mounds E and A form an isosceles triangle, with the two equal sides measuring 260 SU. Bisection of this triangle creates two 3-4-5 right triangles, the fundamental right triangle the world over. The geometry at Watson Brake is phenomenal, with the northern and southern mounds marking pairs of 5-5-6-SMU isosceles triangles enclosed in the paired 6-6-6 equilateral triangles of the vesica. Bisection of the vesica splits all these triangles into 3-5-6 and 3-4-5 right triangles, respectively. These latter triangles record distances of 5 and 7 SMU in their perimeters. Given the arithmetic of the SMU (52 SU), the counts of 260 and 364 will show up for every 5 and 7 SMU. Given the evidence of counting by 4s, 20s, and 13s, honoring the number 260 (20 × 13) by marking significant points along major axes of sites should come as no surprise. The 3-4-5-SMU triangles at Watson Brake represent 12 SMU in perimeter, thus they incorporate both the 260 and 364 counts in the same geometric form. The interior plaza at Watson Brake is defined by four of these 3-4-5 triangles conjoined at their bases.

It is worth stressing that 260 is the sacred day count of all Mesoamerican almanacs, representing the permutation of two cycles of 20 days with 13 number coefficients (see Coe 1999 for clear descriptions). With an SU of 3.333 m, central Poverty Point is 364 units long and 260 units wide. As just described, these same measured intervals are basic to the structure of both Caney Mounds and Watson Brake. These are calendar counts and sacred numbers in Mesoamerica.

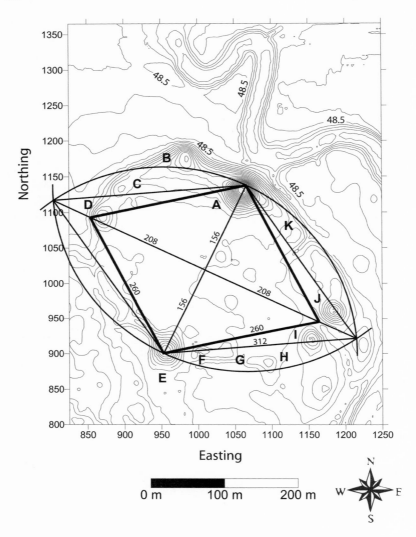

Figure 10.22. Map of Watson Brake showing some distances in the possible native system with the SU calculated at 83.3 cm.

Surely it can be no accident that Poverty Point, Caney Mounds, Watson Brake, and Cedarland have these dimensions, proportions, and numbered counts built into their plazas—however disconcerting this observation might be to Meso-americanists. Distance as number, and number as ritual count, provide some insight into the significance of early Southeast architecture and enclosed spaces. I will not pursue this complex topic here (see Clark 2001), and I raise it only to solicit more and better maps to check the possibility of calendar counts in early mound groups. I find the evidence compelling that the size and arrangements of mounds around the early enclosures represented visual encryptions of calendrical counts and perhaps other ritual numbers. If so, consideration of this deliberate encryption should become part of our thinking about how these enclosures were built and why. If my claim is sound, we might reasonably expect to find lunar, planetary, or even stellar counts in some of these mound arrangements or in mound dimensions. Such evidence would constitute an independent check of my hypothesis.

History Matters

Information and claims presented here have important ramifications for historical issues. I use "history" as a shorthand term for "traditional cultural practices and interactions among peoples through time." As such, "history" is much more than relative chronologies and artifact comparisons (see Pauketat 2000, 2001a, 2001b, 2001c). In terms of broad history, the most significant news lately has been the early dating of mound activity in the American Southeast to 3400 B.C. (Saunders et al. 1997). Later constructions of ceremonial centers in Mesoamerica and Peru evince enough similar features of design, mathematics, and logic that there must be a historic connection. The evidence suggests very old and widely disseminated knowledge about how to build large sites. This building lore persisted remarkably intact for so long that I think we can, and must, assume that it was part of special knowledge tied to ritual practices. The bulk of the evidence points to very old links among cultures receding back beyond Poverty Point times. But it is interesting that Paso de la Amada and Sechín Alto are both at the same scale as Poverty Point, a relatively late scalar innovation in the Southeast, so some shared experience and practices could have been of more recent vintage and have originated in different regions. Much more data will be required before we can better frame or resolve these issues. I hope to have provided sufficient evidence and arguments to raise the possibility of Middle Archaic interaction on a continental scale.

Within the Southeast region, several Middle Archaic mound groups appear to have been constructed at the same time and according to the same principles. Viewing mound building as regional and interactional must clearly be a significant part of any explanation of their existence. On its face, the spatial distribution of the earliest Southeast mounds looks like a competitive, interactional phenomenon. Periodicity is critical here, as argued by Widmer (this volume). Why were some mounds built when they were, and why did mound building cease when it did? I find these questions of fundamental importance but have navigated around them here because their resolution presupposes better knowledge of how the mound groups were actually constructed. The evidence for site planning suggests that early mound enclosures were built fairly quickly as extraordinary community projects. A competitive social milieu may help explain how it was possible for a community leader, or council of leaders, to motivate other coresidents and kin to help build mounds. The other side of this motivation, I believe, came from knowledge that the constructed spaces were being built according to cosmological principles based on venerable knowledge of celestial cycles, sacred numbers, world directions, mythology, and so forth and that the promoted mound complex would better serve the spiritual needs of the community, perhaps in a manner similar to that described by Gibson (1996a, 1996b, 1998b, 2000:61–65; cf. DeBoer 1997) for Poverty Point.

The continental history implied in the preceding discussion presents two conundrums. The first is the spatial extent of architectural and engineering knowledge, such as SMUs, counting by 13s and 20s, use of vesicas and equilateral triangles to measure space and calculate mound emplacements, and so on. Common roots of this knowledge may go back even further than the first construction of earthen mounds in the Southeast—or it could have been shared at any time in the ensuing 20 centuries.

Equally as troublesome as the spread of knowledge and cultural practices over expansive territory is its continuity through long time periods in one place. Of the three large sites considered in the sample (Poverty Point, Paso de la Amada, and Sechín Alto), the similarities between Poverty Point and its Middle Archaic predecessors will be viewed by most scholars as the least problematic because of presumptions of spatial location and cultural traditions (cf. Gibson 1998b:19). There is no good reason to be comfortable with this bias, however. The nearly two-millennium gap between the constructions of Watson Brake and Poverty Point presents as difficult an interpretive problem as finding the Caney triangles in southern Mexico and Peru. One has to presume that knowledge of the building of Caney Mounds and others was passed down through more than 60 generations of non-mound-building peoples with no apparent distortions, loss of measurement accuracy, or shifts in numeration. This is a remarkable feat of cultural memory and practices. This number of generational groups probably exceeds the number of contiguous tribal territories and groups between Watson Brake, Louisiana, and central Peru. So, conceived as a problem of information transmission from group to group (either generational or geographical), Poverty Point was as distant from Watson Brake as it was from Sechín Alto, Peru. How was knowledge of building special centers transmitted and/or preserved across generations and among neighboring groups? What kinds of cultural experiences were involved?

In the brief discussion of Claiborne and Cedarland I suggested one way to bridge the chronological chasm between Caney and Poverty Point, as well as address the equally difficult problem of explaining the Caney Mounds themselves. My thesis is that mound constructions were planned and premeditated and that they were also socially significant and meaningful. If correct, they had to have been meaningful to a hunting-fishing-gathering people with a long tradition of cultural practices and beliefs about identity and their place in the natural, social, and spiritual order of things. I think that Early Archaic base camps and semipermanent villages provided the proximate models for constructing mound enclosures. If so, these would already have to have been imbued with cosmological significance. Constructed mound enclosures represented the basic model of inhabited space, writ large, and memorialized in a more durable medium.

Like their perishable predecessors and counterparts, each mound enclosure was organized in accordance with basic beliefs of the heavens and earth, world directions, distances, number, and elevation, to list the obvious cosmological categories (see DeBoer 1997). I imagine that cultural practices of group living preceded mound building, persisted alongside it, and continued unabated after the first flurry of mound-building activity had dissipated. If true, many of the organizational principles fossilized in the earliest mound groups would have still been in place to inspire and instruct later efforts at mound building, just as they had been prior to the first efforts. This conjecture carries the implication that the order, structure, and meaning of ephemeral villages would also have been viewed as sacred space in a cosmological plan. If so—and I currently can see no viable alternative solutions for conveying information across the chronological gap—then mound enclosures differed from villages, at whatever level of annual permanence, in degree rather than kind. Differences in kind may have developed later with alterations in daily practice, such as reserving special functions and rites for the permanent public spaces captured at mound enclosures. An equally viable alternative suggested by Jim Brown (personal communication, 1998) is that mound enclosures were patterned after domestic dwellings (see also DeBoer 1997:227–230). This excellent suggestion would also account for the persistence of all the basic building knowledge I have been concerned with here. Many of the features of early mound enclosures persisted into the Contact period, as is clear from John White's drawings of the village of Pomeiooc in 1588 Virginia. The village consists of a circular, palisaded enclosure with two principal buildings facing each other across an open central plaza—the temple and the chief's residence (Harriot 1972:67).

Some model for the preservation of basic construction knowledge is needed for explanations of Poverty Point, given the discontinuous history of mound building in the Southeast. If my proposal of cultural practices and traditions is correct, or sufficiently so, then the builders of Poverty Point had at least two sources of proximate inspiration: traditional and meaningful village or house formats and the ancient ruins of earlier builders. Poverty Point peoples may also have preserved, in oral histories or campfire memories, accounts of the building of earthen mountains and the manner and reasons for building them. That Poverty Point builders were aware of ancient mounds is beyond doubt. The entire layout of Greater Poverty Point is calibrated to the position of Lower Jackson, a Middle Archaic mound. All principal measuring grids pass through Lower Jackson, and calculated space appears to have commenced from there (see Figures 10.8–10.11, 10.17). The decision to build Poverty Point in the place chosen probably also had much to do with the earlier mounds marking this area as sacred space.

Function and Meaning

Coming as it does at the end of a long essay of geometric esoterica, my claim that Poverty Point and its honored ancestors were built as sacred spaces is laughably banal. Even a sentient turnip could tell you this from just a glance at these places. I have tried to move a bit beyond the obvious, however. What I have attempted in this chapter is to identify specific ways in which these sites may have been sacred or revered, as well as to identify empirical markers of such special status and function. All of these sites were erected according to strict logic that incorporated calendrical numbers and/or proportions, geometric forms, conjoined alignments, and other special knowledge. I argue for the possibility of mound groups having been patterned after village or house analogs. All the Southeastern mound groups represented large social containers (cf. Mainfort and Sullivan 1998). Encircling mounds delimited and defined interior, public spaces and contained and even protected them. The care taken to measure, mark, and align this space suggests that it was laid out to replicate or even capture features of the cosmos, as culturally perceived, a practice common among most tribal peoples. I expect that individual buildings and earthen platforms were constructed with similar concerns and care. More and better archaeology will be needed to provide a sound evidentiary basis for more explicit considerations of what this cosmic plan may have been.

Construction of ritual space would surely have been critical to site functions, or at least some of them. The striking feature of all the Southeast sites considered here is the demarcation of a central plaza surrounded by mounds or buildings. I suspect the surrounding buildings and houses faced inward, introspectively, with outside walls or mound edges establishing a physical and metaphorical perimeter and/or barrier to the outside (see Gibson 1996a, 1996b, 1998b, 2000). At early mound centers, the perimeter of mounds contained and sheltered the public and/or sacred central area. The notions of centering and centrality are hard to avoid in viewing the configurations of these earthworks (see Brown 1997:476). I refer to centering and centers in a cosmological rather than a political sense, but one of the key questions swirling around the construction of early mounds is whether both senses might not be appropriate. The allocation of mounds along the defined perimeter and their patterned differences in spacing, extent, and height indicate that marking and containing the sacred is only part of the story. As Kenneth Sassaman and Michael Heckenberger (2001) argue, social and political factors of village divisions and statuses may have also been in play.

It is worth stressing that the specific measurement system and site geometry evident in Poverty Point did not continue unchanged into Woodland and Mississippian times, although these features of site layout continued to be major concerns. The Archaic measuring unit appears to have survived into the Adena period (see maps in Clay 1986), but the mound forms and compounds did not. Consequently, Poverty Point represents a terminus rather than a beginning, at least architecturally. Woodland peoples employed a different system of measurements and geometric forms (see Marshall 1980, 1987; Romain 2000). These peoples used a measurement system and geometry derived, at least in part, from Formative Mesoamerica, as argued by Marshall (1978, 1979, 1980, 1987, 1995, 1997, 1999). I address details of the Mesoamerican system in detail elsewhere (Clark 2001). This system used a shorter measuring cord (1.544 m) for the SU and its permutations, but it otherwise preserved many of the traditional counts and arithmetic (i.e., 1 SMU = 52 SU). Also, reliance on triangles was replaced by the use of square grids, and circles and squares, at various SMU increments, as is so evident in Hopewell earthworks (Byers 1991, 1992, 1998; Hively and Horn 1982, 1984; Marshall 1979, 1980, 1987; Romain 2000; Squier and Davis 1848; Thomas 1889). Even with these significant changes, however, there was continuity in laying out sites with regard to some calendrical numbers, such as 364. Continuity of the basic calendrical numbers is more clearly evident, however, in Formative Mesoamerican sites (Clark 2001). The persistence of foundational numerology in the face of an ancient metric and geometric reform suggests that such counts were of extreme importance for all the centers involved, both early and late. In turn, this surviving continuity further implicates these counts in the question of site functions and meanings. An especially created space with ample room for public theater, laid out with cosmic numbers and perhaps celestial benchmarks, should be seen as sacred space. What is clear with Hopewell enclosures is equally patent for Middle Archaic mound enclosures. Building mound groups to the proper specifications, in short, probably served to capture or retain a portion of the sacred for community use. And this possibility helps explain why they were built in the first place.

CONCLUDING REMARKS

I have tried to make several simple points in this essay about Archaic measuring systems, site planning, and the ritual significance of early mound enclosures. As argued, given the specificity of the basic patterns and their temporal and spatial extent, several critical issues of historic contact among ancient New World peoples are implicated. Many of the site-planning details presented here are a fresh result of my latest analysis, and others have already had the benefit of a few critiques following public and hallway presentations. Judging from the reception of these ideas by my colleagues, I presume that many readers who have had the patience to work their way this far and have pondered the accompanying illustrations and math find themselves in an anxious state. What I have argued is incredible, and so a serious decision must be made whether to believe it or not. In other fora, most listeners have followed the arguments quite easily, but they have followed the data to a simpler conclusion: that I am crazy, or the like. Joseph Heller demonstrated the catch-22 futility of arguing questions of personal sanity, so I offer none here. The larger issue is why, when confronted with detailed evidence and illustrations, many colleagues find a disbelieve-the-messenger response more comfortable than believing Archaic peoples had the superior cultural IQ advocated. If my arguments are correct, all that is at stake academically is prejudice against "primitive" tribes.

One reason for presenting a detailed case here, as well as elsewhere (Clark 2001), is that I have difficulty believing some of the implications of my analyses myself. I present them as hypotheses requiring more thorough testing with more rigorous and accurate field data and maps. Implications of my hypothesis are explicit and precise to the centimeter, so there should be no problem sorting out cases that fit and those that do not—once we determine acceptable degrees of modern and ancient measurement error (for discussion of issues of error and statistical tests of site patterns, see Heggie 1981 and Davis 1983). My experience is that the more accurate the maps, the better the fit for the systems presented here. Whether this trend continues to hold remains to be seen.

In quizzing the incredulous, I have been presented with a series of objections to my analyses that bear recitation here. The three strongest objections have been against my assertions of the levels of precision built into ancient sites, the spatial distribution of the Archaic measuring system, and attempts to translate distances into native units. Along the way I have found the greatest resistance among self-confessed math-phobes. I have had the hardest case selling geometry because nobody does this anymore, and few people remember much about it from junior high school. Basic unease with my compass geometry has generated the divergent accusations that either the level of precision is too much or it could have happened by accident. Both objections are just ignorance in its normal guise of personal opinion. Math is ruthless, uncompromising, and frigidly logical. It will be the final arbiter of whether specific proposals for any given site work or not.

A strength of my analysis is that the specific proposals for an Archaic system were worked out with a different dataset than I rely on here to test them. The only logical reason that one could expect to find any concordance between my model and foreign sites is if the sites were built by peoples with some shared knowledge based on contemporaneous or past shared experience. I rely entirely on maps made by others, with the scales indicated. These are not negotiable or malleable data. Once I confirm on the basis of internal evidence of specific descriptions that map data and scale are accurate, I convert spatial distances on these maps into numbers based on the proposed Archaic measuring units and hypothetical layouts based on simple pole-and-cord geometry. I have not changed the lengths, widths, or configurations of any of the sites considered to fit my ideas. Given an accurate map, it is a simple mechanical exercise to determine whether its limits and/or internal structure is spaced by intervals of 86.63 m, 80.29 m, 60 m, or some other system. In short, the hypothesis can be easily falsified. It merits mention that I have no particular desire to find a pervasive pattern, and when I began the work such a result was not even imagined. I expected to find dozens or even hundreds of systems that were culturally specific in time and place. I find it interesting and important that the reality of early site layouts in North and South America has proved otherwise. Thus far, I have only seen evidence of three distinct measuring systems in all of the Americas. I suspect there are others. But the limited number, given possibilities of thousands, is hugely significant.

In some illustrations, there are sufficient orientation lines (see Figures 10.12 and 10.17) that other critics have opined I have created so many grids and lines that I am bound to hit something of architectural significance. True. But there is no reason that I should consistently chance upon significant points such as Lower Jackson, Mounds E, A, and B, and Motley Mound at Greater Poverty Point. I have tried to keep the illustrations simple and show each subsystem by itself before presenting a simplified version approaching a total system. Those colleagues who follow me this far in the argument bring up the objection that my maps are too neat and too precise, with the implication being that I have imposed a rationality on a past phenomenon that it did not have in reality. With this crowd, I find another troublesome bias: most of them know little about building or basic craftsmanship, and so they have a vague notion that it is not that difficult to build something. Carpenters, masons, or architects would have little trouble believing that something as complex and regular as the mound groups discussed here must have been premeditated. These same skeptical colleagues have less trouble believing my arguments for the necessary, sequential technological steps for chipping an arrowhead or forming a pot, which may include dozens of steps. So why the difficulty in believing that constructing a site may have required necessary, sequential, and even difficult steps? Perhaps one difference is that potential risks for belief are so different with insignificant objects, such as arrowheads, and communal, cooperative constructions such as sacred centers. Having stated this, it should be obvious that ancient peoples may have shared our concerns and have taken greater care with those things that mattered most: their sacred centers. The modern bias of privileging small objects over site construction is completely backwards to past reality.

My two counterclaims for deflecting critics appear to thrust me into the same camp as they, resorting to ad hominem assumptions about the knowledge or experience of messengers to dismiss arguments. This is not quite the case. The credibility that individual listeners, and presumably readers, accord my arguments has as much, or more, to do with their personal knowledge and practical experience in their worlds as it does with any ancient evidence. It depends on one's personal views of technical complexity, its difficulty, and its probability. I am not tampering with evidence. Rather I am taking it out of publications and overlaying it with proposed templates of site planning that are highly arbitrary and precise. Most critics object to those aspects of the argument that are furthest from their personal experience. To date, I have yet to receive a satisfactory answer from colleagues as to why they are bothered by the precision in site planning I attribute to Middle Archaic and later peoples. I ask three questions in this regard. Why should we be troubled with evidence that demonstrates the ancients knew more, and at an earlier date, than we presumed they did? How could the ancients have built their sites without planning? If the sites were planned, would this not have included a measuring system, decisions about orientations, counting of units, and simple devices for doing so? At this point, these discussions can take an unpleasant turn as further questioning reveals that the primal objection to my analysis is not against the evidence of planning and precision, per se, only its early date.

What I propose here about ancient practices, knowledge, and concerns violates cherished academic notions of the imagined primitive tribes we have slotted into our narratives for the Middle and Late Archaic period. If the sites were from another time and place, say Formative Mesoamerica, no one would run for the Alka-Seltzer over the issues I raise. I assert that as scholars, most of us have severely underestimated the abilities and practices of Archaic peoples of the New World. Rather than our trying to force the evidence to fit the profession's evolutionist expectations, mound building ought to count as evidence of the knowledge, skills, and concerns of peoples who built and used them. This is my foundational assumption. Analysis of technical details and mechanical and energy concerns reveals that the massive mound groups as executed constructions are coherent, precise, and planned. Specifically, measured intervals represented precise counts, indicating that ritual matters were also of basic concern. Relying on a "watchmaker" argument (i.e., a watch testifies of a maker), I propose that the designs of mound groups required knowledgeable designers, in accord with the intricacy of the designs. If this claim runs counter to prevailing prejudice concerning ancient fishers and muckrakers of the Maçon Ridge, then maybe we should rethink cherished biases concerning their accomplishments, abilities, and way of life.

My argument is that the early mound groups such as Watson Brake were planned as totalities before they were built and that whole complexes were laid out and built according to master plans. Overall, layouts of early mound groups conform to some basic principles of geometry that were widely shared in North and South America in Archaic times. The layout of these early sites demonstrates the uniform use of basic measurement modules and units of 43.32 and 86.63 m and of specific proportions and numbers that, in later times, were associated with the design of sacred space and day counts. Similarities among mound groups through time and space also suggest greater historic contact among Archaic collectors than is generally thought. Considerations of the physical construction of mound complexes, as technical projects, demonstrated the coherence of overall plans and the knowledge involved. All of these further indicate planning and well-executed, rather short-term building projects associated with the encirclement of sacred space. The special knowledge involved in the construction of these mound enclosures further indicates a sacred/ritual function for these spaces.

The primary evidence for claiming the sacred or ritual character of Southeast mound enclosures is the numbers built into them. For most readers, this will be the most difficult part of the argument to evaluate and/or accept. Currently, the specificity of these numbers for Southeast sites exceeds that which can be verified archaeologically, so these conjectures remain to be tested against data of building sizes and locations known to be accurate to within 2 m over distances of 200 m. If my claim holds up, one implication will be that early sites are rife with calendrical numbers, including the rather odd count of 260 days characteristic of Mesoamerica. There are several ways to react to this information. The charitable assumption ought to be that some measured spaces did represent calendar counts as early as Middle Archaic times. If true, many aspects of Mesoamerican calendars must represent very ancient knowledge that was later incorporated into their system of counting days, lunar and planetary cycles, solar years, stellar intervals, and 52 great year cycles. As discussed, evidence for counting by 13s, 20s, 52s, 260s, 360s, and 364s are fossilized in the remains of Watson Brake, Caney Mounds, Poverty Point, and others (including Paso de la Amada and Sechín Alto).

If early peoples had sophisticated day counts and used significant cyclical numbers from them to plan and lay out ritual space, what does this imply about their knowledge, concerns, culture, and spirituality? I believe the evidence from the mound configurations themselves shows that the ancients did indeed have such knowledge, and they deployed it in organizing cultural and cosmic space.

They cared about these issues; they had the technical means and social motivation to plan special sanctuaries, and they actually created them. Theirs is a significant achievement meriting our continued respect and detailed study.

ACKNOWLEDGMENTS

This chapter has benefited greatly from colleagues who provided access to data, maps, commentary, and ideas. I especially appreciate the efforts and generosity of Jim Brown, Norm Davis, Jon Gibson, T. R. Kidder, James Marshall, Noel Reynolds, Ken Sassaman, and Joe Saunders. Their blinding hospitality to a Mesoamerican wanderer sojourning in the Southeast should not be taken as evidence of any degree of complicity or accord with the current product, unless otherwise avowed.

NOTES

1. Two major issues to be resolved concern the procedures for verifying measurement units and any historic connections among measurement systems. Earlier drafts of this chapter dealt with these issues at length, and while the material is not included here, it can be obtained by request.

2. My purpose here is to make a case for geometric, metrological, and mathematical regularities in early mounds. The obvious question to arise from identification of patterning concerns its purpose. Others have suggested that specific alignments of mounds relate to astronomical observations. I would not be surprised if such were the case, but I am unqualified to enter into such arguments, and I have not investigated this promising area of research. Gibson (1996a) and Brown (1997) summarize some of the astronomical studies done for Poverty Point, and Romain's (2000) recent book is an excellent guide for sites of the Woodland period. At Jon Gibson's request, Norm Davis looked over maps and proposed alignments included in this chapter and suggested many intriguing solar, stellar, and lunar alignments and regularities among the different sites. I am convinced, as he argues, that planned azimuths and celestial observations for calendrical purposes (both lunar and solar) were involved in constructing mound centers. Precise dating of centers will be required to match alignments to the changing heavens. In this regard, it is of interest to recall that the base date of the Mesoamerican long-count calendars is August 13, 3114 B.C. (see Malmström 1997:116), a date that Mesoamericanists find difficult to account for because it precedes by over a millennium any evidence of planned centers there. Maybe we are looking in the wrong place for early astronomy in the Americas. The bottom line for any astronomical arguments is that if they are found to be viable and consistent, they only increase the magnitude of difficulty in planning and building these early centers.

3. Given my purpose to infer and test ancient measurement systems, it is imperative

to use the most accurate maps and measurement data available. Evaluation of previous maps of the Poverty Point rings indicated the possible promise for analyzing this site at a more precise level of accuracy. The base map presented here was composed from different sources using Photoshop and working on the image in different layers that could be superimposed and matched. Michelle Knoll did the technical work of drawing the final map. We used the official topographic maps for the region in order to plot precisely the locations of Motley Mound and Lower Jackson vis-à-vis Mound A, Mound B, and the river. We then adjusted Kidder's detailed topographic map of Poverty Point to this scale and made the most accurate fit possible by overlaying it on the base map. The road traversing the rings on both maps was a great help in making a precise match at the same scale. Most maps of the rings at Poverty Point show the details as they are perceived to have been rather than as they actually are. Many of the rings are clearly indicated on Kidder's map, especially in the central portion, but the northern and southern rings have been extensively damaged and do not show up well in the current topography. To capture possible locations of rings, we superimposed the map on the 1934 aerial photograph that shows the rings (illustrated in Gibson 2000:81, fig. 5.2). Not all hypothesized rings are evident on this photograph because of vegetation cover, but there is critical information that complements Kidder's map. On our drawings we have outlined the rings so they show up better. Once the appropriate scalar adjustments were made, we matched Kidder's topography with the photograph of the rings, and we were able to follow the rings on the photograph into areas of Poverty Point that have been leveled since the photo was taken. For plotting the approximate location of the steatite cache, located southwest of Mound A, we superimposed our working map over the map made by Webb (1982:17, fig. 9) and made the best adjustment we could to the locations of the obvious features. For the locations of Dunbar Mound and Sarah's Mount we relied on Gibson's maps (2000:95, fig. 5.9) and Kidder's map. We inferred the locations of some of the avenues and the possible causeway from the Kidder map, taking clues as to their location from Gibson's maps. Given our procedure for amalgamation, not all features of the map are plotted with the same level of accuracy. Locations of major features are the most accurate, with the minor features less so. I suspect that the steatite cache placement is only approximate. The force of my argument comes from correlation over long distances of the prominent features, those most likely to be accurately plotted. I expect more detailed mapping to corroborate the claims made here.

4. The mounds mentioned in this alignment are not contemporaneous in their creation but they could have experienced contemporaneous use, with the earlier mounds continuing in use into later time periods. They clearly form a logical alignment. Of course, it will never be possible to prove beyond dedicated doubt that the peoples who built the rings of Poverty Point took this older power axis into account in building their site. Joe Saunders and his associates (2001) raise the issue that it may be impossible to prove this point. My argument is that the alignment is only part of the pattern that has to be explained. The incremental distances are also important. If I am correct that all

major axial alignments pass through Lower Jackson, the information on its earlier construction becomes compelling evidence that the builders of Poverty Point were well aware that Lower Jackson was where it was, and that it was early. They incorporated this mound, and probably others, into their grand scheme. If true, this is clear evidence of the esteem in which they held earlier works. Naturalistic explanations of fortuitous concordance push the envelope on mathematical probabilities of chance occurrences to their breaking point and significantly blunt Occam's razor (see Gibson 2000). To me, the easier explanation is the obvious one that all the mounds were part of the same configuration, with older mounds setting critical parameters for the planning of the later earthworks.

5. My comments on the steatite cache presume that the vessels were used in this area of the site in conjunction with food preparation and/or serving. Gibson (1998a: 304) suggests that the fragments of steatite vessels were put in a special dump location and were fragments of vessels used in the occupation zone of the rings. Over 2,200 fragments of steatite vessels were found in an oval pit 2.5 m long by 2 m wide and about 60 cm deep. The floor of the pit was burned. Gibson notes that some vessel fragments recovered from the rings conjoin with steatite fragments from the cache—thus his interpretation that the cache was always a collection of discarded fragments. That whole vessels have not been reconstructed from the cache fragments perhaps supports his argument. It is worth pointing out, however, that his hypothesis presumes that it is more likely that conjoining pieces from the two different areas originated from vessels broken in the rings and that fragments were moved to this special refuse location. It would seem to be equally probable that vessels were used in the area of the steatite cache and that fragments could have been taken back to residences as tokens of the occasion.

6. Swanton (1928a:179, n. 81a) cites Hitchcock's interesting information with regard to a scalar model for building a "Round House":

It seems that the architect was Tukabahchee miko, a well-known Upper Creek leader and at that time its leading medicine maker. After giving the dimensions of the buildings as "about 60 feet in diameter and 30 feet high," [Hitchcock] says that Tukabahchee miko "cut sticks in miniature of every log required in the construction of the building, and distributed them proportionately among the residents of the town, whose duty it was to cut logs corresponding with their sticks, and deliver them upon the ground appropriated for the building, at a given time. At the raising of the house, not a log was cut or changed from its original destination; all came together in their appropriate places, as intended by the designer. During the planning of this building, which occupied him six days, he did not partake of the least particle of food" [Smithson. Misc. Colls., no. 53, p. 12].

7. I have portrayed the hypothetical, minimal case of mound building as using daily sweepings to pile up a mound. Some minor earthworks appear to have had this origin.

A substantial oval embankment enclosure about 1 m in height was an unintentional byproduct of sweeping the dance ground or plaza in purification ceremonies for the Creek Indians of the Historic period (Swanton 1928a:190, 1928b:498, 501, fig. 4). This feature resulted from repeated sweepings or scrapings of the grounds and moving the loose dirt, grass, and weeds to the edges of the delimited space. Knight (1989) reviews native beliefs about mounds and argues that it was a common practice ritually to clean plaza areas and then to place removed dirt as a thin mantle on some mounds in a ritual of renewal. Removed dirt was called *tadjo*. Earthworks built or augmented by or with *tadjo* can be expected to show fine laminations. To my knowledge there is no evidence that Archaic mounds were built or augmented in this way, but some Mississippian mounds show evidence of periodic, thin accretions (see Pauketat 2000:120).

8. Analysis of the sizes of Archaic mounds remains to be done. The published sizes for the largest mounds at Greater Poverty Point are of interest in terms of the proposed Archaic measuring system. Motley Mound is 15.5 m high and 121 by 170 m at the base (Ford and Webb 1956:17; Gibson 1996a:289). Mound A is 21.5 m high and 194 by 216 m at its base (Ford and Webb 1956:15; Gibson 1996a:295). Both mounds are described as possible bird effigies; I think describing them as cruciform mounds would be more appropriate because they could be effigies of crosses, trees, men, or birds. In terms of a base unit of 83.3 cm, Mound A measures precisely 26 units in height, 260 in length, and 232 in width. These distances, of course, are arguable based on Ford and Webb's (1956:15) topographic maps and the problem of delimiting the true edges of the mound. The mound could easily be as wide as long (260 SMU), depending on how one reads contours. Identification of mound edges could decide this issue rather easily. On the basis of published dimensions, the mound is 260 SU or 5 SMU in length, the count of ritual days in the Mesoamerican system. Of course, were we to invoke the longer unit of 1.666 m, the numerology would not work as nicely. In turn, if we halved the original unit to the 41.65 cm cubit and looked at the numbers, then Mound A would be 10 large units long, or 520 cubits. In this system, the crosspiece of the cruciform mound marks the division between 7 and 3 large units, this being the division between 364 and 156 small units. It is conceivable, therefore, that at nested scales both the ritual count of 260 and the solar count of 364 were built into the basic plan of Mound A. In the 83.3 cm SU system (SMU = 43.32 m), Motley Mound is about 3 by 4 SMU. The basic rectangle, then, would be comprised of two 3-4-5 right triangles. The diagonal of the mound is 5 SMU, or 260 SU, the length of Mound A, and the circumference of the rectangle is a double year count of 14 SMU (2 × 364 SU). Ford and Webb (1956:18) demonstrate that these are a complementary pair of mounds in size, shape, and alignment. They also share the basic numerology found in all the mound groups and sites considered here. Gibson (1987:20) proposed a 43-m unit for Poverty Point. He observed that most of the rings at this site are placed 43 m apart, crest to crest. My proposal is independent of his observations and based on different information.

11

Crossing the Symbolic Rubicon
in the Southeast

Kenneth E. Sassaman and Michael J. Heckenberger

With the discovery of earthen mounds dating to the sixth millennium before present in the American Southeast, the enduring anthropological question of the emergence of cultural complexity returns to an unusual setting. Although the Poverty Point complex of northeast Louisiana once garnered its share of attention as regards emergent complexity (Ford and Webb 1956; Gibson 1974), recent archaeological discourse over its genesis and organization has downplayed the level of sociopolitical development attending mound construction and long-distance exchange (e.g., Gibson 1996c, 2000; Jackson 1991). This change in perspective is owed, in part, to the empirical results of modern research: Poverty Point simply has not produced evidence for the suite of traits expected of complex societies, notably food production, social hierarchy, and political authority. Even population and degree of settlement permanence have been downgraded from earlier estimates. The Poverty Point culture and now the Middle Archaic societies that preceded it throw into question the structural linkages among demography, economy, and politics that have characterized cultural evolutionary models for decades. In these precocious cultural developments, we see a hint of complexity (monumentality) coupled with an economy (generalized foraging) and form of sociality (egalitarianism) that are presumed antecedents of complex society. While this contradiction alone exposes the shortcomings of modern perspectives on complexity, the tendency on some fronts has been to suggest that complex society is not necessary for building mounds (Russo 1994b; Saunders, this volume; White, this volume). This is similar to the argument used to undermine claims for monumentality in the Shell Mound Archaic (Milner and Jefferies 1998; Crothers, this volume). Without supporting evidence for economic and political change accompanying the construction of monuments, the mounds themselves are dismissed as simply de facto piles of earth and shell or, worse, "wasteful behavior" (Hamilton 1999).

Middle Archaic mound complexes of northeast Louisiana—Watson Brake, Caney, and others—like Poverty Point, were anything but incidental or haphazard constructions. As John Clark demonstrates in Chapter 10, these early mounds were constructed according to a plan. This plan required not only design, engineering, and labor coordination, but it also embodied and reproduced, we submit, a hierarchical form of sociality. The central plazas that were a part of this plan have ethnographic parallels that mirror and reproduce social hierarchy in cases worldwide.

Reticence on the part of archaeologists to accept an advanced level of cultural complexity on the basis of Archaic mounds alone can be traced to a priori assumptions about primitive society (Russo 1994b). Despite three decades of critical commentary on the evolutionary status of the world's foraging societies, archaeologists continue to assume that the antecedents of complex societies were akin to the food-sharing, egalitarian, generalized foragers of the ethnographic present. If we release these ethnographic ideals from their subordinate position in a sequence of cultural evolutionary stages, we are free to explore how hierarchical forms of sociality emerge apart from economic and political change, as a symbolic transformation of forager society, which, in turn, formed the ideological basis for material change.

We suggest that a major threshold, a Rubicon, was crossed in the early sixth millennium B.P. of northeast Louisiana. The result was a fundamental symbolic transformation of society wherein inequality based on difference from the other (culture vs. nature; us vs. them; insider vs. outsider) was turned inward, resulting in ranking or hierarchy among coresident groups. The mounds and central plazas they define are themselves testimony to this transformation. That it was not precipitated or accompanied by economic or demographic change makes the transformation no less significant, however, because once it took place—once the Rubicon was crossed—there was no turning back. This new structural principle was now on the landscape, encoded permanently in earth, and carried forward and transformed through practice. It would later become the ontological basis for dramatic economic and political change. As James Ford (1969) anticipated, it was the emergence of new ideas, a Theocratic Formative, that forever changed the American Southeast. Had he known how old monuments and central plazas were in the Southeast, Ford would not have had to turn to South America for the source of these new ideas.

We have several objectives in this chapter. We begin with a critical examination of the concept of primitive communism, arguing that there is little that is primitive about it and thus there is no reason to assume a priori that the antecedents of so-called complex society were necessarily egalitarian structures. We next summarize briefly the evidence for site plans among the Middle Archaic mound complexes of northeast Louisiana, corroborating and building on the observations of Clark (this volume). We then reiterate the points we have made elsewhere (Sassaman and Heckenberger 2001) about the symbolic significance of mounds and central plazas for social hierarchy. We conclude with some tentative thoughts on the origins of the symbolic transformation we infer from the empirical record of mounds and plazas.

THE ANTHROPOLOGICAL CREATION
OF PRIMITIVE COMMUNISTS

Inquiry into the emergence of cultural complexity presupposes some sense of what constitutes complex society and, less obviously, knowledge about antecedent conditions. Whereas anthropologists of all theoretical stripes would agree that over the course of human history societies became larger and more differentiated (i.e., more complex), they depart company on the essential qualities of complexity and causes for its genesis and reproduction. One of the more prolific writers on hunter-gatherer complexity in the Americas, Jeanne Arnold (1996b:79), indicates that complexity is found only among societies with certain organizational qualities, namely, (1) institutionalized labor relations whereby some people must perform work for others under the direction of nonkin and (2) inherited privileged status. It follows that antecedent societies lack these qualities and thus consist of autonomous members whose social differences do not transcend individual experience. Power, then, has a transient quality in antecedent societies, as no individuals have the authority to impose their will over others or, if they do, that authority dies with them. In theoretical paradigms ranging from nineteenth-century evolutionism to modern Darwinian selectionism, the real power in societies before "complexity" resided in nature's dominion over humans: society in a state of nature (Clastres 1974; Ingold 1999).

Thus, conceptions of primitive society entail more than simply the absence of attributes of complexity. Rather, they involve ontological premises about societal evolution that derive from unwarranted assumptions about human nature stripped of institutions (i.e., humans without society [Ingold 1999]), which, in turn, are traceable to uncritical uses of ethnographic cultures as analogs for primitiveness. When we foreground our conception of the "primitive" for critical analysis, an ironic twist emerges, namely, that the ethnographic material used to construct knowledge of social conditions before the "emergence" of complexity was derived from societies whose internal dynamics, serving to mitigate tendencies for the accumulation of power, are historical consequences of very powerful, institutionalized forces. In other words, "primitive" societies—constituted foremost through ethnographic analogy—are derivative of complex societies.

Although the anthropological creation of the "primitive" has a long history (Diamond 1974), we regard the Kalahari Project of the 1960s as *the* paradigm-defining context for modern knowledge about "primitiveness." From its National Science Foundation–funded beginnings in 1963, the Kalahari Project had as its aim the collection of data about a living hunter-gatherer group that might shed light on the evolution of human behavior (Lee 1976:10). Whereas the incursions of modern nation-states were acknowledged from the beginning of the project (Lee 1979:xvii), the effects of outside contact (i.e., history) could be "filtered out" if the research took an explicitly ecological orientation, emphasizing human adaptation to environmental properties that were potentially generalizable to a wide range of analogical circumstances.

As the Kalahari Project began to draw criticism for its ahistorical and eco-functionalist bent (e.g., Schrire 1980), Lee and his colleague, Eleanor Leacock, published papers from the 1978 Conference on Hunter-Gatherer Societies in Paris that showcased the range of political and historical circumstances affecting hunter-gatherers worldwide (Leacock and Lee 1982). The structural Marxist orientation of these studies is patently obvious (Bender and Morris 1988), for the goal of the editors was to define, despite recent impingements by capitalist nations, a mode of production original to hunter-gatherers. The introductory chapter by Leacock and Lee (1982:8–9) lists the features found in a "forager mode of production." Among them are collective ownership of the means of production; right to reciprocal access to resources; little emphasis on accumulation; total sharing; and equal access to the forces of production. Whereas Leacock and Lee stopped short of erecting the "forager mode" as an evolutionary paradigm, it is clear from Leacock's substantial ethnohistoric research on the Montagnais that these were the very features transformed by contact with Jesuits and French fur traders (Leacock 1954, 1980, 1982); hence they were regarded as antecedent to "complexity."

Lee (1988, 1990) himself later codified the forager mode as an evolutionary model in his resurrection and elaboration of Morgan's (1965 [1881]) and Engels's (1972 [1884]) arguments about the evolutionary status of primitive communism. For Morgan (1965 [1881]:63), "communism in living" was inherent to "the necessities of the family, which, prior to the Later Period of barbarism, was too weak in organization to face alone the struggle of life." This was the age when the Law of Hospitality ruled, according to Morgan, a sense of sociality somewhat akin to the relations based on trust that Ingold (1988) contrasts with relations of domination. Behavioral ecologists offered mathematical proof for the adaptive advantage of communal relations, hospitality, and trust, showing that net energy returns for foragers in unpredictable environments are greatest when they cooperate with other foragers (Dyson-Hudson and Smith 1978; Kelly 1995:168–201; Winterhalder 1986).

When skeptics of the evolutionary status of Kalahari foragers took center stage in the 1980s (Denbow 1984; Gordon 1984; Schrire 1980, 1984; Wilmsen

1983, 1989), Lee and his colleagues rallied behind primitive communism as an especially resilient and self-reproducing mode of production (Lee 1988, 1990). Its internal dynamic of leveling mechanisms was an effective barrier to the accumulation of power or wealth, keeping would-be big men in check even under circumstances of especially abundant resources (cf. Hayden 1994). Parenthetically, this defense of primitive communism posed the conundrum for explaining how societies so equipped to avoid "directional change" did indeed undergo structural transformation in prehistoric times (see Lee [1990] for his thoughts on this problem).

Lee's retreat into evolutionary modeling side-stepped the issues raised by the revisionists by simply noting that the primitive communist mode in places like the Kalahari was able to thwart "outside" influences because its internal dynamic was well equipped for that very purpose. Yet, this further underscored the question of the primitiveness of primitive communism. Polly Wiessner's (1982b) work on Hxaro exchange, one of the key leveling mechanisms of Lee's primitive communism, showed that exchanges between people intensified when they were threatened by encroachments of market economies. Solway and Lee (1990:122) acknowledged that certain Kalahari groups were able to use mobility and foraging to avoid the impingements on autonomy by herders, traders, and slavers of the recent past—that foragers had in fact "resisted the temptation (or threat) to become like us." And, in places throughout his writing, Lee (1992:43) agrees with his critics that the egalitarian relations of his forager mode are asserted, not inevitable or natural to a people under a given set of environmental circumstances. The evolutionary nature of primitive communism, be it an extension of Morgan's Law of Hospitality or the de facto state of a people without power or politics (Mann 1986), was not evolutionary at all, but historical, the outcome of deliberate human action in a matrix of competing regional or global forces.

This indeed is the conclusion reached by the so-called revisionists of Kalahari ethnography, and it is one embedded in the larger program of historicizing "primitives" worldwide (Headland and Reid 1989; Ingold et al. 1988; Wolf 1982). In its extreme formulation, a political-economic perspective on modern foragers places them squarely in the nexus of global economies, the rural proletariat of a capitalist world system (Wilmsen 1989). Others have instead emphasized the self-determination of foragers as resistant traditions (Asch 1982; Sassaman 2001; Schrire 1984). Either way, archaeological data suggest that the ethnogenesis of many foragers can be traced to histories of interaction with farmers and herders centuries before capitalism (Denbow 1984; Denbow and Wilmsen 1983, 1986; cf. debate about evolutionary status of tropical foragers [Bailey et al. 1989]). In response, the defenders of an evolutionary perspective on primitive communism refuse to accept the proposition that ethnographic foragers can be reduced to "societal impoverishment resulting from exploitation by larger and more powerful societies" (Lee 1992:39). Proponents on either side of the debate have accused the other of robbing foragers of their histories; in point of fact, the revisionists have simply liberated foragers from their evolution-ary past, a past that has not been empirically verified with archaeological data unaffected by what Trigger (1990b) calls the "ensured significance" of ethno-graphic data (see also Wobst 1978).

There is ample reason to conclude that primitive communism is not primitive at all but instead an outcome of power struggles within and between "complex" societies. It follows that without "primitives," so conceived, we lack a touchstone for recognizing the emergence of anything of relatively greater complexity. Ob-viously, social formations of some sort existed before the first conch shell was traded from the Gulf Coast to the Green River or before the first pile of dirt was mounded at Watson Brake. However, are we justified in assuming that these an-tecedent formations were somehow relatively less complex than what followed them? Arnold (1996b) is absolutely correct in pointing out the dangers in pick-ing a few traits like long-distance exchange or mound building as measures of social complexity. But her criteria for labor control and ascribed status overshoot the target of emergent complexity by a large margin. That is, between the insti-tutions of power Arnold insists define complex societies on the one hand and the primitive communism that eschews accumulations of power on the other lies a whole range of social variations that may not have much structural specificity (and hence are hard to classify) but embody a variety of actions that determined the pace and direction of social change.

Structural power such as that found in the institutions of authority Arnold emphasizes masks the actions of agents that simultaneously reproduce and alter those very structures. To think of power as an emergent property of institutional authority would merely reify complex culture or society as a unified whole. If we instead treat power in the relational terms advocated by Eric Wolf (1990, 1999:66), then "different relationships will shape power differently." If we like-wise decouple the exercise of power from the material resources that Arnold finds among the Chumash, for instance, and consider the relationship between power and ideas, we can begin to understand how phenomena like the land-scapes of Watson Brake and Poverty Point embody the genesis and reproduction of symbolic capital. Manipulation of symbolic capital by incipient leaders could form the rationale, if left unchecked, for the accumulation of wealth, control over labor, and assertion of exclusive hereditary rights.

In sum, the relevance of the foregoing discussion to our understanding of "emergent complexity" in the American Southeast turns on three points: (1) forager societies of the ethnographic present that are typically held up as evolu-tionary models of the antecedents of "complex" society are instead historical consequences of complex society; (2) the social reproduction of "primitive communism" involves the subversion of tendencies for accumulating power and is thus derived ontologically from structures of power (i.e., primitive communism is the antithesis of institutionalized power); and (3) liberating "primitive communists" from their evolutionary status as antecedents of complex society opens up a realm of alternative sociohistorical circumstances in which potential for the development of institutionalized power is not determined by material conditions (e.g., food supply, population) but by the ideas that enable and naturalize the exercise of authority. This final point underscores the essential role of archaeological research in furthering anthropological understanding of social variation and change. No archaeological resource in recent years has made this point any clearer than Watson Brake and other Middle Archaic mounds of the Lower Mississippi Valley.

THE PLAN OF ARCHAIC MOUND COMPLEXES

The discoveries that renewed interest in emergent complexity in the Southeast are themselves archaeological "facts" whose significance lies not so much in the labor needed to erect them as in the ideas needed to conceive of them. As John Clark demonstrates in Chapter 10, an Archaic numerical system can be inferred from the arrangement and orientation of mounds at particular sites. We build on Clark's argument to suggest that plans for mound complexes embodied principles of ranking or hierarchy—principles that may have been inspired by "nature" but that nonetheless mirrored and reproduced social difference. An essential aspect to these complexes is the space created by the circular or elliptical arrangement of mounds, that is, central plazas. What is more, there is suggestive evidence that mound complexes were components of a regional landscape of constructed spaces, themselves possibly ranked, which likely mirrored and reproduced a higher order of social difference. Although we cannot specify the particular content of these symbolic structures, some tentative interpretations are inspired from ethnographic examples from the Amazon and elsewhere (Heckenberger 1995, 1998, 1999a, 1999b, 2000a, 2000b, 2003; Sassaman and Heckenberger 2001).

The plan we infer from the spatial arrangement of Archaic mounds consists of a series of proportional and geometric regularities, including (1) a "terrace" line of three or more earthen mounds oriented along an alluvial terrace escarpment; (2) placement of the largest mound of each complex in the terrace-edge group, typically in a central position; (3) placement of the second-largest mound back from the largest mound at a distance roughly 1.4 times that between distal members of the terrace-edge group; (4) a line connecting the largest and second-largest, or backset, mound (herein referred to as the "baseline")

set at an angle that deviates roughly 10 degrees from a line orthogonal to the
terrace line; and (5) an equilateral triangle oriented to the baseline that intercepts other mounds of the complex and appears to have formed a basic unit of
proportionality (cf. Clark, this volume). In addition to these site-specific relationships, variations in the orientation of terrace lines and baselines with respect
to cardinal directions suggest that individual complexes were part of a regional
landscape of monument construction (see Figure 1.1 for site locations). Four
mound complexes and an early component of the Poverty Point complex constitute the extant elements of this regional landscape.

Watson Brake

Watson Brake, an 11-mound elliptical complex some 370 m in length and
280 m wide (Figure 11.1), has been thoroughly documented by Saunders et al.
(1997). The largest mound (Mound A) is 7.5 m high. Opposite the largest
mound is a 4.5-m-high backset mound (Mound E). All the mounds, including
nine subordinate mounds, are linked in a meter-high ridge defining an elliptical
central plaza area. Like all the mound complexes described herein, Watson
Brake is situated on the edge of an alluvial escarpment, in this case a Pleistocene-
age terrace overlooking the Ouachita River. Its absolute chronology is well established with 27 carbon 14 dates. Assays on charcoal samples taken from buried
A horizons beneath mounds and ridges range from 5880 to 5450 cal B.P. Assays
on charcoal taken from the initial stages of ridges and mounds suggest that construction began at Watson Brake between 5400 and 5300 cal B.P. Although
later components were added to mounds and ridges, the major components of
the complex were laid out, if not actually built, simultaneously (i.e., according
to an intentional ground plan).

Watson Brake exemplifies the spatial regularities noted above: three mounds
are placed in a line paralleling the terrace escarpment (Mounds A, B, and K);
the largest, Mound A, occupies the central position, with the lesser, distal components situated some 90 m on either side; the second-largest mound, Mound E,
is set back from the terrace edge approximately 1.4 times the distance between
the distal mounds of the terrace-edge group (illustrated in Figure 11.1 as the
ratio of lines a and a'); and the baseline adjoining Mounds A and E (a') deviates
about 10 degrees from a line orthogonal to the terrace-edge line (a) and originating at the apex of Mound A.

A related pattern at Watson Brake involves the relationship of paired mounds
at the southeast end of the complex (Mounds J and I) to Mounds A and E. An
orthogonal line emanating from the midpoint of the Mound A–E baseline bisects evenly the distance between the paired mounds. Two additional lines originating from Mounds A and E intersect each of the paired mounds and converge

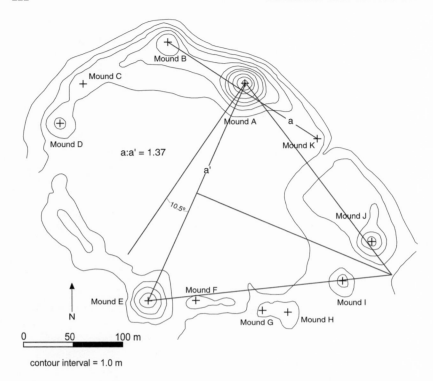

Figure 11.1. Topographic map of Watson Brake (16OU175). Apexes of 11 mounds marked by + (after Saunders et al. 1997:fig. 1).

on the orthogonal line to form an equilateral triangle whose scale is determined by the distance between Mounds A and E.

Caney

Caney Mounds is a six-mound complex in an arc nearly 400 m in maximum dimension (Figure 11.2). First recorded in 1933, Caney has been investigated intermittently ever since (Gibson 1991), most recently by Saunders et al. (2000), who remapped it, cored all the mounds, collected surface finds, and obtained samples for radiometric dating. The results of dating provide convincing evidence for the Middle Archaic inception of mound construction at Caney. The 2-sigma age estimates from samples in buried A horizons of two mounds range from ca. 5600 to 5300 cal B.P. (Saunders et al. 2000). The high degree of similarity in overall plan between Caney and Watson Brake further supports the contemporaneity of the two sites.

The plan of Caney Mounds duplicates the relative positions of the major

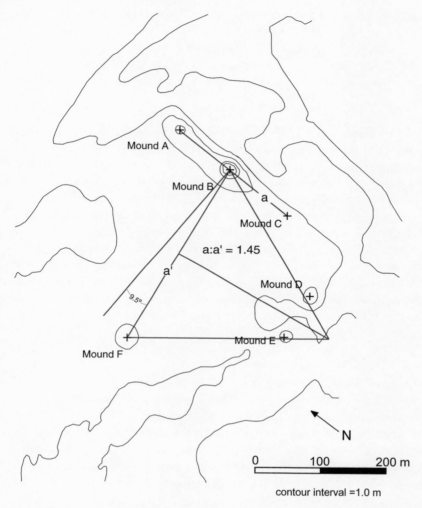

Figure 11.2. Topographic map of Caney Mounds (16CT5). Apexes of six mounds marked by + (after Saunders et al. 2000:fig. 1).

mounds at Watson Brake. Three mounds (A–C) form a line paralleling the escarpment, with the largest of the complex, Mound B, occupying the central position. The backset mound, Mound F, lies 305 m from the apex of Mound B, approximately 1.4 times the distance between the distal components of the terrace-edge mounds. Again the line connecting the two largest mounds (a') deviates about 10 degrees from an orthogonal line emanating from the terrace-edge line (a). An equilateral triangle determined by the orientation and distance between Mounds B and F intercepts the paired mounds (D and E) at the south end of the complex. In addition to the geometric similarities between Caney and Watson Brake, the relative heights of mounds at both sites are identical. Missing from the Caney complex are the mounds opposite the paired mounds and the lesser constructions between the paired mounds and Mound E at Watson Brake.

Frenchman's Bend

Frenchman's Bend, a third Middle Archaic mound complex securely dated to ca. 5500–5300 cal B.P. (Saunders et al. 1994), bears geometric similarity to Watson Brake and Caney, albeit with fewer mounds (Figure 11.3). Four mounds occupy the edge of a terrace escarpment, but the largest is also the southernmost and its linear relationship to the others is ambiguous. Still, a line connecting it with the next-largest mound along the terrace parallels the escarpment. The ratio of this line (a) to a line (a') connecting the largest terrace-edge mound with the only backset mound is similar to respective ratios at Watson Brake and Caney. As at the other complexes, this latter line deviates from a line orthogonal to the terrace-edge line, in this case by a few degrees more than the others (13 degrees). Moreover, the absolute distance between the largest terrace-edge mound and the backset mound at Frenchman's Bend is identical to that at Watson Brake.

Insley

Insley Mounds, located just south of Poverty Point (Kidder 1991), is an elliptical complex of 12 mounds with a plan highly reminiscent of Watson Brake (Figure 11.4). Although dating is uncertain and later Poverty Point and younger components are apparently present at the site, the overall similarity in plan between Watson Brake and the significantly larger Insley complex suggests initial mound construction during the Middle Archaic period. The geometric affinities between Insley and Watson Brake are unequivocal. Five mounds occupy the steep terrace escarpment at Insley, with the largest, Mound A, positioned at the center. A line joining Mound A to its nearest neighbors parallels the escarpment and the proportion of its length (a) to the baseline (a') is identical to that at Watson Brake (1.37). Lacking from the complex are the paired mounds seen at Watson Brake and Caney. Nevertheless, equilateral triangles founded on the line connecting Mounds A and H intercept single mounds at either end of the ellipse in positions similar to those of the paired-mound groups.

Scalar Rank and Regional Integration

Scalar elements of an Archaic mathematical system, consistent with those described by Clark (this volume), can be inferred from regularities in placement of mounds across these sites. When superimposed at the same scale, georeferenced

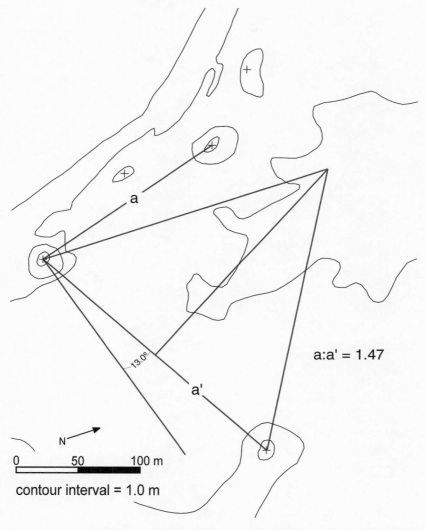

Figure 11.3. Topographic map of Frenchman's Bend (16OU269). Apexes of five mounds marked by + (after Russo 1996a:fig. 14-9).

to the largest mound, and oriented along the axis joining the largest mound with its backset counterpart, the equilateral-triangle components of each complex assume a ranked order (Figure 11.5, top). At approximately 260 m on a side, Watson Brake and Frenchman's Bend are the smallest. Caney is another 20 percent larger, at slightly over 300 m, whereas Insley, at 520 m, is twice the minimal size.

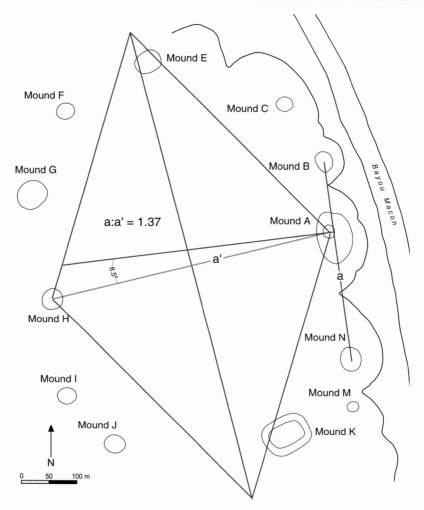

Figure 11.4. Plan of Insley Mounds (16FR2) (after Kidder 1991:fig. 4).

That the ratio of distance between terrace-edge mounds and the major axis of each triangle is virtually constant across all sites (ca. 1:1.4) suggests that lines of sight from the backset mounds to terrace-edge mounds were standardized for purposes of astronomical or calendrical observations. The varied orientation of mound complexes to cardinal directions, however, precludes such a possibility. Instead, a more complex arrangement across sites is suggested by the regional pattern of cardinality. Georeferencing all sites to the respective largest mounds and orienting each to magnetic north, a pattern of geometric integration is re-

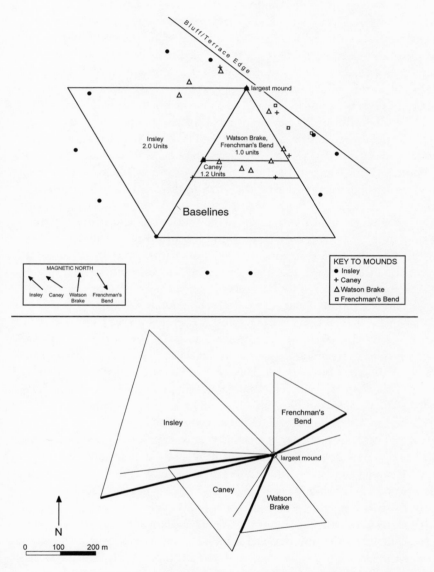

Figure 11.5. Archaic mound complexes georeferenced to largest mound and base lines (top) to show scalar differences, as well as to largest mound and azimuth (bottom) to show integration. Note: baselines (*a′*) are emboldened.

vealed (Figure 11.5, bottom). The major axis of the triangle at Watson Brake conforms precisely to one of the lesser axes of the Caney triangle, both at 23 degrees east of magnetic north. The major axis at Caney in turn conforms to the orthogonal of the terrace-edge line at Insley, while the major axis at Insley conforms to the orthogonal of the terrace-edge line at Frenchman's Bend. This arrangement clearly is not fortuitous. Rather, the integration of all four sites into a regional pattern of alignment suggests that entire landscapes of monumental architecture, and not just individual sites, were planned constructions.

The relationship of Poverty Point to all of this is uncertain but provocative. As long suspected, some elements of the Poverty Point complex were apparently constructed during the late Middle Archaic period. Located 2.2 km south of Poverty Point, the 3-m-high conical Lower Jackson Mound has produced evidence for construction during the sixth millennium B.P. (Saunders et al. 2001). Lower Jackson is aligned with Mounds A, B, and E (Ballcourt Mound) on a 352-degree azimuth. A second parallel line to the east connects Dunbar Mound, in the plaza at Poverty Point, with Motley Mound, 1.6 km to the north. Interestingly, the terrace alignment of mounds at Insley likewise lies on a 352-degree azimuth. Following the same geometric logic inferred from Insley and the other complexes, the distance between the terrace-edge (Dunbar, Motley) and backset lines at Poverty Point (Lower Jackson, Mounds A, B, E) is equivalent to the baselines of the other sites. The distance of this inferred line is just over 600 m, or roughly 2.4 times the minimal unit and twice the length of the Caney baseline. Analyzing these data in different fashion, Clark (this volume) arrives at the same proportional differences. The significance here is that elements of the Poverty Point complex were constructed in Middle Archaic times and the knowledge and surveying techniques for laying out mounds were carried forward some 1,500 years to complete the complex.

Taking these observations one step further, we suggest that the regional layout of mound complexes mirrors the layout of mounds at individual sites. In this sense, Poverty Point, Insley, and Caney are large-scale equivalents of a terrace-edge mound group, while Watson Brake and Frenchman's Bend constitute backset units. It is hardly coincidental that a line joining Frenchman's Bend and Insley is precisely perpendicular to the line intersecting all three of the "terrace-edge" complexes. The proportional distance between Frenchman's Bend and Insley, however, is far shorter than the 1.4 ratio between backset and terrace-edge mounds observed at individual sites.

We further suggest that these geometric patterns will be evident in the arrangement of domestic structures at nonmound sites, assuming that such locations are preserved, located, and excavated. As Clark (this volume) suggests, the implementation of this plan at the domestic level is one way that such knowledge

was reproduced over the many centuries between late Middle Archaic and Poverty Point times when mounds apparently ceased to be constructed.

MOUNDS, PLAZAS, AND HIERARCHY

A broad range of relations about nature and society are symbolized in the construction and use of monuments worldwide. Central plazas are especially notable
for their highly public and open quality, defined not by a singularity but the relation of other structures that impinge upon them. Plazas, like other monuments, represent the social relations of the people who build, maintain, or simply
appear in them. They are fixed, or marked, points that not only reflect social
relations but also perpetuate or "sediment" these relations in place.

Lévi-Strauss (1963) was among the first to consider circular plaza villages
in terms of the relations, social and cultural, that they generally embody, which
are equally applicable, he felt (and we agree), to the Great Lakes Winnebago,
the Gê and Bororo peoples of central Brazil, or Poverty Point and many other
great temple centers of the Americas (see also Lathrap 1985). Circular plaza
villages have been viewed as a reflection of unity—perhaps a reflection of structural opposition between equal halves, a dialectic relation between moieties, for
instance, but equality nonetheless. What they also embody, however, as Lévi-
Strauss clearly noted, is difference, or inequality. Seldom is such inequality un-
ranked, merely representing two equal halves, but instead it is related to a hierarchy of values, represented in the qualitative distinction between inner (public
and sacred) and outer (domestic and profane) space.

The central Brazilian Bororo, Lévi-Strauss's example, are divided into more
or less equal halves (moieties); both have four clans that are internally ranked
from lower (west) to upper (east) and one moiety is ranked socially slightly
above the other, since it is associated with the hereditary chiefs. They exemplify,
as Lévi-Strauss notes, the fact that "most dialectic structures, in *apparent* contradiction to their nature [symmetrical or equal], present an asymmetrical character, one which places them midway between those *rare* diametric forms that
are absolutely symmetrical and the concentric forms, which are always asymmetrical" (Lévi-Strauss 1963:136, emphasis added).

The Xinguanos of central Brazil provide a slightly different model (Heckenberger 1999a)—one that more clearly reflects a "concentric" logic and one, due
to its "monumentality," that may provide a better analog for Middle Archaic
mounds than the Gê-Bororo archetype. Xinguanos have no moieties or clans,
but they are divided. The division is that between "center-people," men, generally, and chiefly individuals, specifically. The person of the primary chief, as well
as one or two secondary chiefs, is objectified in his special residence, situated on

the village ring but larger than the rest and situated in a special place (a cardinal direction), with special trappings of form and decoration and particular materials that are used to construct it. This house, the *tajïfe*, is a container of power, as are the other large houses located at prime locations along the house ring (often at other cardinal points) that are occupied by the other primary chiefs.

The center of power in the village is the plaza center (*hugogo*); it too is a container of power. It is a forum for the negotiations between people and social groups and their alter egos, a place where people dance with spirits, where social, political, sportive, and ethnic rivals compete, and where, occasionally, men speak with the authority of divine ancestors. This power is subjectified in the collective of "chiefly" persons (*anetï*), generally, and, specifically, in the *hugogó òto*, the chief who "owns the center." The primary chiefs are incarnations of lines of ancestral power, dependent on the transmission of chiefly "substance" —e.g., names—based on primogeniture. Chiefs are, metaphorically, social vertices, binding people together and tying this "moral body," this composite person, to others like it.

As a container of symbolic power, then, the plaza village is a node in a larger regional landscape between society and its alter egos, its "Others." In its most schematic form, it separates culture from nature, inside from outside, but it does so gradually, concentrically. The plaza center invariably forms a primary *axis mundi* simultaneously linking the community, through privileged beings (chiefs), to the upper world, the cosmos, and, physically, as a gateway, to other communities in regional landscapes.

The plaza is a stage where the major social dramas are played out, dramas that mirror and reproduce the primary dimensions of sociality. The plaza is about the public, but not everyone has equal access to the plaza (women often have limited access, for instance). It is also about the extraordinary; it is, even in its most seemingly mundane aspects, ritualized. The plaza thus separates things in an obvious way: public from domestic, male from female, sacred from profane, chief from commoner.

That the plan at Middle Archaic mounds necessitates hierarchy will no doubt be controversial. In fact, Archaic mounds, generally, have tended to be viewed not as proof of hierarchy but as proof that mound building does not, as is commonly assumed, require hierarchy. A related problem has been the lack of ancillary evidence for inequality (Saunders, this volume). None of the excavations of mounds to date "has so far revealed any evidence of hierarchical social ranking in terms of differential burials or structures placed within or on top of the mounds" (Russo 1996a:286). The lack of supporting evidence for hierarchy, the "trappings of chiefs," has caused some analysts to suggest that social equality be assumed until it is demonstrated otherwise (e.g., White, this volume).

From what we know of similar configurations, archaeological and ethnographic, however, the opposite conclusion seems more apt: we should expect hierarchy. We just barely scratch the surface of known ethnographic variability to say that, in some cases, plaza villages represent an egalitarian social structure. The simple ethnographic fact is that such configurations more commonly and more forcefully represent inequality: they separate men and women, old and young, center and periphery, sacred and profane, and, according to a relatively precise calculus, culture from nature.

We are far less certain about the apparent integration of mound complexes at the regional scale, although scalar differences among the complexes suggest that regional integration was itself hierarchical. In this respect, human movement through the landscape may have recapitulated and amplified spatial metaphors for hierarchy manifest at particular sites, lending a multiscalar, fractal quality to the symbolism and ritual of Archaic monumentality.

CONCLUSION

Monuments, astronomy, mathematics, engineering, writing, and the like are commonly viewed as cultural "advancements," which like cities and commodities are seen as natural outgrowths, epiphenomena, of the development of civil society. The significance of the Archaic mound and plaza complexes is that, like the Late Preceramic of Peru, Chavin, and the Olmec, they suggest that the State, in its initial form of "petty" chiefdoms or kingdoms, rose out of the very same spatial and social metaphors that were already present in preexisting social formations, in this case the plaza village.

A discussion of ultimate origins of plaza villages and the social relations they embody is beyond the scope of this chapter, but it is important to briefly consider what factors resulted in the transition from what Giddens (1984) calls an "existential contradiction," in which collective identities are constituted vis-à-vis an alterity with the outside, to a "structural contradiction," in which that alterity is internalized (see Heckenberger [2003] for fuller discussion).

Giddens (1981:94–97) saw the city as the "real" container of power, as the root of the structural contradiction, the initiation of a city-countryside dichotomy. For our purposes, however, Giddens, along with a host of social theorists, sets the mark too high and based too literally on Western historical experience, specifically feudal Europe. The structural contradiction, the point after which society was no longer modeled simply after the contours of nature, was rooted in the control of symbolic resources that, in the case of Archaic mounds, resided in the inner-outer dichotomy of the plaza village. Jon Gibson (2000) offers some intriguing insights on the symbolic content of this dichotomy at Poverty Point. It remains to consider how those symbols were appropriated as a model for social difference within the community. We can be fairly certain that this had little to do with economics, specifically economic innovation or demographic growth. Rather, this transformation was about social identities and philosophies. This "early great revolution," the "rank revolution" according to Flannery (1994:104), "lay not in a new way of producing food, but in a new ideology in which chiefly individuals and commoners had separate genealogical origins."

Earlier efforts to trace the origins of this new ideology in the Southeast were primarily diffusionist in orientation (Ford 1969; Lathrap 1985). For Ford (1969), this new ideology, the Theocratic Formative, arrived like a virus into western Ecuador, from whence it spread to the circum-Caribbean, Mesoamerica, the Southeast, and elsewhere. The demonstrable antiquity of mounds and plazas in the Southeast warrants serious consideration of the particular historical circumstances that led to a symbolic transformation among indigenous populations.

Rejecting the single-source diffusionist explanation (but not the process of "secondary" diffusion), we must assume that there is some emergent property of social life in general that, under particular historical circumstances, results in the emergence of the structural contradiction. As we emphasized in the first half of this chapter, such an emergent property, an "internal" capacity for change, will not be found in the social formations of "primitive communists." Rather, these sorts of social formations, and the ideologies of egalitarianism that underwrite them, are a consequence, not a precursor, of the structural contradiction writ large. But in coming to grips with the historical circumstances that give rise to primitive communists, we find inspiration for modeling symbolic transformations of the ancient past. Specifically, we can envision how collectivism constituted on an alterity with the outside (culture vs. nature; us vs. them) is derived, metaphorically, from differences existing in all social formations, those of gender and age. When alterity with the "Other" is constituted along lines of age and/or gender, the difference is at once internal and external. Grinker's (1994) study of ethnicity among the Efe and Lese of the Congo provides one illustration of how gender operates metaphorically to naturalize inequality. An example involving age may be seen in the fission-fusion process of Mississippian societies described by Blitz (1999). In both cases, and others worldwide, these ethnogenetic processes, these transformations, were embedded in regional or global power struggles and thus cannot be understood apart from larger-scale, longer-term historical processes.

The challenge for Southeastern archaeologists is to reconstruct the specific historical circumstances leading to the symbolic transformation manifested in the mounds and plazas of northeast Louisiana. While these monuments may not reflect the actual historical moment when society was changed fundamentally— when the symbolic Rubicon was crossed—they do indeed represent our empirical touchstone to a complex sociality. We at least now have a model of society to compare against the more cryptic residues of domesticate spaces, land-use patterns, and ritualized practices of everyday life in the Middle Archaic, where practice and structure converged.

ACKNOWLEDGMENTS

Our thanks to Jon Gibson and Phil Carr for inviting us to contribute to this provocative volume and for their patience with us over the long delay in finalizing the manuscript. Comments on an earlier version of this chapter by Jon and Phil, as well as discussions with David Anderson, Joe Saunders, Mike Russo, and John Clark, greatly improved the logic and flow of our argument. Portions of this chapter were adapted from a paper presented at the 2002 Visiting Scholar Conference at Southern Illinois University organized by George Crothers.

12
Explaining Sociopolitical Complexity in the Foraging Adaptations of the Southeastern United States

The Roles of Demography, Kinship, and Ecology in Sociocultural Evolution

Randolph J. Widmer

With the discovery of the Watson Brake mound complex in Louisiana (Saunders et al. 1997), archaeologists have had to reevaluate causal factors in the rise of sociocultural complexity in North America. Previously, archaeologists have been strongly influenced by the stage concept of cultural development that sees the rise of sociopolitical complexity as a series of gradual, linear, steplike developments culminating in the Mississippian Tradition (Willey and Phillips 1958). This was further supported by the sequential development of two agricultural systems, with the second being more productive. The first development was based on indigenous cultivated starchy seeds and rose out of a collecting base originally focused on these wild seeds (Smith 1987, 1989, 1990, 1994; Smith, ed. 1992). This was later followed by the adoption of an imported tropical cultivar, maize, which became the staple shortly after A.D. 900 throughout much of the eastern United States.

RISE OF SOCIOCULTURAL COMPLEXITY

The development of sociocultural complexity has been linked in some way or other, implicitly if not explicitly, to these agricultural developments. Of course, Poverty Point has long been an "anomaly" that challenged this traditional viewpoint. However, it could readily be explained by diffusion or migration from the precocious Mesoamerican Formative, which was contemporary with it (Ford 1969). The nonagricultural Calusa and their Woodland period archaeological counterpart also developed a complex chiefdom, although much later in time than the Archaic period Poverty Point. This complexity could be conveniently "explained away" by a historical connection and therefore diffusion of traits from more complex, and agricultural, Mississippian societies (Phillips 1973:xvii). Of course, diffusion was the prime mover of cultural development in the eastern United States up through the 1960s.

In the 1970s, it was recognized that an earlier independent and indigenous agricultural complex developed in the Midwest out of collecting adaptation focused on wild starchy seeds (Smith 1987, 1989, 1990, 1994; Smith, ed. 1992). Ironically, although this minimized the importance of a Mesoamerican source for the origin of agriculture or sociopolitical complexity, it actually reinforced the notion of lineal thinking on sociopolitical complexity; it merely shifted the prime mover, agriculture, from a foreign origin to an indigenous one. The Poverty Point site now comes into line, since it is within the time span of agriculture and plant domestication—and, of course, the atypical Calusa can still be explained away by diffusion.

The Watson Brake mound complex has changed all that and has forced us to abandon our lineal "gradualist" models of sociocultural development in the southeastern United States and instead adopt "punctuated" models of sociocultural complexity. This is not a new idea or concept in archaeological thinking in the southeastern United States. There are examples of cycling of political complexity throughout the trajectories of Mississippian chiefdoms in the Southeast (Anderson 1994a). Cahokia, the largest Mississippian site in North America, is even characterized by a rise and fall (Milner 1998). However, it seems that little attention is paid to the initial origins and underlying seeds of complexity and, more important, how they affect the political structure of societies. Recently, a number of studies have focused on the political economy of chiefdom societies (Anderson 1994a; Earle 1997; Muller 1997), and there has been a surge of interest in praxis and agency theory in the development of power and social inequality in the eastern United States (Emerson 1997). Typically, these discussions focus on the emergence of social inequality and chiefdoms from an underlying agrarian sedentary community base and imply the existence of kin-based social groups, namely, clans and/or lineages. More fundamental questions are typically ignored in these discussions. How do these kin-based social units emerge in the first place? Why is it that social inequality and power emerge only after these social situations are in place? It is recognized that the striving for control of power and differential social status is an underlying inherent trait of human beings (Earle 1997:208) and therefore operates at many different scales regardless of the type of society, including that of foragers (Hayden 1996). Granting this, why is it that such differences are only seen at various times in the historical trajectories of cultural areas? Is this simply due to the problems of scale (Chapman 1996; Price and Brown 1985)? I think not. Instead, I maintain that it is because there is not a clearly focused understanding of the basic origin of power and the mechanism by which it is channeled in nonstate societies, be they composed of foragers or not, and this is one of the problems in dealing with the rise of sociopolitical complexity.

I disagree with Earle (1997:208) that complexity is a "problematic" concept. It is a clear and succinct concept. First, something is more complex than something else if it has more parts and, second, something is more complex than something else if there are more different parts. Of course, this is an organic model of complexity, but this does not make it problematic. The critical first step in understanding the emergence of complexity is to identify the different parts in what you are studying and then count or quantify them. Next, one sees how they change in frequency through time. This becomes "multiscalar" (cf. Chapman 1996; Price and Brown 1985) when one defines the levels (local, regional, domestic, social, political, ideological, and so forth) to which these various parts belong. The focus in this study is the social and political aspects of culture, and so the domestic sphere is of little concern since it need not be complex relative to other social or political institutions that include a degree of differential power. It makes sense to investigate this within the context of regions so that all potential expressions can be observed.

In my own research on the Calusa, I clearly recognized that a developmental trajectory of sociocultural complexity was in no way linked to agriculture or the diffusion of cultural traits from either the Woodland or Mississippian tradition—or anywhere else. Instead, I saw the development of the chiefdoms on the southwest Florida coast as an indigenous internal process that occurred over a span of approximately 500 years, once the appropriate environmental conditions were present. In effect, I modeled this development, in lieu of any data to the contrary, as a slow, linear, or "gradualist" rise in sociopolitical complexity (Widmer 1988). This model was based on what now would be classified as a voluntarist, adaptationist theoretical model rooted in cultural ecology (Earle 1997:68). The model was based on an assumption of an increasing population size and density expanding in a newly formed food-rich environment.

The Watson Brake mound complex utterly shatters this notion of lineal culture development. If we cannot use the continued increase in the efficiency and productivity of subsistence technology, i.e., agriculture, as a means of explaining sociocultural development, then what are we to use? Of course, we could use a variety of praxis or agency theory (cf. Arnold 1996a; Arnold, ed. 1996; Dobres and Robb 2000) to argue that sociocultural development is based on control of the political economy and sources of power such as finance, ideology, and military might. This assumes, of course, that there is a political economy, and here, in lieu of any real agricultural production, only trade and exchange can produce wealth and provide the resources for control. Trade and exchange can involve elite prestige goods, as is typically seen in chiefly exchange, or even more substantive economic resources such as stone or food. An example of this is seen in the absence of any lithic raw material in the Poverty Point area and so the need for importation of this material both in raw form and in the form of finished tools (Gibson 2000:170–181). The ability to obtain this valued, perhaps essential commodity, stone, through trade may lead to differential power relationships within the polity if access to it is controlled by an elite few. It is apparent that whoever needed stone in the Poverty Point polity got it (Gibson 2000:180). The real key to an understanding of the development of sociopolitical complexity is the differential basis for the *sources of power*, not how those resources were controlled and centralized (Earle 1997). These are two completely different questions, and most studies of the development of complexity focus on the latter, not the former. Here, I will examine how the sources of power arise as opposed to how they are used, manipulated, or controlled. I do not underplay the importance of agency or praxis theory in understanding the history of power and changing political economy, but such can only profitably be employed after a discussion of how the sources of power first come to be in a cultural system.

Another more important question brought to light by the Watson Brake mound complex, although this site is by no means an isolated example, is why is it that the history of development of sociocultural complexity in the southeastern United States is characterized by the waxing and waning of monumental mound construction through time? I offer two examples based on foraging adaptations that illustrate this point. The Watson Brake mound complex is abandoned, and there is neither any more mound construction nor use in Louisiana until Poverty Point times, some 1,900 years later. Then, Poverty Point and associated sites seem to flourish and then wane. Mound construction is present in the subsequent Early Woodland period Tchula phase, but the construction is not at the scale in either size or number as seen in the later Middle Woodland period. In southwest Florida, there is mound construction and sedentary houses are present during the preceramic, Late Archaic period on Horr's Island (Russo 1994a, 1996a). This construction is clearly contemporary with the Watson Brake site (Russo 1994a:90, table 1; Saunders et al. 1997:1798, table 1). However, there are no examples of either mound construction or sedentary residences in the subsequent fiber-tempered-ceramics Pre-Glades periods on the southwest Florida coast. Instead, what is seen is a shift to small seasonal campsites without any mound construction. My original formulation of a model of cultural complexity for southwest Florida included a linear, gradualist population rise and concurrent settlement model, based on a constantly rising sea level. The Horr's Island scenario demands readdressing this model and taking into account this precocious sociocultural complexity. Clearly, this sedentary habitation and mound construction development on Horr's Island was short lived and did not in any way contribute to the sociopolitical complexity that later developed in the Glades period after A.D. 500. I would like to propose here a model that can ac-

count for the rise and fall of sociopolitical complexity without the use of agriculture or even that of continued improvement of subsistence technology. This
model will also account for the waxing and waning of complexity under agricultural regimes as well. Since I argue that this model is vested in kinship, it will
require a thorough understanding of kinship dynamics.

KINSHIP AND SOCIOCULTURAL COMPLEXITY

There is universal acceptance that sociopolitical complexity among prehistoric
societies within the southeastern United States, however classified or labeled, be
it chiefdom or hierarchical, heterarchical, or complex society, is kin-based. This
is equally true for all prehistoric cultures to include less complex foraging and
horticultural societies as well. It would seem logical to investigate how this sociopolitical complexity, differential power, and sociopolitical inequality develops and
operates within a framework of kinship. Agency theory, although clearly recognizing the kin basis of political economy, seems to ignore or underplay the importance of kinship in both the economic and political spheres. The reason for
this is quite apparent. Earle (1997:6) argues that kinship is a weak source of
power because it permits a strategy for all to ask for aid and, as such, acts as
a great equalizer of resources, not a concentrator of resources. He goes on to
state that stratification is accomplished by the subjugation of kinship to other
forms of power. Families and other corporate kin-based groups would tend to be
resource-leveling institutions and as such would be unlikely candidates for the
development of differential access to resources and power. This is supported by
Arnold's (1996a) extensive survey of potential labor for appropriation in intermediate societies. In this, there is no discussion of how labor is vested within
unilineal descent groups. The most important processes to her are how certain intensive labor activities are removed from kin-group management (Arnold
1996a:61). But what about the potential sources of power that can arise from
kinship? And how far can differential sources of power be expanded within the
framework of kinship? I argue that while these may not be useful in explaining
the development of more complex forms of inequality and stratification alone,
they do have considerable utility for the investigation of the nascent aspects of
sociopolitical complexity. In fact, I maintain that they form the basic foundation
for all subsequent sociopolitical change regardless of the variable causal factors
that might be used to explain such changes.

Since both the economic and political spheres of the prehistoric societies
of the southeastern United States, regardless of their temporal position, were
clearly grounded in kinship, I feel it is essential to focus on how these kin factors
integrate with the political and economic workings of sociopolitical complexity.
Crucial to my argument is that kinship systems are the outcome of demographic

processes and that production in kin-based societies is equal to reproduction (Goody 1976), meaning, simply, that the number of people in a kin group (the output of reproduction) translates directly into the productive potential of that corporate group. This production is the ultimate source of power, be it military, staple finance, wealth finance, or ideology, and as such it must initially be associated with these kin groups. It is possible, therefore, for unilineal kin groups to differentially develop true sources of power compared with other equivalent kin groups simply by having more members relative to other such kin groups. The importance of this is that the basis of differential power can emerge without any structural change in kinship organization, which is the basis of the social organization and the domestic economy. The corollary to this is that the real important social structural change is the shift from bilateral forms of kinship to unilineal forms of kinship. I argue that this shift, once it occurs, will create the social framework for all subsequent sociopolitical change in nonstate polities. I will now discuss how this works.

Wobst (1978) is correct about the tyranny of ethnographic analogy in his discussion of the suitability of using the few marginal and atypical contemporary foragers, who are situated in poor environments or are in close proximity to horticultural groups, as typical models for those in the past. However, there are structural features in the kinship systems of mobile foragers that undermine their ability to develop the sources for power at any scale. I refer here to the "lineal" or Eskimo terminological system (Fox 1967; Murdock 1949). This kinship terminological system is identical to that which we use in the culture of the United States. This system is distinct in that it terminologically differentiates lineal from collateral kin. Lineal kin are one's direct ancestors and sibs to include grandparents, parents, children, and grandchildren. These relatives are terminologically distinguished from one's collateral kin, namely, one's aunts and uncles, nieces and nephews, and cousins. What is the rational for this classificatory system? The reason for this system is that one's collateral relatives are rarely associated residentially or occur too infrequently to form larger kin groups beyond the nuclear family. The terminological system therefore reflects the nuclear family as the basic social, economic, and residential unit, as it is in our culture today. Mobile foragers, although theoretically able to attain high levels of fertility, rarely realize this in completed family size, through time having instead, typically, only two children that reach reproductive age. This means that on average there will rarely be more than two siblings of the same sex over a *number of consecutive generations* (Howell 1976). These two conditions—multiple siblings of the same sex and same-sex siblings produced over a number of consecutive generations— are essential for the formation of corporate unilineal descent groups, be they matrilineal or patrilineal. Inability to fulfill these conditions negates the ability to form close residential group affiliations of collateral kin since there will rarely

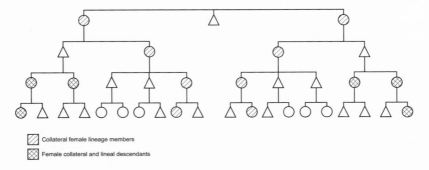

Figure 12.1. Female lineal and collateral descents with population replacement.

be same-sexed siblings in families and the incest taboo will result in opposite-sexed siblings forming new and distinct nuclear families, and this, together with the high flexibility in residential mobility, results in collateral kin becoming residentially dispersed. Because collateral kin do not typically associate residentially with lineal kin they are terminologically distinguished. Figure 12.1 illustrates how small family size with only two children per couple undermines the ability to form corporate kin groups.

For unilineal groups to form, mothers need to consistently have four or more children that grow up to adulthood and produce children of their own. The number four comes from the fact that to have two sibs of the same sex *on average* requires four children who grow up to be adults. Only when these conditions are met at least once will it make sense to develop kinship systems based on collateral rather than lineal principles, since there are no collateral kin of the same sex to form a descent group. This becomes even more apparent when we compare lineal kinship terminology systems to the kinship terminology systems typically associated with sedentary tribal and chiefdom societies: "bifurcate merging" or Iroquois and "generational" or Hawaiian. In the Iroquois and Hawaiian systems, the terms for lineal and collateral relatives within the same generation are merged and hence the same. The existence of these terms suggests that collateral kin of the same sex are present in each generation, and because they are categorically the same, it further suggests that they have similar roles and are in close proximity, so much so that typical domestic terms like mother and father are extended to aunts and uncles. This suggests that there is domestic and economic redundancy in the functions and roles of such individuals and therefore their corporate identity based on kinship emerges. Furthermore, for these terms to be meaningful, there needs to be a continual production of collateral kin in each new generation. Figure 12.1 illustrates how lineal systems of kinship terminology will remain constant though four generations and not lead to new terminological systems, because the threshold of family size is not consistently breached. It also illustrates how collateral principles, if they do emerge, will dissolve over time when sibships are of the opposite sex or else multiple male or female sibships occur but not for a consecutive number of generations to ensure the structural formation of consistent collateral kinship groupings. Figure 12.2 illustrates how Iroquoian and Hawaiian kinship terminological systems, and unilineal descent groups in general, permit collateral kin to form social coherency and corporate grouping, which expands in size through time.

What we see, then, is the development of a corporate group of collaterally related kin with membership reckoned consanguinally and unilineally through either the male or female line. This corporate group becomes a unit of production providing labor. This labor in turn is a direct source of economic power and can be used to form a military force or to produce power through the production of staple or wealth finance. If unilineal descent groups increase in population numbers, then their economic power increases as well. If one unilineal descent group increases in size relative to another, then its power will be greater than that of the other without any other change in political control, structure, or institution. While I concede that this precludes the formation of even more complex forms of control, centralization, and political institutions, I maintain that the control of power will emerge from voluntaristic, cooperative processes—those associated with kinship—before it will develop from coercive forces typically associated with agency theory, i.e., aggrandizers or accumulators. Therefore, if we are looking at the initial appearance of sociopolitical complexity in a region, it makes sense to examine the kin-based source of power instead of those processes that tend to co-opt control of those resources from their kin-based roots.

I further argue that these initial unilineal kin groups are lineages rather than clans. The reasons for this are obvious. First, the actual founding ancestor of the lineage is known, because there is little genealogical depth to the descent group. Second, such a group would have a corporate function, since that is the economic reason for such a social grouping. This also forms a mechanism for the accumulation and concentration of wealth in that group, because that group owns labor and the resources created with that labor. The continued addition of collateral kin to every new generation in a descent group, a situation that is structurally embedded in the kinship terminology, would result in geometric growth of that kin group. Such geometric growth does not have to be realized for more than four generations. Any reduction in the number of offspring surviving to reproductive age that is below the threshold for population growth can still be absorbed by existing established lineages. If lineages grow too large, new lineages will form by budding off through a process called fissioning. I argue that

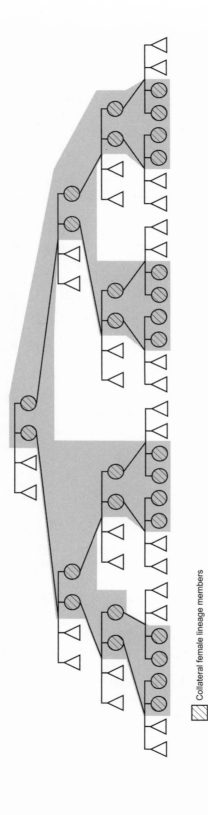

Collateral female lineage members

Corporate matrilineal descent group

Figure 12.2. Formation of corporate matrilineal descent group with population growth.

the lineages that are the largest will be the initial ones formed. They will have more members, because they have more generations to have added members, even if the rate of growth is the same. As the lineage becomes larger, cadet lineages can bud off to form new lineages. This is not just theoretical supposition but has been documented among the Hopi in the southwestern United States. I present a lengthy quote to illustrate this point.

> The lineage group is probably the basic unit for segmentary or formal organization in all the western Pueblos. There is no special name for this unit anywhere—any more than there is for the household—so that it has not had the attention it deserves. The clan is the major grouping in western Pueblo thinking. It has a name, frequently a central residence known as *the* clanhouse, relations with sacred symbols, often control of ceremonies or other territories. Where the clan and the lineage coincide—as they do in perhaps half of the Hopi instances and undoubtedly elsewhere as well—there is no confusion, and either term may be used. But, where the clan is composed of multiple lineages, the distinction is important, since lineages within a clan may vary greatly in status and prestige. The specific mechanisms for inheritance and transmission normally reside in the lineage; the clan is normally the corporate group which holds ritual knowledge and economic goods in trust for future generations.
>
> It is probable that an equivalence of clan and lineage is the earlier pattern, if our reconstruction of Hopi development is reasonably correct and is found to hold for other villages, as well. But with the growth of populations and the widespread migrations of the thirteenth and fourteenth—and later—centuries, the development of multi-lineage clans was almost inevitable in the western Pueblos. Multiple-lineage clans are more stable and organize a larger population, other things being equal, than do single lineages. Where there are several lineages, one of them usually controls the major functions associated with the clan, and the others are subordinate; any tendency to specific allocations of clan functions among the various lineages is made difficult by variations which occur over even a short period of time [Eggan 1950:299–300].

The above discussion does differ somewhat from my argument in that the Pueblo clans are territorial and clans continue to be used even as population grows. I would argue that economic goods reverted to the clan from lineages during the colonial mission era. This was possible because there was no dispersal of population and clans with dwindling populations still resided in sedentary Pueblo communities. Economic and territorial functions of clans would have not been possible for the protohistoric groups of the Southeast nor for sedentary foragers that reverted back to mobile foraging as I argue was the case during the Archaic period.

If the populations of lineages decline systematically over a number of generations, lineages can and do go extinct. If all of the lineages decline over a period of time, what will happen is that lineages will merge into a number of exogamous clans. This happens because lineages under conditions of population decline have no economic utility, if there are no collateral relatives of the same age in them. These clans no longer can trace descent to a known ancestor, and they no longer have corporate or territorial functions. Instead, they serve purely social and religious functions. However, the newly formed concatenation of lineage remnants into clans preserves the rank distinctions of those previous lineages and transfers them to the clans. Thus, what emerges is a number of ranked clans. I can also conceive of the situation in which lineages grow large and do not fission but instead become clans as the lineal descent groups are too large to function in a corporate manner and/or their genealogical depth becomes so deep that the original founding ancestor becomes unknown. This situation is paralleled in the northwest Pacific Coast where warfare resulted in the formation of a larger village by the incorporation of the defeated group into the victorious one. I provide the following Haida example:

> Let us suppose that a village community is strictly homogenous in structure, that is, contains no members that cannot count their descent in either the male or female line from the common ancestor. It is obvious that this state of affairs cannot last indefinitely. The accidents of war will doubtless bring it about that sooner or later some neighboring village community that has suffered at the hands of an enemy and that finds itself subject to extermination at their hands will seek protection from the first village community and, in order to gain this end, will receive permission to take up residence in it. It is immediately apparent that the new enlarged village community, provided it is permanent, will have increased in complexity of structure. Their adherence to their respective traditions will be such that neither of the former village communities will give up its peculiar set of privileges, so that a twofold division of the community, as accentuated by these privileges, will persist. If we imagine this process to have occurred several times, we will gradually arrive at a community which is subdivided into several smaller units which we may call septs or bands, or perhaps even clans, each of which has its distinct stock of legendary traditions and privileges exercised by its titled representatives and whose former connection with a definite locality is still remembered. The growth of the village community does not need, of course, to have taken place only in this fashion. Many other factors may be at work. The group added to the

original community may be the survivors of a conquered village who are given a subordinate place. Furthermore, a member of another tribe or community that has married into the community may, if he (or she) has sufficient prestige, be able to assert the higher rank that he (she) brings with him (her) and found a new line of descent which will take its place side by side with those already represented. We see, then, a number of ways in which the typical division of a tribe into clans, such as we find among the Haida, may be expected to originate [Sapir 1915:365].

Hierarchical ranked matriclans are the social organization that is characteristic of eighteenth-century aboriginal groups east of the Mississippi (Knight 1990). I am convinced that they developed through the process of lineage attrition and coalescence into clans brought about by population decline that started in the sixteenth century and extended through the eighteenth century (Widmer 1992). During this period, lineages undoubtedly went extinct or dwindled in size to a point where they could no longer maintain collateral kin in corporate groups. Furthermore, as populations were becoming displaced on the landscape, it was impossible for kin groups to control land and, more important, pass it on to kin of the next generation. A number of hierarchical ranked clans were formed. The ranking was based on the former ranks of the lineage. It was often the case that a prominent lineage within the clan might retain its lineage status for "dynastic" purposes of determining future leaders through ascription. Thus, I see a sequence to kin-group formation starting from exclusively nuclear families to unilineal descent groups characterized by lineage to ranked clans. Once the unilineal descent groups are initially established, they may bud and fission as they grow and produce a number of hierarchical ranked lineages. The ranks of these lineages correspond to the distances from the apical ancestor at which the lineages split.

POPULATION SIZE/DENSITY AND SOCIOCULTURAL COMPLEXITY

Robert Carneiro (1967) made a very important and powerful observation with regard to the development of sociopolitical complexity. He performed a simple cross-cultural comparison of a number of cultural features associated with complexity and ran correlation regressions on them. What he found was that the most important and strongest correlation with sociopolitical complexity was population size and density. In other words, as the population size and density increased, so did the degree of complexity in that culture. There we have it, a nice covering-law theory to explain the rise of sociocultural complexity! As the population size and density of a culture increases, so then does the sociopolitical complexity of that culture. Conversely, if population size and density decreases, then conversely sociopolitical complexity should also decrease as well. In other words, there is a direct positive correlation between population size and density and sociopolitical complexity.

Unfortunately, correlation is not causation, and other causal factors or explanations can be evoked to account for the correlation. The real problem, however, shifts to the following question. Under what circumstances do cultures increase their population size and density? Why is it that for long periods of time there appears to be little increase in population size and density in an area, while at certain times population grows and during other times declines? Is it simply a question of food supply, or is it attributable to other economic, social, or political factors? Regardless, the problem shifts to one of demography, and it is here where we can obtain an understanding of the waxing and waning of sociopolitical complexity.

In fact, nonagricultural societies and cultural histories are much more informative than others for the study of the emergence of complexity, precisely because food production via agriculture can be factored out as a causal variable. Thus, other variables and factors, whether they are environmental, technological, or political, are ultimately responsible for any changes in sociopolitical complexity. It must be emphasized that all of these factors must somehow relate to demographic processes.

ENVIRONMENT AND DEMOGRAPHY

When all cultures, including foragers, have the capability of increasing their population, why is it that they do not all do so? I argue that cultures will increase their numbers when it is beneficial to that group to do so, or at least when mortality levels drop to the point that populations can grow. It is easy to see how this would happen if there is a shift from foraging to agriculture, because the seasonal vagaries of food supply can be mitigated through storage and increased food production, i.e., planting more crops. But, how is it that a foraging population should increase to the point where at least four children on average survive through adulthood for at least four generations, the conditions that I maintain are necessary for the formation of unilineal corporate groups?

The answer for nonagricultural subsistence systems is clearly environmental change. In an agricultural subsistence system, it is possible to increase the food supply by either putting more land into production or changing cultigens, or both. Fluctuations in food supply can also be evened out through storage. In nonagricultural subsistence systems it is, of course, possible to modify the environment to improve the availability of desirable food sources through selective burning. This is a common strategy among Australian aborigines and might

have been practiced in the southeastern United States as well during preagricul-
tural periods. It is also possible to improve the hunting, trapping, collecting, fishing, and food-processing/storage technology to increase the carrying capacity of
groups within an existing environment. However, it is doubted that such technological changes in foraging adaptations *alone* could have resulted in increases
in carrying capacity to permit increases in population size and density, which is
what is required in the model I am presenting here. This is because foraging
adaptations rely on naturally occurring resources whose frequencies, if not distributions, are ultimately controlled by local ecological and climatic conditions.
Increased effectiveness of technology can increase the ability to obtain food but
cannot dramatically increase the absolute amount of food available in an environment.

Therefore, it is environmental change at either the local, regional, or global
level that is ultimately responsible for shifts in carrying capacity that result in
demographic shifts that influence shifts in sociopolitical complexity. Global climatic changes have affected temperature and moisture regimes, providing a
change in faunal and floral distributions and, more important, their frequencies.
Some of these, like sea level change, are global but have impacts that are regional
in nature; sea level change, specifically, primarily affects the hydrology of coastlines, but in the case of south Florida, the water table and interior wetlands are
also affected. Local changes can occur because of changing river dynamics as
river channels meander and shift, creating and destroying associated swamps
and oxbow lakes through their constant movement. The ever-changing track of
these meanders through time changes the timing and location of resource areas.
This is particularly the case for the lower Mississippi River and the tributaries
that flow into it (Saucier 1974).

Furthermore, as sea level rose through time it resulted in the backing up of
major drainages like the Mississippi and their tributaries. This in turn created
more swamp and aquatic environments with an overwhelmingly rich natural
food resource base for exploitation, a richness such that sedentism and population growth were easily achievable. I am convinced that this is the reason the
Watson Brake and Poverty Point sites achieved such a high degree of sociopolitical complexity. Of course, this can also explain the hiatus and decline as well.
If river systems change in ways that reduce the size or location of aquatic environments and hence the available food supply, the carrying capacity will change.
These changes can be temporal or spatial in nature, or both. We know the Mississippi River drainage is an incredibly dynamic river system and has been this
way since the end of the Pleistocene (Saucier 1974). For it, two factors are at
play. One is the increase in food supply through time as more swampland is created by the sea level rise. The second factor is that there is swampland in turn
being regionally "drained" as the river dynamics shift the locations of the wet-

lands. This is actually one of the reasons given for the abandonment of the Watson Brake site (Saunders et al. 1997:1797).

When this happens, the large dense populations that formed during food-rich periods in certain areas shift back to more mobile foraging with less fertility, and hence the complexity is not maintained. However, the seeds for the reemergence of complexity are present, because once unilineal kinship is established, nonterritorial clans that still maintain ritual and marriage functions can form from earlier lineages. Lineages can then reemerge out of a clan-based social structure when food again becomes plentiful.

SOUTHEAST EXAMPLES

If environments become "better," then they would be capable of supporting larger numbers of people. But how is it that they become "better," and what constitutes a high-quality environment—one that is different from that typically seen throughout the eastern United States during the Archaic period and in the nonagricultural Woodland adaptations of south Florida? I have already intimated this feature and will now more specifically describe it. If one looks at the Watson Brake site, the sites on Horr's Island, Poverty Point sites, and the South Florida (Glades) tradition, they are all seen to share one characteristic: they are all adaptations based on aquatic resources. In the case of the Watson Brake site and the Poverty Point phase, the aquatic environment is riverine with associated swamp and small stream resources (Gibson 1994a, 1996a, 2000; Saunders et al. 1997; Webb 1982). In the case of the Preceramic Archaic period Horr's Island sites and the South Florida tradition of the Woodland period, the resources are those of a tropical estuarine environment (Russo 1991, 1992b, 1994b, 1996a; Widmer 1988, 2002).

I believe that all four of these examples of sociopolitical complexity, three of which are Archaic period and one that dates to the Woodland period, arise from a common environmental shift, namely, the rise of sea level to a position at or *above* where it is today. This results in both the backing up of rivers and concurrent formation of swamps and small streams, plus the formation of large expanses of estuaries on the coastal margins caused by greater freshwater runoff mixed with a higher sea stand and brackish water or by bounding of the freshwater by barrier islands (Coastal Environments, Inc. 1977; Widmer 1988). In the case of Horr's Island, it seems that sea level was at a higher stand than during the period before or for close to 1,200 years after its occurrence and this corresponds to the Older Peron Submergence (Fairbridge 1984:431, table 1). In the case of the riverine examples from Louisiana, this rising sea level backed up the rivers to provide backswamp areas adjacent to the meander belts of the Mississippi and Arkansas Rivers (Saucier 1974:12) with increased quantities of aquatic resources probably not available in such large quantities prior to this time. Even more salient is the fact that both Watson Brake and Poverty Point correspond exactly to sea level stands that were higher than today. The 6000–4700 B.P. (uncorrected) plus-four-meter Older Peron Submergence sea level transgression corresponds to the dated occupation of Watson Brake and Horr's Island, as well as other Archaic period mound sites in Louisiana (Russo 1994b; Saunders 1994), while the 4300–3400 B.P. (uncorrected) plus-three-meter Younger Peron Submergence transgression corresponds to Poverty Point. The hiatus between Watson Brake and Poverty Point also corresponds to the minus-one-meter sea level regression known as the Pelham Bay Emergence at 3400–2800 B.P. (uncorrected) (Fairbridge 1984:431). Furthermore, the dates for Watson Brake are associated with Mississippi River Meander Belt No. 3 and the contemporary Arkansas River Meander Belt No. 4, while Poverty Point is associated with Mississippi River Meander Belt No. 4 and Arkansas River Meander Belt No. 5 (Saucier 1974:21). Thus, it is possible to link the occurrence and disappearance of cultural complexity of these two settlement systems with shifts in the meander belts that were probably triggered by falling eustatic sea level and the reduction in area of high-quality aquatic environments.

The result of this environmental change, ultimately resulting from sea level rise, locally or regionally manifested, is an increase in available resources within a relatively restricted area. This means that there is higher carrying capacity. The cultural response to this situation is, I believe, a demographic one. Namely, people within a culture will aggregate into a denser population through a readjustment of the settlement pattern. This will result in sites having larger numbers of individuals and the individuals residing in these sites for a longer period of time. All of this can occur without any necessary change in fertility or mortality scheduling within the adaptation. This aggregation alone will increase the population density in an area, even though the population size may not change. This is important, because it is the combination of both population size *and* density, not just size alone, that correlates with sociopolitical complexity. However, I believe that it is imperative that sedentism emerge in such a setting of high-quality aquatic resources for true sociopolitical complexity and, more important, mound construction to appear—mound building being the feature that all four examples have in common. The reason for this, from my perspective, is a demographic one that has a profound effect on social structure. I believe that a change in social structure must accompany any demographic increase in population, if sociopolitical complexity and, particularly, mound construction are to emerge. Sedentism is the necessary condition for both of these factors to arise, and the formation of aquatic ecosystems facilitates this development.

I believe that sedentism is present in all four of the archaeological examples I have mentioned. I know that the authors of the Watson Brake site suggest that the site was seasonally occupied on the basis of the plant and animal remains that were recovered (Saunders et al. 1997, Saunders, this volume). However, the reconstruction does not take into account storage—and what plants would be available during winter for collection? Additionally, a recent study of seasonality utilizing catfish otoliths from the Watson Brake site indicates that they were taken during all seasons of the year (Stringer et al. 2002), further supporting a sedentary occupation of the site. The multiple mound complex, all mounds of which appear to be contemporary, is consonant with a sedentary community configuration. Of course, what is the effect of sedentism? The effect is once again demographic.

With sedentism, populations can grow quickly, because birth spacing can decrease as storable foods provide an early weaning food and females experience increased years of fertility as a result of steadier nutrition and less wear and tear from infant mortality (Howell 1976). Not only does this result in an increase in population growth, where previously there was none, but it also results in a more important change in social organization. All of a sudden, there are collateral kin who can be incorporated into the kinship and family structure. This is improbable in zero-population-growth or even low-growth mobile foraging societies, because this growth has to be sustained over four generations. Additionally, the fact that the kinship terminology system of mobile foragers differentiates lineal from collateral kin would seem to imply that traditional fertility rates among mobile foragers are low enough to preclude the use of kinship terms that merge collateral and lineal kin. This is in spite of the fact that higher rates could be realized (see Bently et al. 1993 for range of fertility rates among foragers).

The consistent and regular increase in fertility, if maintained over time, results not only in increased population but also, more important, in a new social structure, namely, lineages. I am not arguing here that mobile foragers are incapable of having collateral kin under most circumstances. In fact, I suggest that this probably happens frequently, but it must happen consistently and regularly enough over time for this to be structurally important enough to be incorporated into the kinship system. This typically would occur when sedentism, or a more limited and restricted settlement mobility, allowed for four generations of population growth. I would go on to suggest that indeed it did happen, and that it is probably characteristic of many, if not most, of the societies throughout the southeastern United States during the Late Archaic period. One of the very great lacunae that we have as archaeologists is the lack of any ethnographic analogs for foragers in high-quality natural environments who were subsequently replaced by groups demonstrating horticulturalist adaptations. The aboriginal groups in California are our best examples, but even here the population decline resulting from European contact has preempted our ability to see these cultures under intact demographic regimes. Nonetheless, it has to be the case that Watson Brake and Poverty Point are not anomalies and, further, that fertility to facilitate low to moderate population growth during the Late Archaic period, if not earlier, occurred on more than one occasion. When it did happen, there were fundamental changes in social structure, as I have discussed above—most notably, the appearance of unilineal descent groups in the form of lineages. The emergence of these lineages whenever and wherever it occurred marked a new era in social transformation and permitted more complex sociopolitical developments and power relationships.

LINEAGES AND MOUNDS

What would be the function of these newly formed lineages and what does this have to do with social complexity or anything else? Lineages as a source of labor are also a source of power. This labor was channeled into ideological power in the form of mound construction. Mounds are a means of conveying wealth and power, since they are the end products in the control of labor (Trigger 1990a). Mounds then become the materialization of the ideological power of heads of lineages, since there is no necessary political position that exists outside of kinship and lineages. Because these leaders are probably determined on principles of primogeniture and inheritance, the mounds become "public symbols" (Geertz 1980) of the sanctity as well as power of lineage heads. The mounds therefore are created by the corporate labor of lineages to express the ideological power of lineages as vested in their ancestors. The reason for the Middle and Late Archaic mound construction, which I have discussed briefly above, is as ancestral shrines. Corporate kin groups, of course, own such mounds and this ownership must be transferred through time via inheritance. As such, mounds are the means of institutionally codifying the power and importance of lineages. The central public plazas associated with them become the stages on which rituals are continually enacted to reinforce the meaning originally created during the initial construction of the mound (Dillehay 1990; Earle 1991, 1997). All of the mound complexes, except Poverty Point, seem to lack residential debris and even residences, although there might be some skeletal remains associated with one of the Horr's Island mounds (Russo 1996a). The reason that mounds are constructed is to venerate ancestors. Interestingly, a residential structure was found at the base of a mound at another Archaic period mound site, Monte Sano, that dates to 6220 × 140 B.P. (Gibson and Shenkel 1988:8). This mound was built over a structure that contained a fire pit with remains of a human cremation (Saunders 1994). This episode can be interpreted as the death of the apical ancestor of this lineage with the mound constructed on this feature as an ancestral

shrine. This is not a new notion in the southeastern United States and, in point
of fact, was suggested by Jim Knight as a function of Mississippian mounds
(Knight 1986).

Mounds symbolically represent lineages. Two features of lineages are that they
are territorial and can trace descent to a known ancestor. The mounds, in effect,
provide the symbol of territorial ownership embedded in the original founding
ancestor's claim to that territory. This is also not a new idea in the southeastern
United States and was originally proposed by Gibson (1994a), as well as earlier
in the Midwest for Late Archaic mounds (Charles and Buikstra 1983). Such a
model is commonly applied in other culture areas, including the Preclassic Maya
of Mesoamerica (McAnany 1995), the Neolithic of Britain (Thomas 1991),
and the Mapuche of Chile (Dillehay 1990). If we suggest that each mound indicates a lineage, then Watson Brake would have 11 lineages represented. I also
envision that the size of the mound is correlated with the size of the lineage
and/or its generation depth. That is why mounds at Watson Brake are of variable
sizes.

CONCLUSIONS

I do not argue that all groups that develop lineages will build mounds or demonstrate the sociopolitical complexity that we associate with chiefdoms. However,
the seeds are there for such development, because in kin-based social groupings
there is a built-in corporate structure for pooling and coordinating labor. This
is more easily accomplished under an existing kin-group structure than in one
that would require the group to develop principles that crosscut kinship. In addition, differential social statuses are more likely to be already present within a
family than among families, since such heterogeneous relationships are already
extant, based on primogeniture and generational differences. Also, the higher
social status of one kin member, even though at the detriment to that of the rest
of the kin, can come to reflect the group as a whole. Thus, logically, the higher
status kin member acts as an agent for the group as a whole and raises all members' status.

As population continues to increase, new lineages will form by budding off
from old lineages. For lineages to thrive and continue budding, they must constantly grow, but this is not what necessarily happens. Actually, we see a hiatus
in mound construction after Watson Brake and, more than likely, a decrease in
population, at least in the site's region. Later, Poverty Point emerges as the primary center in the area, along with additional lower ranked centers not seen
in the Watson Brake settlement system. What happened to the lineages in the
intervening period? More than likely, many lineages went extinct, and populations had to relocate or adjust their territory as resource availability changed in

the area. In such a case, it would be likely that lineage fragments would coalesce into clans.

My model can account not only for the rise of sociopolitical complexity within a foraging society but also for its decline. It also illustrates how the social-structural seeds are in place to allow for future development of complexity. I argue that population increase will favor the development and proliferation of lineages, and that population decrease and/or dispersal will favor the formation of clans from these lineage remnants. These clans will take on the rank of the former highest ranked lineage. Thus the clans become ranked, as was characteristic of the eighteenth-century aboriginal groups in the southeast United States (Knight 1990). The model accounts for the cycling of political centers characteristic of the Mississippian period (Anderson 1994a) and for the appearance and disappearance of mound construction. Furthermore, my model, although demographically based, complements agency and praxis theory and actually accounts for the source of power for the political economy that later becomes contested by competing interests. Although my theoretical approach is based on culture ecology and demography, which might be now considered "tired" or no longer "cutting edge," there is no need to ignore an "outdated" or "unpopular" theory for the latest and greatest new "rave" or "hip" theory. We have to remember that a three-hundred-year-old theory and model, gravity and Newtonian mechanics, were all that was necessary to put a man on the moon in spite of new advances such as the theory of relativity. Culture ecology is alive and well; it still has utility. Of course, it cannot explain all sociocultural change. However, I argue that it needs to be utilized initially, and then when it does not seem to account for the change, other models and theoretical paradigms should be brought to bear. This is how we can achieve a more robust epistemological framework for explaining past cultures.

13

The Power of Beneficent Obligation in First Mound-Building Societies

Jon L. Gibson

Mound building began in the Lower Mississippi Valley and Florida more than fifty-five hundred years ago. Some mounds were large, and sometimes they were strung together in arrangements that lead us to think the unthinkable. Images of mounds as territorial and identity markers, as cosmic sociograms and creation metaphors, and even as massive earthen calendars aligned with the stars and moon creep into our consciousness (Byers 1998; Charles and Buikstra 1983; Clark, this volume; Norman Davis, personal communication, 2001; Gibson 1994a, 1996b, 1998b, 2000; Hively and Horn 1984; Romain 2000). Could such meanings really inhere in mounds as old as these? Their builders were Archaic fisher-hunter-gatherers! We are not even sure how large or sedentary their communities were, how they marshaled and sustained the requisite labor, or how organizationally sophisticated they were. They obviously possessed the leadership, organization, and wherewithal to pull off such feats. The mounds themselves stand as testaments.

There is profit to pursuing the ancient knowledge angle for researchers who know the stars, the math, and the lore, but I ask after another dimension of Archaic mound building—its source or sources of power. And I look for that power in social contexts lacking usual material indicators of power and prestige (Peebles and Kus 1977). I ask, can mounds be built via a communal call with voluntary, freely given labor or must there always be social inequality and an aggrandizing ethic lurking in their shadows?

POWER HAS SHADES OF MEANING

Power has several shades of meaning. Power entails motive, as in what inspires or prompts people to act—a cause, an idea, a pretty flower, or inane happening—just about anything that produces an emotional reaction. But it also entails a person's ability to get another person to act a certain way. Morton Fried (1967: 13) distinguishes power from authority. To Fried, power is backed by threat and sanction, authority is not. He sees authority simply as the ability to gain another person's assent. To me, however, authority carries sanctions just as surely, no matter how mild, deeply embedded, and nonthreatening they may be. A mother's love for a child, for example, is just as powerful withheld as given, a father's praise as motivational as a limber switch, although maybe not as quick to bring action. A renowned hunter works on Lower Jackson Mound just as hard as the unsuccessful hunter, not because he hopes to win greater admiration but because if he does not he stands to lose face, as well as sanctity and security. I cannot think of a single action in life that is not predicated on some authorization or that does not carry sanctions, though many times they are subtle, implicit, or taken for granted.

The path to exposing social power is well traveled and paved with enough theory and terminology to keep graduate seminars and learned symposia busy for a professional lifetime. Why add my voice to the clatter? It's simple. None of this theory and terminology fully explores the social and political contexts of first mound–building groups. Why? Because not even prophets among us expected monumental architecture to be so early or so imbued with cosmic symbolism, as Clark uncovers in Chapter 10. We have come to accept that builders of first mounds were fisher-hunter-gatherers (Russo 1996a; Saunders et al. 1997). Most of us would agree that early mound builders were richer materially than Spartan Bushman bands (see Lee and DeVore 1968)—if nothing else, mound builders had mounds. But we cannot lose sight of the fact that mound builders were mainstream fisher-hunter-gatherers living in one of the richest riparian strips in the Americas, not stragglers trying to survive on the harshest land in the world.

Despite our best intentions, we still tend to regard Archaic mound builders as Bushman clones or else we reach too far in the other direction and expropriate models developed for complex social formations, which are then applied to mound societies like last Christmas's wrapping paper. Neither view works, completely. Why? Because first-mound builders are without ethnographic counterparts. The pristine wilderness and social conditions that brought them into the world have not existed for thousands of years.

The link between monumental architecture and complex society is one of archaeology's most sacred tenets (Trigger 1990a). Dare we question its veracity by suggesting that egalitarian societies living in a land of milk and honey had the capacity to build mounds too? Take away the earthworks and the material signs of social discrimination and you remove the most widely implicated markers of social complexity in first mound–building formations (see Saunders, this volume). Even Poverty Point, centuries later, does not have too much to show besides the massiveness of its earthworks and the long reach and intensity of its exchange program (Gibson 2000). It goes without saying that something dramatically drove up the scale of Poverty Point's works and multiplied the volume of its local and foreign exchanges, and that something was or at least took issue from its social and political-economic organization and ideology.

Signs of distinction and exclusion are easy to spot, but signs of hereditary inequalities are next to impossible to detect within groups whose primary social interactions were geared, I maintain, to suppress them. We cannot use presence or absence of earthworks and public architecture alone as evidence for hierarchical social inequalities among first mound–building societies lacking the usual material markers of social distinctions (see Blanton et al. 1996; Renfrew 1974).

Our dilemma is simple, really. We have big mounds and multimound complexes being built by fisher-hunter-gatherers long assumed to be without the social and political infrastructure required to mount and carry out large, labor-intensive projects. So, were first-mound builders more socially complex than we assumed? Or were big mounds and big mound complexes built by egalitarian peoples? Or does an either-or answer oversimplify the issue (Saitta 1997)?

FROM ORGANIZATION TO POWER

Searching for an answer requires that we shift our attention from organization to power—to the power fund or funds that sponsored first-mound building. Bruce Trigger (1990a:128) avows that control of energy represents the most fundamental measure of political power. He writes: "[T]he most basic way in which power can be symbolically reinforced is through the conspicuous consumption of energy." Without doubt, monumental architecture is one of the most conspicuous consumers of energy most societies ever sponsored (Trigger 1990a:128).

Just how mound building relates to political power or vice versa is at issue here. The first thing that usually comes to mind is, did Archaic leaders broker political power (Earle 1997; Mills 2000)? Can we recognize their intentions and actions under the tons of dirt piled at Hedgepeth, Watson Brake, Stelly Mounds, and, especially, Poverty Point? Or under the tons of shell at Horr's Island, Tick Island, and Tokoma? We do not have their lavish graves. We do not have mounded graves at all. As much as we might like to think of first mounds as tombs, we need to think again (see Gibson 1994a, 1996a, 1996b, 1998b, 2000). Tombs they were not.

What about other indications of leadership? Take away the mounds and we find ourselves lost in a monotonous world of flakes, points, and fire-cracked rock. This does not mean necessarily that leadership signs are not there; more likely it is telling us that we would not know them if they were. Would we recognize clues of leadership among six-thousand-year-old mound builders? We have not yet. But clueless or not, I am disinclined to invest Archaic leaders with the ability to pull off such feats—feasts, yes; feats like building mounds, no. Why? Primarily because I have serious doubts about how successful Archaic leaders would have been at making people do something they did not want to do in the first place. And, if people were already willing and able, then leadership cannot be fingered as the power behind mound building. The real power already existed—hardly a ringing endorsement for the power vested in Archaic leadership. Power rested with the people, and it was ready for unleashing when strong sentiments filled the group and created exuberance for the occasion.

Power, raw power, wonder-working power, is often delivered through the word and the messenger, particularly when people already agree with the message. And if first mounds and mound building were nothing else, they represented new ideas—maybe not radically different visions but certainly new ways of upholding old beliefs. Though first mounds may be nothing more than symbols of people's ancient past cast in a new medium—mounded dirt—they manifest the power of the people, the power of all people who labored in unison for a common goal. Leadership was only part of the overall mound-building process, not the source of power.

In my view, the real power behind first-mound building came out of the group mind (see Saitta 1997). The power of which I speak undergirded practice and custom. It not only touched the core of Archaic society, it was the core. I am talking about those beliefs and attitudes that made people who they were and fired their deepest passions—those notions and feelings fated to bring action, communalistic action, and those that can transform individuals into single-minded social dynamos. I am talking about the power of beneficent obligation, or debt of gratitude.

DEBT OF GRATITUDE

Obligation as a power fund is so familiar, so taken for granted, that its potential for causing and influencing social action largely has been overlooked, except in cases where it results in competition between individuals striving to gain profit or enhance reputation. Competition-generating obligation is often lauded as a primary means of creating or deepening social inequalities—the very heart of social complexity (Clark and Blake 1994; Hayden 1995). But as Joe Saunders (this volume) contends, early mound-building societies are bereft of recognizable signs of inequalities in those material dimensions considered most likely to reveal them, e.g., cemeteries and elaborate graves, houses and house sizes, and exchange and differential access to exchange goods as revealed through differential distributions and associations.

For example, previous analyses of Poverty Point rock exchanges show that they were guided by need, not greed (Gibson 1994a, 1999, 2000; Gibson and Griffing 1994), and need-based exchanges are not what we expect to find in political economies dominated by exclusionary and proprietary principles, the principles we associate with complex societies. Need-based exchange implies beneficent transfers among folks simply trying to do their jobs, folks who are not busy acquiring a stash or putting another bead on their neck chain. In Chapter 8, Phil Carr and Lee Stewart show how rock exchange might have been organized. Of course, nonexclusionary exchange does not necessarily pre-empt social complexity, especially complexity based on communalistic ideals (see Blanton et al. 1996; Feinman 1995, 2000; Saitta 1997), but it sure does make it much harder for us to recognize. And adding to our difficulty is the realization that pre–Poverty Point mound builders did not carry on exchange in durable goods at all.

So what is left to make the case for social inequality and cultural complexity but mounds, big mounds—monumental public architecture? And you simply cannot use mounds to prove the existence of the very phenomenon they are assumed to represent, at least not their presence or absence, a point Nancy White (this volume) drives home about mounded shell heaps on northwestern Florida's Apalachicola River.

Lacking the smoking or even the smoldering gun implicating competition-based obligation and its exclusionary effects on first mound–building societies, I turn to the other side of obligation, its beneficent side. I think this side of obligation is a power fund as potent as competitive obligation, but we have been slow in recognizing its potency because its potentially showy side effects are down-played, deliberately. Drawing attention to gifting and gaining materially from it would undermine the very tenets on which beneficence rests. Show and gain are consequences of competition-based obligation. To see whether we can get an inkling of the potency of beneficent obligation, we need to step outside the simplicity-complexity impasse, at least for a moment, to see whether there is ample power therein to build mounds (see Saitta 1997:8).

Thanking a donor of a gift, whether for goods or a service, is the lesser moment of obligation, although it is crucial to acknowledging the receipt and acceptance of the gift. The heart of debt of gratitude lies in the implicit or avowed understanding between donor and recipient that gifts will be paid back, appropriately and in due time. But beneficent obligation is not the same as reciprocity. Reciprocity is an economic transaction, a transfer of goods or a service without contract (Harris 1993:239). Beneficent obligation is more than economic reciprocity. It is a prevailing ethic that touches every aspect of peoples' lives and psyches.

Whether we are talking economics or ethics, obligation—both competitive and beneficent—carries checks and balances. Not only does the donor expect return on the goods or service (Sahlins 1972), but also what is returned will be subjected to valuation relative to the original gift. Whether it rates as equivalent to, greater than, or less than the original can, and usually does, make a world of difference. A gift not repaid or underpaid places the recipient at risk of incurring the condescension of the original donor and of being socially low rated. In addition, slackers who wait too long to pay back a gift of goods or a service risk being branded as freeloaders or misers, and both kinds of slackers face big trouble in the immediate- or delayed-return political-economic arrangements that likely existed among first mound–building hunter-gatherers. By failing to reciprocate as expected, freeloaders sooner or later get left out and must fend for themselves, if they can. Misers, on the other hand, can expect a worse fate. As Marcel Mauss (1990; see also Sahlins 1972) recognizes, the spirit of the gift, or its beneficence, is not to be used for self-elevation or for gaining an edge on friends and neighbors but is to be returned or passed on to others. I have searched ethnohistorical records on Southeastern natives to discover what fate befell such niggardly individuals (e.g., Bartram 1955 [1791]; Du Pratz 1975 [1774]; Swanton 1911, 1928a, 1931), with little success (but see Gideon Lincecum 1904, quoted in Swanton 1931:22–23). It makes me wonder whether repercussions for stinginess or laziness might not have been so onerous that most people chose not to tempt fate.

We should not regard competitive obligation and beneficent obligation as opposites. Competitors sometimes do favors and give gifts that they know will not help them reach the pearly gates of fame and fortune. And selfish motives and hard hearts may prompt individuals to lend a helping hand as a sort of down payment on future corporate returns, in an I-helped-you-now-your-turn-to-help-me mentality. Even nice folks can be calculating and conniving or merely expectant of just return when needed. In a purely social sense, obligation occurs in all societies, egalitarian or transegalitarian, in all places and times. Its limits are imposed by malice, acrimony, inconsiderateness, or miserliness, not territorial boundaries, customs, or laws.

TWO SOURCES OF DEBT OF GRATITUDE

Debt of gratitude springs from at least two sources. It comes from transfers of gifts between two people—any exchange that puts one person in another's debt, such as help with building houses, weaving fishnets, making dugouts, carrying out blood raids, assisting with funerals or marriages, or carrying out dozens of other activities that could not have been finished as easily without help from family, friends, and neighbors (Krause 1989). Although giving and accepting gifts are individual actions, I suggest that the spirit of giving permeates communalistic folk formations, as well as familiar social groups within larger, complex social formations. In this sense, social obligation is a prerogative of small or close-knit groups more concerned with helping one another or finishing a project of common interest than with gaining personal economic or status advantage (Mauss 1990; Service 1975), at least in most situations. Beneficent obligation does not snuff out the fires of competitiveness. On the contrary, I think competitiveness is just as fierce in small and midsized collectivities as in larger groups, but in smaller groups, what can and cannot be competed for is defined unambiguously by public opinion. Individual competition ends where the good of the group begins. For instance, it is perfectly okay to win a foot race and brag about it, but it is not okay to build a tall mound and expect to gain fame or fortune.

In addition to personal gift giving, debt of gratitude also comes from emotion-rich sentiments. Patriotism, ethnic or religious fervor, or other beliefs arising from heart and soul can, and often do, infuse collectivities, causing them to rise above individual differences and, in some instances, foster a kind of hysteria or zeal, especially when there are threats or challenges to homeland, pride, or beliefs. It is this second source of obligation that I propose as the power behind mound building.

How, you ask, does debt of gratitude come out of emotional sentiment? Essentially, it comes the same way it does from personal gifts. The difference between them is in the passion engendered. Gifts between individuals leverage return gifts in an unending cycle of grateful give and take. The same is true of the gifts from nation or Great Spirit, only the emotional potency is multiplied manyfold. Though they cannot be seen or touched, gifts from nation or Great Spirit often create feelings that are the most stirring people ever experience, for they touch the core of who people are and what they deem important in life. Good health, good medicine, protection, identity, fine sons and daughters, a good dying, and a host of other good feelings are gifts bestowed by spirit forces and are beyond direct control of individuals. The pride that comes from being Tunica, Koroa, Natchez, Choctaw, or Timucua cannot be held in the hands, but it resides in the heart and is often worn on the sleeve. It is the spirit of the gift of identity conferred by the Great Spirit to first man and woman and passed down to all their descendants. The warm feeling of home is the gift of ancestors, who sanctified the land with their living and dying. It is the spirit of their gift. The thrill of the fisherman finding his net filled and the excitement of the boy hunter standing over his first deer are the spirits of the gifts of water and forest. The sense of security brought by living within enclosures of mounds or rings is the spirit of the gift of protection conferred by the spirit world (Gibson 2000; Hall 1976).

Ideology defines what is important and what is not. But I am not referring only to social norms and proper behavior. After all, an automaton can be programmed to act normally. I am talking about bringing out people's deepest feelings, their laughter, tears, pride, fear, and other primal responses. A gift of a basket of fresh yellow catfish or a dozen Dover flint preforms may be appreciated and earmarked for return in kind later, but gifts of the mounds are felt more deeply. As sociograms and creation metaphors, mounds celebrate life and create a sense of belonging. They give identity to a social collectivity and every one of its members. As barriers against omnipresent dark forces, mounds provide protection for each individual, every family member, and the entire village (Gibson 2000; Hall 1976). And in an animistic world where spirit forces live everywhere from rustling leaves to things that go bump in the night, the security blanket of the mound may be one of the greatest gifts ever conferred by the Great Spirit.

Supernatural gifts such as life's joy and spiritual protection are precisely those that produce the depth of feeling that transcends petty jealousies and evokes an all-consuming communalistic spirit. They are the only gifts, I maintain, capable of assembling a mound-building crew simply with a morning call and keeping it motivated without need of whip-cracking gang pushers or threats from the boss. So, ideology is the lesser part of mound building; grateful duty, as John Clark calls it, is the real force. Gifts of the mound simply are too important—to everyone—for people not to hold them close to the heart. Who would not be consumed with obligation to pay back the greatest gifts ever given?

OBLIGATION AND FIRST-MOUND BUILDING

Showing how debt of gratitude could have empowered first-mound building requires that we look at how mounds were built and why. I have found only one historical account of mound building that suits my purpose, the building of Nanih Waiya, the sacred mound of the Choctaw, and it has been embellished and fictionalized to a considerable extent by Gideon Lincecum (1904, quoted in Swanton 1931:12–26). True, Lincecum's account records an eighteenth-century Choctaw story and can be thought of as only a contemporary tale tailored to the moment. I lose no sleep over its veracity as a faithful retelling of the vital moment in Choctaw ethnogenesis, but I strongly suspect that it is faithful, because it gives details no Protestant missionary could have known. Archaeological leanings toward a Middle Woodland origin for Nanih Waiya (Carleton 1999) do not controvert its basic storyline, either. Origin stories are among the most enduring in human oral traditions (Campbell 1988). I see no compelling reason that groups whose descendants became the historic Choctaw could not have formed during Middle Woodland or even earlier times or that their origin account could not have survived some 50 to 60 generations. But all concerns about veracity aside, the real crux of the matter is that Lincecum's account furnishes a better model than I could have constructed from theory or my imagination. Not only does it offer a plausible account of how Archaic mound building might have been conducted, but the social contexts and precipitating circumstances are precisely what I would expect of a close-knit, mound-building Archaic group.

The minko's (chief's) proposal to build a mound is a suggestion brought before the entire group and appeals to people's sense of honor and responsibility—their duty to their dead ancestors. The minko did not order mound building; he did not have the authority for giving orders (see Anonymous 1755, quoted in Swanton 1931:90–91, 234–244). Leadership by suggestion typifies small and intermediate societies based on kinship. In the Choctaw case, suggestion works, not because of the minko's winning personality but because his proposal resolves a crisis facing all the people—what to do with the sacks of bones they had been carrying on their years-long migration. The people readily agree to build a protective monument to hold their ancestors' bones, because it is in every burden bearer's best interests. They can lay their burdens down.

Two conclusions raise interest. First, the minko appeals to people's sense of civic and religious responsibility in order to get them interested in mound building. No force is applied, no threats are made, and a tired people rejoice. Second, the majority rules. Consensus decides the course, approbation readily wins because the minko's proposal gives people a way to perform community-service obligations and lift the weight from their own shoulders at the same time. In effect, building Nanih Waiya kills two birds with one stone—it serves the Choctaw nation and the Choctaw person. To me, actions that conflate several heartfelt interests stand the best chance not only of winning endorsement but also of becoming a guiding, even fiercely defended, tenet of the group.

Lincecum's story claims that mounds of earth will protect the sacred relics (bones) forever. Such protection could just mean keeping ancestral bones from loss or destruction, but I suspect it means much more. Coverings of dirt taken from hallowed places (*tadjo* among the Creek, see Knight 1989) or mounded like Nanih Waiya are believed to have supernatural power, thereby affording as much protection for the living as for the bones of the dead. Might not power dirt have been the means of delivering that assurance or of encasing the evil specter of ghosts and shielding the people from harm?

I think mounded dirt does much more than turn away ghost fright. In the dual-creation myth of the Choctaw, Nanih Waiya is identified as the place where human beings originated (Halbert 1899, in Peterson 1985)—the site where people and grasshoppers emerged together out of a tunnel leading from a cave deep underground and lay about drying on Nanih Waiya until scattering in all directions and becoming the various Muskogean tribes. Womb symbolism links Nanih Waiya with the Earth Mother–Earth Island creation thesis. As symbol of the moment and of the place of creation, Nanih Waiya gives identify to Choctaw people. And I do not think such symbolism started at Nanih Waiya.

It is old wisdom, passed down from the ancients. It already is displayed in first mounds, and I suspect it was ancient even then.

Mound arrangements also confer big medicine. Geometric layouts, both enclosures and linear alignments, are widely regarded by Muskogean tribes as "magical shields against an outside world filled with potentially disorderly beings and evil power" (Gibson 2000:185). I do not know of a confirmed case of first-mound building where only one mound was erected. Archaic mounds are always in groups (Gibson 1994a; Russo 1996a; Saunders et al. 1994) and thus exhibit some kind of geometrical pattern and much more (see Clark, Russo, and Sassaman and Heckenberger, this volume).

By offering a source of safety and identity, mounds are precisely the kinds of buildings most likely to enjoy near-unanimous public endorsement. Mound building may be of and for the people collectively, but it has just as much meaning of and for each person privately. I have previously called this dualistic meaning the genius of the mounds (Gibson 2000). If any action were more likely to have brought out a greater sense of commonweal, I do not know what it might have been, and it certainly did not leave a monument to its doing. Mounds are gifts straight from the Great Spirit. By providing protection and identity—gifts of the mounds—to the group and to every individual within the group, mounds become supernatural donors requiring recompense. I contend that the labor that went into their construction and maintenance and the respect paid them afterwards constituted those return gifts. Return thus was immediate, equitable, and long lasting—the beneficence of the mound and the beneficence of the mound builder linked in a perpetual cycle of obligation and reciprocal gifting.

Dean Saitta makes the case for Chacoan political economy being communalistic by arguing that power and labor relations were relatively independent: "What matters is not the degree of hierarchy or specialization, but rather the appropriation of surplus labor" (Saitta 1997:7–8). This is precisely the context in which beneficent obligation can turn into a strong incentive for common action and provide enough muscle to see a project through. And disentangling labor from social and political power can explain why mound-building Middle Archaic and Poverty Point societies lack showy indications of social hierarchy. There is no secret formula for appropriating labor. There need only be the unambiguous belief that mound building rewards every man, woman, and child individually as much as it does their heartfelt communalistic principles, which brought on mound building in the first place.

HOW HIGH CAN THEY GO?

Does consensus-based, communalistic action guided by low-key leadership have what it takes to put up mounds—big mounds? Is the power of beneficent obligation really enough? We recognize signs of competition, aggrandizing, and exclusionary practices and understand how and why hereditary inequalities come from those actions (see Clark and Blake 1994). First mounds do not embody these signs. So, must we presume that they were built by simple folk, organizationally speaking? No, not necessarily. We lack archaeological markers of beneficence, too (Saunders, this volume), but that is because we have no idea what they would look like anyway. It is really not a matter of blaming egalitarian hunter-gatherers for first mounds, it is a matter of trying to figure out whether beneficent obligation—proposed here as an alternative to aggrandizing, competitive obligation—packs enough power to do the job.

Mound building is bound up with motive, power, leadership, and labor. If we take mounds as proof that first-mound builders possessed the essential motive, power, and leadership, we are left with labor as the remaining variable in mound building. Could hunter-gatherers with their presumably small populations have appropriated enough labor? Or must we look, as we did once upon a time, to larger, more complex groups for the essential labor? Or is it really necessary to view these as either-or choices? I can think of times and circumstances when both competitive obligation and beneficent obligation are manifested in all kinds of groups, small and large, poor and rich, simple and complex. Like corporate and exclusionary tactics (see Blanton et al. 1996), competitive obligation and beneficent obligation are merely flip sides of giving and gifting. Besides, they are not antagonistic even when they coexist among varied social practices of the same group (see Saitta 1997).

Again, I turn to Nanih Waiya, for not only does it offer a good model, but also it is the only record of corporate-based mound building I know. If the Nanih Waiya of tribal lore and the mound in Winston County, Mississippi, identified as Nanih Waiya, are one and the same, then we have a means for converting mound dimensions and volume into labor estimates. The Choctaw were basically egalitarian, although ethnohistorical records do suggest that social inequalities existed, especially among warriors and between medicine men and everybody else. Such inequalities were, however, based on achievement and were not inherited. If the Choctaw could build Nanih Waiya with their essentially egalitarian organization, then Archaic groups ought to have been able to perform similar feats with comparably simple organizations.

Calvin Brown (1992:24) records Nanih Waiya's dimensions: basal length and width, 218 by 140 feet; summit plateau length and width, 132 by 56 feet; and height, between 22 and 25 feet. Calculating mound volume geometrically produces a total of 433,622 cubic feet, or 12,278 m^3 (see Jeter 1984:103). In a dirt-moving experiment in Mexico, Charles Erasmus (1965) found that two men can move 1.76 m^3 of dirt in a day. Lincecum (1904, in Swanton 1931) tells us that Nanih Waiya took seven years to build, engaging laborers for about half the year between spring planting and fall dispersal. I have reduced the yearly mound-building period to only five months, because working on the mound was not a full-time occupation, even for the most impassioned Choctaw. As Lincecum acknowledges, piling dirt on Nanih Waiya was an honorable pursuit but nonetheless an after-work pastime. By Lincecum's reckoning, Nanih Waiya took about 35 months to complete.

Given these figures, two men could have dumped about 1,848 m³ of dirt in Nanih Waiya over the life of the project; one person, around 924 m³. This means that Nanih Waiya could have been built by the equivalent of slightly less than a dirty dozen (an average of 11 adults and a kid, 11.3 persons, to be precise) working for the allotted 35 months. I doubt that construction ran continuously for five months every year with an average crew of a dozen; more likely it proceeded by spurts and fits.

Although interrupted work would have meant larger labor gangs, maybe two or three times larger than the average crew estimated as necessary to build Nanih Waiya, the required labor force still would have been within population parameters of known hunter-gatherers, not to mention the likelihood that mainstream hunter-gatherers living on prime land had even larger populations.

Using Nanih Waiya as a standard measure, we can compare first-mound labor equivalents for compatibility. One first-mound site, Frenchman's Bend, has five mounds and contains just over 3,600 m³ of fill (Gibson 1996c:table 2; Saunders et al. 1994). The Nanih Waiya standard measure of one person for every 924 m³ (over a 35-month period) translates to an average labor force of nearly four adults (3.9 people). Watson Brake, the largest of the first-mound complexes, has 11 mounds and contains around 33,900 m³ of fill (see Saunders, this volume). Its biggest mound alone contains 5,400 m³. On the basis of the Nanih Waiya standard, equivalent requisite labor averages around 37 people—between five and six for the big mound by itself.

Poverty Point, on the other hand, jumps off the scale by the Nanih Waiya standard. The amount of dirt that went into its elevated earthworks totals somewhere between 667,000 and 750,000 m³, and an untold but potentially larger amount was required for land fill (Gibson 1987). This massive amount of dirt work equates to the labor of a crew averaging somewhere between 722 and 812 people. The largest bird mound alone contains the labor equivalent of around 195 people and the second-largest, Motley Mound, the labor equivalent of about 106 people.

I emphasize that these numbers are not actual labor estimates but relative figures (calculated in standard Nanih Waiya labor-unit equivalents) for judging whether first mounds could have been built by corporate-based, consensus-guided groups like the Nanih Waiya Choctaw. The labor-equivalent figures are heuristic only, standardized by factoring in the acknowledged seven-year (35-

month) Nanih Waiya completion span. Labor equivalents for first mounds anywhere close to the Nanih Waiya standard of about a dozen workers make a compelling case that fairly small, corporate-based groups were able to put up some
pretty big mounds.

Frenchman's Bend and Watson Brake are close enough to the Nanih Waiya
standard, but Poverty Point is so much bigger that I am agape at the implications.
The simplest explanation is, of course, for Poverty Point's construction to have
been drawn out over many decades or several generations (for possibilities, see
Gibson 1987:table 2). I can live with decades or even a generation or two, but
not longer (Gibson 2000), although even that would make Poverty Point's work
crews larger than any contemporary hunter-gatherers were able to field. The alternative to an extended building span is that Poverty Point represents the
handiwork of an altogether different kind of society, not simply a small-scale society grown large. Long ago, I claimed Poverty Point to be mainland North
America's first chiefdom (Gibson 1974). I find myself suffering déjà vu all over
again.

I remind myself, however, that Poverty Point was not built by first-mound
builders but by later Archaic people 1,800 years after the nearby first mounds.
Actually that is not entirely true. At least one of the mounds incorporated
in Poverty Point's earthworks, Lower Jackson Mound (and possibly Ballcourt
Mound too), is a first mound (Gibson 2000:91; Saunders et al. 2001). First-
mound builders already were at work on Poverty Point grounds before the massive building program started 18 centuries later. Having brought up the problem
with Poverty Point, I now choose to ignore it.

Another way of looking at these labor-equivalent figures is in terms of how
large hunter-gatherer groups had to be to be able to muster the requisite labor for
mound building. Contemporary nomadic hunter-gatherers live in groups numbering between 15 and 75 people, while sedentary hunter-gatherer groups number between 33 and 1,500 (Kelly 1995:table 6-2). Robert Kelly (1995:213) discovered that among an average hunter-gatherer group of 25, only about seven or
eight were able-bodied adults; the others were too young, too old, or too sick to
work. Applying this percentage to Nanih Waiya's labor-equivalent force, our
standard measure, suggests a total population of between 37 and 42 people,
clearly within the population ranges of both nomadic and sedentary hunter-
gatherers (even though by definition the Choctaw were farmers, or at least they
grew some corn in the spring to go along with their hunting and gathering during the rest of the year). By the same measure, the Frenchman's Bend group
would have been small, numbering between 11 and 13 people, only about a
third as large as the Nanih Waiya Choctaw. Watson Brake's group would have
been about two and a half to three and a half times the size of Nanih Waiya's,

numbering between 116 and 132 people, a size that falls near the upper limits
of nomadic hunter-gatherers but well within limits of sedentary hunter-gatherers.

If we use the same conversion factor to estimate Poverty Point's equivalent
population, we come up with between 2,022 and 2,594 people, and that is 50
to 70 times larger than Nanih Waiya's. Clearly, Poverty Point is off the scale.
The reasons for its grandiosity are embedded in its history and its propitious
location, but they are of its own making.

WAS THERE SUFFICIENT POTENCY
IN BENEFICENT OBLIGATION?

By now you are wondering, what is all the fuss about beneficent obligation? Most
of us recognize its potential for eliciting action, and if you have ever gotten all
puffed up when the national anthem is played or been in the huddle when the
quarterback calls the final play that will determine whether you win or lose the
district championship, you understand the depth of emotion that communalistic feelings can unleash. Egos fall away, and the good of the group becomes all-
consuming. Few feelings are more passionate, certainly not the sting of a limber
switch, the admonition of a supervisor, or the challenge of a rival. But what does
beneficent obligation mean for the smoldering issue of just how complexly organized early mound-building formations really were?

On first glance it seems to sidestep it, but what it really does is decouple labor
appropriation and motive from the political-economic power structure, as Dean
Saitta (1997) recommends for Chacoan sociality. It allows us to take the pulse
of first mound–building societies without having to worry about the shape and
size of their sociopolitical-economic infrastructure. What we know about these
ancient societies actually is pretty basic: some 55 centuries ago, a few lower Mississippi and Florida coastal natives built mounds and rings, some big, some small,
that were steeped in cosmic design and imbued with ritual meaning. And those
builders left few material signs of being rife with hierarchical social inequalities,
especially of the inheritable kind. This does not necessarily mean that they were
nonhierarchical; they could have been. But it does reveal that first mound–
building sociality was not dominated by a competitive-aggrandizer ethos bent on
showy self-appreciation, else there would be telltale signs of exclusion and proprietary wealth. Mound building, if not Archaic societies as a whole, was predicated on communalistic principles and interpersonal relationships.

My interest in beneficent obligation is simple: Was it capable of empower-
ing mound building? I think it was, and not just first mounds but even Poverty Point's towering mounds and mighty rings, the largest earthworks ever
constructed by Native American fisher-hunter-gatherers. Earthworks endowed

their builders with elevated senses of patriotism, home, identity, and security—communalistic passions linked directly to motive, labor, and concerted action. But where does obligation come in? How did a person repay a mound for its gifts? The most obvious and immediate way was in giving time and muscle for its construction. Yet mounds were enduring monuments and would have continually elicited return on the spirit of their gifts. Building new mounds would have been one way to repay obligations, and groups of mounds may reflect this means of payment. But repaying one mound's gifts by building yet another would have produced an unending cycle, and first-mound building did come to an end. In fact, there was a hiatus of nearly 1,800 years between first mounds at Watson Break, Frenchman's Bend, and other places and the next cycle of mound building at Poverty Point. But the beneficence of the mounds also could have been passed directly to people, not merely returned to the mounds and the supernatural forces they embodied. A mother teaching a daughter to be a good wife and mother, a father showing his son how to move stealthily through the woods so there will always be venison in the pot and glory on the warpath, a shaman revealing the tricks of his profession to his apprentice so that one day he will be able to turn away the spirit darkness brought by the north wind and heal the sick—these and other favors and lessons passed on to the young, the feeble, and even the able are the kinds of payback I envision. They are returns on the spirit of the mounds.

But why mounds? Easy—mounds are sociograms and cosmic metaphors that manifest the spirit of the people. No greater symbols of nationalism and ethnic pride were ever raised. And if flag-waving was not enough, mounds also conferred magical protection in an animistic world full of spirits, ghosts, and evil forces. Instead of asking why mounds, one might legitimately ask what other than mounds.

The query behind this essay—was there sufficient potency in obligation to have underpinned first-mound building—is nearly as easy to answer. I say yes. The spirit of the gift is both motive and source of raw, self-generated, and sustainable power. The power of beneficent obligation worked for the Choctaw. Would it have done any less for first-mound builders?

ACKNOWLEDGMENTS

I am much obliged to Phil Carr, John Clark, George Milner, and Vin Steponaitis for their helpful thoughts on this chapter. Peer reviewers Jay Johnson and John Kelly asked tough questions and gently pointed out frayed edges. John Clark went through several incarnations of this essay, catching logical blunders and muddled thinking—sufficiently, I hope, to make what remains intelligible. Joe Saunders has tried to temper my elan with calls for proof. But alas, it is the burden of proof that I seek to circumvent by essay writing instead of awaiting cold, hard facts, which remain as elusive as will-o'-the-wisps. And I deny any credibility to whispers coming out of certain learned circles that it is not facts I circumvent but reason. I wish to thank my mamma and daddy, grandma and grandpa, other members of my extended family, and all the fine folks I grew up with for showing me the power of beneficent obligation and the miracles it works.

14

Archaic Mounds and the Archaeology of Southeastern Tribal Societies

David G. Anderson

> It is rare that archaeologists ever find something that so totally changes our picture of the past, as is true for this case.
>
> Vincas P. Steponaitis, commenting on the Watson
> Brake site in the journal *Science* (Pringle 1997:1761)

The recognition a decade ago that Southeastern societies engaged in complex shell and earthen mound building more than 5,000 years ago is revolutionizing our thinking about the archaeology of the region. In this chapter I discuss some of the implications of this research and where it will take us in the years to come.[1] In brief, the discovery of Archaic mounds has forced us to confront head-on how tribal societies operate; this is an organizational form that has received little serious research attention in the Southeast. What we are now coming to realize is that the tribal formation was the dominant means of organizing and integrating people for thousands of years, from at least as far back as the Middle Archaic period, when monumental Archaic mounds appear amid a backdrop of presumed band-level, residentially mobile foraging populations, through the later Woodland and Mississippian periods, when chiefdom-level societies characterized by intensive agriculture and sedentary village life appear widely across the region. How these societies operated is a subject that Southeastern archaeologists will be exploring in great detail in the years to come and in the process making major contributions to anthropological theory.

The discovery that Middle Archaic populations were capable of far more complex collective action than previously deemed possible has also caused us to question traditional unilineal evolutionary models of how change occurred over the region. It is no longer possible to see the Southeastern landscape as one of organizationally more or less identical populations evolving in lockstep from Paleoindian and Archaic period band-level groups to terminal Late Archaic and Woodland period tribal societies that were, in turn, replaced by later Woodland and Mississippian period chiefdoms. At the very least, we now know that our dating of at least one of these organizational shifts was off by thousands of years.

Even more important, the discovery of ancient mounds is forcing us to confront the variability evident within and between the region's Archaic period societies. We now know that contemporaneous groups integrated at very different levels of complexity were present in different parts of the region. This is most clearly shown by the fact that Archaic peoples were erecting large mound complexes in some areas while in other parts of the region there is no evidence whatsoever for such collective action (e.g., see Brookes, this volume, and White, this volume). Appreciable organizational variability is also evident within as well as between these societies. Individual groups were organized quite differently at different times, depending on, among other things, whether they were aggregated or dispersed, at peace or in conflict, or in times of resource abundance or shortfall. Tribal social organization is highly flexible and capable of undergoing great changes in form or structural pose over short periods of time, making examination of the wide range of Archaic social formations a daunting challenge. Yet documenting and explaining organizational variability in the region's Archaic and Woodland tribal societies is receiving increasing attention and will, I predict, be the focus of much exciting and informative research in the years to come.

THE NATURE OF TRIBAL SOCIETIES

To understand the kind of societies that may have been present in the prehistoric Southeast, we need to evaluate the available archaeological evidence and make comparisons with known organizational forms. I believe that the existing data, particularly those for monumentality and large-scale interaction summarized in this volume, indicate that tribal social formations were present in the Southeast from at least the Middle Archaic period onward (see also Anderson 2002). But what does this mean, and why is such an inference important? We must ask what a tribal society is, and what it is not, and use this information to help us explore and interpret the archaeological record.[2] Tribal societies are characterized by economically autonomous groups of people, or segments, bound together by institutions crosscutting these segments (Sahlins 1968b; Service 1962). As Marshall Sahlins noted:

A band is a simple association of families, but a tribe is an association of kin groups which are themselves composed of families. A tribe is a segmental organization. It is composed of a number of equivalent, unspecialized multifamily groups, each the structural duplicate of the other: a tribe is a congeries of equal kin group blocks. . . . It is sometimes possible to speak of several levels of segmentation. . . . "Primary tribal segment" is defined as the smallest multifamily group that collectively exploits an area of tribal resources and forms a residential entity all or most of the year. . . . In most cases the primary segment seems to fall between 50 and 250 people. . . . Small localized—often primary—tribal segments tend to be economically and politically autonomous. A tribe as a whole is normally not a political organization but rather a social-cultural-ethnic identity. It is held together primarily by likenesses among its segments . . . and by pan-tribal institutions, such as a system of intermarrying clans, of age-grades, or military or religious societies, which cross cut the primary segments. Pan tribal institutions make a tribe a more integrated social institution (even if weakly so) than a group of intermarrying bands . . . pan tribal social institutions are perhaps the most indicative characteristic of tribal society. Such institutions clearly demarcate the borders of a tribe, separating it as a social (and ethnic) entity [Sahlins 1968b:93–94].

Tribal societies have leaders with varying degrees of wealth, status, prestige, permanence, or power, exercising influence over some or all parts of the religious and secular arenas. But these are achieved and ephemeral roles, occupied at best for a portion of the lives of specific individuals, and not hereditary and multi-generational positions filled by accident of birth rather than ability (although ability is usually crucial to maintaining these positions in even the most complex of societies). Authority is typically cooperative and consensual in tribal societies, rather than absolute or coercive in nature, and almost invariably disappears upon the death, declining ability, or change in fortunes of those in such positions. Decision making and leadership in tribal societies are typically ephemeral, "largely consensus-based, situational, and unstable" (Fowles 2002a:15).

The organization of tribal societies is fluid and situational, meaning they can operate at different geographic and demographic scales, levels of inclusiveness, and degrees of integration depending upon circumstances and historical preconditions. Such societies may change structural poses quickly, making the organizational form particularly flexible and efficient and, hence, giving it potentially appreciable longevity (Fowles 2002a:22–23). It is not an inflexible type defined by one or a few strict precepts. There is, in fact, no one way of being "tribal," even within individual tribal societies. Instead, different kinds of complexity may be present simultaneously within the spatial extent of a "tribal" formation, and these kinds of complexity invariably occur over time. Greater organizational complexity tends to emerge during periods of population aggregation, which may also correspond to times of crisis (i.e., stress caused by warfare, subsistence shortfalls, changing patterns of interaction, or religious/ceremonial events, including participation in monumental construction), and fades quickly as population dispersal occurs or when the time of crisis passes (Carneiro 2002: 40–41; Fowles 2002a:17; Parkinson 2002a:7–10, 2002b:394–401). Organizational complexity thus varies depending on the numbers of people interacting at any given time, and these numbers may fluctuate widely. Social boundaries and group affiliation are likewise fluid and flexible in tribal societies, with individual and group movement between segments or larger groupings typically open and unrestrained (Fowles 2002a:20; Hutterer 1991; Snow 2002).

Resistance to domination, both from self-aggrandizing individuals and from the aggressive behavior of other groups, is typically an active part of tribal life (Bender 1990; Flanagan 1989; Fowles 2002a, 2002b; Hayden 1996; Poyer 1991; Redmond 2002; Sassaman 1995, 2001; Woodburn 1982). Typically such resistance derives from an egalitarian ethic in which group activities are agreed upon and entered into willingly and not dictated or coerced. When attempts at domination occur, people may simply ignore the instigator, vote with their feet and move away from the group, or actively resist the challenge, and they may meet attempts at coercion or force with a like response. As Fowles (2002a:25) has noted, the ability "to respond to social conflict with mobility rather than the institutionalization of strong positions of leadership has undoubtedly played a critical role in keeping many tribal groups 'tribal' over the long run" (Kent 1989; Trigger 1990c). Fowles (2002b:91–92) also argues that "egalitarian rebellions" overturn trends toward inequality and emergent hierarchy and are one means by which tribal societies can maintain themselves over the long term, even in regions where more complex societies may be present. Leadership and authority in tribal societies wax and wane over time, rather than holding constant, and changes can occur both over the short run, during seasonal patterns of aggregation and dispersal, as well as over much longer intervals, in what Fowles (2002a: 26) calls "multi-generational cycles of leadership." The expression "nothing recedes like excess" can be considered something of a truism about the difficulties aggrandizing leaders have holding on to their position in tribal societies.[3]

THE ARCHAEOLOGICAL RECOGNITION OF TRIBAL SOCIETIES

As Robert Carneiro (2002:49) argues, a central question facing archaeologists is how to recognize tribal societies in the archaeological record. How do archaeologists recognize pan-tribal institutions or sodalities, such as clans, age-grades, or military or religious societies? The organizational structure of tribal societies, specifically the way they are held together, is complex and multivariate with integration typically occurring in many different ways and at many different scales (Fowles 2002a:24–28). Analyses must be directed to multiple spatial, demographic, and temporal scales to explore fully these societies. Explanation is itself scalar dependent, that is, approaches and results satisfying at one temporal or geographic scale do not necessarily work well or at all at another, and historical events, practice, and trajectories as well as broad cultural processes must be recognized and brought to bear in this interpretive effort (Fowles 2002a; Neitzel and Anderson 1999; Pauketat 2001a, 2001c). Recognizing collective ceremony and ritual and, specifically, looking for evidence for feasting behavior and of how monumental construction occurred are two avenues currently being explored in detail at Southeastern Archaic shell midden and earthen mound sites, as several authors have noted in this book (see also Knight 2001, Pauketat et al. 2002, and Welch and Scarry 1995 for examples of research directed to feasting in later periods).

Architectural evidence is most commonly used by archaeologists to infer the existence of tribal social organization in many parts of the world (e.g., Adler 2002; Fowles 2002a; Johnson 1989). In the Southwest, for example, kivas or household clusters are sometimes used to identify possible tribal segments, while in the Southeast individual mounds or discrete plaza areas within mound groups may represent the same thing. Kenneth E. Sassaman and Michael J. Heckenberger's arguments (this volume) about the symbolic and social role of plazas at Archaic mound centers have also been advanced for Southeastern sites of later periods, such as Woodland period Swift Creek ring middens (Bense 1998:270–273) and Mississippian mound/plaza complexes (Holley et al. 1993; Kidder 2002). Michael Russo (this volume) argues that the larger the shell ring, the more complex its architectural plan seems to become. To him, the presence of attached or nearby rings and open areas (presumed plazas) of varying sizes, asymmetries in the amounts of shell and earthen material employed, and the occasional presence of avenues or causeways are clear evidence for a far greater social complexity than we have traditionally granted the peoples creating these monuments. The relationship between the size and internal variation of monumental architecture and the organizational complexity of the societies creating it is a major research challenge. What makes Russo's argument particularly convincing is the sheer mass of primary mapping and architectural data he and his colleagues are compiling from coastal Archaic shell ring and midden sites to explore these questions. We need much more primary fieldwork like this if we are to understand how these early mound groups were created and used.

Demographic analyses can provide clues about the kinds of organization present at a site or in a given area. The populations living at some Archaic mound centers, for example, were much larger than those assumed to be coresident in band-level societies. In Chapter 3, for example, Russo estimates the sizes of groups creating U- and ring-shaped shell middens on the Gulf and Atlantic coasts by calculating the number of households that could be located on the ring and by varying the average number of inhabitants per household. Even the smallest Southeastern Archaic shell ring middens, ca. 30 m in diameter, could have held upwards of 50 people, well beyond the approximately 25 individuals who make up typical band-level coresident groups. The presence of large settled communities may well point to organizational forms beyond the band level, but since such numbers are within the range of aggregation loci of both band and tribal societies, great care must be taken to ensure that these occupations were long term and not transitory and that the inferred living areas were occupied contemporaneously. Russo (1991), for example, additionally examined paleosubsistence data to make the case for extensive, year-round resource procurement at the Horr's Island shell midden in Florida and hence probable permanent residence.

Paleosubsistence data can also be used to explore feasting behavior, which is an effective means of integrating people in societies of all kinds (Dietler 2001; Dietler and Hayden 2001; Dietler and Herbich 2001; Hayden 2001; Knight 2001; Russo, this volume). At Watson Brake, for example, large numbers of bone fragments were found in Stage I and in the submound area of Mound B that were interpreted as indicating seasonal site use and that could also, given the quantity of material recovered, reflect feasting behavior associated with mound construction (Saunders, this volume; Saunders et al. 1994; Saunders et al. 1997). Resource-rich areas of the Southeast, such as the lower Mississippi alluvial valley or the estuarine areas of the Gulf and Atlantic coasts where people could marshal large quantities of food to support feasting behavior, would be areas where the development of complex Archaic cultures was more probable. Accordingly, where people were present in large numbers on the Archaic Southeastern landscape and food surpluses or massive temporary accumulations were possible, we must look for evidence of complexity or else for a deliberate opting out of such developments.

Given their importance in the historic era, lineages and clans were undoubtedly critical constituents of tribal social organization in the Southeast and likely defined or crosscut tribal segments, respectively (Hudson 1976; Knight 1990; Widmer, this volume). Tribal segments, consisting of coresident groups, likely consisted of related kin, perhaps from one or a few lineages. Clans, in contrast, may have included people from a number of segments. The archaeological recognition of coresident groups, or groups tied to specific territories or areas, or members of specific sodalities, of course, will require appreciable effort.

Burial data can be profitably examined to learn how individuals in tribal societies were perceived. Among tribal societies, wealth or status markers are typically buried with individuals rather than passed on to subsequent generations (Carneiro 2002:44). How the dead were treated and what was interred with them offer important clues about how these societies were organized (Yerkes 2002:238–239). Elaborate burials may be present in tribal settings, but these reflect the achieved status of individuals and the esteem in which their relatives and friends held them rather than evidence for hereditary positions. Where are the dead of the people who created the Middle Archaic mounds of Louisiana? We are not certain, but they were possibly buried at or near where they lived, if the recently discovered Conly site is any indication (Girard 2000). At Conly, a dense habitation midden with well-preserved charcoal and bone, including human burials and subsistence remains, was found, together with an extensive lithic assemblage that included both chipped- and ground-stone tools. Eight radiocarbon dates securely place the midden between ca. 7500 and 8000 B.P. (Girard 2000:62). We urgently need to find the residences and physical remains of the people who built the mound complexes.

Examining the distribution of artifacts such as hafted bifaces, bannerstones, or bone pins across the Middle and Late Archaic Southeast might be one way to infer the existence of sodalities or subgroups/segments within local tribal societies or, possibly, to identify and differentiate such societies over the larger region (i.e., Brookes, this volume; Jefferies 1995, 1996, this volume; Johnson and Brookes 1989). Why are bannerstones, shell beads, possibly bone pins, and other items unevenly distributed over the Southeastern landscape (e.g., Crothers, this volume; Sassaman 1996)? What are the archaeological contexts in which items such as hypertrophic Benton points, bone pins, or zoomorphic beads occur? The differing distributions are, of course, partially due to differential preservation conditions but also may occur because discrete groups used varying means of signaling group affiliation or individual status, most of which were likely perishable. If differentiating people was becoming increasingly important, as the evidence for the emergence of group territories and conflict suggests, hairstyles, clothing, or tattoos likely differed appreciably over the region.

Palynological data may be able to help us in the study of these early societies. Did Archaic mound-building societies, for example, encourage the growth of nut trees, particularly near ceremonial centers where they would have provided an additional feasting food resource for groups aggregating there? A profitable area for research might be exploring this question through an examination of plant macrofossil remains or pollen cores. A few years of casually picking up pecans in my backyard has certainly inspired me to encourage their growth and replacement, and I cannot imagine Archaic populations acting less practically. Areas with unusual densities of nut crop trees at various times in the past may well have been a direct result of human action, and they may signal areas where large numbers of people lived or aggregated.

Finally, it is difficult to recognize that which we do not believe exists. For a number of years Russo (1994a, 1994b, 1996a, 1996b, this volume) has been telling us how our theoretical blinders (i.e., the use of unilineal evolutionary stages and assumptions about developmental possibilities within each) have prevented us from seeing what has been in front of our eyes all along: that there are early mound sites and that these sites evince appreciable internal variability that is potentially indicative of differential status. Early maps of shell rings, presented in his chapter, typically depict them as uniform in height and width. The variability that was present was apparently discounted as minimal or unimportant.

The close-interval systematic contour mapping that Russo and his colleagues have been undertaking at many of these sites in recent years, in contrast, shows them to be anything but uniform. Indeed, at some sites the difference in shell extent and volume from one part of the ring to another may differ by as much as an order of magnitude.

The early mapping of Archaic shell rings is a classic case of how theoretical assumptions dictated not only archaeological interpretations but also field methods and recording procedures. Our theoretical underpinning shapes the kind of work we do far more than we might think. We expected to see undifferentiated ringlike structures, reinforcing our view that they reflected the remains of relatively uncomplicated, egalitarian foraging groups, and that is exactly what many archaeologists saw, or reported, even in those few cases where their maps showed otherwise.[4] We must do our basic archaeological homework, but from a perspective informed by anthropological and archaeological theory and ethnographic and ethnohistoric analogy. We will never think to look for evidence for differential feasting behavior or status within Archaic sites, for example, unless we realize such variability might exist. Because a society is considered egalitarian does not mean it is characterized by a dull uniformity or homogeneity.

The fact that widely divergent opinions can be offered about the organization and operation of the groups that created Southeastern Archaic mounds highlights the need for focused, theoretically well-conceived research. Russo's work on shell ring sites, with its explicit problem orientation and research questions, concern for relevant theory, use of ethnographic analogy, and innovative field and analytical strategies, is exemplary in this regard. He first asks the questions: (a) are shell rings incidental refuse accumulations or intentional public architecture and (b) did the ring shape reinforce an egalitarian ethic or reflect inequality within the community using it? Through the detailed mapping and testing of shell rings, Russo and his colleagues have shown that they are not uniform accumulations but possess appreciable internal variation in the distribution and content of shell and earth fill. Coupled with this he also explores whether feasting behavior could have occurred and, if so, how it may have delimited social relationships. With Joe Saunders's (this volume; Saunders et al. 1994; Saunders et al. 1997) work on earthen mounds in Louisiana, this work stands as an excellent example of how to make use of archaeological data to explore these early mound-building societies.

WHAT DO WE MEAN BY COMPLEXITY?

The presence of Archaic mounds has forced us to consider what we mean by cultural complexity in the Southeast. What we have learned, as Saunders (this volume) demonstrates quite nicely, is that the construction of monumental architecture by large numbers of people working together can occur in the apparent absence of many traditional attributes of complexity, such as hereditary inequality, coercive control over labor, tribute mobilization, prestige-goods display, storage, craft specialization, long-distance exchange, and agriculture. To Saunders, this suggests that the societies that built the early mounds were essentially egalitarian.[5] While the absence of some of these attributes may be the result of sampling error or preservation, since we have really excavated only small parts of these sites, particularly for the early mounds in Louisiana, it is unlikely that all of these observations will be overturned. The Southeastern archaeological record is thus demonstrating that the presence of monumental architecture, by itself, is not sufficient to infer the existence of a nonegalitarian form of social organization (see also Yerkes 2002:227). But what was present? Bands? Macrobands? "Transegalitarian" societies?[6]

Elsewhere I have argued that an organizational transformation occurred during the Middle Archaic in some parts of the Southeast. Tribal social forms emerged, with potentially all the behaviors that acting tribally encompasses (Anderson 2002). If this is indeed the case, we must come to a better understanding of how tribal societies are organized and what people within them are capable of doing. As noted above, acting tribally can include the integration of large numbers of people who collectively do remarkable things, including the building of large mound complexes. These were not simple egalitarian societies with uncomplicated worldviews, even though a strong egalitarian ethos likely prevailed and many traditional beliefs were retained. Leaders were present, as were followers, at least at some times and in some places. To Sassaman and Heckenberger (this volume), the construction of Archaic mound/plaza complexes reflected a major symbolic transformation, a Rubicon that once crossed forever changed and enlarged the Southeastern social and cosmological landscape. Russo's chapter (this volume, and as discussed below) reinforces this view: evidence for inequality in these societies is literally piled up in front of us in the differential accumulations that make up these mound/midden groups. This suggests that some people and groups were larger or held higher status than others and possibly, through sheer weight of numbers, had greater access to resources. As these and other researchers have stressed in this book, the layouts of some Archaic mound/plaza complexes appear to embody principles of relative social ranking or hierarchy, of the way people use structures and space to position and define themselves with regard to one another.

What empowered Archaic mound building? What were the ideologies and labor relationships that motivated and enabled people to create such complexes? How do we explore these topics archaeologically? Recognizing that the early Southeastern mound complexes were probably put together by tribal societies, and not chiefdoms, and examining them accordingly is a good place to start.

Ideologies legitimizing the sanctity or coercive power of hereditary elites were not in place. But sacred knowledge and ideologies stressing its importance were undoubtedly present and could have inspired collective action to acknowledge and commemorate it. Sassaman and Heckenberger (this volume) suggest that symbolic power channeled into the hands of a few is an effective way of mobilizing labor, even if such authority is not vested in a hereditary leadership. Ritual and collective ceremony are important integrative mechanisms in tribal society, and as John Clark (this volume) argues, at least some of these early mound centers appear to have been physical embodiments of powerful special knowledge (i.e., sacred numerology/calendrical systems, standard units of measurement or design). Legitimizing group action and labor mobilization through appeals or linkages to deeply held beliefs occurs in societies of all kinds and at all levels of complexity. Early centers were thus not simply arenas where status differences between individuals and groups emerged and played out. This may have happened, but so too did much else.

Jon L. Gibson (this volume) observes that obligation-generating competition is widely recognized as a powerful motivating force, but he turns the concept on its head, arguing that in the Middle Archaic Southeast a prevailing ethic of "beneficent obligation" or "grateful duty" for the public good was in play rather than, or in addition to, action motivated by a desire for individual status enhancement or wealth. The building or maintenance of monuments would have reinforced group identity and pride, which may have been considered desirable for any number of reasons. Once established as a means of integrating people, it was a strategy that was used for the next several thousand years in the region.

What Gibson is asking, in part, is how societies lacking ranking or hereditary inequality can mobilize people to the collective action needed to build mound centers. This is a major challenge archaeologists have been wrestling with for some time and has led, in part, to the creation and study of concepts like heterarchy (Crumley 1987; Ehrenreich et al. 1995), horizontal as opposed to vertical integration, simultaneous vs. sequential decision making (Johnson 1982), group-oriented vs. individualizing societies (Renfrew 1974), and corporate vs. network strategies (Blanton et al. 1996). Renfrew (2001:17–18) proposes "Locations of High Devotional Expression" as another term for situations "motivated by a powerful belief system" in which unusual amounts of societal energy are directed into such areas as monumental construction. Yoffee, Fish, and Milner (1999:266) propose the term *rituality* for similar expressions: "One means of dealing with the organization of large numbers of people and possibly differing cultural orientations is to invest in ritual behavior, negotiating identity through ceremony, and providing a new, or at least improved, context for community integration" (Yoffee et al. 1999:267). This is a very different way of viewing group organization and collective action from one based on hereditary elites wielding coercive power. It is also not teleological. Tribal organization is not something people do before chiefdoms or states "inevitably" emerge. The Archaic mound-building tradition, which includes both earth and shell mound sites, offers new ways of looking at human integration over the long term, ways that are fully viable and, given the prominence of egalitarian leveling mechanisms, may even be antithetical to the formation of these other organizational forms. In the Southeast we have been too intent on looking backward in time from the tops of Mississippian temple mounds and assuming they were the inevitable result of all that came before. We now know that elaborate artwork occurs deep in humanity's past, upwards of 30,000 years ago. Why do we have such a hard time accepting that organizational complexity can also have appreciable time depth? Understanding and exploring cultural complexity must include examining variation within the tribal formation.

SPECIFIC IMPLICATIONS ABOUT TRIBAL ORGANIZATION DERIVED FROM ARCHAIC MOUND CENTERS

As several of the authors of this book demonstrate, the layout and shape of Archaic mound centers may tell us a great deal about the size, organization, and cultural knowledge of the constituent groups that created them. The horizontal and vertical asymmetry in mounds or middens to Russo, Widmer, and others reflects status and demographic differences between lineages or tribal segments using these differing site areas. The differences in the size of the earth and/or shell accumulations reflect differences in the abilities or numbers of people capable of engaging in feasting behavior and in mobilizing labor. The individual high points within shell rings or mound groups may represent discrete social groups and the ring, plaza, or overall site, the collectivity or whole. A critical challenge will be to determine whether the subareas within these sites actually do reflect the physical locations of discrete social groups, such as tribal segments or alternatively perhaps sodalities crosscutting normal residence groups. I find it interesting that at least one Archaic earthen mound site, Watson Brake, includes a ringlike structure as well as separate mounds on the ring and in general configuration thus resembles many coastal shell ring or U-shaped middens. This suggests a similar organizational structure, indicating that while their settings and subsistence preferences may have been quite different, the Archaic mound-building peoples in interior Louisiana and coastal Florida were likely organized in a similar fashion. As Russo cautions, however, extensive fieldwork will be essential at these sites to determine their internal construction history, including differentiating between changes "wrought by nature, time, and subsequent cultures."

The number of discrete areas within these early centers may also be an important measure of organizational scale and complexity. Human information-processing capabilities appear to limit the number of segments that can coalesce in nonhierarchical societies to roughly six (Johnson 1978, 1982), unless some other organizational principles are employed, such as the combining of progressively larger segments by the Nuer (e.g., Sahlins 1961). Dual or more complex divisions of society potentially capable of linking more tribal segments together are indicated at some Southeastern mound sites. At Watson Brake, where 11 mounds are present, a dual subdivision is suggested by the occurrence of the two largest mounds, A and E, on opposite sides of the ring that links the mounds together. The lesser mounds may have been affiliated with one or the other of these two primary mounds, or the primary mounds may themselves have served as foci for major subdivisions encompassing a number of groups, such as occurs in moiety organization. Some early Southeastern mound groups with six or fewer mounds, and no evidence for a binary construction logic, in contrast, may have represented tribal societies integrating groups at a much smaller geographic and demographic scale than occurred at mound groups with greater numbers of mounds or where evidence for multiple levels of segmentation is evident. Poverty Point, with its six mounds and six sets of concentric rings, which are in turn apparently subdivided into from four to six subdivisions by aisles (Kidder 2002:91, 98, 99), thus may have represented the physical signature of from six to possibly as many as 36 or more tribal segments.

We must also consider the implications of the size as well as the layout of early earthworks/mound complexes. The fact that the volume of fill in the earthworks at Poverty Point is many times that at Watson Brake (Gibson, this volume) is likely telling us something about the relative size and organizational complexity, or scale of integration, of the social groups that built these centers, as well as the amount of time that they engaged in this activity. Mound volume may thus be related to the internal architectural and possible social segmentation of these societies, as Russo (this volume) argues. Perhaps Poverty Point was a regional center, filling the same role that a number of subregional centers did in the preceding Middle Archaic period, a collectivity created by peoples drawn from possibly the same approximate area and in the same numbers but focusing on one site instead of many "smaller" centers.

Russo (this volume) elegantly shows that the use of theory, in this case social space theory, can provide new insight into the interpretation of these early mound centers. Humans position themselves with respect to one another when they operate in groups, and these positions signal relationships in dominance hierarchies (Gron 1991). The observation, following social space theory, that locations accorded higher status by people operating in groups correspond to portions of midden or mound groups where the greatest earth or shell accumulations are present provides complementary evidence that these accumulations reflect status differences. Leaders are at the head of the class in linear or U-shaped seating arrangements or are centered on one side or the other in oval or ring-shaped configurations. Russo's argument as applied to shell middens translates directly and usefully to the interpretation of earthen mound sites. The U-shaped shell midden with one prominent location at the base of the U and nothing opposite it suggests greater control (or less opposition) than at ring centers with multiple mounds of varying sizes, as at Watson Brake (Gron 1991:108; Russo, this volume). The duality exhibited at Watson Brake, where the two largest mounds, A and E, face each other across the ring, suggests these were the locations used by high-status and possibly opposing kin or social groups or individuals. Similar observations can be made from the arrangement of mounds at many other sites in the region, both during the Archaic period and after (e.g., Knight 1998).

As Russo also argues, we must control for site occupational histories through the gathering of specific information on the construction, contents, and duration of mound stages, households, and plaza areas if we are to untangle the social dynamics at such sites. The relative status of households and individuals that may occur in different parts of these sites can be inferred using social space theory and tested using traditional archaeological investigations. Russo and his colleagues (2002) have begun to do this at sites like the Late Archaic Guana shell ring in Florida, dated to ca. 3600–3900 B.P. At this site, testing in different parts of the ring revealed that while pottery and shellfish discard covaried, the occurrence of decorated Orange Incised pottery was proportionally much higher than that of Orange Plain pottery in the areas of greatest shellfish discard, with the reverse (proportionally more plain pottery) in areas of lower shellfish discard (Russo et al. 2002:39). Since decorated pottery was found associated with site areas where the greatest food refuse occurred, it may have been accorded higher status and possibly have been associated with feasting.

HOW QUICKLY WERE THE EARLIEST MOUNDS BUILT?

What do the available archaeological data tell us about how specific Archaic mound groups were created? As Gibson (this volume) suggests, big mounds do not necessarily require large labor forces or continuous long-term effort. For the Middle Archaic earthen mounds in Louisiana, a great deal of labor was apparently invested in their construction over fairly short periods. Mound C at Frenchman's Bend was apparently built in a single episode (Saunders et al. 1994:141). At Hedgepeth Mounds, Mound A was constructed in two stages (Saunders et al. 1994:147). At Hillman's Mound, of possible Middle Archaic age, one or possibly two stages were reported (Saunders et al. 1994:150). At the Stelly Mounds, Mounds B and C were apparently built in a single stage (Russo

1996a:278). At Watson Brake, where the most complex construction history has been documented to date, only four possible construction episodes are indicated in Mounds A, C, and D, over about a 400-year span. Each episode at this site, furthermore, is separated from the next by a fair amount of time, as indicated by the presence of buried A horizons whose development could only occur if the stage surface had been exposed for possibly as much as a century or more (Saunders et al. 1997:1797). These early Louisiana centers thus do not appear to be accretional constructions reflecting multiple thin blankets or filling episodes that could be easily done by small groups operating over a long interval. Instead, a lot of work, probably by fairly large numbers of people, appears to have occurred over a few comparatively brief periods. I suggest these mound centers reflect the action of multiple tribal segments operating collectively and over comparatively brief periods. Clark (this volume) reached a similar conclusion using independent evidence derived from the design of the centers themselves, which indicates they had to have been laid out as totalities, not haphazardly or accretionally.

Of course, as Saunders and his colleagues (Saunders et al. 1994:147; Saunders et al. 1997:1797) have been careful to point out, differentiating and dating filling episodes and stages in mounds upwards of 5,000 years old, with concomitant extensive weathering of the soil profiles, is a challenging task. Nonetheless, their work has shown that it is possible to develop construction histories at some of these sites. Likewise, the sacred aspects of mound construction argued by many of the contributors to this book appear to have had great antiquity in the region. Is ceremony explicitly reflected in the construction itself? Some Woodland and Mississippian mounds were built with colored or cleaned soils with earlier construction episodes carefully demarcated. At present there is very little evidence for the use of such special fills or attendant ceremony in the construction of Middle Archaic mounds in Louisiana. At Horr's Island in Florida, however, Russo (1991) found evidence for stages of ceremonial construction, including the use of clean sand, and a similar pattern was documented at Tick Island (Aten 1999:143–147, 163; Russo 1994b). At both Stelly (Russo and Fogleman 1994) and Horr's Island (Russo 1991) the ground surface was leveled prior to mound construction, which Russo interpreted as reflecting ritual behavior. We need detailed information on the construction effort that went into each mound and (where present) ring segment at these sites, as well as about their associated assemblages, if we are to understand how these early societies operated.

TRIBAL ORGANIZATION AT A REGIONAL SCALE

How Archaic mound centers reflect regional population distributions and organizational relationships is also something that is starting to be explored, as several chapters in this book illustrate. It is tempting to speculate, as Russo, Widmer, and others do, that individual mounds or midden accumulations reflect specific social groups and that the size of the accumulation reflects the prestige, power, or population of the group that built it. Sassaman and Heckenberger (this volume) further argue that mound centers on the larger regional landscape are positioned in relation to one another in fulfillment of social and cosmological belief systems, in a "regional landscape of constructed spaces." These ideas are comparable to those advanced for Mississippian ceremonial centers intimating that the layout and size of mounds and plazas mirror social organization and population distributions (e.g., Blitz 1999; Knight 1998). At the Archaic centers, however, the separate mounds may represent places used by more or less egalitarian clan- or lineage-based tribal segments or sodalities rather than hereditarily ranked clans or lineages or lesser chiefdoms. Southeastern peoples appear to have used a similar strategy of mapping aspects of their social organization into their ceremonial centers for thousands of years, and we should be looking for these constituent populations on the landscape during the Middle and Late Archaic periods, as well as in the subsequent Woodland and Mississippian periods.

It would be interesting, for example, to see whether specific tribal segments were dispersed over the landscape in a way that corresponds to the location of mounds within the larger centers. That is, did the people using mounds on the northern or western portions of these centers come from territories or annual ranges located in those directions? If each center were the ceremonial focus of a particular group, and the centers were indeed linked together in a larger social system, then the largest mound at any one center was probably created and used by the core group occupying that area, and the smaller mounds were created and used by groups from other areas, each with its own center where its dominant role was manifest in the local architecture. This would suggest that peoples across thousands of square miles were tied together, which is in accord with the geographic and demographic scales at which many ethnographically documented tribal societies operated (e.g., Arnold 1996a; Carneiro 2002; Feinman and Neitzel 1984; Fowles 2002b; Parkinson 2002a, 2002b; Sahlins 1968b). Alternatively, the centers may have been only loosely linked together with little intervisitation and with individual accumulations and mounds reflecting demographic- and status-based asymmetries in locally based lineages/tribal segments/populations. Regardless of the scale of the organization, however, we should begin thinking about how the entire landscape was used and whether any direct ties can be made between outlying settlements and specific mounds. Of course, the whole argument becomes more difficult if the mounds represented clans or sodalities whose membership crosscut specific settlements or territorially focused groups. In fact, use of mounds in such a fashion to bring people together from different tribal segments would serve a valuable integrative function. All of these ideas, as Russo's work exemplifies, are amenable to testing with archaeological data.

Sassaman and Heckenberger (this volume) argue that terminal Middle Archaic mound building in northern Louisiana was planned at a regional scale. This is clearly the case in later Woodland and Mississippian societies in the region (e.g., Blitz 1999; Hally 1993, 1995; Steponaitis 1978; Williams and Freer Harris 1998). We know that there were trail networks linking societies across the east for millennia (Anderson 1994b; Tanner 1989); were any present linking these Archaic period centers, and were some of these trails sacred in nature, as has been documented in the later southwestern archaeological record in areas like Chaco Canyon (Nials et al. 1987; Roney 1992)? The contemporaneity of Watson Brake, Caney, and Frenchman's Bend has been suggested by radiocarbon and other forms of absolute dating (i.e., all date to within a few centuries of 5000 B.P.), and Insley appears to be part of this larger system. If these mounds were laid out about the same time and according to the same principles, it is reasonable to suppose their use was coordinated as well—that each did not operate in isolation. That is, each mound center likely served as the ceremonial center for a subregional group, probably people from the immediately surrounding area. Or did peoples from across the area use these centers, with aggregation rotating from one to another, perhaps as part of a ceremonial cycle? Rotating use would have facilitated the renewal of resources that might have become locally depressed. Alternatively, this may not have been much of a problem, and rotation of use may have been solely to help bind peoples together at a regional scale.

What caused periodic aggregation and feasting behavior that could have led to monumental construction? For the earliest Paleoindian groups, aggregation was essential for group survival, through the information exchange, mating network regulation, and affiliations between individuals and kin groups that it promoted.[7] Aggregation is also thought to have been associated with collective ritual and feasting at these and indeed all time levels in the Eastern Woodlands. Throughout later prehistory aggregation events continued to be an important means of bringing and binding people together, and while the associated reasons, ceremonies, and activities may have changed, the basic process of aggregation itself appears to have been universal. To some peoples the place where aggregation events occurred was apparently sufficient unto itself, and monumental construction never occurred. Among other peoples, monumental architecture developed through the accretion of subsistence remains like shellfish and the recognition that the debris could be used to create landscape features of surprising permanence. And in some societies the importance of the location was reinforced through construction using nonsubsistence remains like wood or earth.

Monumental construction is obviously not universal in human society, but given the many different groups that occupied the Southeastern landscape over the past 13,500 and more years, we should not be at all surprised that it occurred. Once underway anywhere, monumentality could have been emulated everywhere. What is as interesting as the presence of Archaic mound building in some parts of the region (once monuments did appear), however, is its *absence* in other areas. Monumental construction became a tradition that grew like topsy in some areas but that never happened or may have even been deliberately avoided in other areas. Given the appreciable individual, family, and group movements that occur in tribal society, I do not think the differential distribution of mound complexes was due to factors of geographic isolation or a lack of knowledge. Specific historical events and people started the process, and in some areas historical trajectories favored its continuation, in others its resistance, and in still others cycles between periods of mound building and no mound building.

WHY MOUNDS IN THE TERMINAL MIDDLE ARCHAIC?

A number of reasons have been advanced to explain why Southeastern peoples organized tribally and built large mounds, but why did this happen at ca. 5500–5000 B.P. and not appreciably before or after? The need for risk minimization or the existence of alliance networks has been used to explain the origin of tribal societies in the Eastern Woodlands (e.g., Bender 1985b; Braun and Plog 1982), but these are not time dependent. During the terminal Middle Archaic/initial Late Archaic from ca. 5400–4600 B.P. an apparent explosion in mound building occurred in the lower Mississippi alluvial valley and along the Florida Atlantic and Gulf coasts (e.g., Russo 1994a, 1996a, 1996b; Russo and Heide 2001). There was a general amelioration of global climate about this time, which marked the end of the Hypsithermal, and sea levels stabilized close to modern levels with only minor fluctuations thereafter. Precipitation and lake levels rose over the preceding period (Webb et al. 1993:454–457), and flooding increased, as did channel migration in major river systems (Knox 1983:33, 39). Compared to the harsher conditions of the Hypsithermal, these changes, particularly the formation of extensive riverine/backswamp environments, could have meant wild food resources were more prevalent (Anderson 2001; Brookes, this volume; Widmer, this volume).

    The end of the Middle Holocene also witnessed an increase in the occurrence and intensity of El Niño (e.g., Rodbell et al. 1999; Sandweiss et al. 1996, 1999), which could have resulted in highly variable climatic conditions in eastern North America and possibly greater and more serious flooding, prompting groups to come together to overcome the resulting uncertainty (Hamilton 1999). None of these explanations is very satisfying, however, since mound building occurred in only a few areas and does not appear to have been widely adopted, at least during the Middle and initial Late Archaic periods. Resort to climatic effects is also unsatisfying because the lower Mississippi alluvial valley is one of the richest areas in North America in terms of wild plant and animal food resources and probably has been throughout the period of human occupation. The food resources that would have permitted aggregations of the size and duration needed to produce monumental architecture were likely readily available, particularly if the environment became especially favored following the Hypsithermal. Exactly what local climate and biota were like when the earliest mounds were being constructed, however, is uncertain and must be better resolved. Were conditions for group survival bad, prompting greater integration as a risk minimization/leveling strategy, or were they good, allowing for easy aggregation and feasting behavior, with subsistence risk minimization considered essentially unimportant? Likewise, given appropriate technology, formerly poor environments may become productive; were there changes in technology at this time that created new subsistence landscapes? We simply do not know at present.

Sassaman and Heckenberger (this volume), taking a somewhat different tack, argue that complexity may be an "emergent property of social life in general," which develops "under particular historical circumstances." That is, once regional population density and resource availability or uncertainty reach certain levels, increases in system complexity become inevitable but are still highly contingent on historical factors (cf. Binford 2001:378–379, 424–464; Carneiro 1967; Feinman and Neitzel 1984; Kosse 1996). Could the terminal Middle Archaic be a time when regional population density reached a point where people in many areas were forced to stake out resources for themselves and mark their control through conspicuous display? If so, this action took different forms in different areas and was apparently in highly perishable media in many parts of the region, if it even occurred at all. Are there Middle and Late Archaic tribal territories and buffer zones like those we know existed in later Mississippian times? If so, were they actively defended, and how? Is it possible that these early mounds are spectacular examples of territorial markers? The distributional maps of all known Middle and Late Archaic Southeastern sites compiled a few years ago show that some areas have large numbers of sites and others comparatively few, but what these distributions mean is not well understood (Anderson 1996, 2002:259–262).

Is the evidence for increased conflict observed in the Middle Archaic (Smith 1996) indicative of a need for larger scale interaction and integration in order to maintain defensive (or offensive) alliances? That is, once regional population density and resource uncertainty reach certain levels is conflict and territorial marking inevitable? This is a somewhat grimmer view of the ultimate causes of mound building than the beneficent proximate causes Gibson proposes, of course, but the two perspectives are not necessarily incompatible. Mounds likely did all the positive things for the people who built them that Gibson describes, such as promote group security, well being, and identity, and their construction may well have been the "grateful duty" of many people. But they may simultaneously have been produced because they were a means of solving difficult challenges facing these peoples, notably, how to allocate rights to resources in an increasingly populous human landscape or defend people from aggressive neighbors.

ARCHAIC MEASUREMENT AND DESIGN SYSTEMS

If the arguments advanced by Clark (this volume) hold up to testing, namely, that Archaic societies over large areas of the New World shared common ritual, calendrical, and cosmological underpinnings, expressed in systems used to delimit space and mark time, it will be quite literally a paradigm-shaking event forcing us to reconsider our ideas about New World archaeology. As Clark puts it, "My principal inference . . . is that the Middle and Late Archaic inhabitants of North and South America shared a common measurement system and logic." Regardless of whether commonalities of measurement and design existed at a hemispherical scale, discussion of which I will defer for the moment, Clark has, to my mind, convincingly shown how Middle Archaic peoples could have designed and laid out their ceremonial centers in a simple and straightforward manner using readily available technology, a consistent system of measurement, and equilateral triangles formed from multiples of standard measurement units. I strongly suspect, in fact, that they did it pretty much the way he describes.

Clark provides clear ways to test his ideas by noting that marker posts, unusual artifact caches or special offerings, or other elaborate features might be found at strategic design/layout points at these centers, such as the steatite caches found at such locations as Poverty Point and Claiborne. Clark explicitly calls for archaeologists working at these centers to carefully examine these locations, test implications of remarkable specificity. Furthermore, he argues that with increasingly precise site mapping, the fit between the expectations from his proposed measurement system and logic and what is actually present on the ground should get progressively better, controlling of course for postconstruction modification. Furthermore, if, as he suggests, this measurement system and design logic are also to be found in village construction, then archaeological excavation and inspection of these site types should reveal its presence. Clark's idea that mound sites are "special 'villages' projected to a cosmic plane in a more permanent form" helps us understand the rationale for the design of these centers as the physical representation of community plan and relationships between individual households (or tribal segments) writ large (see also DeBoer 1997; Sassaman and Heckenberger, this volume). Societal energies could have been directed to large human or animal effigies, sacred road or trail systems, or some other manner of activity. Accordingly, if ceremonial centers are eventually found employing perishable technologies in those parts of the region where none are currently known to exist, they too might be expected to employ the logic of community representation, only constructing edifices of wood or (metaphorically) of sand and earth.

While I accept the evidence Clark proposes for the intentional design of some of these centers according to preconceived plans and procedures, I have greater difficulty accepting the necessity for the measurement system and design logic to be directly and continuously preserved in village construction practices and then brought out after hundreds or thousands of years to guide the construction of new centers. The reason is not that I deny the possibility that sacred knowledge embodying principles of astronomy, calendrical systems, measurement, and design could have existed—it probably did and had great time depth and resilience. Rather, there is very little evidence to support the idea that Southeastern Archaic peoples lived in such population aggregates/village communities. Instead, they appear to have been dispersed in small groups and were additionally fairly mobile much of the year (admitting, of course, that our evidence for this perspective for the Middle Archaic period in the Southeast is fairly limited and based more on inferences from stone tools and human ecology than from actual site plans). It would be worthwhile examining whether there are ethnographic cases in which this kind of planning is employed or evident in village construction. That is, are there any surviving New World societies in which such information about measurement systems or design logic remains preserved implicitly or explicitly in the memories and actions of individuals? Or is this information to be found in noncenter (i.e., mundane) village plans, be the data ethnographic or archaeological in origin? If so, this kind of evidence would markedly strengthen Clark's case. Likewise, if the design logic was indeed so deeply rooted in everyday life, why and how could it change in the subsequent Woodland period as Clark argues? If the new measurement/design system was imported from Mesoamerica, as Clark suggests, could it be that cultural influence was now flowing in this direction, a reversal of the trend a few thousand years earlier? Might these be early examples of what has been called "the law of cultural dominance" (e.g., Kaplan 1960; Sahlins and Service 1960:444),[8] with developments in the Archaic Southeast influencing less complex societies to the south in Mesoamerica and the reverse happening later?

Dramatic examples of monumentality were right in front of these later peoples, as Clark himself points out. That is, once the terminal Middle Archaic mounds were constructed, their design logic would be there seemingly for all time. If Poverty Point evinces the design logic of nearby ancient, dramatic, and presumably sacred places, I find it just as plausible that the people responsible for the creation of that center carefully studied and put to use what their predecessors in the same immediate part of the region had done as it is that the knowledge was passed down for over a thousand years embedded in everyday practice.[9] If the people who built Poverty Point were adventurous enough to do whatever it took to obtain lithic raw materials from across large parts of the Eastern Woodlands (Carr and Stewart, this volume), trips of no more than a few tens of kilometers to ancient ceremonial centers would not have been beyond them. The fact that, as Clark (this volume) himself argues, "the positions of all the mounds and rings at Poverty Point were dependent for their placement on the antecedent position of [the presumed Middle Archaic period] Lower Jackson Mound," which is on the Poverty Point site, clearly shows these people were well aware of the construction feats of their ancestors and, at this site, apparently made extensive use of the information. Of course, they would have been greatly aided in any such analysis by a continuity of basic knowledge embedded in myth, ritual, or cosmology or, as Clark suggests, if the measurement system and design logic had been routinized into everyday life. Standard units of measurement and their multiples, especially when linked with calendrical systems or construction practices, would have been fairly easy to retain and use. This type of knowledge, tied to fundamental cultural values and beliefs, would have also been more likely preserved over time and space than explicit instructions on how to lay out mound groups. Such instructions, if present, were clearly ignored over large parts of the region where mound were never built. Even in the heartland where the design logic saw its greatest expression, in northeast Louisiana, there is little indication that mound building was occurring for upwards of a millennium after the initial centers like Watson Brake were erected, from ca. 5000 to 4000 B.P.

The archaeological evidence noted previously for construction history available from the Louisiana Middle Archaic mounds, while fairly minimal, supports some of Clark's (this volume) assertions based on independent evidence about design logic and standard measurements that "these sites were planned as totalities, at high levels of precision, and constructed over relatively short periods of time." There is nothing complex or mystical about the procedures Clark describes to lay out sites. Greater argument may attend his belief that a standard unit of measurement occurred widely across the New World and was linked to ritual/calendrical numbering systems. Ultimately what he is arguing is, to use his words, that "constructed spaces were . . . built according to cosmological principles based on venerable knowledge of celestial cycles, sacred numbers, world directions, mythology, and so forth."[10] Leadership for the building of monumental architecture may have been somewhat ephemeral, but the ritual knowledge that these leaders made use of was anything but, if Clark's arguments are correct. Indeed, the development of precise calendrically based measurement and design systems would seemingly require the collective knowledge of generations of specialized practitioners. I do not view this as at all improbable, since shamanistic practices date back to the Paleolithic and basic astronomical knowledge likely came with the first peoples into the Americas. People with repeated views of the night sky are likely to pick up on and be impressed by the trends occurring therein.

Clark's idea that the layout of at least some of the larger Archaic mound centers was carefully planned is compellingly argued and appears more plausible to me than that they grew accretionally (i.e., mound by mound) in a haphazard fashion. I thus believe Clark's ideas are credible and worthy of consideration and testing along the lines he suggests, as well as those his critics are likely to raise. His arguments cannot be dismissed out of hand, nor should they be. To do so would be to deny the potential of the most sacred sites of the Archaic Southeast and the accomplishments of the peoples who built them.[11]

LONG-TERM TRENDS IN THE TRIBAL SOUTHEAST

Fowles (2002a:19–28) has argued that instead of just trying to recognize the existence of discrete types of neoevolutionary stages in the archaeological record, such as band, tribe, or chiefdom, given our control over vast stretches of time archaeologists should also be trying to recognize types of cultural processes or historical trajectories. That is, what types of societies were present, and how and why did they change through time? The Southeastern archaeological record is characterized by numerous differing tribal social trajectories (sensu Parkinson 2002a:9; Fowles 2002a:22), and archaeology's ability to examine these societies over great intervals of time and to identify broad patterns of change offers great research promise. Some initial observations at the very broadest of scales are briefly advanced here (see also Anderson 2002).

The tribal societies of the Archaic and Woodland Southeast appear to have been characterized by fairly fluid (i.e., structurally variable) organizational systems that fluctuated between periods of greater or lesser integration and had relatively impermanent centralized authority structures/leadership positions. Indeed, authority appears to have been centralized and pronounced only when people came together; the public offices and organizational structures evident or implied by activities occurring during periods of nucleation may have been all but nonexistent the rest of the time. Leadership was thus achieved and transitory and consensual in foundation, rather than hereditary and more or less permanent and deriving from sacred authority and/or secular coercion. This "tribal" pattern of organizational flexibility—with differing structural poses adopted at different times for differing reasons, with populations living in dispersed small groups much of the time and aggregating in much larger groups on occasion and probably only in some areas—continued for thousands of years in the Southeast. It was present in every area save perhaps in portions of coastal Florida, where Russo (1991, 1994b, 1996b, this volume; Russo and Heide 2001) has documented year-round occupation, with little use of the surrounding interior areas, around sites such as Horr's Island, Bonita Bay, Joseph Reed, and Oxeye. Not until late in the Woodland period do nucleated population/ceremonial centers occupied for much or all of the year appear in many parts of the region, however, replacing the earlier pattern of occasional nucleation by dispersed populations.

At a much larger temporal and geographic scale, what one sees in many parts of the Southeast is the emergence and decline of ritual/ceremonial centers formed through the temporary aggregation of residentially mobile and presumably widely dispersed foraging (and later agricultural) populations. In a few areas, in contrast, such as along the lower south Atlantic and Florida Gulf coasts, extended multiseasonal or year-round occupation by larger groups, probable true sedentism, appears to have emerged very early. The settlement and hence organizational structure(s) of these coastal Archaic peoples thus likely differed somewhat from the trends occurring in the lower Mississippi valley and elsewhere in the interior. This is not to say that periodic aggregation by large numbers of peoples, including people from other areas, may not have also occurred at these coastal sites. Only in the Woodland period in some areas does agricultural food production appear to have made an important contribution to the diet, and nucleated settlements occupied much of the year do not appear until toward the very end of that period, roughly coeval with the adoption of intensive agriculture. Over the several thousand years tribal societies are assumed to have been present in the Southeast, there is little evidence for long-term continuity within specific areas of societies engaging in complex behavior (i.e., monumental construction, long-distance exchange). While centers with appreciable monumental construction were sometimes reused by later peoples, at no center and apparently in no area was monumental construction continuous throughout the period tribal societies are assumed to have been present. That some areas or centers were used for several hundred years, however, is itself a remarkable and enduring achievement. Why some sites and areas were used for greater and lesser intervals and how this relates to tribal social organization and longevity is a major research challenge facing Southeastern archaeologists. Delimiting the geographic extent and temporal duration of Southeastern tribal societies should prove as fruitful and important as it has been for Mississippian societies (e.g., Hally 1993, 1995).

Why were the first earthen mounds erected during such a comparatively short time, with construction not resuming in some areas for a thousand or more years? In Florida, for example, following the Late Archaic period, ring middens do not reappear until well into the Woodland period in the Swift Creek culture (Bense 1998; Stephenson et al. 2002). The height of Poverty Point culture was 1,500 years after the abandonment of centers like Watson Brake (Gibson and Carr, this volume). Instead of earthen mounds, were other means of signaling tribal affiliation or collective social action used, such as creation of shell middens in the Midsouth and Gulf and Atlantic coasts or use of wooden or other perishable types of structures? Were peoples organized tribally in many areas but in ways that did not leave pronounced archaeological signatures? Wooden ceremonial structures, for example, might have taken as much labor as earthen mounds but would be far less likely to survive or be detected, especially by archaeologists focusing most of their energies on areas or site types with obvious monumental architecture. Alternatively, as Sassaman (1991, 1995, 2001) has variously suggested, in some areas people appear to have consciously opted completely out of this collective, quasihierarchical approach to social organization and ceremony.

Sassaman and Heckenberger discuss James A. Ford's (1969) ideas about the Theocratic Formative, notably his belief that Mesoamerica was a source area for appreciable social complexity in the New World, and rightly suggest (as does Clark, this volume) that this perspective needs to be rethought. Given the dating of Southeastern Archaic mounds and the symbolic and ritual aspects of their construction, as documented by them and Clark, a plausible case can be made that the Southeast may have been the source for ritual and calendrical systems and for the design and layout of monumental architecture that are observed to the south in Mesoamerica some 2,000 years later.[12] If Clark's arguments about the kind of sacred knowledge incorporated into the construction of these centers are correct, the Southeast, and the lower Mississippi valley in particular, was a center of innovation during the Middle Archaic.

Finally, I believe that the societies characterized by monumental construction (i.e., big mounds) that are discussed in this book were probably not the region's first tribal societies, just the first such societies that are currently readily visible and acceptable to many archaeologists. Late Paleoindian period Dalton culture in the central Mississippi valley with its inferred "Cult of the Long Blade" (Walthall and Koldehoff 1998), formal cemeteries, and relatively dense populations (e.g., Morse 1997) may have been an early experiment at a tribal society (see also Anderson 2002 and Brookes, this volume). Likewise, I also believe that after chiefdoms became established across much of the region, tribal societies continued in some areas, particularly on the margins (e.g., Emerson 1999; see also Creamer and Haas 1985). Variability in and between organizational forms characterizes the regional archaeological record over time and space.

CONTRIBUTIONS OF ARCHAIC MOUND RESEARCH TO GENERAL ARCHAEOLOGICAL THEORY

The Southeast with its massive and well-documented archaeological record is one of the world's premier laboratories from which to explore tribal social organization over the thousands of years it appears to have been present. This record can be used to explore how change occurred in these societies, by following historical trajectories at a number of temporal and geographic scales. In the process important contributions to ethnological theory can be made. In particular, the Southeast offers a valuable alternative perspective to traditional ethnographic models of what it means to behave tribally. Tribal social organization is traditionally closely associated with sedentism, autonomous village life, and agriculture (e.g., Carneiro 2002; Service 1962). In the Archaic Southeast, as the chapters in this book demonstrate, these attributes are not particularly accurate or useful (see also Fowles 2002a:16–17 and Herr and Clark 2002 for additional critiques of these attributes from global and southwestern perspectives, respectively). In the Eastern Woodlands, in contrast, tribal societies appear to have existed for thousands of years, typically amid dispersed and residentially mobile hunter-gatherer populations, who came together in larger numbers for collective ceremony, ritual exchange, or warfare only infrequently (save, as noted, in some coastal areas, an important exception). Intensive agriculture was nonexistent, and domesticates themselves appear to have been important in the diet only after the onset of the Woodland at ca. 3000 B.P., and even then only in some areas. Archaeological evidence for individual Archaic houses, much less organized villages, is minimal (Sassaman and Ledbetter 1996). Evidence for sedentism has been found at some shell midden sites in coastal areas (Russo 1996a, this volume), but sedentism does not appear to have been present beyond this setting (e.g., Saunders, this volume).

As Gibson emphasizes in Chapter 13, the first mound–building societies in the Southeast also appear to represent pristine tribal formations and not secondary constructs formed through interactions with chiefdoms or state-level societies. There are few ethnographic counterparts for this type of society, and thus the Southeastern archaeological record can teach us much about what these societies were like. I have no doubt that exploration of the region's early tribal societies will be accorded the same research attention we now devote here and in other parts of the world to areas of primary chiefdom or state formation or initial agricultural food production. Why, for example, did tribal societies apparently quickly give way to chiefdoms in some parts of the world, such as in Mesoamerica (Clark and Cheetham 2002), but apparently not in the Southeast until much later?

Approaches such as Russo's (this volume) offer us the means to examine over the long perspective archaeology has to offer how humans make use of space to position themselves within communities with respect to one another. Sassaman and Heckenberger (this volume), in turn, suggest that these spatial relationships may have been shaped at an even larger scale, over regional landscapes. We know this is the case in hierarchical societies like chiefdoms or states, where communities and centers are positioned to facilitate tribute flow and domination; the same is true in market economies in order to efficiently bring resources to consumers. What we are seeing in the Southeast is specific information on how populations in tribal societies may have shaped and used the regional landscape. Comparison with settlement and center distributions in other parts of the world, such as Neolithic Europe or portions of pre-eighteenth-century sub-Saharan Africa, can and should be drawn.

Russo's chapter, as discussed previously, also shows how careful examination of the Southeastern archaeological record can lead to a better understanding of feasting behavior, an important means by which humans develop, maintain, and convey information about their relative wealth, status, and alliances. Hayden's (2001) inference that rare or labor-intensive items are likely to be present at large-scale feasts, for example, was not found to hold up at Southeastern shell midden sites, indicating the inference may only be valid in fairly complex societies, as Hayden himself suggests. Instead, oysters were apparently a staple of feasts. Russo quite logically argues that if one is to feed large numbers of people, common and abundant resources had to be used. Rarer items, he argues, are more likely to show up in daily meals, reflecting their occasional procurement as part of generalized foraging. This is not to critique Hayden's approach. Without his model, we would have nothing to evaluate, and it is also clear that in some cases, rare and unusual items are important items in feasts, conveying great information about the wealth and/or power of the participants.[13] Theoretically based arguments must be tested and accepted or rejected based on how well they fit real-world data. Indeed, often, it is by finding exceptions to our models that new perspectives emerge. Russo, for example, notes that everyday foods can become special when served in unusual contexts, such as when they accompany ceremony or ritual.

Widmer's (this volume) argument associating the appearance of unilineal kin groups with the emergence of larger corporate groups and labor sources, a threshold leading to tribal organization, is particularly elegant, indicating the kinds of insights archaeological inquiry can generate. In brief, Widmer suggests that Middle Archaic tribal organization and mound building were facilitated by the emergence of lineage-based collateral kinship systems (i.e., bifurcate merging/Iroquoian, generational/Hawaiian), which replaced the less inclusive lineal (i.e., Eskimo) kinship systems typically used by mobile band-level foraging populations. Changes in kinship systems thus helped create and maintain the labor base essential to large-scale cooperative endeavors, such as Archaic mound building. Widmer further argues that the differential reproductive success of individual tribal segments or lineages, shaped by varying environmental productivity and initial population size and density, translated into differential political success, which can be directly measured by the size of individual mounds and the status value of associated material remains in and near these mounds within multimound complexes (see also Russo, this volume). Knowing the kinds of kin-based systems, feasting practices, or status distinctions that may have potentially been in place in these societies is a first step toward exploring and testing these subjects archaeologically.

CONCLUSIONS

In this chapter and elsewhere I have argued that societies best described as tribal were present across much of the Southeast from the Middle Archaic period onward. Furthermore, appreciable variability was present within and between these societies. Why this was the case is an important and challenging area for research. In the Archaic Southeast, band-level society was transcended much earlier than we thought by societies with organizational forms operating at geographic and demographic scales we never dreamed possible as recently as 10 years ago (e.g., Bense 1994).[14] Monumental architecture is an enduring legacy of these early examples of tribal ethnogenesis in the region and a valuable and readily accessible archaeological record that can be used to explore how tribal societies emerged and changed over time.

The chapters in this book demonstrate just how far our thinking about Archaic social organization and use of monumental architecture has come in a few short years. We also, however, have the unusual situation whereby differing authors can come up with radically different interpretations of the same data, specifically with regard to the level of social complexity represented by sites such as Watson Brake (cf. Saunders vs. Sassaman and Heckenberger, this volume). The current debate is healthy and is going in a number of directions. The disparate and sometimes seemingly contradictory views being espoused, however, also show us that we have a lot of work to do in the field and lab and in our theorizing before we will approach a consensus about what was going on in the Archaic Southeast. There is nothing wrong with this, however, since we are in the exciting era of scientific exploration that always occurs following a major paradigm shift (sensu Kuhn 1962), which is what the recognition of Archaic mound building has been. As we come to grips with tribal social organization in the Southeast, however, we need to discard outmoded views of hunter-gatherers as symbolically, technically, and organizationally impoverished egalitarian foragers and begin to explore the richly laden world that really existed. The Archaic Southeast, as the chapters in this book have shown us, was a far richer and more fascinating place than we previously imagined. As Clark (this volume) notes, the people of the Southeast "knew much more, and much earlier, than we give them credit for."

ACKNOWLEDGMENTS

This chapter has benefited from extensive discussions with and comments by Philip J. Carr, John E. Clark, Severin A. Fowles, Jon L. Gibson, William A.

Parkinson, Michael Russo, Kenneth E. Sassaman, Joe Saunders, and Randolph J. Widmer. Most of the ideas expressed within this essay, in fact, originated with one or more of these scholars, as the subject of Archaic mounds has occupied our increasing research attention and thinking in recent years in the Southeast. An earlier publication (Anderson 2002) explored some of the ideas recounted here in appreciably more detail, but the writing herein is original and reflects some changes in my thinking in the two years since that paper was completed. So quickly are our ideas about Southeastern Archaic mounds changing that I expect the chapters herein will be viewed as historical curiosities in 20 years or less, and a new volume on Archaic mounds will be needed to encompass the data and ideas being generated.

NOTES

1. This essay complements an earlier paper entitled "The Evolution of Tribal Social Organization in the Southeastern United States" that appears in *The Archaeology of Tribal Societies*, edited by William A. Parkinson, a volume that appeared in 2002 and that explores this topic from theoretical, ethnographic, and archaeological perspectives, with case studies drawn from around the world. I recommend it highly for those interested in exploring the organization and operation of Archaic and Woodland societies in the Eastern Woodlands.

2. Critiques of the tribal concept (e.g., Fried 1968, 1975) are acknowledged but are considered irrelevant here, since it remains a useful heuristic for guiding research, as admirably argued by Parkinson (2002a:3–7). Additionally, substitute terminology that has been proposed (i.e., midlevel societies, middle-range societies, and so on) has its own problems of inclusiveness and appropriateness.

3. This will be my sole attempt to emulate Jon Gibson's unique and humorous delivery style and ability to turn memorable phrases, which I have long admired. Jon is the latest in a Louisiana tradition of remarkable educators with silver tongues such as Stu Neitzel and Bill Haag. As such, he is a classic example of a charismatic tribal leader, held in high esteem by his peers and able to get them to do a great deal of work (e.g., as the writers of this book can testify), yet lacking the perks of a "chiefly" position, such as ascribed wealth or status or (as far as we know) multiple wives or a residence atop a temple mound!

4. A classic example of how worldview/theoretical perspective can literally shape what we see is recounted by James A. Michener (1983:707–709) in his description of the supernova of A.D. 1054, which for 23 days blazed almost as bright as the sun in the constellation Taurus, visible in broad daylight and overwhelming by night. It was recorded by peoples everywhere—in China, the Islamic world, and even in the American Southwest—but went largely unreported in western Europe, where the immutability of the heavens was fixed in religious dogma. As Michener (1983:709) observed, "An age is called Dark not because the light fails to shine, but because people refuse to see it."

While this is a singularly dramatic example, science is full of cases where the obvious appears so only once people have had it pointed out to them enough times and they are finally predisposed to accept it. From Middle Archaic mound groups to Middle Woodland platform mounds, neither of which received serious acceptance until fairly recently, Southeastern archaeology is replete with examples such as these (Knight 2001; Russo 1994a, 1994b).

5. Crothers (this volume) and also Saunders (this volume) provide what might be called minimalist perspectives about the level of complexity apparent in Archaic mound-building societies, with Crothers going so far as to say the shell middens in the Archaic Midsouth are little more than chance accumulations created through generations of use. Ritual and collective ceremony, although present, were in this view fairly minimal aspects of the behavior associated with these middens (see also Hensley 1994; Milner and Jefferies 1998). An opposite perspective has been advanced by Claassen (1991b, 1991c, 1996a), who sees many larger shell middens as loci of great ceremony and sacred meaning.

6. The term *transegalitarian* was proposed by Clark and Blake (1994:18) and elaborated upon by Hayden (1995:17–18) to describe societies intermediate between more or less egalitarian bands and societies characterized by hereditary inequality, like chiefdoms. Fried's (1967:109) concept of rank society "in which positions of valued status are somehow limited so that not all those of sufficient talent to occupy such statuses actually achieve them" comes close to what is meant by the term. But since rank societies as defined by Fried can include stratified societies, the term is not entirely satisfying. Staeck (1996; personal communication, 2003) has defined transegalitarian societies as characterized by "groups of people organized beyond the level of the nuclear household who, for various reasons and through a variety of mechanisms, come to have individuals who possess both power and prestige beyond that possessed by individuals of similar sex and age, but among whom the acquisition of power and prestige is not guaranteed through inheritance of either wealth or title." The concept of "tribal society" is used in this chapter to mean essentially what Clark and Blake, Hayden, and Staeck mean by transegalitarian society. I am well aware that the concept of tribe and the use of the term is not universally accepted by anthropologists, but I believe it serves as a useful and more familiar heuristic and organizing concept (cf. Fried 1967:154–182 and Hayden 1995:17 with Fowles 2002a and Parkinson 2002a).

7. Clark (this volume) sees Early Archaic aggregation events and base camps as proximate models for Middle Archaic ceremonial centers. I suspect the roots of this behavior go far deeper in time, well back into the Paleoindian era (see also Anderson 1995; Anderson and Gillam 2001).

8. This so-called law is stated as follows: "a cultural system which more effectively exploits the energy resources of a given environment will tend to spread in that environment at the expense of less effective systems . . . a cultural system will tend to be found precisely in those environments in which it yields a higher energy return per unit of labor than any alternate system available" (Sahlins and Service 1960:444).

9. Clark made the very good point when reviewing an earlier draft of this essay that he found it easier to believe in a design logic and measurement system based on sacred knowledge and embedded in everyday life than to believe that the peoples who built later mounds were able to accurately measure much older sites in presumably densely wooded terrain, abstract their design principles, and then apply them in novel ways and, at Poverty Point, at a much larger spatial scale. I believe that the initial centers served as templates for what came later (as does Clark, of course), but I am also quite certain that later visitors intent on building comparable earthworks had the ability to measure these early centers carefully, if they chose to do so, and come to an understanding of the procedures used to lay them out.

10. Looking at the way things in the sky like the sun, the moon and planets, and the brighter stars move, and divining patterns therein, has a very long history in human society, and there is little doubt many peoples attached sacred meaning to such phenomena. Likewise, social aggregation is an equally important part of human life, also probably with great time depth. That these two activities were combined and made manifest in ceremonial centers in the Archaic Southeast, as they were combined and made manifest in monumentality in many other parts of the world, I find in no way surprising.

11. Clark's (this volume) "Concluding Remarks" section makes this point so forcefully that it should be required reading for all skeptics.

12. Clark's observation that the starting date for the Mesoamerican long count is 3114 B.C., well before any evidence for planned centers there but precisely the time the Louisiana centers were going strong, makes singularly remarkable his assertion that "maybe we are looking in the wrong place for early astronomy in the Americas."

13. Examples are the kinds of foods offered at an upper-class Roman feast or the social engagements of some modern elites, where Beluga caviar and Krug champagne go hand and hand.

14. That even more complex social formations may have been present in the Middle and Late Archaic Southeast, such as chiefdoms, is likewise unknown but considered unlikely at the present by most scholars, given the complete absence of evidence for hereditary inequality, even in areas like the Midsouth or northeastern Florida, where large numbers of burials have been found. Mortuary evidence that could shed light on this further question is, unfortunately, rare at this time level in many parts of the region, particularly in the lower Mississippi valley.

15

Old Mounds, Ancient Hunter-Gatherers, and Modern Archaeologists

George R. Milner

When asked to be a discussant of the symposium that led to this book, I jumped at the chance. The papers promised to be informative and provocative, but I also had another interest in the symposium. I feel research on the hunting-and-gathering societies of the southern Eastern Woodlands is likely to gain momentum in the near future, and these essays can play a big part in defining the trajectory of that work.

For the past decade or so, the Archaic societies in the Southeast and Midwest have not received the same level of attention, especially the external notice, of the much later Mississippian chiefdoms. It is not as if outstanding studies have been lacking. The volumes edited by Anderson and Sassaman (1996; Sassaman and Anderson 1996) are particularly fine examples of scholarship on this subject. Despite this excellent work, the preeminence of hunter-gatherer studies in the 1970s and early 1980s has been eclipsed by the great effort lavished on Mississippian chiefdoms.

Work on Middle to Late Archaic societies has implications for research far beyond the Southeast and Midwest. Topics of special concern include, among others, the early settling down of human populations, the initial steps toward agriculture, the rate and timing of population growth, the first appearance of monumental architecture, the broadening of exchange networks, and the emergence of what is commonly labeled sociopolitical complexity. A strength of this work is its reliance on an enormous amount of solid information on site locations and characteristics. This database, which is already quite large, is expanding rapidly, mostly because of numerous well-funded cultural resource management projects. As a matter of fact, information about archaeological sites is increasing much faster than it can be mined for its full potential. But the greatest reason for my optimism about the prospects of research on the Archaic period has to do with the ever-increasing numbers of energetic and accomplished scholars who bring their considerable talents and divergent perspectives to bear on issues of common concern.

By this point in this book, readers will have found that all contributors do not agree on all points. That is exactly as things should be. Archaeological data by their very nature are incomplete and biased, leading to ambiguous results amenable to different interpretations. The most interesting divergences in opinion are over how we should go about learning about the past and, indeed, even identifying what is worth knowing. For the most part, the contributors direct their attention toward determining how people interacted with one another and, to a lesser extent, with their natural environments. Power relationships—often linked to mound construction—are an important component of that work. One contributor, however, searches for key dimensions and geometric shapes that served as mental templates for site layouts.

BIG MOUND POWER?

One might as well start from the beginning with "Big Mound Power"—the title of the original symposium. This title captures the essence of an enduring debate, so it is perhaps best followed by a question mark. What do mounds tell us about the organization of ancient societies, specifically the control or influence some people held over others? This question, of course, is by no means restricted to the Archaic hunter-gatherers discussed here. In fact, only recently has interest in Middle to Late Archaic mounds quickened, as pointed out by Jon Gibson and Philip Carr (this volume). Other time periods—as well as other parts of the world—have received more than their fair share of speculation about what mounds or other forms of monumental architecture might have meant to ancient people.

When talking about mounds, large is commonly equated with power. The biggest of them—including Monks Mound at Mississippian period Cahokia, but also the Adena Grave Creek mound and Mound A at Late Archaic Poverty Point—have stoked the imaginations of many writers. Almost 200 years ago, Henry Brackenridge (1818:154, 158) drew a direct link from Cahokia's big mounds to an enormous population and an organizationally complex society when he wrote that "a people capable of works requiring so much labour, must be numerous, and if numerous, somewhat advanced in the arts." The site and its immediate environs were inhabited by "a population as numerous as that which once animated the borders of the Nile, or of the Euphrates, or of Mexico and Peru." Better-informed voices did little to dampen the enthusiasm of an impressionable public. Sober appraisals of available evidence rarely prevail when pitted against popularizations of an overly romanticized, but nonexistent, past. That is as true today as it was in Brackenridge's time.

A century ago, Gerard Fowke (1898, 1902) took great pains to point out the problem with extrapolating directly from mounds to population size and societal complexity. An ever-practical man, he noted that 40 hard-working men could, in one day, load a steamboat with 10,000 bushels of corn (Fowke 1902:85). Converting this load to soil, he said that these men would have produced a mound that was 12 m in diameter and 3 m high. A mound of this size is quite respectable. It is larger than the great majority of mounds ever built in eastern North America, although it falls far short of the largest ones, including some dating to the Middle and Late Archaic periods.

There are, of course, a number of difficulties with any such labor estimates. Yet, they provide a sense of scale, which is essential when evaluating inflated claims about the numbers of people required to move dirt from one place to another. We need not become overly concerned with the details of Fowke's example to see how it highlights several issues. First, given sufficient time, small groups of people are capable of building big earthen monuments. The amount of time required to do so need not have been all that great. Second, we require more and much better data on the sizes of mounds and earthworks to refine labor estimates. Surprisingly little of that work has been done, although Joe Saunders (this volume) has calculated the amount of earth moved at Watson Brake, and Gibson (1996a, 2000, this volume) has done it for Poverty Point and Frenchman's Bend. Third, labor estimates require better information on the sources of the earth or stone used in building mounds. Of great interest is how far these materials were carried, since anyone who has dug soil or grubbed rocks out of the ground knows that this work is not as difficult or time consuming as hauling them over anything more than short distances. Fourth, more information is needed on exactly how the fill was deposited. Periodic additions of small loads of soil over many years imply a different kind of labor investment, and perhaps even motivation, than massive deposits laid down all at once. Fifth, overall labor estimates tell us little about the demands on households unless something is also known about the size of the participating population and the duration of construction.

Better estimates of mound size and construction histories only start us down the road toward what we want to know about the societies responsible for mounds. We still would like to determine how the mounds were used and what they meant to the people who built them. To do so, it is necessary to look at the types and layouts of buildings and burials, along with the locations of mounds relative to each other and to nearby sacred and secular spaces. While much still remains to be learned about mounds, their excavation is often impossible because of the current political climate. Yet they will still be dug—the necessities and conveniences of modern life usually weigh more heavily than the integrity of prehistoric sites.

Fortunately, plenty of other work can be done. For example, detailed topographic information for Poverty Point—certainly one of the premier sites in the United States—was only published a few years ago (Kidder 2002). Fieldwork must also be combined with museum-based analyses, as has been shown so well by the long-term research of Patty Jo Watson, her colleagues, and her students (see several chapters in Carstens and Watson 1996; Crothers, this volume). Examinations of old collections are essential as shown by changes in standard osteological methods. It makes little sense, when trying to detect patterning in grave goods and locations, to rely on error-prone age and sex estimates from mid-twentieth-century sources, such as reports on the huge excavations conducted during the Great Depression (see Milner and Jefferies 1987; Powell 1988). That is just one reason museum collections have enduring value, even if the original descriptions of sites and their contents were among the best of their time.

It is perhaps worth reiterating a point raised by contributors such as Nancy White, Michael Russo, and George Crothers: even the word "mound" can cause confusion. When something is labeled a mound, we usually think of deliberately piled-up heaps of earth used for various social and ritual purposes. Yet great piles of debris that accumulated in places where many Archaic hunter-gatherers lived for lengthy periods are also called mounds. The "involuntary builders of . . . refuse heaps"—which is how William S. Webb (1939:14) described the people who produced these mounds, back in the 1930s when many of the sites were dug—sometimes produced impressive piles of debris, the "left-overs from primitive kitchens," along with an abundance of domestic features and burials.

White argues that Late Archaic sites along the Apalachicola and lower Chattahoochee Rivers came from the frequent reoccupation of the same spots by people attracted to resource-rich wetlands. The mounds are accumulations of garbage, so they are more properly considered shell middens. In such swampy environments, it makes sense that exactly the same places were repeatedly reoccupied because rare high spots must have been sought out by people who quite naturally wished to keep their feet dry. They would return as long as the surrounding areas remained plentifully supplied with food and other essential resources. Here I admit to a deep bias: whatever might be said from the comfort of an office armchair does not have nearly the same weight as the practical experience of someone like White who has spent many years mucking about finding and excavating shell heaps.

Much the same could be said about shell and midden mounds along several interior rivers, most notably the Green and Tennessee Rivers. These sites were large piles of refuse where many generations of people camped, just like the 1930s excavators thought (Crothers, this volume; Milner and Jefferies 1998; for another point of view see Claassen 1992, 1996b). Once again, these people relied heavily on wetlands, but Crothers notes that the sites themselves became important components of cultural landscapes. That is, the shell heaps acquired significance beyond being convenient places to settle. Choices about the proper place to live balanced immediate survival needs with perceptions about how certain settings served as stages for a rich social and ritual life.

We must be careful about assigning great significance to the burials found in these middens, some of which are more plentifully supplied with skeletons than others. Accumulations of skeletons in repeatedly occupied campsites should not be confused with formal cemeteries where space is specifically dedicated to burial purposes and graves are laid out according to a fixed plan. We have three possibilities here. First, each mound was principally a burial monument, presumably a single cemetery, as has been proposed by Claassen (1992, 1996b). Second, the sites encompass several small, but discrete and presumably temporally distinct burial areas that were distributed across heavily used areas marked by deep habitation deposits. Third, the skeletons represent an expedient disposal of bodies as people happened to die at a frequently occupied spot. Earlier graves only influenced the placement of later ones when deaths took place in short succession, perhaps over a few years as a group returned repeatedly to the site.

The honest response to the burial question is that we need to know a lot more about mortuary practices at these sites. Nevertheless, there is no indication in the published literature or the unpublished maps I have seen that indicates the first possibility—the mortuary monument scenario—is correct. And the overall distribution of burials at one of these sites, Read, along Kentucky's Green River, is consistent with the third possibility (Milner and Jefferies 1998; Webb 1950c).

Despite fully justified cautions about exaggerating the significance of every bump on the land, there can be no doubt that Archaic hunter-gatherers built mounds in certain places. Several of the most impressive deliberately built mounds are part of the Watson Brake and Poverty Point groups. These sites and others like them capture our attention because they lie close to the heart of debates about complexity and inequality in hunting-and-gathering societies. As Russo, Gibson, Saunders, and others point out, there is little else on which to base arguments.

But why build mounds in the first place? This question is not restricted to mounds dating to Middle and Late Archaic times. Rather than asking why mounds were built in the Eastern Woodlands, it is worth considering why they were such a common feature of so many different cultures around the world.

The answer might actually be rather straightforward, if shorn of the academic blather that typically accompanies discussions of such subjects. First of all, mounds can be impressive—they remain so today, which is why archaeologists spend so much time talking about them. They are visually effective monuments, regardless of how they were initially used and whatever culture-specific meanings they once had. But mounds also have a number of other advantages. Few, if any, special skills or tools are needed to dump dirt in a pile. The labor needed to build mounds is quite modest, considering what can be done in the fullness of time. The results of this work are cumulative, as opposed to the effort spent erecting structures of perishable materials, such as wood, that have to be periodically replaced. More fill can be added as deemed appropriate, enlarging an existing mound to make an even more imposing structure. A mound can be used long before it reaches its final dimensions, and its function can change over that period of time. Mounds become permanent fixtures of cultural landscapes —they are places to visit or to avoid that are associated with particular people, events, or beliefs. What a mound means to people can change as circumstances dictate, memory fails, or new populations replace old ones. In this way, old structures can serve new needs. In short, mounds have the virtues of being cheap, permanent, and conspicuous. These characteristics are attractive to anyone who wants to make a powerful social and political statement. They serve equally well to reinforce the positions of important people and social groups, to mark territories, to underscore common group identity, and the like.

To simplify this discussion, I have drawn a distinction between purposeful mound building and mere waste disposal. Such a contrast, however, is much too stark. Russo, for one, chooses a middle road when he argues that the shell rings or arcs scattered along the Georgia, South Carolina, and Florida coasts tell us something about the nature of the groups that occupied these sites, even though the debris came from innumerable meals. Irregularities in the amount of shell in various parts of the rings are thought to indicate inequalities within these communities, specifically differences in the ability of various families or lineages to marshal the resources needed to orchestrate large feasts. As in many societies, a household's physical position within a community—here they were distributed around an open public area—could have indicated its social standing. If this was indeed true, then some people, presumably key members of situationally and numerically advantaged kin groups, were held in greater esteem than their neighbors. Following this line of reasoning, the form of the debris heaps reveals the existence of inequities within these coastal communities. Russo is to be commended for conducting the laborious fieldwork needed to pursue his provocative ideas. As he notes, this work is challenging because it is hard to separate the refuse of everyday life from the debris produced during ceremonies that involved presentations of food, particularly when there was little spatial separation between them.

Several authors correctly point out that multimound sites were more than simple accumulations of mounds and low ridges. People tend to arrange themselves and their monuments in highly structured ways while they imbue their surroundings with particular meanings. Archaic people presumably did so as well. John Clark goes much further when he argues that sites such as Watson Brake and Poverty Point were built according to a fixed plan based on notions of geometric relationships and suitable dimensions that were shared by people throughout the Americas. Readers can decide for themselves whether this chapter is a brilliant satire of the strange ideas often attached to ancient sites or a curiously quixotic attempt to uncover an underlying structure in how widely distributed sites were laid out.

In Clark's draft, figures consisting of three triangles were superimposed on five maps of sites with either mounds or standing architecture, three of which are in the Southeast.[1] Over one-half of the triangle corners did not land near known mounds or buildings. About the same proportion of the triangles' sides were not anchored by at least two architectural features.

Perhaps getting a good fit with observable features was not the true point of this exercise. Whatever the real reason for delving deeply into numerology, assertions about historical continuities or human universals require better supporting evidence, at least for those of us who are challenged by the prospect of creeping stealthily into the minds of the ancients. It is also necessary to come up with some explanation for why perceptions about site layouts were shared by culturally, geographically, and temporally diverse peoples. I found it difficult to tell whether fixed concepts about proper site arrangements and dimensions supposedly came about through some psychic unity of humankind, a widespread dissemination of ideas about how settlements should be organized, or a lengthy retention of beliefs that originated in a shared ancestry dating to a remote past stretching as far back as the initial peopling of the Americas, if not earlier.

Before leaving this topic, it is worth emphasizing what to most readers will seem to be an obvious point. The complex form of a completed site does not necessarily mean that its various parts—mounds, buildings, and the like—were carefully, consistently, and unerringly positioned in accord with a fixed plan that originated with the first occupants of a particular spot. There are, of course, innumerable historically known towns and cities with readily discernable layouts where the overall organization of space and the significance attached to various places have changed over time as new and unanticipated circumstances presented themselves. Furthermore, the history of earlier construction, especially the locations of large and relatively permanent structures such as mounds, constrains how space can be used during a site's later development. A site layout that superficially appears to have been conceived as an integrated entity at the outset can emerge without an overarching and far-seeing plan as various kinds of buildings, public spaces, and monumental architecture are added to an existing community structure.

As far as the Archaic mound sites are concerned, it is certainly worth seeking out the organizing principles that contributed to their eventual forms. These places probably also evolved over time as needs changed, much like any other long-occupied site that we know about. Later developments at these Archaic sites must have been influenced by prior land use, particularly the existence of mounds.

SOCIETAL COMPLEXITY

Prehistoric hunter-gatherers are commonly viewed primarily in terms of what they did to survive. While the demands of getting food and shelter were no doubt major concerns for the members of Archaic societies—nobody is exempt from such worries—other aspects of life tend to get short shrift. Something like the reverse is true when archaeologists write about life at the most recent end of prehistory. For the Mississippian societies, explanations for what happened and why it did so rely more heavily on ritual and interpersonal relations, especially between chiefs and their followers, than they do on what needed to be done to survive. One might conclude that a miracle occurred somewhere along the line: hunter-gatherers whose interests extended no farther than their corporeal existence were at some point magically transformed into people freed of the burden of everyday concerns.

This tendency means that hunter-gatherer societies that exhibit some degree of sociopolitical complexity are all too often viewed as special cases, as noted by Gibson and Carr. Thus Poverty Point and also the less impressive midden and shell heaps scattered across the Southeast and southern Midwest are dismissed as anomalies that do not fit a hunter-gatherer way of life. Yet as a number of authors, including contributors to this book, have pointed out, there is no such thing as a hunting-and-gathering archetype (e.g., Kelly 1995; Rowley-Conwy 2001; Wobst 1978). In fact, the ethnographic record is badly biased. We know most about near-recent people who often lived in inhospitable areas; more precisely, they occupied places that were not particularly good for agriculture.

Kenneth Sassaman and Michael Heckenberger (this volume) call attention to the fact that modern hunter-gatherers are the product of long histories of interaction with demographically larger and organizationally complex societies. No recent group is a pristine survival of a much older way of life that has somehow remained intact since the days of our distant human ancestors, so modern hunter-gatherers cannot be used as simple analogues for life in prehistoric times. This particular issue, of course, has attracted considerable attention outside archaeology—most particularly in terms of the !Kung of arid southwestern Africa (Lee 2002; Lee and Guenther 1991; Solway and Lee 1990; Wilmsen 1989; Wilmsen and Denbow 1990; Wobst 1978). While not all hunter-gatherers around the world lived their lives just like the !Kung, or any other modern group, our understanding of archaeological information must still be firmly grounded in a comparative ethnographic perspective.[2]

It is widely understood that hunter-gatherers in well-watered temperate areas, including the Midwest and Southeast, are poorly represented in our worldwide sample of ethnographically and historically recorded societies. The contributors to this book move us toward a fuller appreciation of the great diversity among hunter-gatherers by looking at frequently reoccupied camps that were essential elements of cultural landscapes (the shell and midden heaps), the deliberate construction of impressive mounds (such as those at Watson Brake and Poverty Point), and the use and exchange of artifacts imbued with special symbolic significance (including nicely carved bone pins). Archaic life certainly had a richer ceremonial component and a more complex social organization than it does in the way it is commonly portrayed.

What is meant by complexity and how we can identify and measure it with archaeological materials are by no means settled to everyone's satisfaction, as pointed out by Sassaman and Heckenberger (this volume). Inequality is certainly a part of the mix, as noted in several chapters. I am referring to institutionalized inequality among individuals of the same age and sex, not situational advantages based on an individual's skill, differences in how men and women or the young and old are treated, or simple good fortune. Saunders notes that if mounds are evidence of inequality among Middle Archaic communities, then there should be other signs of social distinctions. In short, it is better to argue from multiple lines of evidence than to focus on only one aspect of life, such as a fondness for piling up dirt. He concludes that a bunch of reasonably well off, yet still basically egalitarian, hunter-gatherers could have built the Watson Brake mounds. Not all contributors to this book would agree with such an interpretation. Saunders, however, is on to something here: multifaceted research must be undertaken if we are to pursue the challenging ideas raised in this book's wide-ranging chapters. To do otherwise is to demote papers to the level of Op-Ed pieces where the strength of an argument rests on an author's ability to spout jargon. Moreover, statements about past societies must be based on a careful consideration of all available evidence, not odds and ends selected just because they fit some preconceived notion about what happened in the past.

What exactly do purposefully built mounds tell us about Archaic hunter-gatherers? The answer is not at all obvious, as indicated by the range of opinion expressed by the contributors to this book. It is clear, however, that the early mound builders were not living in small, highly mobile bands that forever busied themselves eking out a meager existence. Russo, among others, believes that something other than an egalitarian ethic operated in some of the Middle to Late Archaic groups. He argues that feasting at coastal shell rings is inconsistent with strictly egalitarian societies. A distinction must be made here between the collection and distribution of food on special occasions by certain segments of the community and the expedient sharing of a big kill by a lucky hunter. If Russo is right, then some families or larger descent groups possessed the where-withal to orchestrate feasts more often than other people. These occasions, which were undoubtedly accompanied by great fanfare, augmented the prestige of the people who organized them. Sassaman and Heckenberger equate mounds with some form of social hierarchy. Russo sees signs of a ranking of individuals or social groups, particularly in the largest shell rings. While key people might have been able to arrange special events, such as feasts, that boosted their local standing, Gibson points out that their ability to exert control over what their neighbors could do was quite limited. The impetus to build mounds came from the people, not from strong leaders who demanded their construction. Leaders were only successful when their followers were pushed in the direction of their own self-interest. There is no evidence in any of these societies for a great deal of power, that is, an ability to coerce people to do something they did not want to do. Randolph Widmer argues that the mounds, by celebrating ties to ances-tors, denoted lineage control over resource-rich places. In terms of a lineage's local standing, bigger was better: a group's size directly affected its productive capacity and, hence, its ability to mount impressive prestige-enhancing displays.[3] For the Archaic mounds, the amount of earth moved would have been related to the size of the contributing population and the number of generations over which they were engaged in this work. The challenge we now face is how to evaluate these ideas, along with any others that might be proposed, with the kinds of data and the amount of information we are likely to have available from various contexts.

When talking about inequality and hierarchy, we must be careful about what differentiates people from one another. To take but one example, everyone would probably agree that important people in chiefdoms were separable from their fol-lowers through a combination of behavior, dress, showy prestige goods, size and location of residences, and association with monumental architecture. There is, however, no consistent osteological signature indicating that the leaders of the late prehistoric chiefdoms in the Eastern Woodlands generally ate a markedly different diet or enjoyed a better standard of health.[4] Even among societies like the Maya of Copan in Honduras, the signal for status-related variation in diet is weak—not nearly as strong as variation attributable to an individual's sex (Reed 1998). Thus, as a general (perhaps universal) rule, measurable differences in wealth and prestige—mounds, fancy ornaments, bigger houses, and the like—appear long before consistent status-related distinctions in diet and health.

Several contributors comment on the overall pattern of cultural evolution. Of special interest is Widmer's criticism of the assumption that the emergence of sociopolitical complexity was gradual. The applicability to specific cases of a gradualist perspective, so common in archaeological thinking, needs to be carefully evaluated. Widmer adopts a more punctuated view that also accommodates the possibility of sequential periods of greater and lesser complexity. There is a general point to be made here: it is simply wrong to equate evolution with gradual, progressive change—there is nothing in the former that necessitates the latter.

INTERACTION

In this book, intergroup interaction is folded into discussions of sociopolitical complexity. How one goes about measuring the magnitude and nature of such contacts remains a problem for archaeologists everywhere. Identifying where materials and artifacts came from is difficult, but it is even harder to determine how they ended up far from where they originated. These issues are important because it is commonly understood that the long-distance exchange of various items, including stone and shell, had increased by Late Archaic times, as pointed out by Philip Carr and Lee Stewart; Prentice Thomas, Janice Campbell, and James Morehead; and Richard Jefferies, among others.

Carr and Stewart's chapter is particularly interesting because of the unusual nature of the Poverty Point site. It has long been recognized that stone tools and ornaments, including beads and tiny carved animals, are abundant at Poverty Point, even though the immediately surrounding area lacks naturally occurring stones suitable for making them. Carr and Stewart point out that we need to know where the artifacts and raw materials came from if we are going to talk about the nature of exchange systems and what they might mean in terms of social organization. Care must be taken to avoid the assumption that when materials are widely distributed—even lots of them—they indicate tightly integrated exchange networks. When Highland New Guinea was first visited in the 1930s, the people who lived there had no earthly idea where their widely traded and greatly valued marine shells came from (Leahy 1991).

While detailed, quantitatively based studies of the distribution of various raw materials will occupy researchers for many years, Carr and Stewart have made an excellent start for Poverty Point. When dealing with raw material identifications, they run headlong into the problem of whether categories should be narrowly or broadly defined. The first choice results in many rocks from a particular source remaining unidentified; the second in specimens often being placed in wrong categories. In expanding this essential work, it would be desirable to obtain quantitative estimates of both sensitivity and specificity—the epidemiological literature provides a good guide for dealing with such problems (e.g., Austin and Werner 1974; Holland 1998).

Jefferies's work with bone pins makes a significant contribution to our knowledge about interaction among Middle to Late Archaic hunter-gatherers. Samuel Brookes's work with Benton and other chipped-stone artifacts is also important in this regard. In Jefferies's various articles, he has plotted the distribution of ornamental bone pins to define broad geographical areas where widely separated groups of people must have maintained reasonably frequent interactions with one another (also see Jefferies 1995, 1997). It is unlikely that exchanging large pins worn in the hair or on clothing was the principal reason people were so intent on maintaining contact with one another. Instead, Jefferies reasonably argues that the pins identified people who maintained friendly or cooperative relationships with members of neighboring groups. Why that would have been necessary is an interesting question, although it probably had something to do with the real needs of people in an uncertain environment.

Before leaving the issue of contacts among different groups of people, it is worth noting that attention should be directed at conflict as well as at cooperation. Over the past decade or so warfare has become something of a growth industry in archaeology, although not long ago the subject was all but ignored in the Eastern Woodlands and elsewhere in the world (Keeley 1996). Fortunately, we now have a good idea about the tactics employed for fighting in the Eastern Woodlands—they are what we would expect from the ethnographic and historical literature—and we even know something about geographical and temporal variation in the intensity of warfare (Milner 1999; Milner et al. 1991). The available skeletal evidence indicates that people in Middle and Late Archaic times occasionally fought one another. In fact, signs of trauma that include projectile point injuries and mutilated bodies are more common in museum collections than the existing literature would suggest (Mensforth 2001; Smith 1995, 1997). The situation improved about 2,000 years ago in the Middle Woodland period, only to worsen yet again in Late Woodland and later times. At this point, we only have a foggy notion about why the chances of conflicts breaking out varied so much over time and space. It most likely had something to do with population pressure and how these societies were organized. Whatever happened, systematic studies of warfare are required if we are to reach a fuller understanding of life in Middle to Late Archaic times.

FOOD AND PEOPLE

The hunter-gatherers responsible for many of the sites discussed in these chapters —those who lived at Watson Brake, Poverty Point, and other sites with fewer mounds—had a strong aquatic orientation (Saunders and Widmer, this volume). This statement could be extended to include the societies that left the midden and shell heaps from southern Illinois to northern Alabama, as well as those along the south Atlantic and Gulf coasts (Crothers, Russo, White, and Widmer, this volume). Much later societies, including those dating to Middle Woodland and Mississippian times, retained this wetlands orientation in many places, especially in broad river bottomlands and coastal settings (Milner 1998; Smith 1992b; Widmer 1988). Nobody would argue that living in proximity to wetlands prompted people to build mounds (or do the other things that people in so-called complex societies often do). Yet resource-rich places, including wetlands, were essential for numerous people to settle down in long-lasting or frequently reoccupied camps. These sites were not just used for long periods— many of them also were marked with large mounds. In short, resources that were productive and, most important, stable from one year to the next were essential.

Despite their importance, one should not exaggerate the material benefits of living next to oxbow lakes, backwater swamps, mussel shoals, and coastal marshes and lagoons. Arguments that invoke a simplistic reading of Sahlins's (1972:1) "original affluent society" rest on flimsy evidence. Cooperative these people might have been, but "affluent" they most certainly were not.[5] Particularly gripping accounts of the precarious existence of hunter-gatherers can be found in Hill and Hurtado's (1996) critique of the affluent-society myth (also see Jenike 2001). Despite evidence to the contrary, overly rosy views of hunter-gatherer life are common, perhaps even dominant, in scholarly and popular writing. They are especially prominent in the frequently cited stepwise deterioration in health that is said to have accompanied the shift to the drudgery of an agricultural existence and, ultimately, to the miseries of civilization (Cohen 1989; Cohen and Armelagos 1984). This is an important topic, but because it is only referred to obliquely in this book it is sufficient to mention just three problems with the health-decline idea. First, a unidirectional shift implies there was some uniformity in health among the societies within broadly defined categories such as hunter-gatherer and agriculturist. Note that contributors to this book emphasize the wide diversity in hunter-gatherer societies, and the same could be said about subsistence agriculturists. Second, the currently popular scenario does not account for the rise in population growth, a common indication of success, that took place while health supposedly deteriorated. Third, the interpretation of osteological data—the basis of this model—is problematic (Wood et al. 1992). While I could go on at great length, the bottom line is that one should be cautious about basing any argument on the "original affluent society" notion with its decidedly Rousseauian overtones.

Widmer looks at another population-related issue when he emphasizes the centrality of demographic processes to change over time in sociopolitical complexity. This work builds squarely on a large body of literature, including Keeley's (1988) study of recent hunter-gatherers and population pressure. Widmer argues that in low-energy nonagricultural systems, it is local to global environmental change that has the greatest effect on carrying capacity, hence population size (more importantly, density) and, ultimately, sociopolitical complexity. Population size, density, and pressure should not be confused; while related to one another, they are distinctly different. What concerns us most is pressure; that is, demands placed by a population on a ceiling set by a particular system of production in a certain environment.

Widmer's chapter deserves careful reading because it highlights the importance of population histories and how little we really know about them. It is possible, however, to make a first step toward understanding population change by looking at sites from a wide variety of environmental settings. Figure 15.1 shows the distribution of about 83,000 components dating to the past 10,000 years from sites in the computerized files for Alabama, Arkansas, Illinois, Kentucky, Mississippi, New York, Tennessee, and Wisconsin (also see Galloway 1994 and Williams 1994). Collectively, these sites are probably representative of much of the Eastern Woodlands, especially the Midwest and Southeast. In Figure 15.1, components that lasted for short periods are assigned to the appropriate 500-year interval, and the components with long durations are divided among the intervals they spanned. Common understandings of the duration of various cultural periods, based mostly on uncalibrated radiocarbon dates and guesswork, were converted to calibrated (or calendar) dates. There are, of course, serious problems with extrapolating from sites to people. They include differential site preservation and visibility, along with differences in settlement longevity and occupancy. Nevertheless, the state site files are the best data assembled so far for the large geographical coverage needed for such an exercise. Because of the nature of this information, it is best to look at general trends, not minor peaks and valleys in the site distribution. When that is done, there appears to have been a long period of near stasis followed by a growth phase in which the annual increase in sites was 0.06 percent. It would be wrong to think that any such figure can be applied uniformly to the Eastern Woodlands. Local groups certainly went through periods of expansion and decline, even extinction, but such varied population histories are masked by overall trends in the aggregate data.

If numbers of sites bear any relation to population size, then the last several thousand years of prehistory were generally a time of increasing pressure on resources. This pressure could only be lessened by technological and social innovations that enhanced productivity, assuming there were no drastic changes in ecological settings that increased resource yield and reliability. The large midden and shell heaps began to develop alongside both riverine and coastal wetlands toward the end of a long period of population stagnation. This was a time when people in some places reduced their mobility and occupied sites repeatedly and for longer periods of time. During the Late Archaic—about the time when domesticated varieties of several native plants first appeared (Smith 1989)—population growth accelerated. The overall rate of increase remained relatively

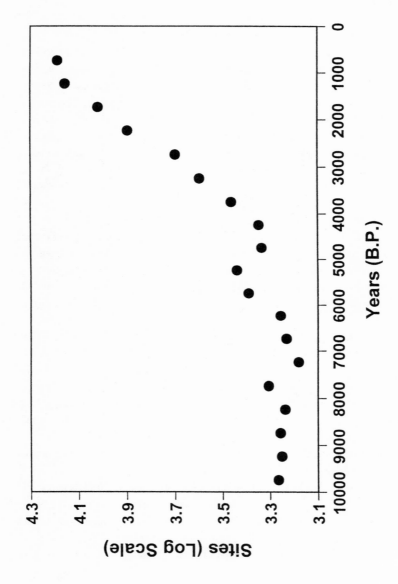

Figure 15.1. Approximately 83,000 components from the site files for eight states plotted on a log scale to facilitate comparisons of rates of change. Two general periods are represented: stagnation and growth.

fixed from that time onward. For those of us who spend our time looking at cultural developments in late prehistory, it appears that we must broaden our gaze to include much longer sweeps of time, extending deep into the Archaic.

FINAL REMARKS

I make no claims about being able to foresee the future by gazing into crystal balls—even the colorful yard-art variety—but there is every reason to believe that we will see a marked increase in Archaic hunter-gatherer studies over the next decade or so. These chapters, individually and collectively, set the stage for that work. The relevance of this research extends far beyond finding out what life was like in Middle to Late Archaic times. That is because it squarely addresses the identification and interpretation of the archaeological signatures for what are often labeled complex hunter-gatherer societies.

ACKNOWLEDGMENTS

Jon Gibson and Phil Carr kindly invited me to participate in their symposium and volume. This essay benefited greatly by comments from Richard W. Jefferies and Claire McHale Milner. The site data cited were collected and maintained through the hard work of innumerable people—I am grateful that this information was made available to me.

NOTES

1. The Southeastern sites with mounds are Poverty Point, Watson Brake, and Caney Mounds. Two other sites with midden rings are not included in this tally.

2. Incidentally, the same point could be made about the Yanomamo of tropical lowland South America, who are sometimes viewed as a classic example of village agriculturists.

3. These events can be impressive productions, as I have seen for myself at a funeral on a Micronesian island where huge quantities of food were laid out.

4. A distinction should be made between more of the same food and diets that were measurably different in content.

5. "Original" in the "original affluent society" has also come under criticism (Rowley-Conwy 2001), so the only part that is not controversial is "society."

References Cited

Abrams, E. M.

1989   Architecture and Energy: An Evolutionary Perspective. In *Archeological Method and Theory*, vol. 1, edited by M. B. Schiffer, pp. 47–87. University of Arizona Press, Tucson.

Adler, M. A.

2002   Building Consensus: Tribes, Architecture, and Typology in the American Southwest. In *The Archaeology of Tribal Societies*, edited by W. A. Parkinson, pp. 155–172. Archaeological Series 15, International Monographs in Prehistory, Ann Arbor, Michigan.

Adler, M. A., and R. H. Wilshusen

1990   Large-Scale Integrative Facilities in Tribal Societies: Cross-Cultural and Southwestern United States Examples. *World Archaeology* 22(2):133–146.

Ahler, S. R.

1991   Modoc Matting and Beads. *The Living Museum* 53(1):3–6.

Allen, C.

1996   Preliminary Floral Analysis at Watson Brake. Paper presented at the 53rd Annual Meeting of the Southeastern Archaeological Conference, Birmingham, Alabama.

Ames, K. M.

1994   The Northwest Coast: Complex Hunter-Gatherers, Ecology, and Social Evolution. *Annual Review of Anthropology* 34:209–229.

Anderson, D. G.

1990   The Paleoindian Colonization of Eastern North America: A View from the Southeastern United States. In *Early Paleoindian Economies of Eastern North America*, edited by K. B. Tankersley and B. L. Isaac, pp. 163–216. Research in Economic Anthropology, Supplement 5, JAI Press, Greenwich, Connecticut.

1994a   *The Savannah River Chiefdoms*. University of Alabama Press, Tuscaloosa.

1994b   Exploring the Antiquity of Interaction Networks in the Eastern Woodlands. Paper presented at the 51st Annual Meeting of the Southeastern Archaeological Conference and the 39th Annual Meeting of the Midwest Archaeological Conference, Lexington, Kentucky.

1995   Paleoindian Interaction Networks in the Eastern Woodlands. In *Native American Interactions: Multiscalar Analyses and Interpretations in the Eastern Woodlands*, edited by M. S. Nassaney and K. E. Sassaman, pp. 3–26. University of Tennessee Press, Knoxville.

1996   Approaches to Modeling Regional Settlement in the Archaic Period Southeast. In *Archaeology of the Mid-Holocene Southeast*, edited by K. E. Sassaman and D. G. Anderson, pp. 157–176. University Press of Florida, Gainesville.

2001   Climate and Culture Change in Prehistoric and Early Historic Eastern North America. *Archaeology of Eastern North America* 29:143–186.

2002   The Evolution of Tribal Social Organization in the Southeastern United States. In *The Archaeology of Tribal Societies*, edited by W. A. Parkinson, pp. 246–277. Archaeological Series 15, International Monographs in Prehistory, Ann Arbor, Michigan.

Anderson, D. G., and J. C. Gillam

2001   Paleoindian Interaction and Mating Networks: Reply to Moore and Moseley. *American Antiquity* 66(3):530–535.

Anderson, D. G., and K. E. Sassaman (editors)

1996   *The Paleoindian and Early Archaic Southeast*. University of Alabama Press, Tuscaloosa.

Anonymous

1755   Relation de la Louisiane. In *Source Material for the Social and Ceremonial Life of the Choctaw Indians*, by J. R. Swanton, pp. 243–270. Bulletin 103, Bureau of American Ethnology, Smithsonian Institution Press, Washington, D.C.

Arnold, J. E.

1987   *Craft Specialization in the Prehistoric Channel Islands, California*. University of California Press, Berkeley.

1995   Social Inequality, Marginalization, and Economic Process. In *Foundations of Social Inequality*, edited by T. D. Price and G. M. Feinman, pp. 87–104. Plenum Press, New York.

1996a   Organizational Transformations: Power and Labor among Complex Hunter-Gatherers and Other Intermediate Societies. In *Emergent Complexity: The Evolution of Intermediate Societies*, edited by J. E. Arnold, pp. 59–73. Archaeological Series 9, International Monographs in Prehistory, Ann Arbor, Michigan.

1996b   The Archaeology of Complex Hunter-Gatherers. *Journal of Archaeological Method and Theory* 3(2):77–126.

Arnold, J. E. (editor)

1996   *Emergent Complexity: The Evolution of Intermediate Societies*. Archaeological Series 9, International Monographs in Prehistory, Ann Arbor, Michigan.

Asch, M. I.

1982   Dene Self-Determination and the Study of Hunter-Gatherers in the Modern World. In *Politics and History in Band Societies*, edited by E. Leacock and R. Lee, pp. 347–372. Cambridge University Press, Cambridge, U.K.

Aten, L. E.

1999   Middle Archaic Ceremonialism at Tick Island, Florida: Ripley P. Bullen's 1961 Excavations at the Harris Creek Site. *The Florida Anthropologist* 52:131–200.

Atkinson, J. R.

1974   Appendix A, Test Excavations at the Vaughan Mound Site. In *An Archaeological
Survey and Test Excavations in the Upper-Central Tombigbee River Valley: Aliceville
Columbus Lock and Dam and Impoundment Areas, Alabama and Mississippi*, by
M. D. Rucker. Submitted to the National Park Service. Copies available from De-
partment of Anthropology, Mississippi State University, Mississippi State.

Austin, D. F., and S. B. Werner

1974   *Epidemiology for the Health Sciences*. C. C. Thomas, Springfield, Illinois.

Bader, A. T.

1992   An Analysis of Bone and Antler Tool Use Patterns from the Kentucky Air National
Guard Site. Unpublished Master's thesis, Department of Anthropology, University
of Kentucky, Lexington.

Bailey, R. C., G. Head, M. R. Jenike, B. Owen, R. Rechtman, and E. Zechenter

1989   Hunting and Gathering in Tropical Rain Forest: Is It Possible? *American Anthropologist* 91:59–82.

Bartram, W.

1955   [1791] *Travels through North & South Carolina, Georgia, East & West Florida, the
Cherokee Country, the Extensive Territories of the Muscogulges, or Creek Confederacy,
and the Country of the Chactaws; Containing an Account of the Soil and Natural
Productions of those Regions, Together with Observations on the Manners of the Indians*. Reissued as *Travels of William Bartram*, edited by M. Van Doren. Dover Publications, New York.

Bass, S.

1981   A Closer Examination of Local Lithic Sources for Tool Manufacture at the Poverty
Point Site. Unpublished Master's thesis, Louisiana State University, Baton Rouge.

Bender, B.

1985a   Prehistoric Developments in the American Midcontinent and in Brittany, Northwest France. In *Prehistoric Hunter-Gatherers: The Emergence of Cultural Complexity*,
edited by T. D. Price and J. A. Brown, pp. 21–57. Academic Press, New York.

1985b   Emergent Tribal Formation in the American Midcontinent. *American Antiquity*
50:52–62.

1990   The Dynamics of Nonhierarchical Societies. In *The Evolution of Political Systems:
Sociopolitics in Small Scale Sedentary Societies*, edited by S. Upham, pp. 247–263.
Cambridge University Press, New York.

Bender, B., and B. Morris

1988   Twenty Years of History, Evolution and Social Change in Gatherer-Hunter Studies.
In *Hunters and Gatherers*, vol. 1, *History, Evolution and Social Change*, edited by
T. Ingold, D. Riches, and J. Woodburn, pp. 4–14. Berg, London.

Benderly, B. L.

1982   Rape Free or Rape Prone. *Science 82* 3(8):40–43.

Bense, J. A.
    1998   Santa Rosa–Swift Creek in Northwestern Florida. In *A World Engraved: Archae-ology of the Swift Creek Culture*, edited by M. Williams and D. T. Elliott, pp. 247–273. University of Alabama Press, Tuscaloosa.
    1994   *Archaeology of the Southeastern United States: Paleoindian to World War I*. Academic Press, San Diego, California.
Bense, J. A. (editor)
    1987   *Midden Mound Project*. Reports of Investigations No. 6, Office of Cultural and Ar-chaeological Research, University of West Florida, Pensacola.
Bently, G. R., T. Goldberg, and G. Jasienska
    1993   The Fertility of Agricultural and Non-Agricultural Traditional Societies. *Population Studies* 47:269–281.
Bernbeck, R.
    1991   Crisis in the Foraging Mode of Production: Long-Term Cyclical Processes in Hunter-Gatherer Societies. In *Foragers in Context: Long-Term, Regional, and Historical Perspectives in Hunter-Gatherer Studies*, edited by P. T. Miracle, L. E. Fisher, and J. Brown, pp. 47–62. Michigan Discussions in Anthropology Vol. 10, University of Michigan, Ann Arbor.
Binford, L. R.
    1979   Organization and Formation Processes: Looking at Curated Technologies. *Journal of Anthropological Research* 35:255–273.
    1980   Willow Smoke and Dogs' Tails: Hunter-Gatherer Settlement Systems and Archaeo-logical Site Formation. *American Antiquity* 45:4–28.
    2001   *Constructing Frames of Reference: An Analytical Method for Archaeological Theory Building using Hunter-Gatherer and Environmental Data Sets*. University of Califor-nia Press, Berkeley.
Bird-David, N.
    1990   The Giving Environment: Another Perspective on the Economic System of Gatherer-Hunters. *Current Anthropology* 31:189–196.
    1998   Beyond "The Original Affluent Society": A Culturalist Reformulation. In *Limited Wants, Unlimited Means: A Reader on Hunter-Gatherer Economics and the Environ-ment*, edited by J. Gowdy, pp. 115–137. Island Press, Washington, D.C. Originally published 1992, *Current Anthropology* 33:25–34.
Blake, M.
    1991   An Emerging Early Formative Chiefdom at Paso de la Amada, Chiapas, Mexico. In *The Formation of Complex Society in Southeastern Mesoamerica*, edited by W. R. Fowler, Jr., pp. 27–46. CRC Press, Boca Raton, Florida.
Blanton, R. E., G. M. Feinman, S. A. Kowalewski, and P. N. Peregrine
    1996   A Dual-Processual Theory for the Emergence of Mesoamerican Civilization. *Cur-rent Anthropology* 37:1–14.
Blitz, J. H.
    1999   Mississippian Chiefdoms and the Fission-Fusion Process. *American Antiquity* 64:577–592.

Brackenridge, H. M.

1818   On the Population and Tumuli of the Aborigines of North America. *Transactions of the American Philosophical Society* 1:151–159.

Braun, D. P., and S. Plog

1982   Evolution of "Tribal" Social Networks: Theory and Prehistoric North American Evidence. *American Antiquity* 47:504–525.

Breitburg, E.

1982   Analysis of Area A Fauna. In *The Carrier Mills Archaeological Project: Human Adaptation in the Saline Valley, Illinois,* edited by R. W. Jefferies and B. M. Butler, pp. 863–952. Research Paper 33, Center for Archaeological Investigations, Southern Illinois University, Carbondale.

Brookes, S. O.

1997   Aspects of the Middle Archaic: The Atassa. In *Results of Recent Archaeological Investigations in the Greater Mid-South: Proceedings of the 17th Annual Mid-South Archaeological Conference, Memphis, Tennessee, June 29–30, 1996,* edited by C. H. McNutt. Occasional Paper No. 18, Anthropological Research Center, University of Memphis, Memphis, Tennessee.

Brose, D. S.

1979   A Speculative Model of the Role of Exchange in the Prehistory of the Eastern Woodlands. In *Hopewell Archaeology: The Chillicothe Conference,* edited by D. Brose and N. Greber, pp. 3–8. Kent State University Press, Kent, Ohio.

Brown, C. S.

1992   *Archaeology of Mississippi.* Reprinted. University Press of Mississippi, Jackson. Originally published 1926, Mississippi Geological Survey, University of Mississippi, University.

Brown, I. W.

1999   Contact, Communication, and Exchange: Some Thoughts on the Rapid Movement of Ideas and Objects. In *Raw Materials and Exchange in the Mid-South: Proceedings of the 16th Annual Mid-South Archaeological Conference, Jackson, Mississippi, June 3–4, 1995,* edited by E. Peacock and S. O. Brookes, pp. 132–141. Archaeological Report No. 29, Mississippi Department of Archives and History, Jackson.

Brown, J. A.

1985   Long-Term Trends to Sedentism and the Emergence of Complexity in the American Midwest. In *Prehistoric Hunter-Gatherers: The Emergence of Cultural Complexity,* edited by T. D. Price and J. A. Brown, pp. 201–231. Academic Press, New York.

1996   *Spiro Ceremonial Center: The Archaeology of Arkansas Valley Caddoan Culture in Eastern Oklahoma.* Memoirs of the Museum of Anthropology No. 29, University of Michigan, Ann Arbor.

1997   The Archaeology of Ancient Religion in the Eastern Woodlands. *Annual Review of Anthropology* 26:465–485.

Brown, J. A., and T. D. Price

1985   Complex Hunter-Gatherers: Retrospect and Prospect. In *Prehistoric Hunter-Gatherers:*

The Emergence of Cultural Complexity, edited by T. D. Price and J. A. Brown, pp. 436–442. Academic Press, New York.

Brown, J. A., and R. K. Vierra

  1983   What Happened in the Middle Archaic? In *Archaic Hunters and Gatherers in the American Midwest*, edited by J. L. Phillips and J. A. Brown, pp. 165–195. Academic Press, New York.

Bruhns, K. O.

  1991   Sexual Activities: Some Thoughts on the Sexual Division of Labor and Archaeological Interpretation. In *The Archaeology of Gender: Proceedings of the 22nd Annual Conference of the Archaeological Association of the University of Calgary*, edited by D. Walde and N. Willows, pp. 420–429. Archaeological Association of the University of Calgary, Calgary, Alberta, Canada.

Bruhns, K. O., and K. E. Stothert

  1999   *Women in Ancient America*. University of Oklahoma Press, Norman.

Brumbach, H. J., and R. Jarvenpa

  1997   Woman the Hunter: Ethnoarchaeological Lessons from Chipewyan Life-Cycle Dynamics. In *Women in Prehistory: North America and Mesoamerica*, edited by C. Claassen and R. Joyce, pp. 17–32. University of Pennsylvania Press, Philadelphia.

Brumfiel, E. M., and T. K. Earle

  1987   Specialization, Exchange, and Complex Societies: An Introduction. In *Specialization, Exchange, and Complex Societies*, edited by E. M. Brumfiel and T. K. Earle, pp. 1–9. Cambridge University Press, Cambridge, U.K.

Bruseth, J. E.

  1991   Poverty Point Development as Seen at the Cedarland and Claiborne Sites, Southern Mississippi. In *The Poverty Point Culture: Local Manifestations, Subsistence Practices, and Trade Networks*, edited by K. M. Byrd, pp. 7–25. Geoscience and Man Vol. 29, Louisiana State University, Baton Rouge.

Buckley, T.

  1988   Menstruation and the Power of Yurok Women. In *Blood Magic: The Anthropology of Menstruation*, edited by T. Buckley and A. Gottlieb, pp. 188–209. University of California Press, Berkeley.

Bullen, R. P.

  1958   *Six Sites near the Chattahoochee River in the Jim Woodruff Reservoir Area, Florida*. River Basin Surveys Papers No. 14, pp. 316–358. Bulletin 169, Bureau of American Ethnology, Smithsonian Institution Press, Washington, D.C.

  1961   Indian Burials at Tick Island. *American Philosophical Society Yearbook 1961*, pp. 477–480.

Burger, R. L.

  1992   *Chavin and the Origins of Andean Civilization*. Thames and Hudson, London.

Bushnell, D. I., Jr.

  1909   *The Choctaw of Bayou Lacomb, St. Tammany Parish, Louisiana*. Bulletin 48, Bureau of American Ethnology, Smithsonian Institution Press, Washington, D.C.

Byers, A. M.

1991   Structure, Meaning, Action and Things: The Duality of Material Culture Media-
        tion. *Journal for the Theory of Social Behaviour* 21:1–29.

1992   The Action-Constitutive Theory of Monuments: A Strong Pragmatic Version.
        Journal for the Theory of Social Behaviour 22:403–446.

1998   Is the Newark Circle-Octagon the Ohio Hopewell "Rosetta Stone"?: A Question of
        Archaeological Interpretation. In *Ancient Earthen Enclosures of the Eastern Wood-
        lands,* edited by R. C. Mainfort, Jr., and L. P. Sullivan, pp. 135–153. University
        Press of Florida, Gainesville.

Cable, J. S.

1995   *Intensive Archaeology Survey of Salt Pond, South Tibwin, Palmetto Plantation, and
        Brick Church Tracts, Wambaw Ranger District, Francis Marion National Forest,
        Charleston County, South Carolina.* Submitted to Francis Marion and Sumter Na-
        tional Forests, National Forest Service, U.S. Department of Agriculture, McClel-
        lanville, South Carolina. Cultural Resource Management Report 94-07, Technical
        Report 243, New South Associates, Stone Mountain, Georgia.

1997   The Ceremonial Mound Theory: New Evidence for the Possible Ceremonial Func-
        tion of Shell Rings. From South Carolina Archaeology Week poster *Shell Rings of
        the Late Archaic.* South Carolina Institute of Archaeology and Anthropology, Uni-
        versity of South Carolina, Columbia.

Caldwell, J. R.

1958   *Trend and Tradition in the Prehistory of the Eastern United States.* Illinois State Mu-
        seum, Springfield.

Callender, C., and L. M. Kochems

1983   The Native American Berdache. *Current Anthropology* 24:443–470.

Calmes, A.

1967   Test Excavations at Two Late Archaic Sites on Hilton Head Island. Manuscript on
        file, South Carolina Institute of Archaeology and Anthropology, University of
        South Carolina, Columbia.

1968   Test Excavations at Three Late Archaic Shell-Ring Mounds on Hilton Head Island,
        South Carolina. *Southeastern Archaeological Conference Bulletin* 8:45–48.

Campbell, J.

1988   *Historical Atlas of World Mythology.* Vol. 1, *The Way of the Animal Powers,* pt. 1,
        Mythologies of the Primitive Hunters and Gatherers. Harper & Row, New York.

Carleton, K. H.

1999   Nanih Waiya (22WI500): An Historical and Archaeological Overview. *Mississippi
        Archaeology* 34:125–155.

Carneiro, R. L.

1967   On the Relationship between Size of Population and Complexity of Social Organi-
        zation. *Southwestern Journal of Anthropology* 23:234–243.

2002   The Tribal Village and Its Culture: An Evolutionary Stage in the History of Hu-
        man Society. In *The Archaeology of Tribal Societies,* edited by W. A. Parkinson,
        pp. 34–52. Archaeological Series 15, International Monographs in Prehistory, Ann
        Arbor, Michigan.

Carr, P. J.
  1994   The Organization of Technology: Impact and Potential. In *The Organization of North American Prehistoric Chipped Stone Tool Technologies*, edited by P. J. Carr, pp. 1–8. Archaeological Series 7, International Monographs in Prehistory, Ann Arbor, Michigan.

Carr, P. J., and A. P. Bradbury
  2001   Flake Debris Analysis, Levels of Production, and the Organization of Technology. In *Lithic Debitage: Context, Form, and Meaning*, edited by W. Andrefsky, Jr., pp. 126–146. University of Utah Press, Salt Lake City.

Carstens, K. C., and P. J. Watson (editors)
  1996   *Of Caves and Shell Mounds.* University of Alabama Press, Tuscaloosa.

Chagnon, N. A.
  1968   *Y•nomamö: The Fierce People.* Holt, Rinehart, and Winston, New York.

Chang, K.
  1958   Study of the Neolithic Social Grouping: Examples from the New World. *American Anthropologist* 60:298–334.

Chapman, R. W.
  1996   Problems of Scale in the Emergence of Complexity. In *Emergent Complexity: The Evolution of Intermediate Societies*, edited by J. E. Arnold, pp. 35–49. Archaeological Series 9, International Monographs in Prehistory, Ann Arbor, Michigan.

Chapman, S., E. Breitberg, and N. Lopinot
  1999   *Data Recovery (Mitigation) of Sites 23MI578, 23MI605, 23MI651, 23MI652 and 23MI797 in the New Madrid Floodway, Mississippi County, Missouri.* Submitted to the Memphis District, U.S. Army Corps of Engineers, Memphis, Tennessee, Delivery Order 9.

Charles, D., and J. E. Buikstra
  1983   Archaic Mortuary Sites in the Central Mississippi Drainage: Distribution, Structure, and Behavioral Implications. In *Archaic Hunters and Gatherers in the American Midwest*, edited by J. L. Phillips and J. A. Brown, pp. 66–72. Academic Press, New York.

Claassen, C.
  1991a   Normative Thinking and Shell Bearing Sites. In *Archaeological Method and Theory*, vol. 3, edited by M. A. Schiffer, pp. 249–298. University of Arizona Press, Tucson.
  1991b   Gender, Shellfishing, and the Shell Mound Archaic. In *Engendering Archaeology*, edited by J. Gero and M. Conkey, pp. 276–300. Basil Blackwells, Oxford, U.K.
  1991c   New Hypotheses for the Demise of the Shell Mound Archaic. In *The Archaic Period in the Mid-South*, edited by C. McNutt, pp. 66–72. Archaeological Report No. 24, Mississippi Department of Archives and History, Jackson.
  1992   Shell Mounds as Burial Mounds: A Revision of the Shell Mound Archaic. In *Current Archaeological Research in Kentucky*, vol. 2, edited by D. Pollack and A. G. Henderson, pp. 1–11. Kentucky Heritage Council, Frankfort.
  1996a   A Consideration of the Social Organization of the Shell Mound Archaic. In *Archaeology of the Mid-Holocene Southeast*, edited by K. E. Sassaman and D. G. Anderson, pp. 235–258. University Press of Florida, Gainesville.

1996b Research Problems with Shells from Green River Shell Matrix Sites. In *Of Caves and Shell Mounds,* edited by K. C. Carstens and P. J. Watson, pp. 132–139. University of Alabama Press, Tuscaloosa.

Claflin, W. H., Jr.

1931 *The Stalling's Island Mound, Columbia County, Georgia.* Museum Papers 4(1), Harvard University Peabody Museum, Cambridge, Massachusetts.

Clark, J. E.

2001 Ciudades Tempranas Olmecas. In *Reconstruyendo la Ciudad Maya: El Urbanismo en las Sociedades Antiguas,* edited by A. Ciudad Real, M. J. I. Ponce de León, and M. d. C. Martínez Martínez, pp. 183–210. Sociedad Española de Estudios Mayas, Madrid.

Clark, J. E., and M. Blake

1994 The Power of Prestige: Competitive Generosity and the Emergence of Rank Societies in Lowland Mexico. In *Factional Competition and Political Development in the New World,* edited by E. M. Brumfiel and J. W. Fox, pp. 17–30. Cambridge University Press, Cambridge, U.K.

1996 The Power of Prestige: Competitive Generosity and the Emergence of Rank Societies in Lowland Mesoamerica. In *Contemporary Archaeology in Theory,* edited by R. Preucel and I. Hodder, pp. 258–281. Blackwell, Oxford, U.K.

Clark, J. E., and D. Cheetham

2002 Mesoamerica's Tribal Foundations. In *The Archaeology of Tribal Societies,* edited by W. A. Parkinson, pp. 278–340. Archaeological Series 15, International Monographs in Prehistory, Ann Arbor, Michigan.

Clark, J. E., and R. D. Hansen

2001 The Architecture of Early Kingship: Comparative Perspectives on the Origins of the Maya Royal Court. In *The Maya Royal Court,* edited by T. Inomata and S. D. Houston, pp. 1–45. Westview Press, Boulder, Colorado.

Clark, J. E., and W. J. Parry

1990 *Craft Specialization and Cultural Complexity.* Research in Economic Anthropology 12:289–346. JAI Press, Greenwich, Connecticut.

Clastres, P.

1974 *Society Against the State.* Blackwell, Oxford, U.K.

Clay, R. B.

1986 Adena Ritual Spaces. In *Early Woodland Archeology,* edited by K. B. Farnsworth and T. E. Emerson, pp. 581–595. Center for American Archaeology Press, Kampsville, Illinois.

Coastal Environments, Inc.

1977 *Cultural Resources Evaluation of the Northern Gulf of Mexico Continental Shelf.* Vol. 1, *Prehistoric Cultural Resource Potential.* Submitted to Interagency Archaeological Services, National Park Service, U.S. Department of the Interior, Washington, D.C.

Coe, M. D.

1999 *The Maya,* 6th ed. Thames and Hudson, London.

Cohen, M.

1989 *Health and the Rise of Civilization.* Yale University Press, New Haven, Connecticut.

Cohen, M. N., and G. J. Armelagos
  1984   Paleopathology at the Origins of Agriculture: Editors' Summation. In *Paleopathology at the Origins of Agriculture,* edited by M. N. Cohen and G. J. Armelagos, pp. 585–601. Academic Press, Orlando, Florida.

Conkey, M. W., with S. Williams
  1991   Original Narratives: The Political Economy of Gender in Archaeology. In *Gender at the Crossroads of Knowledge: Feminist Anthropology in the Postmodern Era,* edited by M. DiLeonardo, pp. 102–139. University of California Press, Berkeley.

Conn, T. L.
  1976   The Utilization of Chert at the Poverty Point Site. Unpublished Master's thesis, Louisiana State University, Baton Rouge.

Connaway, J. M.
  1981   The Keenan Bead Cache, Lawrence County, Mississippi. *Louisiana Archaeology* 8:57–71.

Connaway, J. M., with S. O. Brookes and S. O. McGahey
  1977   *The Denton Site: A Middle Archaic Occupation in the Northern Yazoo Basin, Mississippi.* Archaeological Report No. 4, Mississippi Department of Archives and History, Jackson.

Cook, T. G.
  1976   *Koster: An Artifact Analysis of Two Archaic Phases in West-Central Illinois.* Prehistoric Research Records 1, Archaeology Program, Northwestern University, Evanston, Illinois.

Craig, A. B.
  1958   A Dwarf Burial from Limestone County, Alabama. *Journal of Alabama Archaeology* 4:15–17.

Creamer, W., and J. Haas
  1985   Tribe versus Chiefdom in Lower Central America. *American Antiquity* 50:738–754.

Crothers, G. M.
  1999   Prehistoric Hunters and Gatherers, and the Archaic Period Green River Shell Middens of Western Kentucky. Unpublished Ph.D. dissertation, Department of Anthropology, Washington University, St. Louis.

Crothers, G. M., and R. Bernbeck
  2003   The Foraging Mode of Production: The Case of the Green River, Kentucky, Archaic Shell Middens. In *Hunters and Gatherers in Theory and Archaeology,* edited by G. M. Crothers. Occasional Paper No. 31, Center for Archaeological Investigations, Southern Illinois University, Carbondale, in press.

Crumley, C. L.
  1987   A Dialectical Critique of Hierarchy. In *Power Relations and State Formation,* edited by T. C. Patterson and C. W. Gailey, pp. 155–169. American Anthropological Association, Washington, D.C.

Crusoe, D. L., and C. B. DePratter
  1976   A New Look at the Georgia Shell Mound Archaic. *The Florida Anthropologist* 29(1):1–23.

Custer, J. F.
  1987   Core Technology at the Hawthorn Site, New Castle County, Delaware: A Late
          Archaic Hunting Camp. In *The Organization of Core Technology*, edited by J. K.
          Johnson and C. A. Morrow, pp. 45–62. Westview Press, Boulder, Colorado.

Dahlberg, F. (editor)
  1981   *Woman the Gatherer*. Yale University Press, New Haven, Connecticut.

Davis, A.
  1983   Pacing and the Megalithic Yard. *Glasgow Archaeological Journal* 10:7–11.

DeBoer, W. R.
  1997   Ceremonial Centres from the Cayapas (Esmeraldas, Ecuador) to Chillicothe (Ohio,
          USA). *Cambridge Archaeological Journal* 7(2):225–253.

Denbow, J. R.
  1984   Prehistoric Herders and Foragers of the Kalahari: The Evidence for 1500 Years of
          Interaction. In *Past and Present in Hunter-Gatherer Studies*, edited by C. Schrire,
          pp. 175–193. Academic Press, Orlando, Florida.

Denbow, J. R., and E. Wilmsen
  1983   Iron Age Pastoralist Settlements in Botswana. *South African Journal of Science*
          79:405–407.
  1986   Advent and Course of Pastoralism in the Kalahari. *Science* 234:1509–1515.

DePratter, C. B.
  1976   Shellmound Archaic on the Georgia Coast. Unpublished Master's thesis, Univer-
          sity of Georgia, Athens.
  1979   Shellmound Archaic on the Georgia Coast. *South Carolina Antiquities* 11:1–69.

DePratter, C. B., and J. D. Howard
  1980   Indian Occupation and Geological History of the Georgia Coast: A 5,000 Year
          Summary. In *Excursions in Southeastern Geology: The Archaeology-Geology of the
          Georgia Coast*, edited by J. D. Howard, C. B. DePratter, and R. W. Frey, pp. 1–65.
          Georgia Geologic Survey Guidebook 20, Department of Natural Resources, Envi-
          ronmental Protection Division, Atlanta.

Diamond, S.
  1974   *In Search of the Primitive: A Critique of Civilization*. Transaction Books, New Bruns-
          wick, New Jersey.

Dickel, D.
  1992   *An Archaeological and Historical Survey of Bonita Springs, Parcel Three, Lee County,
          Florida*. AHC Technical Report 43, Archaeological and Historical Conservancy,
          Davie, Florida.

Dietler, M.
  2001   Theorizing the Feast: Rituals of Consumption, Commensal Politics, and Power in
          African Contexts. In *Feasts: Archaeological and Ethnographic Perspectives on Food,
          Politics, and Power*, edited by M. Dietler and B. Hayden, pp. 65–114. Smithsonian
          Institution Press, Washington, D.C.

Dietler, M., and B. Hayden (editors)
  2001   *Feasts: Archaeological and Ethnographic Perspectives on Food, Politics, and Power*.
          Smithsonian Institution Press, Washington, D.C.

Dietler, M., and I. Herbich

2001   Feasts and Labor Mobilization Dissecting a Fundamental Economic Practice. In *Feasts: Archaeological and Ethnographic Perspectives on Food, Politics, and Power*, edited by M. Dietler and B. Hayden, pp. 240–264. Smithsonian Institution Press, Washington, D.C.

Dillehay, T.

1990   Mapuche Ceremonial Landscape, Social Recruitment and Resource Rights. *World Archaeology* 22:223–241.

Dillehay, T. (editor)

1997   *Monte Verde: A Late Pleistocene Settlement in Chile*, vol. 2, *The Archaeological Context*. Smithsonian Institution Press, Washington, D.C.

Dobres, M.-A., and J. Robb (editors)

2000   *Agency in Archaeology*. Routledge, New York and London.

Donoghue, J. F., and N. M. White

1994   Late Holocene Sea Level Change and Delta Migration, Apalachicola River Region, Florida. *Journal of Coastal Research* 11(3):651–663.

Douglass, A. E.

1882   A Find of Ceremonial Axes in a Florida Mound. *American Antiquarian and Oriental Journal* 4:100–109.

Dowd, J. T.

1970   A Woodland Burial in Middle Tennessee. *Tennessee Archaeologist* 26:1–14.

1989   *The Anderson Site: Middle Archaic Adaptation in Tennessee's Central Basin*. Miscellaneous Paper No. 13, Tennessee Anthropological Association, Knoxville.

Drayton, J.

1972   [1802] *A View of South Carolina, as Respects Her Natural and Civil Concerns*. W. P. Young, Charleston. The Reprint Company, Spartanburg, South Carolina.

Drennan, R. D.

1996   One for All and All for One: Accounting for Variability without Losing Sight of Regularities in the Development of Complex Society. In *Emergent Complexity: The Evolution of Intermediate Societies*, edited by J. E. Arnold, pp. 25–34. Archaeological Series 9, International Monographs in Prehistory, Ann Arbor, Michigan.

Du Pratz, M. L. P.

1975   [1774] *The History of Louisiana*. Translated and edited by J. G. Tregle, Jr. Louisiana State University Press, Baton Rouge.

Dyson-Hudson, R., and E. A. Smith

1978   Human Territoriality: An Ecological Reassessment. *American Anthropologist* 80: 21–41.

Earle, T.

1991   Property Rights and the Evolution of Chiefdoms. In *Chiefdoms: Power, Economy, and Ideology*, edited by T. Earle, pp. 71–99. Cambridge University Press, Cambridge, U.K.

1997   *How Chiefs Come to Power: The Political Economy in Prehistory*. Stanford University Press, Stanford, California.

Edwards, W. E.

1965   A Preliminary Report on the Sewee Mound Shell Midden, Charleston County, South Carolina. Manuscript on file, South Carolina Institute of Archaeology and Anthropology, University of South Carolina, Columbia.

Eggan, F.

1950   Social Organization of the Western Pueblo. University of Chicago Press, Chicago.

Ehrenreich, R. M., C. L. Crumley, and J. E. Levy (editors)

1995   Heterarchy and the Analysis of Complex Societies. Archeological Papers of the American Anthropological Association No. 6, American Anthropological Association, Arlington, Virginia.

Emerson, T. E.

1997   Cahokia and the Archaeology of Power. University of Alabama Press, Tuscaloosa.

1999   The Langford Tradition and the Process of Tribalization on the Middle Mississippian Borders. Midcontinental Journal of Archaeology 24:3–56.

Engels, F.

1972   [1884] The Origin of the Family, Private Property, and the State. International Publishing, New York.

Erasmus, C. J.

1965   Monument Building: Some Field Experiments. Southwestern Journal of Anthropology 21:277–301.

Estioko-Griffin, A.

1986   Daughters of the Forest. Natural History 95(5):36–43.

Evans-Pritchard, E. E.

1940   The Nuer. Oxford University Press, New York.

Exnicios, J., and D. Woodiel

1990   Poverty Point Excavations, 1980–1982. Louisiana Archaeology 13:73–100.

Fairbridge, R. W.

1984   The Holocene Sea Level Record in South Florida. In Environments of South Florida: Present and Past, II, 2nd ed., edited by P. J. Gleason, pp. 427–436. Miami Geological Society, Coral Gables, Florida.

Faulkner, W.

1954   Untitled. Holiday Magazine 15:34–47.

Feinman, G., and J. Neitzel

1984   Too Many Types: An Overview of Sedentary Prestate Societies in the Americas. In Advances in Archaeological Method and Theory, vol. 7, edited by M. B. Schiffer, pp. 39–102. Academic Press, New York.

Feldman, R. A.

1987   Architectural Evidence for the Development of Nonegalitarian Social Systems in Coastal Peru. In The Origins and Development of the Andean State, edited by J. Haas, S. Pozorski, and T. Pozorski, pp. 9–14. Cambridge University Press, Cambridge, U.K.

Flanagan, J. G.

1989   Hierarchy in Simple "Egalitarian" Societies. Annual Review of Anthropology 18: 245–266.

Flannery, K. V.

1994   Childe the Evolutionist: A Perspective from Nuclear America. In *The Archaeology of V. Gordon Childe*, edited by D. Harris, pp. 101–120. University of Chicago Press, Chicago.

Ford, J. A.

1954   Additional Notes on the Poverty Point Site in Northern Louisiana. *American Antiquity* 19(3):282–285.

1955a   Poverty Point Excavations. *Science* 122(3169):550–551.

1955b   The Puzzle of Poverty Point. *Natural History* 64(9):466–472.

1969   *A Comparison of the Formative Cultures of the Americas*. Smithsonian Contributions to Anthropology Vol. 11, Smithsonian Institution Press, Washington, D.C.

Ford, J. A., P. Phillips, and W. G. Haag

1955   *The Jaketown Site in West-Central Mississippi*. Anthropological Papers Vol. 45, Pt. 1, American Museum of Natural History, New York.

Ford, J. A., and C. H. Webb

1956   *Poverty Point, a Late Archaic Site in Louisiana*. Anthropological Papers Vol. 46, No. 1, American Museum of Natural History, New York.

Ford, J. A., and G. R. Willey

1941   An Interpretation of the Prehistory of the Eastern United States. *American Anthropologist* 43(3):325–363.

Fowke, G.

1898   Some Popular Errors in Regard to Mound Builders and Indians. *Ohio Archaeological and Historical Publications* 2:380–403.

1902   *Archaeological History of Ohio*. Ohio State Archaeological and Historical Society, Columbus.

Fowles, S. M.

2002a   From Social Type to Social Process: Placing "Tribe" in a Historical Framework. In *The Archaeology of Tribal Societies*, edited by W. A. Parkinson, pp. 13–33. Archaeological Series 15, International Monographs in Prehistory, Ann Arbor, Michigan.

2002b   Inequality and Tribal Rebellion: A Tribal Dialect in Tonga History. In *The Archaeology of Tribal Societies*, edited by W. A. Parkinson, pp. 74–96. Archaeological Series 15, International Monographs in Prehistory, Ann Arbor, Michigan.

Fox, R.

1967   *Kinship and Marriage*. Penguin Books, Baltimore.

Fried, M. H.

1967   *The Evolution of Political Society*. Random House, New York.

1968   On the Concepts of "Tribe" and "Tribal Society." In *Essays on the Problem of Tribe*, edited by J. Helm, pp. 3–20. American Ethnological Society, University of Washington Press, Seattle.

1975   *The Notion of Tribe*. Cummings Publishing, Menlo Park, California.

Frink, D. S.

1995   Application of the Oxidizable Carbon Ratio Dating Procedure and Its Implications for Pedogeneic Research. *Soil Science Society of America, Special Publication* 44:95–105.

1999   The Scientific Basis of Oxidizable Carbon Ratio (OCR) Dating. *Bulletin of the Society for American Archaeology* 17(5).

Fryman, M. L., D. Swindell, and J. J. Miller

1980   *Cultural Resource Reconnaissance of Hobe Sound National Wildlife Refuge, Martin County, Florida.* Submitted to Interagency Archeological Services Division (National Park Service), Atlanta, and U.S. Fish and Wildlife Service, Contract A-55034(79). Copies available from Office of the State Historic Preservation Officer, Tallahassee, Florida.

Gagliano, S. M.

1963   *A Survey of Preceramic Occupations in Portions of South Louisiana and Mississippi.* Coastal Studies Institute Contribution No. 63-7, Technical Report No. 16, Pt. E, United States Gulf Coastal Studies, Baton Rouge, Louisiana.

1967   *Occupation Sequence at Avery Island.* Coastal Studies Series No. 22, Louisiana State University Press, Baton Rouge.

Galloway, P.

1994   Prehistoric Population of Mississippi: A First Approximation. *Mississippi Archaeology* 29:44–71.

Gardner, J. W.

1992   *Sewee Fire Survey: Archaeological Survey of 135 Acres in the Sewee Historic Area, Wambaw Ranger District, Francis Marion National Forest, Charleston County, South Carolina.* Submitted to Francis Marion and Sumter National Forests, Contract 43-4670-2-0184, National Forest Service, U.S. Department of Agriculture, McClellanville, South Carolina. Cultural Resource Management Report 92-19, Brockington and Associates, Inc., Atlanta.

Geertz, C.

1980   *Negara: The Theater State in Nineteenth Century Bali.* University of Princeton Press, Princeton, New Jersey.

Gibson, J. L.

1968   Cad Mound: A Stone Bead Locus in East Central Louisiana. *Bulletin of the Texas Archaeological Society* 38:1–17.

1973   Social Systems at Poverty Point, An Analysis of Intersite and Intrasite Variability. Unpublished Ph.D. dissertation, Department of Anthropology, Southern Methodist University, Dallas.

1974   Poverty Point, the First North American Chiefdom. *Archaeology* 27:96–105.

1987   Poverty Point Earthworks Reconsidered. *Mississippi Archaeology* 22(2):14–31.

1989   *Digging on the Dock of the Bay(ou): The 1988 Excavations at Poverty Point.* Center for Archaeological Studies Report No. 8, University of Southwestern Louisiana, Lafayette.

1990   *Search for the Lost Ridge: The 1989 Excavations at Poverty Point.* Center for Archaeological Studies Report No. 9, University of Southwestern Louisiana, Lafayette.

1991   Catahoula—An Amphibious Poverty Point Manifestation in Eastern Louisiana. In *The Poverty Point Culture: Local Manifestations, Subsistence Practices, and Trade Networks*, edited by K. M. Byrd, pp. 61–87. Geoscience and Man Vol. 29, Louisiana State University, Baton Rouge.

1994a   Before Their Time? Early Mounds in the Lower Mississippi Valley. *Southeastern Archaeology* 13:162–181.

1994b   Empirical Characterization of Exchange Systems in Lower Mississippi Valley Prehistory. In *Prehistoric Exchange Systems in North America*, edited by T. G. Baugh and J. E. Ericson, pp. 127–175. Plenum Press, New York.

1994c   Over the Mountain and Across the Sea: Regional Poverty Point Exchange. *Louisiana Archaeology* 17:251–299.

1994d   *Cool Dark Woods, Poison Ivy, and Maringoins: The 1993 Excavations at Poverty Point, Louisiana*. Center for Archaeological Studies Report No. 12, University of Southwestern Louisiana, Lafayette.

1996a   Poverty Point and Greater Southeastern Prehistory: The Culture That Did Not Fit. In *Archaeology of the Mid-Holocene Southeast*, edited by K. E. Sassaman and D. G. Anderson, pp. 288–305. University Press of Florida, Gainesville.

1996b   Religion of the Rings, Poverty Point Iconology and Ceremonialism. In *Mounds, Embankments, and Ceremonialism in the Midsouth*, edited by R. C. Mainfort, Jr., and R. Walling, pp. 1–6. Research Series No. 46, Arkansas Archeological Survey, Fayetteville.

1996c   *Ancient Earthworks of the Ouachita Valley in Louisiana*. Technical Reports No. 5, Southeast Archeological Center, National Park Service, Tallahassee, Florida.

1997   Harder Than It Looks: Poverty Point Organization. Paper presented at the 54th Annual Meeting of the Southeast Archaeological Conference, Baton Rouge, Louisiana.

1998a   *Elements and Organization of Poverty Point Political Economy: High-Water Fish, Exotic Rocks, and Sacred Earth*. Research in Economic Anthropology 19:291–340. JAI Press, Greenwich, Connecticut.

1998b   Broken Circles, Owl Monsters, and Black Earth Midden: Separating Sacred and Secular at Poverty Point. In *Ancient Earthen Enclosures of the Eastern Woodlands*, edited by R. C. Mainfort, Jr., and L. P. Sullivan, pp. 17–30. University Press of Florida, Gainesville.

1999   Swamp Exchange and the Walled Mart: Poverty Point's Rock Business. In *Raw Materials and Exchange in the Mid-South: Proceedings of the 16th Annual Mid-South Archaeological Conference, Jackson, Mississippi, June 3–4, 1995*, edited by E. Peacock and S. O. Brookes, pp. 57–63. Archaeological Report No. 29, Mississippi Department of Archives and History, Jackson.

2000   *The Ancient Mounds of Poverty Point: Place of Rings*. University Press of Florida, Gainesville.

Gibson, J. L., and P. J. Carr

1999   Signs of Power: Why Early Mounds Are Southern and Other Thoughts. Paper presented at the 56th Annual Meeting of the Southeastern Archaeological Conference, Pensacola, Florida.

Gibson, J. L., and D. L. Griffing

1994   Only a Stone's Throw Away: Exchange in the Poverty Point Hinterland. In *Exchange in the Lower Mississippi Valley and Contiguous Areas at 1100 B.C.*, edited by J. L. Gibson, pp. 251–300. Louisiana Archaeology No. 21, Louisiana Archaeological Society, Lafayette.

Gibson, J. L., and J. R. Shenkel

1988   Louisiana Earthworks: Middle Woodland and Predecessors. In *Middle Woodland Settlement and Ceremonialism in the Midsouth and Lower Mississippi Valley*, edited by R. C. Mainfort, Jr., pp. 7–18. Archaeological Report No. 22, Mississippi Department of Archives and History, Jackson.

Giddens, A.

1981   *A Contemporary Critique of Historical Materialism*, vol. 1, *Power, Property and the State*. Macmillan, London.

1984   *The Constitution of Society: Outline of a Theory of Structuration*. Polity Press, Cambridge, U.K.

Girard, J. S.

2000   *Regional Archaeology Program, Management Unit 1, Eleventh Annual Report*. Department of Culture, Recreation, and Tourism, Louisiana Division of Archaeology, Baton Rouge.

Goody, J.

1976   *Production and Reproduction: A Comparative Study of the Domestic Domain*. Cambridge University Press, New York.

Goodyear, A. C.

1974   *The Brand Site: A Techno-Functional Study of a Dalton Site in Northeast Arkansas*. Research Series 7, Arkansas Archaeological Association, Fayetteville.

Gordon, R. J.

1984   The !Kung in the Kalahari Exchange: An Ethnohistorical Perspective. In *Past and Present in Hunter-Gatherer Studies*, edited by C. Schrire, pp. 195–224. Academic Press, Orlando, Florida.

Gregg, S. A. (editor)

1991   *Between Bands and States*. Occasional Paper No. 9, Center for Archaeological Investigations, Southern Illinois University, Carbondale.

Grinker, R. R.

1994   *Houses in the Rainforest: Ethnicity and Inequality among the Farmers and Foragers in Central Africa*. University of California Press, Berkeley.

Grøn, O.

1991   A Method for Reconstruction of Social Structure in Prehistoric Societies and Examples of Practical Application. In *Social Space: Human Spatial Behavior in Dwellings and Settlements, Proceedings of an Interdisciplinary Conference*, edited by O. Grøn, E. Engelstad, and I. Lindblom, pp. 100–117. Odense University Press, Denmark.

Guillemin-Tarayre, E.

1919a   Le Grand Temple de Mexico. *Journal de la Société des Américanistes de Paris*, n.s., 11:97–120.

1919b   Les Temples de l'Anahuac: Conclusions sur l'Unité de Mesure Chinoise Introduite
         au Mexique pour la Construcion des Temples. *Journal de la Société des Américanistes
         de Paris*, n.s., 11:501–512.
Halbert, H. S.
1899   Nanih Waiya, the Sacred Mound of the Choctaws. *Mississippi Historical Society
         Publications* 2:223–234.
Hale, S. H.
1984a   Prehistoric Environmental Exploitation around Lake Okeechobee. *Southeastern Ar-
         chaeology* 3(2):173–187.
1984b   Analysis of Fauna from a Late Archaic and St. Johns I and II Period Site in Volusia
         County, Florida. Paper presented at the 41st Annual Meeting of the Southeastern
         Archaeological Conference, Pensacola, Florida.
Hall, R. L.
1976   Ghosts, Water Barriers, Corn and Sacred Enclosures in the Eastern Woodlands.
         American Antiquity 41:360–364.
1997   *An Archaeology of the Soul, North American Indian Belief and Ritual*. University of
         Illinois Press, Urbana.
Hally, D. J.
1993   The Territorial Size of Mississippian Chiefdoms. In *Archaeology of Eastern North
         America, Papers in Honor of Stephen Williams*, edited by J. B. Stoltman, pp. 143–
         168. Archaeological Report No. 25, Mississippi Department of Archives and His-
         tory, Jackson.
1995   Platform Mound Construction and the Political Stability of Mississippian Chief-
         doms. In *Political Structure and Change in the Prehistoric Southeastern United States*,
         edited by J. F. Scarry, pp. 92–127. University Press of Florida, Gainesville.
Hamilton, F. E.
1999   Southeastern Archaic Mounds: Examples of Elaboration in a Temporally Fluctuat-
         ing Environment. *Journal of Anthropological Archaeology* 18:344–355.
Hare, A. P., and R. F. Bales
1963   Seating Position and Small Group Interaction. *Sociometry* 26(1):480–486.
Harriot, T.
1972   *A Briefe and True Report of the New Found Land of Virginia, The Complete 1590
         Theodor de Bry Edition*. Dover Publications, New York.
Harris, M.
1993   *Culture, People, and Nature*, 6th ed. Harper Collins, New York.
Hayden, B.
1994   Competition, Labor, and Complex Hunter-Gatherers. In *Key Issues in Hunter-
         Gatherer Research*, edited by J. Ernest, S. Burch, Jr., and L. J. Ellanna, pp. 223–242.
         Berg, Oxford, U.K.
1995   Pathways to Power: Principles for Creating Socioeconomic Inequalities. In *Founda-
         tions of Social Inequality*, edited by T. D. Price and G. M. Feinman, pp. 15–86.
         Plenum Press, New York.
1996   Thresholds of Power in Emergent Complex Societies. In *Emergent Complexity: The
         Evolution of Intermediate Societies*, edited by J. E. Arnold, pp. 50–58. Archaeologi-
         cal Series 9, International Monographs in Prehistory, Ann Arbor, Michigan.

2001   Fabulous Feasts: A Prolegomenon to the Importance of Feasting. In *Feasts: Archaeological and Ethnographic Perspectives on Food, Politics, and Power*, edited by M. Dietler and B. Hayden, pp. 23–64. Smithsonian Institution Press, Washington, D.C.

Headland, T. N., and L. A. Reid
1989   Hunter-Gatherers and Their Neighbors from Prehistory to the Present. *Current Anthropology* 30:43–66.

Heckenberger, M. J.
1995   Local Politics and Regional Identity: Social Being and Becoming in the Upper Xingu. Paper presented at the 94th Annual Meeting of the American Anthropological Association, Washington, D.C.
1996   War and Peace in the Shadow of Empire: Sociopolitical Change in the Upper Xingu of Southeastern Amazonia, A.D. 1400–2000. Unpublished Ph.D. dissertation, University of Pittsburgh, Pittsburgh.
1998   Hierarquia e Economia Política em Amazonia: A Construçao de Diferença e Desiqualidade na Política in Xinguana. Paper presented at the 21st Annual Meeting of the Associaçao Brasaileira de Anthropologia, Víctoria, Brazil.
1999a   O Enigma das Grandes Cidades: Corpo Privado e Estado em Amazonia. In *A Outra Margem do Occidente*, edited by A. Novaes, pp. 125–152. Companhia das Letras, Sao Paulo.
1999b   Xinguano History and Hierarchy: An Archaeology of Cultural Meanings. Paper presented at the 98th Meeting of the American Anthropological Association, Chicago.
2000a   Estrutura, História, e Transformaçao: A Cultura Xinguanao na Longue Durée (1000 a 2000 d. C.). In *Os Povos do Alto Xingu: História e Cultura*, edited by B. Franchetto and M. J. Heckenberger. Editori da Universidade Federal do Rio de Janeiro.
2000b   The Archaeology of Experience: Plazas as Symbolic Windows in Amazonia. Paper presented at the Theoretical Archaeology Group, Oxford.
2003   *The Ecology of Power: Archaeology, History and Memory in the Southern Amazon*. Routledge, New York, in press.

Heckenberger, M. J., J. B. Peterson, and E. G. Neves
1999   Village Size and Permanence in Amazonia: Two Archaeological Examples from Brazil. *Latin American Antiquity* 10(4):353–376.

Heggie, D. C.
1981   *Megalithic Science: Ancient Mathematics and Astronomy in North-West Europe*. Thames and Hudson, London.

Heide, G.
2002   Mapping of the Fig Island Shell Rings. In *The Fig Island Ring Complex (38CH42): Coastal Adaptation and the Question of Ring Function in the Late Archaic*, by R. Saunders and M. Russo, pp. 67–84. Grant 45-01-16441, South Carolina Department of Archives and History, Columbia.
2003   The Coosaw Island Shell Ring Complex. Paper presented at the 29th Annual Meeting of the Conference on South Carolina Archaeology, Columbia.

Heimlich, M. D.
  1952   *Guntersville Basin Pottery.* Museum Paper 32, Geological Survey of Alabama, Tus-
          caloosa.
Hemmings, T.
  1970   Preliminary Report of Excavations at Fig Island, South Carolina. *Notebook* 2(9):9–
          15. Institute of Archaeology and Anthropology, University of South Carolina, Co-
          lumbia.
  1989   Cover illustration. In *Studies of Southeastern United States Aboriginal Shell Rings,*
          Part 2, edited by D. R. Lawrence. Department of Geological Sciences, University
          of South Carolina, Columbia.
  1991   Cover illustration. In *Studies of Southeastern United States Aboriginal Shell Rings,*
          Part 4, edited by D. R. Lawrence. Department of Geological Sciences, University
          of South Carolina, Columbia.
Hensley, C. K.
  1994   The Archaic Settlement System of the Middle Green River Valley, Kentucky. Un-
          published Ph.D. dissertation, Department of Anthropology, Washington Univer-
          sity, St. Louis.
Herr, S. A., and J. J. Clark
  2002   Mobility and the Organization of Prehispanic Southwest Communities. In *The Ar-*
          chaeology of Tribal Societies, edited by W. A. Parkinson, pp. 123–154. Archaeologi-
          cal Series 15, International Monographs in Prehistory, Ann Arbor, Michigan.
Hill, K., and A. M. Hurtado
  1996   *Ache Life History: The Ecology and Demography of a Foraging People.* Aldine De
          Gruyter, New York.
Hillman, M. M.
  1986   The 1985 Test Excavations of the "Dock" Area of Poverty Point. *Louisiana Archae-*
          ology 13:133–149.
Hively, R., and R. Horn
  1982   Geometry and Astronomy in Prehistoric Ohio. *Archaeoastronomy* 4:1–20.
  1984   Hopewellian Geometry and Astronomy at High Bank. *Archaeoastronomy* 7:S85–
          S100.
Hobbes, T.
  1968   [1651] *Leviathan.* Edited with an introduction by C. A. MacPherson. Penguin
          Books, Baltimore.
Holland, B. K.
  1998   *Probability without Equations: Concepts for Clinicians.* Johns Hopkins University
          Press, Baltimore.
Holley, G. R., R. A. Dalan, and P. A. Smith
  1993   Investigations in the Cahokia Site Grand Plaza. *American Antiquity* 1993:306–319.
Hopgood, J. F.
  1967   The Burkett Site (23MI20). In *Southeast Missouri Land Leveling Salvage Archeology,*
          by J. R. Williams. Submitted to the National Park Service, Midwest Region, Lin-
          coln, Nebraska.

Houck, B. A.

   1996   *Archaeological Excavations at 8LL717, Bonita Springs, Lee County, Florida. Ar-
           chaeological Historical Conservancy, Technical Report 78* [revision of 1993 report].
           Submitted to Bonita Bay Properties. Copies available from Bureau of Archaeologi-
           cal Research, Florida Division of Historical Resources, Tallahassee.

Howard, J. D., and C. B. DePratter

   1980   Field Trip Guide to the Archaeology-Geology of the Georgia Coast. In *Excursions
           in Southeastern Geology: The Archaeology-Geology of the Georgia Coast,* edited by
           J. D. Howard, C. B. DePratter, and R. W. Frey, pp. 234–253. Georgia Geologic
           Survey Guidebook 20, Department of Natural Resources, Environmental Protec-
           tion Division, Atlanta.

Howard, J. H.

   1968   *The Southeastern Ceremonial Complex and Its Interpretation.* Memoir No. 6, Mis-
           souri Archaeological Society, Columbia.

Howell, N.

   1976   Toward a Uniformitarian Theory of Human Paleodemography. In *The Demographic
           Evolution of Human Populations,* edited by H. T. Ward and K. M. Weiss, pp. 25–40.
           Academic Press, New York.

Howells, L. T., and S. W. Becker

   1962   Seating Arrangement and Leadership Emergence. *Journal of Abnormal and Social
           Psychology* 64(2):148–150.

Hudson, C.

   1976   *The Southeastern Indians.* University of Tennessee Press, Knoxville.

   1984   Elements of Southeastern Indian Religion. In *Iconography of Religions,* edited by
           T. P. van Baaren, L. P. van den Bosch, L. Leertouwer, F. Leemhuis, H. te Velde,
           H. Witte, and H. Buning, pp. 1–36. Section 10: North America, Fascicle 1. Insti-
           tute of Religious Iconography, State University Groningen. E. J. Brill, Leiden,
           Netherlands.

Hughes, D.

   1998   Excavations at 8LL71, Bonita Springs, Florida. Paper presented at the 50th Annual
           Meeting of the Florida Anthropology Society, Gainesville.

Hutterer, K. L.

   1991   Losing Track of the Tribes: Evolutionary Sequences in Southeast Asia. In *Profiles in
           Cultural Evolution: Papers from a Conference in Honor of Elman R. Service,* pp. 219–
           245. Anthropological Papers No. 85, Museum of Anthropology, University of
           Michigan, Ann Arbor.

Iceland, H.

   2000   Joseph Reed Shell Ring Lithics Report. In *Draft: The Joseph Reed Shell Ring,* by
           M. Russo and G. Heide, pp. 87–89. Submitted to Hobe Sound National Wildlife
           Refuge, Stuart, Florida. Copies available from Southeast Archeological Center, Na-
           tional Park Service, Tallahassee, Florida.

Ingold, T.

   1983   The Significance of Storage in Hunting Societies. *Man* 18:553–571.

   1988   Notes on the Foraging Mode of Production. In *Hunters and Gatherers,* vol. 1, *His-*

tory, Evolution and Social Change, edited by T. Ingold, D. Riches, and J. Woodburn, pp. 269–285. Berg, London.

1996   Hunting and Gathering as Ways of Perceiving the Environment. In *Redefining Nature: Ecology, Culture and Domestication*, edited by R. Ellen and K. Fukui, pp. 117–156. Berg, Oxford, U.K.

1999   On the Social Relations of the Hunter-Gatherer Band. In *The Cambridge Encyclopedia of Hunters and Gatherers*, edited by R. B. Lee and R. Daly, pp. 399–410. Cambridge University Press, Cambridge, U.K.

2000   *The Perception of the Environment. Essays in Livelihood, Dwelling and Skill.* Routledge, London.

Ingold, T., D. Riches, and J. Woodburn (editors)

1988   *Hunters and Gatherers*, vol. 1, *History, Evolution and Social Change.* Berg, London.

Isaac, B.

1990   Economy, Ecology, and Analogy: The !Kung San and the Generalized Foraging Model. In *Early Paleoindian Economies of Eastern North America*, edited by B. Isaac and K. Tankersley, pp. 323–335. Research in Economic Anthropology Supplement 5, JAI Press, Greenwich, Connecticut.

Jackson, H. E.

1991   The Trade Fair in Hunter-Gatherer Interaction: The Role of Intersocietal Trade in the Evolution of Poverty Point Culture. In *Between Bands and States*, edited by S. A. Gregg, pp. 265–286. Occasional Paper No. 9, Center for Archaeological Investigations, Southern Illinois University, Carbondale.

1996   Faunal Remains from the Watson Brake Mound Complex: A Preliminary Look at Archaic Subsistence Patterns. Paper presented at the 53rd Annual Meeting of the Southeastern Archaeological Conference, Birmingham, Alabama.

Jackson, H. E., and M. D. Jeter

1994   Preceramic Earthworks in Arkansas: A Report on the Poverty Point Period Lake Enterprise Mound (3AS379). *Southeastern Archaeology* 13(2):153–161.

Jackson, H. E., and S. L. Scott

1995   The Faunal Record of the Southeastern Elite: The Implications of Economy, Social Relations, and Ideology. *Southeastern Archaeology* 14(2):103–119.

2001   Archaic Faunal Utilization in the Louisiana Bottomlands. *Southeastern Archaeology* 20(2):187–196.

Jackson, H. E., S. L. Scott, and M. Sheffield

2001   Faunal Exploitation Strategies and the Emergence of Cultural Complexity in the Lower Mississippi Valley: New Data from Archaic Sites in Louisiana. Poster presentation at the 66th Annual Meeting of the Society for American Archaeology, New Orleans.

Jahn, O. L., and R. P. Bullen

1978   *The Tick Island Site, St. Johns River, Florida.* Publication 10, Florida Anthropological Society, Gainesville.

Jefferies, R. W.

1995   Late Middle Archaic Exchange and Interaction in the North American Midcontinent. In *Native American Interactions: Multiscalar Analyses and Interpretations in the*

Eastern Woodlands, edited by M. S. Nassaney and K. E. Sassaman, pp. 73–99. University of Tennessee Press, Knoxville.

1996 The Emergence of Long-Distance Exchange Networks in the Southeastern United States. In *Archaeology of the Mid-Holocene Southeast,* edited by K. E. Sassaman and D. G. Anderson, pp. 222–234. University Press of Florida, Gainesville.

1997 Middle Archaic Bone Pins: Evidence of Mid-Holocene Regional-Scale Social Groups in the Southern Midwest. *American Antiquity* 62:464–487.

Jenike, M. R.

2001 Nutritional Ecology: Diet, Physical Activity and Body Size. In *Hunter-Gatherers: An Interdisciplinary Perspective,* edited by C. Panter-Brick, R. H. Layton, and P. Rowley-Conwy, pp. 205–238. Cambridge University Press, Cambridge, U.K.

Jeter, M. D.

1984 Mound Volumes, Energy Ratios, Exotic Materials, and Contingency Tables: Comments on Some Recent Analyses of Copena Burial Practices. *Midcontinental Journal of Archaeology* 9(1):91–104.

Jeter, M. D., J. C. Rose, J. G. Ishmael Williams, and A. M. Harmon

1989 *Archeology and Bioarcheology of the Lower Mississippi Valley and Trans-Mississippi South in Arkansas and Louisiana.* Research Series No. 37, Arkansas Archeological Survey, Fayetteville.

Johnson, A. W., and T. Earle

1987 *The Evolution of Human Societies: From Foraging Group to Agrarian State.* Stanford University Press, Stanford, California.

Johnson, G. A.

1978 Information Sources and the Development of Decision-Making Organizations. In *Social Archaeology beyond Subsistence and Dating,* edited by C. L. Redman, M. J. Berman, E. V. Curtin, W. T. Langhorne, Jr., N. M. Versaggi, and J. C. Wanser, pp. 87–112. Academic Press, New York.

1982 Organizational Structure and Scalar Stress. In *Theory and Explanation in Archeology,* edited by C. Renfrew, M. Rowlands, and B. Segraves, pp. 389–422. Academic Press, New York.

1989 Dynamics of Southwestern Prehistory: Far Outside—Looking In. In *The Dynamics of Southwestern Prehistory,* edited by L. Cordell and G. Gumerman, pp. 209–262. Smithsonian Institution Press, Washington, D.C.

Johnson, J. K.

1987 Cahokia Core Technology in Mississippi: The View from the South. In *The Organization of Core Technology,* edited by J. K. Johnson and C. A. Morrow, pp. 187–206. Westview Press, Boulder, Colorado.

1993 Poverty Point Period Quartz Crystal Drill Bits, Microliths, and Social Organization in the Yazoo Basin, Mississippi. *Southeastern Archaeology* 12(1):59–64.

1994 Prehistoric Exchange in the Southeast. In *Prehistoric Exchange Systems in North America,* edited by T. G. Baugh and J. E. Ericson, pp. 99–125. Plenum Press, New York.

1996 Preliminary Analysis of Watson Brake Lithics. Paper presented at the 53rd Annual Meeting of the Southeastern Archaeological Conference, Birmingham, Alabama.

2000   Beads, Microdrills, Bifaces, and Blades from Watson Brake. *Southeastern Archaeology* 19(2):95–104.

Johnson, J. K., and S. O. Brookes

1989   Benton Points, Turkey Tails and Cache Blades: Middle Archaic Exchange in the Southeast. *Southeastern Archaeology* 8:134–145.

Jolly, F., III

1969   Painted Bone Ornament Fragment. *Journal of Alabama Archaeology* 15:67–71.

Jones, B.C.

1993   The Late Archaic Elliott's Point Complex in Northwest Florida. Paper presented at the 45th Annual Meeting of the Florida Anthropological Society, Clearwater.

Kaplan, D.

1960   The Law of Cultural Dominance. In *Evolution and Culture*, edited by M. Sahlins and E. Service, pp. 69–92. University of Michigan Press, Ann Arbor.

Keeley, L. H.

1988   Hunter-Gatherer Economic Complexity and "Population Pressure": A Cross-Cultural Analysis. *Journal of Anthropological Archaeology* 7:373–441.

1996   *War Before Civilization*. Oxford University Press, New York.

Kehoe, A. B.

1999   A Resort to Subtler Contrivances. In *Manifesting Power: Gender and the Interpretation of Power in Archaeology*, edited by T. Sweely, pp. 17–29. Routledge, London.

Keller, E. F.

1985   The Force of the Pacemaker Concept in Theories of Aggregation in Cellular Slime Mold. In *Reflections on Gender and Science*, by E. F. Keller, pp. 150–157. Yale University Press, New Haven, Connecticut.

Kelly, R. L.

1991   Sedentism, Sociopolitical Inequality, and Resource Fluctuations. In *Between Bands and States*, edited by S. A. Gregg, pp. 135–158. Occasional Paper No. 9, Center for Archaeological Investigations, Southern Illinois University, Carbondale.

1992   Mobility/Sedentism: Concepts, Archaeological Measures, and Effects. *Annual Review of Anthropology* 21:43–66.

1995   *The Foraging Spectrum: Diversity in Hunter-Gatherer Lifeways*. Smithsonian Institution Press, Washington, D.C.

Kent, S.

1989   Cross-Cultural Perceptions of Farmers as Hunters and the Value of Meat. In *Farmers as Hunters, The Implications of Sedentism*, edited by S. Kent, pp. 1–17. Cambridge University Press, New York.

1998   Gender and Prehistory in Africa. In *Gender in African Prehistory*, edited by S. Kent, pp. 9–24. AltaMira, Walnut Creek, California.

1999   Egalitarianism, Equality, and Equitable Power. In *Manifesting Power: Gender and the Interpretation of Power in Archaeology*, edited by T. Sweely, pp. 30–48. Routledge, London.

Kidder, T. R.

1991   New Directions in Poverty Point Settlement Archaeology: An Example from Northeast Louisiana. In *The Poverty Point Culture: Local Manifestations, Subsistence*

Practices, and Trade Networks, edited by K. M. Byrd, pp. 27–50. Geoscience and Man Vol. 29, Louisiana State University, Baton Rouge.

2002 Mapping Poverty Point. *American Antiquity* 67:89–101.

Kidder, T. R., and G. J. Fritz

1993 Subsistence and Social Change in the Lower Mississippi Valley: The Reno Brake and Osceola Sites, Louisiana. *Journal of Field Archaeology* 20:281–297.

Killick, D. J., A. J. T. Jull, and G. S. Burr

1999 A Failure to Discriminate: Querying Oxidizable Carbon Ratio (OCR) Dating. *Bulletin of the Society for American Archaeology* 17(5).

Kimbrough, R. M.

1999 A Norwood Simple Stamped Vessel from the Apalachicola National Forest, Florida. Paper presented at the 51st Annual Meeting of the Florida Anthropological Society, Fort Walton Beach.

Knight, V. J.

1986 The Institutional Organization of Mississippian Religion. *American Antiquity* 51: 675–685.

1989 Symbolism of Mississippian Mounds. In *Powhatan's Mantle: Indians in the Colonial Southeast*, edited by P. H. Wood, G. A. Waselkov, and M. T. Hatley, pp. 279–291. University of Nebraska Press, Lincoln.

1990 Social Organization and the Evolution of Hierarchy in Southeastern Chiefdoms. *Journal of Anthropological Research* 46:1–23.

1998 Moundville as a Diagrammatic Ceremonial Center. In *Archaeology of the Moundville Chiefdom*, edited by V. J. Knight, Jr., and V. P. Steponaitis, pp. 44–62. Smithsonian Institution Press, Washington, D.C.

2001 Feasting and the Emergence of Platform Mound Ceremonialism in Eastern North America. In *Feasts: Archaeological and Ethnographic Perspectives on Food, Politics, and Power*, edited by M. Dietler and B. Hayden, pp. 311–333. Smithsonian Institution Press, Washington, D.C.

Knoblock, B. W.

1939 *Bannerstones of the North American Indian*. Self-published, LaGrange, Illinois.

Knox, J. C.

1983 Responses of River Systems to Holocene Climate. In *Late Quaternary Environments of the United States*, pt. 2, *The Holocene*, edited by H. E. Wright, Jr., pp. 26–41. University of Minnesota Press, Minneapolis.

Koldehoff, B.

1987 The Cahokia Flake Tool Industry: Socioeconomic Implications for Late Prehistory in the Central Mississippi Valley. In *The Organization of Core Technology*, edited by J. K. Johnson and C. A. Morrow, pp. 151–186. Westview Press, Boulder, Colorado.

Kosse, K.

1996 Middle Range Societies from a Scalar Perspective. In *Interpreting Southwestern Diversity: Underlying Principles and Overarching Patterns*, edited by P. R. Fish and J. J. Reid, pp. 87–96. Anthropological Research Paper No. 48, Arizona State University, Tempe.

Krause, R. A.
    1989   The Archaic Stage and the Emergence of Hopewellian Ceremonialism in the
            Southeastern United States. *Mississippi Archaeology* 24:17–34.
Kuhn, T. S.
    1962   *The Structure of Scientific Revolutions.* University of Chicago Press, Chicago.
    1970   *The Structure of Scientific Revolutions,* 2nd ed. University of Chicago Press, Chi-
            cago.
Lafferty, R. H., III
    1994   Prehistoric Change in the Lower Mississippi Valley. In *Prehistoric Exchange Systems
            in North America,* edited by T. G. Baugh and J. E. Ericson, pp. 177–214. Plenum
            Press, New York.
    1998   Earthquakes, Ceramics and Chronology in the Cairo Lowland of Southeast Mis-
            souri. Paper presented at the 55th Annual Meeting of the Southeastern Archaeo-
            logical Conference, Greenville, South Carolina.
Lafferty, R. H., III, and K. M. Hess (editors)
    1996   *Archeological Investigations in the New Madrid Floodway.* Report 95-7, Mid-Continental
            Research Associates, Inc., Lowell, Arkansas.
Lakatos, I.
    1970   Falsification and the Methodology of Scientific Research Programmes. In *Criticism
            and the Growth of Knowledge,* edited by I. Lakatos and A. Musgrave, pp. 104–195.
            Cambridge University Press, Cambridge, U.K.
Lathrap, D. W.
    1985   Jaws: The Control of Power in the Early Nuclear American Ceremonial Center. In
            Early Andean Ceremonial Centers, edited by C. Donnan, pp. 241–267. Dumbarton
            Oaks, Washington, D.C.
Lawrence, D. R. (editor)
    1989   *Studies of Southeastern United States Aboriginal Shell Rings, Part 1.* Department of
            Geological Sciences, University of South Carolina, Columbia.
    1991   *Studies of Southeastern United States Aboriginal Shell Rings, Part 4.* Department of
            Geological Sciences, University of South Carolina, Columbia.
Lazarus, W. C.
    1958   A Poverty Point Complex in Florida. *The Florida Anthropologist* 11:23–32.
Leacock, E.
    1954   The Montagnais "Hunting Territory" and the Fur Trade. *American Anthropologist*
            Memoir 78.
    1980   Montagnais Women and the Jesuit Program for Colonization. In *Women and Colo-
            nization: Anthropological Perspectives,* edited by M. Etienne and E. Leacock. Praeger,
            New York.
    1982   Relations of Production in Band Societies. In *Politics and History in Band Societies,*
            edited by E. Leacock and R. B. Lee, pp. 159–170. Cambridge University Press,
            Cambridge, U.K.
Leacock, E., and R. B. Lee (editors)
    1982   *Politics and History in Band Societies.* Cambridge University Press, Cambridge, U.K.

Leahy, M. J.
1991 *Explorations into Highland New Guinea 1930–1935*. Edited by D. E. Jones. University of Alabama Press, Tuscaloosa.

Lee, R. B.
1969 !Kung Bushman Subsistence: An Input-Output Analysis. In *Environment and Cultural Behavior*, edited by A. Vayda, pp. 47–79. Natural History Press, Garden City, New York.
1976 Introduction. In *Kalahari Hunter-Gatherers: Studies of the !Kung San and Their Neighbors*, edited by R. B. Lee and I. DeVore, pp. 3–24. Harvard University Press, Cambridge, Massachusetts.
1979 *The !Kung San: Men, Women, and Work in a Foraging Society*. Cambridge University Press, Cambridge, U.K.
1988 Reflections on Primitive Communism. In *Hunters and Gatherers*, vol. 1, *History, Evolution and Social Change*, edited by T. Ingold, D. Riches, and J. Woodburn, pp. 252–268. Berg, London.
1990 Primitive Communism and the Origin of Social Inequality. In *The Evolution of Political Systems: Sociopolitics in Small Scale Sedentary Societies*, edited by S. Upham, pp. 225–246. Cambridge University Press, New York.
1992 Art, Science, or Politics? The Crisis in Hunter-Gatherer Studies. *American Anthropologist* 94:31–54.
2002 Solitude or Servitude? Ju/'hoansi Images of the Colonial Encounter. In *Ethnicity, Hunter Gatherers, and the "Other": Association or Assimilation in Africa*, edited by S. Kent, pp. 184–205. Smithsonian Institution Press, Washington, D.C.

Lee, R. B., and I. DeVore (editors)
1968 *Man the Hunter*. Aldine, Chicago.

Lee, R. B., and M. Guenther
1991 Oxen or Onions? The Search for Trade (and Truth) in the Kalahari. *Current Anthropology* 32:592–601.

Lehmann, G. R.
1991 Foreign Lithics of the Poverty Point Period in the Yazoo Basin. In *The Poverty Point Culture: Local Manifestations, Subsistence Practices, and Trade Networks*, edited by K. M. Byrd, pp. 187–192. Geoscience and Man Vol. 29, Louisiana State University, Baton Rouge.

Leigh, D. S.
2002 Soils at Fig Island. In *The Fig Island Ring Complex (38CH42): Coastal Adaptation and the Question of Ring Function in the Late Archaic*, by R. Saunders and M. Russo, pp. 184–203. Grant 45-01-16441, South Carolina Department of Archives and History, Columbia.

Lévi-Strauss, C.
1963 *Structural Anthropology*. Basic Books, New York.

Lewis, T. M. N., and M. Kneberg Lewis
1961 *Eva: An Archaic Site*. University of Tennessee Press, Knoxville.

Lincecum, G.
1904 Choctaw Traditions about Their Settlement in Mississippi and the Origin of Their Mounds. *Publications of the Mississippi Historical Society* 8:521–542.

Lorant, S. (editor)

　1946　*The New World: The First Pictures of America*. Duell, Sloan, and Pearce, New York.

McAnany, P. A.

　1995　*Living with the Ancestors: Kinship and Kingship in Ancient Maya Society*. University of Texas Press, Austin.

McGahey, S. O.

　1987　Paleo-Indian Lithic Material: Implications of Distributions in Mississippi. *Mississippi Archaeology* 22(2):1–13.

McGee, R. M., and R. G. Wheeler

　1994　Stratigraphic Excavations at Groves-Orange Midden, Lake Monroe, Volusia County, Florida: Methodology and Results. *The Florida Anthropologist* 47:333–349.

McKinley, W.

　1873　*Mounds in Georgia*. Annual Report for 1872, vol. 22, pp. 422–428, Smithsonian Institution Press, Washington, D.C.

McMichael, A. E.

　1982　A Cultural Resource Assessment of Horr's Island, Collier County, Florida. Unpublished Master's thesis, Department of Anthropology, University of Florida, Gainesville.

Mainfort, R. C., Jr., and L. P. Sullivan

　1998　Explaining Earthen Enclosures. In *Ancient Earthen Enclosures of the Eastern Woodlands*, edited by R. C. Mainfort, Jr., and L. P. Sullivan, pp. 1–16. University Press of Florida, Gainesville.

Malinowski, B.

　1929　*The Sexual Life of Savages in North-Western Melanesia*. Horace Liveright, New York.

Malmström, V. H.

　1997　*Cycles of the Sun, Mysteries of the Moon: The Calendar in Mesoamerican Civilization*. University of Texas Press, Austin.

Mann, M.

　1986　*The Sources of Social Power: A History of Power from the Beginning to A.D. 1760*. Cambridge University Press, Cambridge, U.K.

Manuel, J. O.

　1983　The Hornsby Site—16SH21: An Archaic Occupation in St. Helena Parish, Louisiana. Manuscript on file, Regional Archaeology Program, University of Louisiana, Monroe.

Marquardt, W. H.

　1985　Complexity and Scale in the Study of Fisher-Gatherer-Hunters: An Example from the Eastern United States. In *Prehistoric Hunter-Gatherers: The Emergence of Cultural Complexity*, edited by T. D. Price and J. A. Brown, pp. 59–98. Academic Press, New York.

Marquardt, W. H., and P. J. Watson

　1983　The Shell Mound Archaic of Western Kentucky. In *Archaic Hunters and Gatherers in the American Midwest*, edited by J. L. Phillips and J. A. Brown, pp. 323–339. Academic Press, New York.

Marrinan, R.

1975   Ceramics, Molluscs, and Sedentism: The Late Archaic Period on the Georgia
        Coast. Unpublished Ph.D. dissertation, Department of Anthropology, University
        of Florida, Gainesville.

Marshall, J. A.

1978   American Indian Geometry. *Ohio Archaeologist* 28(1):29–33.

1979   Geometry of the Hopewell Earthworks. *Early Man* (Spring):1–6.

1980   Geometry of the Hopewell Earthworks. *Ohio Archaeologist* 30(2):8–12.

1987   An Atlas of American Indian Geometry. *Ohio Archaeologist* 37(2):36–49.

1995   Astronomical Alignments Claimed to Exist on the Eastern North American Pre-
        historic Earthworks and the Evidence and Arguments against Them. *Ohio Archae-
        ologist* 45(1):4–16.

1997   Defining the Bounds of the Hopewell Core and Periphery Utilizing the Geometric
        Earthworks. *Ohio Archaeologist* 47(4):24–32.

1999   A Rebuttal to the Archaeoastronomers: Science Begins with the Facts. *Ohio Ar-
        chaeologist* 49(1):32–49.

Martin, M. K., and B. Voorhies

1975   *Female of the Species.* Columbia University Press, New York.

Mauss, M.

1990   *The Gift: Forms and Functions of Exchange in Archaic Societies.* Translated by W. D.
        Halls. Reprinted. Originally published 1950, W. W. Norton, New York.

Meehan, B.

1982   *Shell Bed to Shell Midden.* Australian Institute of Aboriginal Studies, Canberra.

Meeks, S. C.

1999   The "Function" of Stone Tools in Prehistoric Exchange Systems: A Look at Benton
        Interaction in the Mid-South. In *Raw Materials and Exchange in the Mid-South:
        Proceedings of the 16th Annual Mid-South Archaeological Conference, Jackson, Mis-
        sissippi, June 3–4, 1995,* edited by E. Peacock and S. O. Brookes, pp. 29–43.
        Archaeological Report No. 29, Mississippi Department of Archives and History,
        Jackson.

Meltzer, D. J.

1989   Was Stone Exchanged among Eastern North American Paleoindians? In *Eastern
        Paleoindian Lithic Resource Use,* edited by C. J. Ellis and J. C. Lothrop, pp. 11–40.
        Westview Press, Boulder, Colorado.

Mensforth, R. P.

2001   Warfare and Trophy Taking in the Archaic Period. In *Archaic Transitions in Ohio
        and Kentucky Prehistory,* edited by O. H. Prufer, S. E. Pedde, and R. S. Meindel,
        pp. 110–138. Kent State University Press, Kent, Ohio.

Michener, J.

1983   *Space.* Random House, New York.

Michie, J. L.

1976   The Daw's Island Shell Midden and Its Significance during the Shell Mound For-
        mative. Paper presented at the 2nd Annual Conference on South Carolina Arche-
        ology, Columbia.

346

Milanich, J. T.

1994   *Archaeology of Precolumbian Florida*. University Press of Florida, Gainesville.

Milanich, J. T., and C. H. Fairbanks

1980   *Florida Archaeology*. Academic Press, New York.

Miller, J. J.

1998   *An Environmental History of Northeast Florida*. University Press of Florida, Gainesville.

Mills, B. J.

2000   Alternative Models, Alternative Strategies, Leadership in the Prehispanic Southwest. In *Alternative Leadership Strategies in the Prehistoric Southwest*, edited by B. J. Mills, pp. 3–18. University of Arizona Press, Tucson.

Milner, G. R.

1998   *The Cahokia Chiefdom: The Archaeology of a Mississippian Society*. Smithsonian Institution Press, Washington, D.C.

1999   Warfare in Prehistoric and Early Historic Eastern North America. *Journal of Archaeological Research* 7:105–151.

Milner, G. R., E. Anderson, and V. G. Smith

1991   Warfare in Late Prehistoric West-Central Illinois. *American Antiquity* 56:581–603.

Milner, G. R., and R. W. Jefferies

1987   A Reevaluation of the WPA Excavation of the Robbins Mound in Boone County, Kentucky. In *Current Archaeological Research in Kentucky*, vol. 1, edited by D. Pollack, pp. 33–42. Kentucky Heritage Council, Frankfort.

1998   The Read Archaic Shell Midden in Kentucky. *Southeastern Archaeology* 17:119–132.

Moore, C. B.

1892   Supplementary Investigations at Tick Island. *American Naturalist* 26:128–143.

1893   Certain Shell Heaps of the St. Johns River, Florida, Hitherto Unexplored. *American Naturalist* 27:8–13, 113–117, 605–624, 708–729.

1894   Certain Sand Mounds of the St. Johns River, Florida, Part II. *Journal of the Academy of Natural Sciences of Philadelphia* 10:129–146.

1897   Certain Aboriginal Mounds of the Georgia Coast. *Journal of the Academy of Natural Sciences of Philadelphia* 11.

1916   Some Aboriginal Sites on Green River, Kentucky. *Journal of the Academy of Natural Sciences of Philadelphia* 16(3).

Moore, J. D.

1996   *Architecture & Power in the Ancient Andes: The Archaeology of Public Buildings*. New Studies in Archaeology. Cambridge University Press, Cambridge.

Morehead, J. R., L. J. Campbell, P. LaHaye, P. D. Bourgeois, Jr., J. H. Mathews, and P. M. Thomas, Jr.

1999   *Fort Polk 45: The Results of a Forty-Fifth Program of Site Testing at Ten Sites, Fort Polk Military Reservation, Vernon Parish, Louisiana*. Prentice Thomas and Associates, Inc., Report of Investigations No. 498, Fort Walton Beach, Florida.

Morey, D. F., and G. M. Crothers

1998   Clearing Up Clouded Waters: Paleoenvironmental Analysis of Freshwater Mussel Assemblages from the Green River Shell Middens, Western Kentucky. *Journal of Archaeological Science* 25:907–926.

Morgan, L. H.

1965 [1881] *Houses and House-Life of the American Aborigines.* University of Chicago Press, Chicago.

Morgan, R. G.

1937 Ohio's Prehistoric "Engineers." *The Ohio State Engineer* 20:2–5.

Morse, D. F.

1973 Dalton Culture in Northeast Arkansas. *The Florida Anthropologist* 26(1):23–38.

Morse, D. F. (editor)

1997 *Sloan: A Paleoindian Period Dalton Cemetery in Arkansas.* Smithsonian Institution Press, Washington, D.C.

Muller, J.

1997 *Mississippian Political Economy.* Plenum, New York.

Murdock, G. P.

1949 *Social Structure.* MacMillan, New York.

Nance, J. D.

1988 The Archaic Period in the Lower Tennessee-Cumberland-Ohio Region. In *Paleoindian and Archaic Research in Kentucky,* edited by C. D. Hockensmith, D. Pollack, and T. N. Sanders, pp. 127–152. Kentucky Heritage Council, Frankfort.

Neitzel, J. E., and D. G. Anderson

1999 Multiscalar Analyses of Middle Range Societies: Comparing the Late Prehistoric Southwest and Southeast. In *Great Towns and Regional Polities in the Prehistoric American Southwest and Southeast,* edited by J. E. Neitzel, pp. 243–254. Amerind Foundation New World Studies Series 3. University of New Mexico Press, Albuquerque.

Nelson, M.

1991 The Study of Technological Organization. In *Archaeological Method and Theory,* vol. 3, edited by M. B. Schiffer, pp. 57–100. University of Arizona Press, Tucson.

Neuman, R. W.

1984 *An Introduction to Louisiana Archaeology.* Louisiana State University Press, Baton Rouge.

1985 *Report on the Soil Core Borings Conducted at the Campus Mounds Site (16EBR6), East Baton Rouge Parish, Louisiana.* Copies available from Regional Archaeology Program, University of Louisiana, Monroe.

Nials, F. L., J. R. Stein, and J. R. Roney

1987 *Chacoan Roads in the Southern Periphery: Results of Phase II of the BLM Chaco Roads Project.* Cultural Resources Series I, Bureau of Land Management, U.S. Department of the Interior, Albuquerque, New Mexico.

North, D. C.

1990 *Institutions, Institutional Change and Economic Performance.* Cambridge University Press, Cambridge, U.K.

Parkington, J., and G. Mills

1991 From Space to Place: The Architecture and Social Organisation of Southern African Mobile Communities. In *Ethnoarchaeological Approaches to Mobile Camp Sites: Hunter-Gatherer and Pastoralist Case Studies,* edited by C. S. Gamble and

W. A. Boismier, pp. 355–370. Ethnological Series 1, International Monographs in Prehistory, Ann Arbor, Michigan.

Parkinson, W. A.

2002a Introduction: Archaeology and Tribal Societies. In *The Archaeology of Tribal Societies,* edited by W. A. Parkinson, pp. 1–12. Archaeological Series 15, International Monographs in Prehistory, Ann Arbor, Michigan.

2002b Integration, Interaction, and Tribal "Cycling": The Transition to the Copper Age on the Great Hungarian Plain. In *The Archaeology of Tribal Societies,* edited by W. A. Parkinson, pp. 391–438. Archaeological Series 15, International Monographs in Prehistory, Ann Arbor, Michigan.

Parry, W. J., and R. L. Kelly

1987 Expedient Core Technology and Sedentism. In *The Organization of Core Technology,* edited by J. K. Johnson and C. A. Morrow, pp. 285–304. Westview Press, Boulder, Colorado.

Pauketat, T. R.

2000 The Tragedy of the Commoners. In *Agency in Archaeology,* edited by M.-A. Dobres and J. Robb, pp. 113–129. Routledge, New York and London.

2001a A New Tradition in Archaeology. In *The Archaeology of Traditions: Agency and History before and after Columbus,* edited by T. R. Pauketat, pp. 1–16. University Press of Florida, Gainesville.

2001b Concluding Thoughts on Tradition, History, and Archaeology. In *The Archaeology of Traditions: Agency and History before and after Columbus,* edited by T. R. Pauketat, pp. 253–256. University Press of Florida, Gainesville.

2001c Practice and History in Archaeology. *Anthropological Theory* 1:73–98.

Pauketat, T. R., L. S. Kelly, G. J. Fritz, N. H. Lopinot, S. Elias, and E. Hargrave

2002 The Residues of Feasting and Public Ritual at Early Cahokia. *American Antiquity* 67:257–279.

Paynter, R.

1989 The Archaeology of Equality and Inequality. *Annual Review of Anthropology* 18: 369–399.

Peebles, C., and S. Kus

1977 Some Archaeological Correlates of Ranked Societies. *American Antiquity* 42:421–448.

Peterson, J. H., Jr. (editor)

1985 *A Choctaw Sourcebook.* Garland, New York.

Phelps, D. S.

1965 The Norwood Series of Fiber-Tempered Ceramics. *Southeastern Archaeological Conference Bulletin* 2:65–69.

Phillips, P.

1970 *Archaeological Survey in the Lower Yazoo Basin, Mississippi, 1949–1955.* Papers of the Peabody Museum of American Archaeology and Ethnology No. 60, Harvard University, Cambridge, Massachusetts.

1973 Introduction. *Exploration of Ancient Key Dweller's Remains on the Gulf Coast of Florida,* by F. H. Cushing. AMS, New York.

Phillips, P., J. A. Ford, and J. B. Griffin

1951 *Archaeological Survey in the Lower Mississippi Alluvial Valley, 1940–1947.* Papers of the Peabody Museum of American Archaeology and Ethnology No. 25, Harvard University, Cambridge, Massachusetts.

Piatek, B. J.

1994 The Tomoka Mound Complex in Northeast Florida. *Southeastern Archaeology* 13:109–118.

Pielou, E. C.

1991 *After the Ice Age: The Return of Life to Glaciated North America.* University of Chicago Press, Chicago.

Pleger, T. C.

2000 Old Copper and Red Ocher Social Complexity. *Midcontinental Journal of Archaeology* 25:169–190.

Porter, D., and M. J. Guccione

1996 Geomorphology of the Cairo Lowland. In *Archaeological Investigations of the New Madrid Floodway,* by Mid-Continental Research Associates, Inc. Submitted to the Memphis District Corps of Engineers. Report 95-7, Mid-Continental Research Associates, Inc., Lowell, Arkansas.

Powell, M. L.

1988 *Status and Health in Prehistory.* Smithsonian Institution Press, Washington, D.C.

Poyer, L.

1991 Maintaining Egalitarianism: Social Equality on a Micronesian Atoll. In *Between Bands and States,* edited by S. A. Gregg, pp. 359–375. Occasional Paper No. 9, Center for Archaeological Investigations, Southern Illinois University, Carbondale.

Pozorski, S., and T. Pozorski

1987 *Early Settlement and Subsistence in the Casma Valley, Peru.* University of Iowa Press, Iowa City.

Price, T. D.

1995 Social Inequality at the Origins of Agriculture. In *Foundations of Social Inequality,* edited by T. D. Price and G. M. Feinman, pp. 129–151. Plenum Press, New York.

Price, T. D., and J. A. Brown (editors)

1985 *Prehistoric Hunter-Gatherers: The Emergence of Cultural Complexity.* Academic Press, New York.

Price, T. D., and G. M. Feinman

1995 Foundations of Prehistoric Social Inequality. In *Foundations of Social Inequality,* edited by T. D. Price and G. M. Feinman, pp. 3–11. Plenum Press, New York.

Pringle, H.

1997 Oldest Mound Complex Found at Louisiana Site. *Science* 277:1761–1762.

Purdy, B. A.

1996 *The Art and Archaeology of Florida's Wetlands.* CRC Press, Boca Raton, Florida.

Quitmyer, I. R., and M. A. Massaro

1999 Seasonality and Subsistence in a Southwest Florida Estuary: A Faunal Analysis of Precolumbian Useppa Island. In *The Archaeology of Useppa Island,* edited by W. H.

Marquardt, pp. 99–128. Monograph 3, Institute of Archaeology and Paleoenvironmental Studies, University of Florida, Gainesville.

Rathje, W. L.
1974   The Garbage Project. A New Way of Looking at the Problems of Archaeology. *Archaeology* 27(4):236–241.

Rau, C.
1878   *The Stock-in-Trade of an Aboriginal Lapidary.* Annual Report for 1877, pp. 291–298, Smithsonian Institution Press, Washington, D.C.

Redmond, E. M.
2002   The Long and Short of a War Leader's Arena. In *The Archaeology of Tribal Societies,* edited by W. A. Parkinson, pp. 53–73. Archaeological Series 15, International Monographs in Prehistory, Ann Arbor, Michigan.

Reed, D. M.
1998   Ancient Maya Diet at Copán, Honduras. Unpublished Ph.D. dissertation, Department of Anthropology, Pennsylvania State University, University Park.

Renfrew, C.
1974   Beyond Subsistence Economy: The Evolution of Social Organization in Prehistoric Europe. In *Reconstructing Complex Societies,* edited by C. B. Moore, pp. 69–85. Bulletin Supplement No. 20, American Schools of Oriental Research, Cambridge, Massachusetts.
2001   Production and Consumption in a Sacred Economy: The Material Correlates of High Devotional Expression at Chaco Canyon. *American Antiquity* 66:14–25.

Renouf, M. A. P.
1991   Sedentary Hunter-Gatherers: A Case for Northern Coasts. In *Between Bands and States,* edited by S. A. Gregg, pp. 89–107. Occasional Paper No. 9, Center for Archaeological Investigations, Southern Illinois University, Carbondale.

Ritchie, W. A.
1932   *The Lamoka Lake Site: The Type Station of the Archaic Algonkin Period in New York.* Researches and Transactions of the New York State Archeological Association Vol. 7, No. 4, Rochester Museum of Arts and Sciences, Rochester, New York.

Rodbell, D. T., G. O. Seltzer, D. M. Anderson, M. B. Abbott, D. B. Enfield, and J. H. Newman
1999   An ~15,000-Year Record of El Niño–Driven Alluviation in Southwestern Ecuador. *Science* 283:516–520.

Rolingson, M. A., and J. M. Howard
1997   Igneous Lithics of Central Arkansas: Identification, Sources, and Artifact Distribution. *Southeastern Archaeology* 16(1):33–50.

Romain, W. F.
2000   *Mysteries of the Hopewell, Astronomers, Geometers, and Magicians of the Eastern Woodlands.* University of Akron Press, Akron, Ohio.

Roney, J. R.
1992   Prehistoric Roads and Regional Integration in the Chacoan System. In *Anasazi Regional Organization and the Chaco System,* edited by D. E. Doyel, pp. 123–131.

Maxwell Museum of Anthropology Anthropological Papers No. 5, University of New Mexico, Albuquerque.

Roosevelt, A. C.

1995   Early Pottery in the Amazon: Twenty Years of Scholarly Obscurity. In *The Emergence of Pottery*, edited by W. Barnett and J. Hoopes, pp. 115–132. Smithsonian Institution Press, Washington, D.C.

Roosevelt, A. C., M. Lima da Costa, C. Lopes Machado, M. Michab, N. Mercier, H. Valladas, J. Feathers, W. Barnett, M. Imazio da Silveira, A. Henderson, J. Sliva, B. Chernoff, D. S. Reese, J. A. Holman, N. Toth, and K. Schick

1996   Paleoindian Cave Dwellers in the Amazon: The Peopling of the Americas. *Science* 272:373–384.

Root, D.

1983   Information Exchange and the Spatial Configurations of Egalitarian Societies. In *Archaeological Hammers and Theories*, edited by J. A. Moore and A. S. Keene, pp. 193–219. Academic Press, Orlando, Florida.

Roshto, J.

1985   Ogeechee River Bodkins. *Central States Archaeological Journal* 33:102–103.

Rothschild, N. A.

1979   Mortuary Behavior and Social Organization. *American Antiquity* 44:658–675.

Rowley-Conwy, P.

2001   Time, Change and the Archaeology of Hunter-Gatherers: How Original Is the "Original Affluent Society." In *Hunter-Gatherers: An Interdisciplinary Perspective*, edited by C. Panter-Brick, R. H. Layton, and P. Rowley-Conwy, pp. 39–72. Cambridge University Press, Cambridge, U.K.

Russo, M.

1991   *Archaic Sedentism on the Florida Coast: A Case Study from Horr's Island*. Ph.D. dissertation, Department of Anthropology, University of Florida. University Microfilms, Ann Arbor, Michigan.

1992a   Chronologies and Cultures of the St. Marys Region of Northeast Florida and Southern Georgia. *The Florida Anthropologist* 45:107–126.

1992b   Characterization and Function of Archaic Shell and Earth Mounds in Southwest Florida. Paper presented at the 49th Annual Meeting of the Southeastern Archaeological Conference, New Orleans.

1994a   A Brief Introduction to the Archaic Mounds in the Southeast. *Southeastern Archaeology* 13:89–93.

1994b   Why We Don't Believe in Archaic Ceremonial Mounds and Why We Should: The Case from Florida. *Southeastern Archaeology* 13:93–108.

1996a   Southeastern Preceramic Archaic Ceremonial Mounds. In *Archaeology of the Mid-Holocene Southeast*, edited by K. E. Sassaman and D. G. Anderson, pp. 259–287. University Press of Florida, Gainesville.

1996b   Southeastern Mid-Holocene Coastal Settlements. In *Archaeology of the Mid-Holocene Southeast*, edited by K. E. Sassaman and D. G. Anderson, pp. 177–199. University Press of Florida, Gainesville.

2002   Architectural Features at Fig Island. In *The Fig Island Ring Complex (38CH42):*

Coastal Adaptation and the Question of Ring Function in the Late Archaic, by R. Saunders and M. Russo, pp. 85–97. Grant 45-01-16441, South Carolina Department of Archives and History, Columbia.

Russo, M., A. S. Cordell, L. A. Newsom, and S. J. Scudder
 1991   *Final Report on Horr's Island: The Archaeology of Archaic and Glades Settlement and Subsistence Patterns.* Submitted to Key Marco Developments. Copies available from Florida Museum of Natural History, Department of Anthropology, Gainesville.

Russo, M., A. S. Cordell, and D. L. Ruhl
 1993   *The Timucuan Ecological and Historic Preserve Phase III, Final Report.* Accession No. 899, Southeast Archeological Center, National Park Service, Tallahassee, Florida.

Russo, M., and J. Fogleman
 1994   Stelly Mounds (16SL1): An Archaic Mound Complex. *Louisiana Archaeology* 21:127–158.

Russo, M., and G. Heide
 2000   *Draft: The Joseph Reed Shell Ring.* Submitted to Hobe Sound National Wildlife Refuge, Stuart, Florida. Copies available from Southeast Archeological Center, National Park Service, Tallahassee, Florida.
 2001   Shell Rings of the Southeast US. *Antiquity* 75(289):491–492.
 2002   The Joseph Reed Shell Ring (8Mt13). *The Florida Anthropologist* 55(2):67–87.

Russo, M., G. Heide, and V. Rolland
 2002   *The Guana Shell Ring.* Historic Preservation Grant F0126, Florida Division of Historical Resources, Bureau of Archaeological Resources, Tallahassee.

Russo, M., and D. Ste. Claire
 1992   Tomoka Stone: Archaic Period Coastal Settlement in East Florida. *The Florida Anthropologist* 45(4):336–346.

Russo, M., and R. Saunders
 1999   *Identifying the Early Use of Coastal Fisheries and the Rise of Social Complexity in Shell Rings and Arcuate Middens on Florida's Northeast Coast.* Submitted to National Geographic Society. Copies available from Southeast Archeological Center, National Park Service, Tallahassee, Florida.

Sahlins, M.
 1961   The Segmentary Lineage: An Organization of Predatory Expansion. *American Anthropologist* 63:332–345.
 1968a   Notes on the Original Affluent Society. In *Man the Hunter,* edited by R. B. Lee and I. DeVore, pp. 85–89. Aldine, Chicago.
 1968b   *Tribesmen.* Prentice-Hall, Englewood Cliffs, New Jersey.
 1972   *Stone Age Economics.* Aldine, Chicago.
 1998   The Original Affluent Society. In *Limited Wants, Unlimited Means: A Reader on Hunter-Gatherer Economics and the Environment,* edited by J. Gowdy, pp. 5–41. Island Press, Washington, D.C. Originally published 1972 in *Stone Age Economics,* by M. Sahlins, Aldine, Chicago.

Sahlins, M., and E. Service
 1960   *Evolution and Culture.* University of Michigan Press, Ann Arbor.

Saitta, D. J.

 1997 Power, Labor, and the Dynamics of Change in Chacoan Political Economy. *American Antiquity* 62:7–26.

Sanday, P. R.

 1981 The Socio-Cultural Context of Rape: A Cross-Cultural Study. *Journal of Social Issues* 37:5–27.

Sandweiss, D. H., K. A. Maasch, D. G. Anderson

 1999 Climate and Culture: Transitions in the Mid-Holocene. *Science* 283:499–500.

Sandweiss, D. H., J. B. Richardson III, E. J. Reitz, H. B. Rollins, and K. A. Maasch

 1996 Geoarchaeological Evidence from Peru for a 5000 Years B. P. Onset of El Niño. *Science* 273:1531–1533.

Sapir, E.

 1915 The Social Organization of the West Coast Tribes. *Proceedings and Transactions of the Royal Society of Canada* 9:355–374.

Sassaman, K. E.

 1991 Adaptive Flexibility in the Morrow Mountain Phase of the Middle Archaic Period. *South Carolina Antiquities* 23:31–41.

 1993 *Early Pottery Technology in the Southeast: Tradition and Innovation in Cooking Technology.* University of Alabama Press, Tuscaloosa.

 1994 Production for Exchange in the Mid-Holocene Southeast: A Savannah River Valley Example. *Lithic Technology* 19:42–51.

 1995 The Cultural Diversity of Interactions among Mid-Holocene Societies of the American Southeast. In *Native American Interactions: Multiscalar Analyses and Interpretations in the Eastern Woodlands*, edited by M. S. Nassaney and K. E. Sassaman, pp. 174–204. University of Tennessee Press, Knoxville.

 1996 Technological Innovations in Economic and Social Contexts. In *Archaeology of the Mid-Holocene Southeast*, edited by K. E. Sassaman and D. G. Anderson, pp. 57–74. University Press of Florida, Gainesville.

 1997 The Symbolism of Circles: The Stalling's Culture. From South Carolina Archaeology Week poster *Shell Rings of the Late Archaic*. South Carolina Institute of Archaeology and Anthropology, University of South Carolina, Columbia.

 2001 Hunter-Gatherers and Traditions of Resistance. In *The Archaeology of Traditions: Agency and History before and after Columbus*, edited by T. R. Pauketat, pp. 218–236. University Press of Florida, Gainesville.

Sassaman, K. E., and D. G. Anderson (editors)

 1996 *Archaeology of the Mid-Holocene Southeast.* University Press of Florida, Gainesville.

Sassaman, K. E., G. T. Hanson, and T. Charles

 1988 Raw Material Procurement and Reduction of Hunter-Gatherer Range in the Savannah River Valley. *Southeastern Archaeology* 7:79–94.

Sassaman, K. E., and M. J. Heckenberger

 2001 Roots of the Theocratic Formative of the Archaic Southeast. Paper presented at Hunters and Gatherers in Theory and Archaeological Research, the SIU Visiting Scholar Conference, Carbondale, Illinois.

Sassaman, K. E., and R. J. Ledbetter
  1996   Middle and Late Archaic Architecture. In *Archaeology of the Mid-Holocene South-east,* edited by K. E. Sassaman and D. G. Anderson, pp. 75–95. University Press of Florida, Gainesville.

Saucier, R. T.
  1974   *Quaternary Geology of the Lower Mississippi Valley.* Research Series No. 6, Arkansas Archeological Survey, Fayetteville.
  1990   Relationship of the Beckwith's Fort Site (23MI2) (Towosahgy State Historic Site) to the Physical Environment. In *Archeological Investigations in Three Areas of the Towosahgy State Historic Site, 23MI2, Mississippi County, Missouri, 1989,* by J. E. Price, G. L. Fox, and R. T. Saucier. Submitted to Division of Parks, Recreation and Historic Preservation. Copies available from American Archaeology Division, University of Missouri, Columbia.
  1994   *Geomorphology and Quaternary Geologic History of the Lower Mississippi Valley I.* U.S. Army Engineer Waterways Experiment Station, Vicksburg, Mississippi.

Saunders, J. W.
  1993   *1993 Annual Report for Management Unit 2.* College of Pure and Applied Sciences, Department of Geosciences, University of Louisiana, Monroe.

Saunders, J. W., and E. T. Allen
  1994   Hedgepeth Mounds: An Archaic Mound Complex in North-Central Louisiana. *American Antiquity* 59(3):471–489.
  1998   The Archaic Period. *Louisiana Archaeology* 22:1–30.

Saunders, J. W., E. T. Allen, R. Jones, and G. Swoveland
  2000   Caney Mounds (16CT5). *Louisiana Archaeological Society Newsletter* 27:14–21.

Saunders, J. W., E. T. Allen, D. LaBatt, R. Jones, and D. L. Griffing
  2001   An Assessment of the Antiquity of the Lower Jackson Mound South of Poverty Point. *Southeastern Archaeology* 20:67–77.

Saunders, J. W., E. T. Allen, and R. T. Saucier
  1994   Four Archaic? Mound Complexes in Northeast Louisiana. *Southeastern Archaeology* 13:134–153.

Saunders, J. W., R. Jones, K. Moorhead, and B. Davis
  1998   "Watson Brake Objects," an Unusual Artifact Type from Northeast Louisiana. *Southeastern Archaeology* 17:72–79.

Saunders, J. W., R. D. Mandel, R. T. Saucier, E. T. Allen, C. T. Hallmark, J. K. Johnson, E. H. Jackson, C. M. Allen, G. L. Stringer, D. S. Frink, J. K. Feathers, S. Williams, K. J. Gremillion, M. F. Vidrine, and R. Jones
  1997   A Mound Complex in Louisiana at 5400–5000 Years before Present. *Science* 277:1796–1799.

Saunders, R.
  1994   The Case for Archaic Period Mounds in Southeast Louisiana. *Southeastern Archaeology* 13:118–134.
  1999   Feast or Quotidian Fare? Rollins Shell Ring and the Question of Ring Function. Paper presented at the 56th Annual Meeting of the Southeastern Archaeological Conference, Pensacola, Florida.

2002a   Field Excavations: Methods and Results. In *The Fig Island Ring Complex (38CH42):* *Coastal Adaptation and the Question of Ring Function in the Late Archaic*, by R. Saunders and M. Russo, pp. 98–140. Grant 45-01-16441, South Carolina Department of Archives and History, Columbia.

2002b   Summary and Conclusions. In *The Fig Island Ring Complex (38CH42): Coastal Adaptation and the Question of Ring Function in the Late Archaic*, by R. Saunders and M. Russo, pp. 154–159. Grant 45-01-16441, South Carolina Department of Archives and History, Columbia.

2003   Feast or Quotidian Fare? Rollins Shell Ring and the Question of Ring Function. Manuscript in the possession of the author.

Saunders, R., and M. Russo

2002   *The Fig Island Ring Complex (38CH42): Coastal Adaptation and the Question of Ring Function in the Late Archaic*. Grant 45-01-16441, South Carolina Department of Archives and History, Columbia.

Schiefenhövel, W., and I. Bell-Krannhals

1996   Of Harvests and Hierarchies: Securing Staple Food and Social Position in the Trobriand Islands. In *Food and Status Quest: An Interdisciplinary Perspective*, edited by P. Weissner and W. Schiefenhövel, pp. 235–352. Berghahn Books, Providence, Rhode Island.

Scholten de D'Éneth, M.

1954   Geometría y Geográfica Humana en Sudamerica. *Revista del Museo Nacional* 23: 241–259.

1956   Geometría y Geográfica Humana en Sudamerica II.—La Barra Mágica. *Revista del Museo Nacional* 25:264–274.

1958   Un Posible Sistema de la Antropo-Geografía del Perú Antiguo. *Actas y Trabajos del II Congreso Nacional de Historia del Perú: Epoca Prehispánica*, p. 339.

1970   La Unidad de Medida en América Pre-hispánica. *XXXIX Congreso Internacional de Americanistas*, Lima, Peru.

1977   *La Ruta de Wirakocha*. Editorial Juan Mejía Baca, Lima, Peru.

1980   *Chavin de Huantar: 1. Deseño Arquetectónico del Conjunto Arqueológico*. Editorial Juan Mejía Baca, Lima, Peru.

1981   *Chavin de Huantar: 2. Piedras Esculpidas*. Editorial Juan Mejía Baca, Lima, Peru.

1985   *TUPU: Symbol of Integration* (Bilengual). Editorial Juan Mejía Baca, Lima, Peru.

Schrire, C.

1980   An Enquiry in the Evolutionary Status and Apparent Identity of San Hunter-Gatherers. *Human Ecology* 8(1):9–32.

1984   Wild Surmises on Savage Thoughts. In *Past and Present in Hunter-Gatherer Studies*, edited by C. Schrire, pp. 1–25. Academic Press, Orlando, Florida.

Service, E. R.

1962   *Primitive Social Organization*. Random House, New York.

1975   *Origins of the State and Civilization: The Process of Cultural Evolution*. W. W. Norton, New York.

Shannon, G. W., Jr.

1986   The Southeastern Fiber-Tempered Ceramic Tradition Reconsidered. In *Papers in Ceramic Analysis*, edited by P. M. Rice, pp. 47–80. Ceramic Notes No. 3, Occasional Publications of the Ceramic Technology Laboratory, Florida State Museum, Gainesville.

1987   A Reconsideration of Formative Cultural Development in the Southeastern United States. Unpublished Ph.D. dissertation, Department of Anthropology, Michigan State University, East Lansing.

Shott, M. J.

1990   Stone Tools and Economics: Great Lakes Paleoindian Examples. In *Early Paleoindian Economies of Eastern North America,* edited by K. B. Tankersley and B. L. Isaac, pp. 3–44. Research in Economic Anthropology, Supplement 5, JAI Press, Greenwich, Connecticut.

Simpkins, D. L.

1975   A Preliminary Report on Test Excavations at the Sapelo Island Shell Ring, 1975. *Early Georgia* 3:15–37.

Small, J. F

1966   Additional Information on Poverty Point Baked Clay Objects. *The Florida Anthropologist* 19:65–76.

Smith, B. D.

1986   The Archaeology of the Southeastern United States: From Dalton to deSoto, 10,500 to 500 BP. *Advances in World Archaeology* 5:1–92.

1987   The Independent Domestication of Indigenous Seed-Bearing Plants in Eastern North America. In *Emergent Horticultural Economies of the Eastern Woodlands,* edited by W. T. Keegan, pp. 3–47. Occasional Paper No. 7, Center for Archaeological Investigations, Southern Illinois University, Carbondale.

1989   Origins of Agriculture in Eastern North America. *Science* 246:1566–1571.

1990   *The Mississippian Emergence.* Smithsonian Institution Press, Washington, D.C.

1992a   Prehistoric Plant Husbandry in Eastern North America. In *The Origins of Agriculture: An International Perspective,* edited by C. W. Cowan and P. J. Watson, pp. 101–119. Smithsonian Institution Press, Washington, D.C.

1992b   Hopewellian Farmers of Eastern North America. In *Rivers of Change: Essays on Early Agriculture in Eastern North America,* edited by B. D. Smith, pp. 201–248. Smithsonian Institution Press, Washington, D.C.

1994   *The Emergence of Agriculture.* Scientific American Library, New York.

Smith, B. D. (editor)

1992   *Rivers of Change: Essays on Early Agriculture in Eastern North America.* Smithsonian Institution Press, Washington, D.C.

Smith, B. D., W. Cowan, and M. P. Hoffman

1992   Is It an Indigene or a Foreigner? In *Rivers of Change: Essays on Early Agriculture in Eastern North America,* edited by B. D. Smith, pp. 67–100. Smithsonian Institution Press, Washington, D.C.

Smith, B. W.

1991   The Late Archaic–Poverty Point Trade Network. In *The Poverty Point Culture: Local Manifestations, Subsistence Practices, and Trade Networks,* edited by K. M. Byrd, pp. 173–180. Geoscience and Man Vol. 29, Louisiana State University, Baton Rouge.

Smith, H. M.

1969   The Murdock Mound: Cahokia Site. In *Explorations into Cahokia Archaeology*, edited by M. L. Fowler, pp. 49–88. Bulletin 7, Illinois Archaeological Survey, Urbana.

Smith, M. O.

1995   Scalping in the Archaic Period: Evidence from the Western Tennessee Valley. *Southeastern Archaeology* 14:60–68.

1996   Bioarchaeological Inquiry into Archaic Period Populations of the Southeast: Trauma and Occupational Stress. In *Archaeology of the Mid-Holocene Southeast*, edited by K. E. Sassaman and D. G. Anderson, pp. 134–154. University Press of Florida, Gainesville.

1997   Osteological Indications of Warfare in the Archaic Period of the Western Tennessee Valley. In *Troubled Times: Violence and Warfare in the Past*, edited by D. L. Martin and D. W. Frayer. Gordon and Breach, Amsterdam, The Netherlands.

Snow, D. R.

2002   The Dynamics of Ethnicity in Tribal Society: A Penobscot Case Study. In *The Archaeology of Tribal Societies*, edited by W. A. Parkinson, pp. 97–108. Archaeological Series 15, International Monographs in Prehistory, Ann Arbor, Michigan.

Solway, J. S., and R. B. Lee

1990   Foragers, Genuine or Spurious? Situating the Kalahari San in History. *Current Anthropology* 31:109–146.

Sommer, R.

1961   Leadership and Group Geography. *Sociometry* 24(1):99–110.

Sparks, J. T.

1987   *Prehistoric Settlement Patterns in Clay County, Mississippi.* Archaeological Report No. 20, Mississippi Department of Archives and History, Jackson.

Speth, J. D.

1990   Seasonality, Resource Stress, and Food Sharing in So-Called "Egalitarian" Foraging Societies. *Journal of Anthropological Archaeology* 9:148–188.

Spinden, H. J.

1917   The Origin and Distribution of Agriculture in America. In *Proceedings of the 19th Annual International Congress of Americanists*, pp. 269–278. Washington, D.C.

Squier, E. G., and E. H. Davis

1848   *Ancient Monuments of the Mississippi Valley.* Smithsonian Contributions to Knowledge Vol. 1, Smithsonian Institution Press, Washington, D.C.

Staeck, J. P.

1996   Ranking, Marriage, and Power: Reflections of Ho-Chunk (Winnebago) Oral Traditions on Effigy Mound Transegalitarian Strategies for Developing Power and Prestige. Paper presented at the Midwest Archaeological Conference, Beloit, Wisconsin. Available on-line at http://www.cod.edu/people/faculty/staeck/mac96.htm.

Stange, M. Z.

1998   *Woman the Hunter.* Beacon Press, Boston.

Steinzor, B.

1950   The Spatial Factor in Face-to-Face Discussion Groups. *Journal of Abnormal and Social Psychology* 45:552–555.

Stephenson, K., J. Bense, and F. Snow
2002   Aspects of Deptford and Swift Creek of the South Atlantic and Gulf Coastal Plains. In *The Woodland Southeast,* edited by D. G. Anderson and R. C. Mainfort, Jr., pp. 318–351. University of Alabama Press, Tuscaloosa.

Steponaitis, V. P.
1978   Location Theory and Complex Chiefdoms: A Mississippian Example. In *Mississippian Settlement Patterns,* edited by B. D. Smith, pp. 417–453. Academic Press, New York.

Stoltman, J. B.
1992   The Concept of Archaic in Eastern North American Prehistory. *Revista de Arqueología Americana* 5:101–118.

Stringer, G. L.
2001   Analysis of Fish Otoliths from Watson Brake. Manuscript on file, Regional Archaeology Program, University of Louisiana, Monroe.

Stringer, G. L., W. P. Patterson, and C. Strickland
2002   Seasonality and Paleotemperatures of Louisiana Archaic Sites as Indicated by Fish Otoliths. Paper presented at the 59th Annual Meeting of the Southeastern Archaeological Conference, Biloxi, Mississippi.

Sugiyama, S.
1993   Worldview Materialized in Teotihuacan, Mexico. *Latin American Antiquity* 4:103–129.

Swanton, J. R.
1911   *Indian Tribes of the Lower Mississippi Valley and Adjacent Coast of the Gulf of Mexico.* Bulletin 43, Bureau of American Ethnology, Smithsonian Institution Press, Washington, D.C.

1928a   *Social Organization and Social Usages of the Indians of the Creek Confederacy.* Forty-Second Annual Report, Bureau of American Ethnology, Smithsonian Institution Press, Washington, D.C.

1928b   *The Interpretation of Aboriginal Mounds by Means of Creek Indian Customs.* Annual Report for 1927, Smithsonian Institution, Smithsonian Institution Press, Washington, D.C.

1931   *Source Material for the Social and Ceremonial Life of the Choctaw Indians.* Bulletin 103, Bureau of American Ethnology, Smithsonian Institution Press, Washington, D.C.

Tanner, H. H.
1989   The Land and Water Communication Systems of the Southeastern Indians. In *Powhatan's Mantle: Indians in the Colonial Southeast,* edited by P. H. Wood, G. A. Waselkov, and M. T. Hatley, pp. 6–20. University of Nebraska Press, Lincoln.

Testart, A.
1982   The Significance of Food Storage among Hunter-Gatherers: Residence Patterns, Population Densities, and Social Inequalities. *Current Anthropology* 25:523–537.

Thomas, C.
1889   *The Circular, Square, and Octagonal Earthworks of Ohio.* Smithsonian Institution Press, Washington, D.C.

Thomas, J.
 1991   *Rethinking the Neolithic*. Cambridge University Press, Cambridge, U.K.

Thompson, V., M. Reynolds, B. Haley, R. Jefferies, J. Johnson, and C. Humphries
 2002   The Sapelo Shell Rings Site: Remote Sensing on a Georgia Island. Paper presented
        at the 59th Annual Meeting of the Southeastern Archaeological Conference,
        Biloxi, Mississippi.

Trigger, B.
 1990a Monumental Architecture: A Thermodynamic Explanation of Symbolic Behavior.
        World Archaeology 22:119–132.
 1990b Comment on Foragers, Genuine or Spurious? Situating the Kalahari San in His-
        tory. *Current Anthropology* 31:135.
 1990c Maintaining Economic Equality in Opposition to Complexity: An Iroquoian Case
        Study. In *The Evolution of Political Systems: Sociopolitics in Small Scale Sedentary
        Societies*, edited by S. Upham, pp. 119–145. Cambridge University Press, New
        York.

Trinkley, M. B.
 1980   Investigation of the Woodland Period along the South Carolina Coast. Unpub-
        lished Ph.D. dissertation, Department of Anthropology, University of North Caro-
        lina, Chapel Hill.
 1985   The Form and Function of South Carolina's Early Woodland Shell Rings. In *Struc-
        ture and Process in Southeastern Archaeology*, edited by R. S. Dickens, Jr., and H. T.
        Ward, pp. 102–118. University of Alabama Press, Tuscaloosa.
 1997   The Gradual Accumulation Theory: The Lighthouse Point and Stratton Place
        Shell Rings. From South Carolina Archaeology Week poster *Shell Rings of the Late
        Archaic*. South Carolina Institute of Archaeology and Anthropology, University of
        South Carolina, Columbia.

Trocolli, R.
 1999   Women Leaders in Native North American Societies. In *Manifesting Power: Gender
        and the Interpretation of Power in Archaeology*, edited by T. Sweely, pp. 49–61. Rout-
        ledge, London.

Tuttle, Martitia
 2002   Report on Paleoseismology Study at the Burkett Archeological Site. Presented to
        Prentice Thomas and Associates, Inc. Copies available from Prentice Thomas and
        Associates, Inc., Mary Esther, Florida.

VanDerwarker, A. M.
 1999   Feasting and Status at the Toqua Site. *Southeastern Archaeology* 18(1):24–34.

Voorhies, B., G. H. Michaels, and G. M. Riser
 1991   Ancient Shrimp Fishery. *National Geographic Research and Exploration* 7(1):20–35.

Walker, K. J.
 2000   The Material Culture of Precolumbian Fishing: Artifacts and Fish Remains from
        Coastal Southwest Florida. *Southeastern Archaeology* 19:24–45.

Walthall, J. A., and B. Koldehoff
 1998   Hunter-Gatherer Interaction and Alliance Formation: Dalton and the Cult of the
        Long Blade. *Plains Anthropologist* 43(165):257–273.

Walthall, J. A., C. H. Webb, S. H. Stow, and S. I. Goad
  1982   Galena Analysis and Poverty Point Trade. *Midcontinental Journal of Archaeology*
          7(1):131–148.
Waring, A. J., Jr.
  1968a   The Archaic Hunting and Gathering Cultures, the Archaic and Some Shell Rings.
          In *The Waring Papers: The Collected Works of Antonio J. Waring, Jr.*, edited by S. B.
          Williams, pp. 243–246. Papers of the Peabody Museum of Archaeology and Eth-
          nology No. 58, Harvard University, Cambridge, Massachusetts.
  1968b   The Bilbo Site, Chatham County, Georgia. In *The Waring Papers: The Collected
          Works of Antonio J. Waring, Jr.*, edited by S. B. Williams, pp. 152–197. Papers of
          the Peabody Museum of Archaeology and Ethnology No. 58, Harvard University,
          Cambridge, Massachusetts.
Waring, A. J., Jr., and L. Larson
  1968   The Shell Ring on Sapelo Island. In *The Waring Papers: The Collected Works of
          Antonio J. Waring, Jr.*, edited by S. B. Williams, pp. 263–278. Papers of the Pea-
          body Museum of Archaeology and Ethnology No. 58, Harvard University, Cam-
          bridge, Massachusetts.
Waselkov, G. A.
  1987   Shellfish Gathering and Shell Midden Archaeology. In *Advances in Archaeological
          Method and Theory*, vol. 10, edited by M. A. Schiffer, pp. 93–210. Academic Press,
          Orlando, Florida.
Wason, P. K.
  1994   *The Archaeology of Rank*. Cambridge University Press, London.
Webb, C. H.
  1968   Extent and Content of Poverty Point Culture. *American Antiquity* 33:297–331.
  1970   Settlement Patterns in the Poverty Point Cultural Complex. In *The Poverty Point
          Culture*, edited by B. Broyles and C. H. Webb, pp. 3–12. Bulletin 12, Southeastern
          Archaeological Conference, Morgantown, West Virginia.
  1971   Archaic and Poverty Point Zoomorphic Locust Beads. *American Antiquity* 36:105–114.
  1977   *The Poverty Point Culture*. Geoscience and Man Vol. 17, Louisiana State Univer-
          sity, Baton Rouge.
  1982   *The Poverty Point Culture*, rev. ed. Geoscience and Man Vol. 17, Louisiana State
          University, Baton Rouge.
  1991   Poverty Point Culture and Site: Definitions. In *The Poverty Point Culture: Local
          Manifestations, Subsistence Practices, and Trade Networks*, edited by K. M. Byrd,
          pp. 3–6. Geoscience and Man Vol. 29, Louisiana State University, Baton Rouge.
Webb, T., III, P. J. Bartlein, S. P. Harrison, and K. H. Anderson
  1993   Vegetation, Lake Levels, and Climate in Eastern North America for the Past
          18,000 Years. In *Global Climate since the Last Glacial Maximum*, edited by H. E.
          Wright, Jr., J. E. Kutzbach, T. Webb III, W. F. Ruddiman, F. A. Street-Perrott, and
          P. J. Bartlein, pp. 415–467. University of Minnesota Press, Minneapolis.
Webb, W. S.
  1939   *An Archaeological Survey of Wheeler Basin on the Tennessee River in Northern Ala-
          bama*. Bulletin 112, Bureau of American Ethnology, Smithsonian Institution Press,
          Washington, D.C.

1946 *Indian Knoll, Site Oh 2, Ohio County, Kentucky.* Reports in Anthropology and Archaeology Vol. 4, No. 3, Pt. 1, University of Kentucky, Lexington.

1950a *The Read Shell Midden, Site 10, Butler County, Kentucky.* Reports in Anthropology and Archaeology Vol. 7, No. 5, University of Kentucky, Lexington.

1950b *The Carlston Annis Mound, Site 5, Butler County, Kentucky.* Reports in Anthropology and Archaeology Vol. 7, No. 4, University of Kentucky, Lexington.

1950c *The Read Shell Midden, Site 10, Butler County, Kentucky.* Reports in Anthropology and Archaeology Vol. 6, No. 5, University of Kentucky, Lexington.

1974 *Indian Knoll.* Reprinted. University of Tennessee Press, Knoxville. Originally published 1946 as *Indian Knoll, Site Oh 2, Ohio County, Kentucky,* Reports in Anthropology and Archaeology Vol. 4, No. 3, Pt. 1, University of Kentucky, Lexington.

Webb, W. S., and D. L. DeJarnette

1942 *An Archaeological Survey of Pickwick Basin in the Adjacent Portions of the States of Alabama, Mississippi, and Tennessee.* Bulletin 129, Bureau of American Ethnology, Smithsonian Institution Press, Washington, D.C.

Webb, W. S., and W. G. Haag

1939 *The Chiggerville Site, Site 1, Ohio County, Kentucky.* Reports in Anthropology and Archaeology Vol. 4, No. 1, University of Kentucky, Lexington.

1940 *The Cypress Creek Villages, Sites 11 and 12, McLean County, Kentucky.* Reports in Anthropology and Archaeology Vol. 4, No. 12, University of Kentucky, Lexington.

Welch, P. D., and C. M. Scarry

1995 Status-Related Variation in Foodways in the Moundville Chiefdom. *American Antiquity* 60:397–419.

White, N. M.

1992 Shell Mounds of the Lower Apalachicola River Swamp, Northwest Florida. *Journal of Alabama Archaeology* 38:113–162.

1994a *Archaeological Investigations at Six Sites in the Apalachicola River Valley, Northwest Florida.* NOAA Technical Memorandum NOS SRD 26, National Oceanic and Atmospheric Administration, Washington, D.C.

1994b *Apalachicola Shell Mound Excavations, 1993.* Submitted to the Florida Division of Historical Resources, Tallahassee. Copies available from Department of Anthropology, University of South Florida, Tampa.

1999 Reflections and Speculations on Putting Women into Southeastern Archaeology. In *Grit-Tempered: Early Women Archaeologists in the Southeastern United States,* edited by N. White, L. Sullivan, and R. Marrinnan, pp. 315–336. University Press of Florida, Gainesville.

2003a Testing Partially Submerged Shell Middens in the Apalachicola Estuarine Wetlands, Franklin County, Florida. *The Florida Anthropologist* 56(1):15–45.

2003b Late Archaic in the Apalachicola/Lower Chattahoochee Valley of Northwest Florida, Southwest Georgia, Southeast Alabama. *The Florida Anthropologist* 56(2): 69–90.

White, N. M., and R. W. Estabrook

1994 Sam's Cutoff Shell Mound and the Late Archaic Elliott's Point Complex in the Apalachicola Delta, Northwest Florida. *The Florida Anthropologist* 47:61–78.

White, N. M. (editor), with C. Ho Lee and J. A. Bense
  1983   *Final Interim Report, Archaeological Excavations in the Upper Tombigbee Valley, Phase II.* Report of Investigations No. 4, Office of Cultural and Archaeological Research, University of West Florida, Pensacola.

Widmer, R. J.
  1988   *The Evolution of the Calusa: A Nonagricultural Chiefdom on the Southwest Florida Coast.* University of Alabama Press, Tuscaloosa.
  1992   The Structure of Southeastern Chiefdoms. In *The Forgotten Centuries: Indians and Europeans in the American South 1521–1704,* edited by C. Hudson and C. Chaves Tesser, pp. 125–155. University of Georgia Press, Athens.
  2002   The Woodland Archaeology of South Florida. In *The Woodland Southeast,* edited by D. G. Anderson and R. C. Mainfort, Jr., pp. 373–397. University of Alabama Press, Tuscaloosa.

Wiessner, P.
  1982a Beyond Willow Smoke and Dogs' Tails: A Comment on Binford's Analysis of Hunter-Gatherer Settlement Systems. *American Antiquity* 47:171–178.
  1982b Risk, Reciprocity and Social Influences on !Kung San Economics. In *Politics and History in Band Societies,* edited by E. Leacock and R. B. Lee, pp. 61–84. Cambridge University Press, Cambridge, U.K.

Willey, G. R.
  1949   *Archeology of the Florida Gulf Coast.* Smithsonian Miscellaneous Collections 111, Smithsonian Institution Press, Washington, D.C. Reprinted 1999, University Press of Florida, Gainesville.

Willey, G. R., and P. Phillips
  1958   *Method and Theory in American Archaeology.* University of Chicago Press, Chicago.

Williams, J. R.
  1967   *Southeast Missouri Land Leveling Salvage Archeology.* Submitted to the National Park Service, Midwest Region, Lincoln, Nebraska.

Williams, M.
  1994   Archaeological Site Distributions in Georgia, 1994. *Early Georgia* 22:35–76.

Williams, M., and J. Freer Harris
  1998   Shrines of the Prehistoric South: Patterning in Middle Woodland Mound Distribution. In *A World Engraved: Archaeology of the Swift Creek Culture,* edited by M. Williams and D. T. Elliott, pp. 36–47. University of Alabama Press, Tuscaloosa.

Williams, S.
  1954   An Archeological Study of the Mississippian Culture in Southeast Missouri. Unpublished Ph.D. dissertation, Department of Anthropology, Yale University, New Haven, Connecticut.
  1991   Poverty Point North and Some Thoughts on Origins. In *The Poverty Point Culture: Local Manifestations, Subsistence Practices, and Trade Networks,* edited by K. M. Byrd, pp. 95–102. Geoscience and Man Vol. 29, Louisiana State University, Baton Rouge, Louisiana.

Williams, S., and J. P. Brain
  1983   *Excavations at the Lake George Site Yazoo County, Mississippi 1958–1960.* Papers of

the Peabody Museum of Archaeology and Ethnology No. 74, Harvard University, Cambridge, Massachusetts.

Wilmsen, E. N.

1983   The Ecology of Illusion: Anthropological Foraging in the Kalahari. *Reviews in Anthropology* 10(1):9–20.

1989   *Land Filled with Flies: A Political Economy of the Kalahari.* University of Chicago Press, Chicago.

Wilmsen, E. N., and J. R. Denbow

1990   Paradigmatic History of San-Speaking Peoples and Current Attempts at Revision. *Current Anthropology* 31:489–534.

Winterhalder, B.

1986   Diet Choice, Risk, and Food Sharing in a Stochastic Environment. *Journal of Anthropological Archaeology* 5:369–392.

Winters, H. D.

1968   Value Systems and Trade Cycles of the Late Archaic in the Midwest. In *New Perspectives in Archaeology*, edited by S. R. Binford and L. R. Binford, pp. 175–221. Aldine, Chicago.

Wobst, H. M.

1977   Stylistic Behavior and Information Exchange. In *For the Director: Research Essays in Honor of James B. Griffin*, edited by C. E. Cleland, pp. 317–342. Anthropological Papers No. 61, Museum of Anthropology, University of Michigan, Ann Arbor.

1978   The Archaeo-Ethnology of Hunter-Gatherers or the Tyranny of the Ethnographic Record in Archaeology. *American Antiquity* 43:303–309.

Wolf, E. R.

1982   *Europe and the People without History.* University of California Press, Berkeley.

1990   Distinguished Lecture: Facing Power. *American Anthropologist* 92:586–596.

1999   *Envisioning Power.* University of California Press, Berkeley.

Wood, J. W., G. R. Milner, H. C. Harpending, and K. M. Weiss

1992   The Osteological Paradox: Problems of Inferring Prehistoric Health from Skeletal Samples. *Current Anthropology* 33:343–370.

Woodburn, J.

1980   Hunters and Gatherers Today and Reconstruction of the Past. In *Soviet and Western Anthropology*, edited by E. Gellner, pp. 95–117. Columbia University Press, New York.

1982   Egalitarian Societies. *Man* 17:431–451.

Yerkes, R. W.

2002   Hopewell Tribes: A Study of Middle Woodland Social Organization in the Ohio River Valley. In *The Archaeology of Tribal Societies*, edited by W. A. Parkinson, pp. 227–245. Archaeological Series 15, International Monographs in Prehistory, Ann Arbor, Michigan.

Yerkes, R. W., and L. M. Gaertner

1997   Microwear Analysis of Dalton Artifacts. In *Sloan: A Paleoindian Dalton Cemetery in Arkansas*, edited by D. F. Morse, pp. 58–71. Smithsonian Institution Press, Washington, D.C.

Yoffee, N., S. K. Fish, and G. R. Milner
  1999   Comunidades, Ritualities, Chiefdoms: Social Evolution in the American Southwest
          and Southeast. In *Great Towns and Regional Polities in the Prehistoric American
          Southwest and Southeast,* edited by J. E. Neitzel, pp. 261–271. Amerind Founda-
          tion, Dragoon, Arizona, and University of New Mexico Press, Albuquerque.
Young, M. W.
  1971   *Fighting with Food: Leadership, Values, and Social Control in a Massim Society.* Cam-
          bridge University Press, Cambridge, U.K.

Contributors

DAVID G. ANDERSON
Department of Anthropology
University of Tennessee
250 South Stadium Hall
Knoxville, Tennessee 37996

SAMUEL O. BROOKES
USDA Forest Service
100 West Capitol Street, Suite 1141
Jackson, Mississippi 39269

L. JANICE CAMPBELL
Prentice Thomas & Associates
425 E. Hollywood Boulevard
Mary Esther, Florida 32569

PHILIP J. CARR
Department of Sociology and Anthropology
HUMB 34
University of South Alabama
Mobile, Alabama 36688

JOHN E. CLARK
Anthropology Department
950 SWKT
Brigham Young University
Provo, Utah 84602

GEORGE M. CROTHERS
William S. Webb Museum of Anthropology
University of Kentucky
1020A Export Street
Lexington, Kentucky 40506

JON L. GIBSON
Lake Claiborne
355 Coleman Loop
Homer, Louisiana 71040

MICHAEL J. HECKENBERGER
Department of Anthropology
1112 Turlington Hall
University of Florida
Gainesville, Florida 32611

RICHARD W. JEFFERIES
Department of Anthropology
211 Lafferty Hall
University of Kentucky
Lexington, Kentucky 40506

GEORGE R. MILNER
Department of Anthropology
409 Carpenter Building
Pennsylvania State University
University Park, Pennsylvania 16802

JAMES R. MOREHEAD
Prentice Thomas & Associates
425 E. Hollywood Boulevard
Mary Esther, Florida 32569

MICHAEL RUSSO
Southeast Archeological Center
2035 East Paul Dirac Drive
Johnson Building, Suite 120
Tallahassee, Florida 32310

KENNETH E. SASSAMAN
Department of Anthropology
1112 Turlington Hall
University of Florida
Gainesville, Florida 32611

JOE SAUNDERS
Department of Geosciences
University of Louisiana at Monroe
Monroe, Louisiana 71209

LEE H. STEWART
USDA Forest Service
Pineville, Louisiana 71360

PRENTICE J. THOMAS, JR.
Prentice Thomas & Associates
425 E. Hollywood Boulevard
Mary Esther, Florida 32569

NANCY MARIE WHITE
Department of Anthropology
4202 E. Fowler Avenue
University of South Florida
Tampa, Florida 33620

RANDOLPH J. WIDMER
Department of Anthropology
University of Houston
Houston, Texas 77204

Index